AF840059

The Dismissal of Gough Whitlam and the Australian Constitutional Crisis of 1975

The Dismissal of Gough Whitlam and the Australian Constitutional Crisis of 1975

When No One Knew the Rules

Ian Killey

Foreword by Matt Harvey

LEXINGTON BOOKS
Lanham • Boulder • New York • London

Lexington Books
Bloomsbury Publishing Inc, 1385 Broadway, New York, NY 10018, USA
Bloomsbury Publishing Plc, 50 Bedford Square, London, WC1B 3DP, UK
Bloomsbury Publishing Ireland, 29 Earlsfort Terrace, Dublin 2, D02 AY28, Ireland
www.rowman.com

Copyright © 2025 by The Rowman & Littlefield Publishing Group, Inc.

All rights reserved. No part of this publication may be: i) reproduced or transmitted in any form, electronic or mechanical, including photocopying, recording or by means of any information storage or retrieval system without prior permission in writing from the publishers; or ii) used or reproduced in any way for the training, development or operation of artificial intelligence (AI) technologies, including generative AI technologies. The rights holders expressly reserve this publication from the text and data mining exception as per Article 4(3) of the Digital Single Market Directive (EU) 2019/790.

British Library Cataloguing in Publication Information Available

Library of Congress Cataloging-in-Publication Data

Names: Killey, Ian, author.
Title: The dismissal of Gough Whitlam and the Australian constitutional crisis of 1975: when no one knew the rules / Ian Killey.
Other titles: Australian constitutional crisis of 1975.
Description: Lanham: Lexington Books, 2025. | Includes bibliographical references and index.
Identifiers: LCCN 2024054528 (print) | LCCN 2024054529 (ebook) | ISBN 9781666930320 (cloth) | ISBN 9781666930337 (ebook)
Subjects: LCSH: Constitutional history—Australia—20th century. | Australia—Politics and government—20th century.
Classification: LCC KU1760. K56 2025 (print) | LCC KU1760 (ebook) | DDC 342.9402/9—dc23/eng/20250108
LC record available at https://lccn.loc.gov/2024054528
LC ebook record available at https://lccn.loc.gov/2024054529

For product safety related questions contact productsafety@bloomsbury.com.

To Asher, the new addition to the family

Figure 0.1 ALP Political Badges from the 1970s from the Collection of the Author.
Source: Image taken by the author.

Contents

Foreword

1975

The dismissal of the Whitlam government by the Governor-General Sir John Kerr happened nearly 50 years ago. Whitlam urged his supporters to 'maintain your rage', but Ian Killey argues in this book that the rage is misplaced.

For quite a while, scholarly responses fell roughly into two camps: the governor-general did as he was entitled to do by the Constitution, dismissing a government that could not obtain supply, or the governor-general committed a coup against democracy, dismissing a duly elected government that still held a majority in the House of Representatives.

Ian Killey has found a third way, arguing that no one really knew what they were doing. Kerr forgot his duty to warn Whitlam before dismissing him. Whitlam failed to alert his Senate colleagues, and the supply bills were passed when they could have been blocked in the Senate or not certified by the Speaker of the House of Representatives. A written Constitution that leaves the most important elements unsaid, combined with a governor-general choosing to take their written powers literally, makes a great recipe for a crisis.

At one level, the crisis was resolved by the overwhelming victory of the Coalition in the subsequent election. At another, it has remained unresolved for fifty years and still divides and confuses. Although not 'unprecedented', the element of surprise will be missing if similar circumstances occur again, but the words of the Constitution are still the same.

This book meticulously analyses all aspects of the crisis and its resolution. Not only does it demonstrate that many scholars and commentators have gotten key aspects wrong, but it also demonstrates that the main players did as well.

Although prospects of constitutional reform remain dim, this book will help to ensure that if we ever do get a republic, we must state the rules, especially the powers of the head of state, more clearly in the Constitution.

Matt Harvey
Senior Lecturer and Convenor of Constitutional Law,
Victoria Law School, Victoria University

Preface

1975

This work examines the fifty-year history of the dismissal of the Whitlam government that occurred on November 11, 1975. Its origin derives from my own limited and confused involvement in the events and consequences of that event many years ago. Then, as a young law student in Melbourne, like most Australians, I tried to make sense of what was happening to my country and its government as a result of the actions taken by an appointed man, a man whom most had never heard of, using powers that even fewer knew of or accepted as existing, when he decided to dismiss a twice-elected prime minister.

That has led to many arguments that condemn those actions, but as this work will demonstrate, many of those popular views of that dismissal are just flawed. And that has largely occurred because, as the former chief justice of the high court, Harry Gibbs recognized in 1997 much of the comment regarding the dismissal of the Whitlam government is both 'erroneous and distorted', as the media has 'so little knowledge of the constitutional principles that they have expounded so confidently'.

This review of what occurred leading up to and on November 11, 1975, has examined the various criticisms that have been made of the 1975 events and has led to conclusions that contradict much of what is widely believed. That is:

- The powers exercised by Sir John Kerr to dismiss Gough Whitlam, the reserve powers, were then well established, if unknown to most.
- There was no constitutional or legal reason preventing Kerr from consulting with either Sir Garfield Barwick or Anthony Mason regarding the reserve

powers or requiring those judicial officials to have advised Whitlam of Kerr's plans or to withdraw from advising Kerr.
- Kerr was not engaged in any 'conspiracy' or 'coup' with Malcolm Fraser or Garfield Barwick to dismiss Whitlam but was seeking, as Whitlam's successor as leader of the ALP, Bill Hayden concluded, 'to do what he believed was right and proper'.
- Kerr was also not operating under any instructions from either Barwick or Mason.
- And finally, neither the Palace nor the CIA knew that Kerr had decided to sack Whitlam and neither instructed nor directed him to take that action.

Nonetheless, other widely held criticisms can and should be made of both Kerr and Barwick. Barwick, largely because the constitutional basis of his advice to Kerr, was inadequate and defective; and Kerr because he acted far too early, well before the supply had run out, and he did so with no effective warning to Whitlam of his intended actions. In addition, Kerr should be criticized for his unwillingness to discuss his views with the prime minister and for his very selective use of material in his accounts, including in his correspondence with the Palace, which includes his failure to make any reference to the advice that he had received from the experienced governors of New South Wales and Victoria and from Justice Mason that he should have warned Whitlam.

But this work also concludes that, despite the many flaws in Kerr's approach, the end result of November 11, 1975, may well have been significantly different had the dismissed prime minister, Gough Whitlam, acted very differently. That is, had Whitlam appreciated the powers that he still had in hand, even after he was dismissed, his successor as prime minister, Malcolm Fraser, may well have been prevented from providing the supply bills to Kerr for assent. As one of Fraser's leading colleagues, Ian Sinclair,[1] later said: 'If we didn't have supply, there was no government'. And without supply, Kerr would have been left with few alternatives other than reappointing the dismissed prime minister.

But as this work will demonstrate, all that required for Whitlam to have appreciated was that 'the devil is in the detail'. But he did not, and as a result, that was the end of his government and his career as prime minister. Whitlam should, therefore, be remembered, as will be seen, not only as the ambushed and deceived prime minister but also as the prime minister whose ultimate fate was determined by his own failures when he ignored his last chance of success when he, to adapt a football idiom, 'dropped the prime-ministerial ball'.

Ian Killey PSM
Bastille Day, 2024

NOTE

1. In 1975, Sinclair was the Opposition Spokesperson for Primary Industry, and later, the Leader of the National Party (1984–1989).

Central Characters in the 1975 Dismissal

THE SACKED GOVERNMENT

The Prime Minister

Gough Whitlam – Australia's twenty-first prime minister, famous for his reformist political style, was the dismissed prime minister in 1975. He was born in Kew in Melbourne, brought up in Canberra, the son of Australia's Crown solicitor, and had been a barrister since 1947, being made a Queens Counsel in 1962.[1] He has also been a quiz champion, having won the Australian National Quiz Championships in both 1948 and 1949 and runner up in 1950.[2] He joined the ALP in 1945, and in 1952 he became a member of Federal Parliament[3] when he won the seat of Werriwa in the state of New South Wales, a seat he held until 1978. He became the ALP's deputy parliamentary leader in 1960 under the new leadership of Arthur Calwell, which lasted until 1967 when Calwell retired. He then became the party leader, holding that office until 1977 and was the first ALP leader to win consecutive elections (1972 and 1974). Although Whitlam's relationship with Calwell was poor, Calwell considering that 'Whitlam is not true Labor man' as he 'only uses the party for himself'.[4] Whitlam's reformist activities as prime minister have led most others to reach very different views. That included John Kerr's predecessor as governor-general, Paul Hasluck, who had predicted that Whitlam 'would be one of our great prime ministers and certainly the first leader of distinction and capacity since Menzies'.[5]

Whitlam died in 2014 at the age of 98.

Deputy Prime Ministers

Lance Barnard – He had been the first deputy prime minister in the Whitlam government from December 1972 to June 1974, having been the deputy leader of the ALP since 1967. He held the Tasmanian seat of Bass in the House of Representatives, a seat he secured in 1954 and held until June 1975. In the newly elected Whitlam government in 1972, in its first fortnight, Barnard initially held fourteen ministerial portfolios in Whitlam's duumvirate government between December 5 and 19. After that, when a full ministry was established, Barnard became Minister for Defence, an office he held until June 1975 when he retired from Parliament. Barnard's retirement occurred once he was not able to remain deputy leader and deputy prime minister after the 1974 election when Jim Cairns replaced him. Barnard then went on to become the Ambassador to Sweden, an office he held until 1978. However, the by-election in Bass saw Labor lose that seat with a large swing (discussed in chapter 5).

Barnard was not only a political colleague of Whitlam but also his close friend. Whitlam has described Barnard as 'my oldest and best mate'[6] and that 'No Labor leader ever had a better deputy or a better friend'.[7]

Barnard died on August 6, 1997, at the age of 78.

Jim Cairns was possibly the most interesting person in the Whitlam government, other than Whitlam, and was a man of contradictions.

He was the second deputy prime minister in the Whitlam government (between June 1974 and July 1975). He was also the second treasurer in that government (between December 1974 and June 1975). However, he was also one of the few Australian treasurers who never delivered a budget, as he was removed from that office due to his unapproved loan-making activities (as discussed in chapter 4). He was also removed from his deputy prime ministership for misleading Parliament (as also discussed in chapter 4).

Cairns was a highly trained and qualified left-wing economic historian who came from a poor background. At a time when university training in Australia was largely confined to the wealthy, Cairns gained his undergraduate education through part-time study while employed. His employment was as a policeman, an unusual position for a man from the political left. Nonetheless, he was one of the first Victorian policemen to hold a tertiary degree – studying part-time for his economics degree at the University of Melbourne. He was, however, a good student, as he was able to leave the police in 1944 and then went on to work as tutor and lecturer at Melbourne University before completing his PhD at Oxford in 1957.

Politically, Cairns was an unequivocal socialist, and he even sought to become a member of the Communist Party. That party, however, rejected his application, as it believed that he may well be a 'police agent'.[8] As a result, he then joined the ALP in 1947, and he soon gained preselection for a safe seat, being elected as the Member for the Victorian seat of Yarra in the House of Representatives in 1955. He held that seat until 1969 when that seat was abolished. He was then elected in another very safe seat, Lalor, holding that seat until 1977.

Cairns was popular in the ALP, particularly among those on the left and was a strong leader of the anti-Vietnam War campaigns in the 1960s. But he was, as observed by Fred Daly, who was from the right of the party, 'a strange fellow' in that his behaviour did not match the normal behaviour in the party, which was 'if I didn't agree with you I didn't want to know you'. With Cairns that distinction did not operate as, despite differences between factions, he was still 'a man you could talk to'.[9]

But even so, Cairns was not close to Whitlam and was the only member of the ALP who could challenge Whitlam for leadership of the party, almost winning it in 1968 when he lost by a relatively narrow margin of six votes, 38 to 32.[10] He also just missed out on winning the deputy leadership in 1967, losing to Barnard by just two votes, 33–35. But after the 1974 election, Cairns reversed that result, convincingly defeating Barnard – 54 to 42.[11]

That was the peak of Cairns' political success, as his performance during his one year as deputy prime minister and his seven months as treasurer was not a triumph due to both his very public relationship with his Office Co-ordinator, Junie Morosi, and his involvement in unauthorized loan activities, both of which are discussed in chapter 4.

After Cairns left politics, he largely devoted himself to the counterculture and to selling his books at local markets. He did, however, seek a Senate seat in 1983, but as an independent, he was significantly unsuccessful. The Labor Party did not expel him for that venture but largely ignored him until it made him a Life Member of the Labor Party later in life, in 2000. He died three years later, at the age of 89, in October 2003. He was then accorded a State Funeral at St John's Anglican Church in Toorak, the home of the wealthy. An odd end for a man who had earlier described himself as having:

> never believed myself to be anything that I can attach a name to. I wasn't a Christian. I didn't regard myself as a humanist or a socialist. I was something: what I am, and it didn't have a name.[12]

Frank Crean was the third-deputy prime minister in the Whitlam government, from July 1975. He had been the first treasurer in that government and later became minister for Overseas Trade from November 1974. He had held the seat of Melbourne Ports since 1951 until November 1977.

He died in 2008 at the age of 92.

The Treasurer

Bill Hayden had been the minister for Social Security in the Whitlam government, between December 19, 1972, and June 6, 1975, and was responsible for the development and enactment of Australia's first system of universal medical insurance, Medibank. He then became the third treasurer in Whitlam's government, after Jim Cairns, serving from June 6 until November 11 and was responsible for the Supply Bills rejected by the Opposition.

Hayden was born in Queensland in 1933 and had been a policeman prior to his entry into Parliament in 1961 at the young age of 28, for the seat of Oxley, in Queensland, and held that seat until 1988. After the December 1975 election, he was left as the only Labor member in Queensland. He succeeded Whitlam as party leader in 1977, a post he held until 1983, when he was succeeded by Bob Hawke shortly before the 1983 election. After that election and the return of the Bob Hawke Labor Government, Hayden became Australia's foreign minister, a post he retained until 1988 when he retired from the House of Representatives. He was then appointed Australia's twenty-first governor-general in February 1989 and held that post for seven years until February 1996, the second-longest term of any Australian governor-general.

He died in October 2023 at the age of 90.

Attorney-General

Lionel Murphy was the first attorney-general in the Whitlam government, between December 1972 and February 9, 1975. He had trained as both an organic chemist and lawyer but worked as a barrister, being made a Queens Counsel in 1960. He then became a Senator from New South Wales, serving from 1962 to 1975. In that House, he was the leader of the government in the Senate between December 2, 1972, and February 9, 1975, when Murphy was appointed to the High Court. When he left the Senate, the casual vacancy created was used to appoint a replacement who was not from the ALP, Cleaver Bunton, a process that was part of the procedure that allowed the Opposition to delay, but not reject, supply.

Murphy's term on the High Court was notable for a number of reasons. Not only was Murphy the last High Court Justice to have served as a Member of Parliament, and the last politician appointed to the High Court, but he was very activist in his judgments during his term. He was also convicted in 1985 of perverting the course of justice, based on allegations made by the Chief Magistrate of New South Wales, that Murphy had attempted to influence a court case against Morgan Ryan, whom Murphy referred to as 'my little mate'. An appeal to the Court of Appeal quashed that conviction, and in a subsequent trial, Murphy was acquitted. Nonetheless, a Parliamentary Commission of

Inquiry had been established, made up of three retired judges, with the task of examining 'whether any conduct of the Honourable Lionel Keith Murphy has been such as to amount, in its opinion, to proved misbehaviour within the meaning of section 72 of the *Constitution*'. Murphy, however, announced in July 1986 that he was dying of terminal cancer, with the result that the Commission did not conclude its role and its legislation was repealed. Murphy remained a High Court justice until his death on October 21, 1986, aged 64.

Kep Enderby was the second attorney-general in the Whitlam government, serving between February 10 and November 11, 1975. He had been made a Queen's Counsel in 1973, and prior to being made the attorney-general, he held other ministerial posts in the Whitlam government since 1972. He held the seat of Australian Capital Territory (between May 30, 1970, and May 18, 1974), and then the new seat of Canberra, between May 18, 1974, and December 13, 1975. He lost that seat in the election after Whitlam's dismissal and then returned to the bar in Sydney.

He later became a Judge of the Supreme Court of New South Wales, between 1982 and 1992.

He died in 2015 at the age of 89.

Leader of Government in the Senate

Ken Wriedt became the leader of the government in the Senate, succeeding Lionel Murphy. He held this office from February 1975 until the dismissal of the government on November 11, 1975. He had been a Senator from the state of Tasmania since 1968 and remained party leader in that House until September 1980. He had been Minister for Primary Industries and Agriculture for most of the Whitlam government and succeeded Rex Connor as Minister for Minerals and Energy in October 1975. He, like all other Labor senators, was not consulted by Whitlam after his dismissal. What occurred in the Senate on November 11 is discussed in chapter 10.

After leaving the federal Parliament in 1980, he became a member of the Tasmanian Lower House in 1982 and became Leader of the Opposition from 1982 to 1986. Later, he became a Minister in the Tasmanian Labor Government from 1989 to 1990.

He died in 2010 at the age of 83.

Other Ministers

Rex Connor – known in the ALP with the nickname of 'the Strangler', had been the Minister for Mineral and Energy in the Whitlam government, between December 1972 and October 14, 1975. He saw his role as expanding

Australia's ownership of its minerals, and his role in the 1975 dismissal was in establishing its cause, due to his failed activities in seeking a very large loan from the Middle East financiers through very unusual methods to finance his form of economic nationalism. Those activities, which became known as the 'loans affair', are discussed in chapter 4. But they also led Connor to mislead the House of Representatives regarding his dealings with the financial intermediary that Connor used in his failed attempts to secure the loan, Tirath Khemlani, the event that required Whitlam to seek his ministerial resignation.

After his resignation from the ministry, Connor remained a member of the House of Representatives, holding the seat that he had held since 1963, the New South Wales seat of Cunningham, until his death in August 1977. He died at the age of 70.

Fred Daly – He became the Father of the House, having served in ALP governments under Prime Ministers Curtin and Chifley, before being a minister in the Whitlam government. In that government, he was also the leader of the House (the minister responsible for the management of government business in the Lower House). His ministries under Whitlam were: Minister for Urban and Regional Development (from December 1972 to June 1974) and then Minister for Property Services, then Minister for Services and Property (to October 1975), and then minister for administrative services (from October to November 1975).

Daly was first elected to the House of Representatives in 1943, representing the seat of Martin in New South Wales. In 1949, he moved to the safer seat of Grayndler, a seat he held until his retirement from politics in 1975. He was one of the few colleagues whom Whitlam consulted after his dismissal at the Lodge meeting discussed in chapter 10.

After his retirement from politics, he published volumes of humorous memoirs, including *From Curtin to Hawke* (1984), *The Politician Who Laughed* (1982) and the *A to Z of Politics* (1978).

He died in 1995, aged 83.

Jim McClelland – He had been a Senator from New South Wales between March 1971 and July 1978. He was also a junior minister in the Whitlam government (Minister for Manufacturing Industry, between February and June 1975 and then Minister for Labor and Immigration, since June 1975). His role in the dismissal was minimal, but he has been included here as it has been claimed that he was part of Whitlam's Lodge meeting after his dismissal. But, as chapter 10 and McClelland's own memoirs demonstrate, those accounts of his participation in the meeting with Whitlam at the Lodge after his dismissal cannot be true.

After he left the Senate, McClelland became the first chief judge of the New South Wales Environment Court between 1980 and 1985, and in 1984, he was the president of the Royal Commission into British nuclear tests in Australia.

He died in January 1999, aged 83.

Speaker of the House of Representatives

Gordon Scholes – He was the Speaker of the House of Representatives from February 27, 1975, until February 16, 1976. Prior to his election to Parliament, he was a railway engineer and a talented amateur boxer, being the Victorian heavyweight champion in 1949. He was the member for the seat of Corio in the federal Lower House from July 1967, and he held that seat until February 1993. His particular relevance to the events of the dismissal concerns what he could have done, with the powers of the Lower House over the Supply Bills, to hamper and possibly prevent the dismissal of Whitlam from being successful. This is discussed in chapter 10.

After the dismissal of the Whitlam government, Scholes became the manager of Opposition Business in the House of Representatives in 1976 and 1977. Later, he became a minister under the Hawke government, serving as Minister for Defence between 1983 and 1984 and Minister for Territories between 1984 and 1987.

He died in December 2018 at the age of 87.[13]

Solicitor-General

Sir Maurice Byers – Byers was Commonwealth solicitor-general from 1973 to 1983 with a long and successful career as an advocate in the High Court, beginning in 1946. He later served as a member of the Constitutional Commission (between 1985 and 1988) reviewing the *Australian Constitution*, proposing referendum proposals. His advice to the government was central to the position taken by the Whitlam government, although, as will be seen in chapter 3, he has been incorrectly taken as arguing that the reserve powers exercised by the governor-general do not exist. He was described in the *Sydney Morning Herald* as 'the finest lawyer never to have been appointed to the High Court'.[14]

He died in 1999, aged 81.

Public Servants and Government Advisers

Sir Clarrie Harders – A senior public servant, best known for being secretary of the attorney-general's department during the 1970s. His advice was central to the decisions made during the Whitlam government. He was described by the Liberal Party Attorney-General when he was appointed, Tom Hughes QC, and by Gough Whitlam as being 'fearless in providing frank (and sometimes unpalatable advice) to the governments and ministers he served' and that 'By any standards, Harders was a first-class public lawyer, both constitutional and international'. In their view, 'Undoubtedly, Australia is a better place for the life of Sir Clarrie Harders'.[15] He died in February 1997, aged 81.

John Menadue was the secretary of the Department of Prime Minister and Cabinet in 1975 and 1976, working under both Prime Ministers Whitlam and Fraser. He was one of Whitlam's key advisers and was one of the first people that Whitlam wanted to consult with after he had been dismissed (see chapter 10). He had previously been the private secretary to Whitlam when he was deputy leader of the Opposition.

He subsequently was made ambassador to Japan (1977 to 1980), after which he was secretary to the Department of Immigration and Ethnic Affairs (1980 to 1983). Later, he became secretary to the Department of the Special Minister of State and the secretary of the Department of Trade. He was also the chief executive officer of Qantas from 1986 to 1989.

More recently, he has written his autobiography, *Things You Learn Along the Way* (1999), and publicizes a blogsite, *Pearls and Irritations*.

He was born in 1935, is still alive, and is currently 89 years old.

John Mant – A lawyer and town planner who, after the election of the Whitlam government in 1972, became a member of the personal staff of Minister Tom Uren (minister for Urban and Regional Development). He then became assistant secretary of the Department of Urban and Regional Development until five months before the November 11 dismissal, when he acquired a position central to observe that dismissal and its effects, as the Principal Private Secretary to the Prime Minister.

After the dismissal, Mant occupied a number of private and government functions; the latter included being South Australia's director-general of the Department of Housing, Urban and Regional Affairs, acting town planning commissioner in Western Australia, serving on Paul Keating's Urban Design Task Force, and as assistant and acting commissioner of the NSW Independent Commission Against Corruption in 1994. He also undertook an inquiry into the NSW Department of Housing and was central to the rewriting and modernization of the NSW *Local Government Act*. He also served on the Sydney Council between 2012 and 2016.

He died in July 2021 aged 84.[16]

Michael Sexton – In 1975, he had been an adviser in the attorney-general's office. Previously, he had been an associate to Justice McTiernan on the High Court, having studied law at the University of Melbourne, and later obtained a Master of Laws from the University of Virginia.

He was not central to the decisions made on November 11 but has argued that Whitlam did consult with at least one Senator on that day, an argument examined and rejected in chapter 10. He has also argued that the failure of the Speaker to provide the Supply Bills 'would not have prevented the Bills being taken to the governor-general for his assent'. This argument is examined in chapter 10.

After the events of November 11, 1975, Sexton went to the Bar, became a senior counsel in 1998, and in that year he was made the solicitor-general of New South Wales, an office that he still holds 25 years later. He is currently 77 years of age.

Graham Freudenberg – The speech-writer for Labor leaders until Whitlam, he was the drafter of Whitlam's 'It's Time' speech in 1972. He was also the author of a number of books, including the first biography of Gough Whitlam, *A Certain Grandeur.* He was also close to Whitlam and was one of the few whom Whitlam consulted after he had been dismissed at the Lodge meeting, which is discussed in chapter 10.

He died in 2019 at the age of 85.

The Caretaker Government

Malcolm Fraser – Australia's twenty-second prime minister – had been the federal Parliamentary leader of the Liberal Party, and leader of the Opposition since March 1975. More biographical details of Fraser are provided in chapter 5.

He became the caretaker prime minister on November 11, 1975, leading the conservative coalition to a complete routing of the Labor government at the election held on December 13.

Fraser remained prime minister until March 1983 when he was defeated by the Labor Party led by Bob Hawke. Fraser resigned his seat of Wannon and became progressively more and more distant from the party that he had once led, leading to his resignation in 2010, considering that the party was no longer a liberal party but had become a conservative party.[17]

He died in 2015 at the age of 84.

Reg Withers – Known as the 'Toe-cutter', he had been the leader of the Opposition in the Senate during the Whitlam government and was, as chapter 5 demonstrates, the first, from as early as 1973, to develop the supply blockage method as a means of bringing the Liberal/Country Party coalition back into power.

He was a Senator from Western Australia, initially in 1966, when he filled that office due to the death of an elected Senator. Although he lost the special Senate election later that year, he was re-elected to the Senate the following year. He remained a Senator from 1968 until 1987.

After the 1975 election, Withers held a number of ministerial roles in Fraser's government until 1978 when Fraser dismissed him as a result of a Report of a Royal Commission that stated Withers, while not acting illegally, had acted 'with impropriety' when he had suggested to the chief electoral officer that the names of two newly constituted electorates be changed.[18]

After he retired from the Commonwealth Parliament, Withers later became the Lord Mayor of Perth between 1991 and 1994 and was a delegate to the Constitutional Convention in 1998.

He died in 2014, aged 90.

Robert Ellicott – He was the Commonwealth's solicitor-general between 1969 and 1973 and then a member of the House of Representatives, holding the New South Wales seat of Wentworth from 1974 to 1981. He was also the cousin of the Chief Justice of the High Court, Garfield Barwick.

Prior to the 1975 dismissal, despite what some assert, he had not been the shadow attorney-general but had held a lesser role in the Opposition (the shadow minister for Aboriginal Affairs and for Tasmania). However, he still used his extensive legal skills, playing his most important role in the 1975 dismissal when he released, on October 16, 1975, a 'press release' that was, in effect, his legal opinion on the governor-general's reserve powers. As discussed in chapter 8, his view was that if the governor-general was satisfied that the government was left 'without funds to carry on', then he considered that it would be the governor-general's 'duty to dismiss his ministers and appoint others', and that was the course adopted by the governor-general.

After the 1975 election, he became the attorney-general in Fraser's government, which lasted until 1977, and then held other ministerial roles. He retired from politics in 1981 and became a judge of the Federal Court but resigned from that court two years later to allow him to return to the bar and to take part in public affairs again.[19]

Ellicott died on October 31, 2022 at the age of 95.

The Crown

John Kerr – Australia's eighteenth governor-general who dismissed Prime Minister Whitlam. He served in that office between July 1974 and December 1977. More biographical details are found in chapter 6.

He died in 1991, aged 76.

Paul Hasluck was Kerr's predecessor as governor-general. He served in that office between April 1969 and July 1974. Although he had been a Liberal Party senior minister (between 1951 and 1969), and one that Whitlam had thrown a glass of water over (see chapter 5) in a fit of pique, Hasluck became

Whitlam's first preference to continue in office from July 1974. He was both an astute political observer and author, whose works include his short but accurate study from 1979, *The Office of the Governor-General.*

He died in January 1993, aged 87.

David Smith – Public servant, who served as official secretary to the governor-general, John Kerr. He first served in that role under Paul Hasluck and continued under later governors-general, Sir Zelman Cowen, Sir Ninian Stephen and Bill Hayden up until 1990. His most famous role in the dismissal events included his reading of the governor-general's dissolution proclamation on the steps of Parliament House while being towered over by the dismissed former prime minister.

After his retirement from the public service, he was made a visiting fellow in the Faculty of Law at the Australian National University in 1998 and 1999 and was also a member of the 1998 Constitutional Convention (arguing against a republic).

He also spent much of his time defending the actions of Kerr in 1975, as can be seen in his 2005 book, *Head of State: The Governor-General, the Monarchy, the Republic and the Dismissal.*

He died in 2022, aged 89.

Martin Charteris – The younger brother of an Earl[20] and a former military official, he was the Queen's Private Secretary who conducted extensive correspondence with Governor-General Kerr, both before and after Whitlam's dismissal, discussed in chapters 11 and 12.

His role in the Palace was long-standing, going back to 1950 when he was appointed as private secretary to Princess Elizabeth, then heir presumptive to the British throne. From her accession in 1952 until 1972, he served as the Queen's assistant private secretary and was then promoted to her private secretary. He held that post until his retirement in 1977, when he returned to Eton as its Provost. He was also made a life peer in 1978.

He died in 1999, aged 86.

The High Court

Garfield Barwick – The seventh chief justice of Australia's high court, serving in that office for a longer period than any other, 16 years and 9 months, between 1964 and February 1981. There are more biographical details of Barwick in chapter 8.

His role in the dismissal events is largely because he advised the governor-general from November 9, 1975, and provide his written advice on the following day, November 10. As seen in chapter 8, as well as in his two books on the subject, *Sir John Did His Duty* (1983)[21] and in his later 1995 autobiography, *A Radical Tory*[22] he strongly supported Kerr's actions taken on November 11.

He died in July 1997, aged 94.

Anthony Mason was a justice of the High Court between August 1972 and 1987 and later became Australia's ninth chief justice, serving between 1987 and 1992. He was, in Whitlam's view, 'the first adequate chief justice in Australia for more than seventy years'.[23]

He had previously been a justice of the Supreme Court of New South Wales, between 1969 and 1972, and was both a colleague and a friend of John Kerr. His importance to the 1975 dismissal is that he had a series of conversations with Kerr discussing options regarding the supply blockage and the availability and use of the reserve powers that began as early as August 1975. Those conversations were not, however, publicly known until 2012, and there have been allegations that Mason had used those conversations to instruct and manipulate Kerr, assuming 'personal power in public office'.[24] Mason, however, released his own view of what those conversations were in August 2012, but otherwise, his view is that 'I owe history nothing'.[25] These matters are discussed in more detail in chapter 8.

Mason is one of the few centrally involved in the 1975 events who is still alive in 2024 and is aged 99.

NOTES

1. Jenny Hocking, *Gough Whitlam, A Moment in History* (Carlton, Victoria: Miegunyah Press, 2008), 115.
2. Hocking, *A Moment*, 109.
3. Graham Freudenberg, *A Certain Grandeur, Gough Whitlam's Life in Politics* (South Melbourne, Victoria: Sun Books, 1978), 63.
4. Paul Hasluck, *The Chance of Politics* (Melbourne: Text Publishing, 1997), 199.
5. Hasluck, *The Chance,* 202.
6. E. G. Whitlam, "Gough Whitlam's Eulogy for Lance Barnard: 'My Oldest and Best Mate.'" WhitlamDismissal.com, accessed June 22, 2024, https://whitlamdismissal.com/1997/08/15/whitlam-eulogy-for-lance-barnard.html.
7. Gough Whitlam, *The Truth of the Matter* (Carlton, Victoria: Melbourne University Press, 2005), 83.
8. Robin Hughes, "Australian Biography: Jim Cairns – Transcript," National Films and Sound Archive of Australia. NFSA 420890, 1998, https://www.nfsa.gov.au/collection/curated/asset/99785-australian-biography-jim-cairns.
9. Quoted in Paul Strangio, *Keeper of the Faith* (Carlton, Victoria: Melbourne University Press, 2002), 121.

10. Freudenberg, *Certain Grandeur*, 136.

11. Troy Bramston, "Prologue, The Whitlam Ascendency," in *The Whitlam Legacy,* ed. Troy Bramston (Leichardt, NSW: Federation, 2015), 1, 9.

12. Hughes, "Australian Biography: Jim Cairns – Transcript."

13. Jenny Hocking, "Scholes, Gordon Glen (1931–2018)," Australian Dictionary of Biography, National Centre of Biography, Australian National University, https://adb.anu.edu.au/biography/scholes-gordon-glen-28243/text35926, published online 2021, accessed online June 23, 2024.

14. Bernard Langan, "Pickwickian Figure Helped Shape Nation; OBITUARY," *Sydney Morning Herald,* January 19, 1999, 4.

15. Gough Whitlam & Tom Hughes, "An Adviser Who Gave his All," *Sydney Morning Herald,* March 10, 1997, 17.

16. City of Sydney, Resolution of Council, Item 3.1. "Vale John Hayward Mant AM" July 26, 2021. "John Mant, Tribute to Gough Whitlam," in *Pearls and Irritations*, John Menadue's Public Policy Journal, November 19, 2014, https://johnmenadue.com/john-mant-tribute-to-gough-whitlam/, accessed June 23, 2024. Robert Freestone and Richard Whitington, "Urban Planner and Policy Leader 'made a difference,'" *Sydney Morning Herald*, July 19, 2021.

17. Peter Hartcher, "It's Not My Party and I'll Quit if I Want To," *Sydney Morning Herald,* May 27, 2010, 15.

18. David Hough and Kay Walsh, "Withers, Reginald Grieve," *The Biographical Dictionary of the Australian Senate*, Online Edition. This biography was first published in *The Biographical Dictionary of the Australian Senate*, Vol. 4, 1983-2002, Department of the Senate, Canberra, 2017, 472–477.

19. Jack Waterford, "Ellicott Resigns from the Bench," *Canberra Times,* January 19, 1983, 1.

20. The 12th Earl of Wemyss.

21. Garfield Barwick, *Sir John Did His Duty* (Wahroonga, NSW: Serendip Publications, 1983).

22. Garfield Barwick, *A Radical Tory* (Annandale, NSW: Federation Press, 1996).

23. Jenny Hocking, *Gough Whitlam, His Time* (Carlton, Victoria: Miegunyah Press, 2014), Kindle. 574.

24. Hocking, *His Time* (2014), 575.

25. Hocking, *His Time* (2014), 359 & 575.

Timeline

1975 Dismissal and the Events Leading to It

1972
December 2 – The ALP won the federal election

1973
March 8 – Leader of the Opposition in the Senate, Reg Withers, announced the plan to use the Senate's powers to bring down the Whitlam government

1974
April 10 – First attempt at supply blockage by the Senate
April 11 – Both houses were dissolved
May 18 – Whitlam government re-elected
June 10 – Jim Cairns elected deputy leader
November 21 – Jim Cairns appointed as treasurer
December 13 – Executive Council authorizes Connor to raise a $US4,000 million loan

1975
January 7 – Connor's loan authority revoked
January 28 – Connor's loan authority reinstated at $US2,000 million
February 3 – ALP conference at Terrigal
February 9 – Lionel Murphy appointed to the High Court
February 10

- Jim McClelland elected to ministry
- Ken Wriedt becomes ALP Senate leader
- NSW Premier announces that Murphy will be replaced by a non-Labor successor

February 27 – Cleaver Bunton became senator to replace Lionel Murphy

March 7–10 – Cairns provides George Harris with two loan letters
March 21 – Fraser replaced Snedden as Leader of the Opposition
April 15 – Cairns provides George Harris with the remaining two loan letters
May 20 – Connor's loan authority of $US2,000 million revoked
May 30 – Barnard retires from politics
June 6 – Cairns is replaced as treasurer by Hayden
June 28 – Bass by-election, a heavy labor loss
July 2 – Cairns removed from ministry
July 14 – Crean appointed as ALP deputy leader
August – Kerr began a series of private discussion with Mason regarding the supply crisis and reserve powers available to him
August 19 – Hayden announces budget
September 9 – Albert Field sworn in to Senate to replace Queensland's senator Milliner
October 1 – Albert Field was served with a High Court writ challenging his right to occupy his position in the Senate, and he was granted leave from the Senate
October 14 – Connor resigns from ministry
October 15

- The Coalition leadership group decided unanimously to block the budget.
- Labor Caucus met and supported Whitlam in his defiant stance, and approved the calling of a half-Senate election at a time of the prime minister's choosing.

October 16

- The Senate deferred the supply bills.
- Ellicott press release.
- Government House dinner with Malaysian prime minister, Tun Abdul Razak, when Whitlam made his observation: 'it all depends who gets to the phone first, he to dismiss me or I to have him recalled'.
- Kerr met with Fraser, which left Fraser with the conclusion that he 'believed' that 'the governor-general . . . will sack the prime minister'.

October 19 – Kerr asked the prime minister to confer with the chief justice – which was refused.
October 20

- Kerr asked to meet with Fraser so as to allow him to 'ascertain the likely course of future events', a meeting that occurred on October 21.
- Kerr conferred with the NSW Governor, Sir Roden Cutler VC.

October 21 – Kerr asked the prime minister for the opinions of the attorney-general and solicitor-general.
October 30 – Whitlam also approved of Kerr having further meetings with Fraser, the first of which occurred that day.

November 3

- Fraser advised the governor-general that he was prepared to pass supply, but only if Whitlam also agreed to a House of Representatives election at the same time as the Senate poll.
- Kerr conferred with the governors of New South Wales and Victoria, and both advised that Whitlam should be warned.

November 6

- The Senate repeated its deferral of the supply bills.
- The draft and unsigned legal opinion, dated November 4, of the attorney-general and the solicitor-general, was given to the governor-general.
- Kerr met separately with Fraser and Hayden, and the latter advised him that the supply will last until around November 27.
- Whitlam advised the governor-general that he would 'probably . . . advise a half-Senate election on 13 December, which was the last practical day on which an election could be held before Christmas'.
- Kerr treated this day as the '*decisive day*', the day when he knew that: 'I must make up my mind as to the actions to be taken by me, and follow that decision through'.
- Hayden warned Whitlam that he believed that 'he's going to sack us', which Whitlam rejected.
- Meanwhile, Whitlam still considered that 'Kerr is the best appointment we've made'.

November 9

- Kerr had 'made up my mind as to what I must do if the two leaders were still in a deadlock when 11 November came up, inexorably, on the calendar'. That is, he had made up his mind 'conclusively' that if there was going to be a general election before Christmas, '11 November would be the last day for decision'.
- Kerr conferred with Chief Justice Barwick.

November 10

- Kerr and Barwick met.
- Barwick prepared and provided his advice to Kerr

November 11

- 9.45 am – Kerr spoke to Barwick by phone to discuss 'tactical issues'.
- 9.55 am – Fraser/Kerr telephone conversation.
- 11.00 am – The governor-general attended the Remembrance Day ceremony in Canberra.
- 1.00 pm – 1.30pm – Kerr dismisses Whitlam and appoints Fraser as prime minister subject to caretaker restrictions, and with the immediate obligation of securing supply.

- 1.00–2.00 pm – Whitlam returned to the Lodge for a steak lunch and had a short meeting with colleagues regarding the response to his dismissal, but no Senators were invited.
- 2.23 pm – Supply approved by Senate, but ALP Senators were not aware that Whitlam had been dismissed
- 2.34 pm – Fraser advised the House the Representatives that he had been appointed as prime minister.
- 3.00–3.15 pm – A no confidence motion in the new Fraser government was passed by the House of Representatives.
- 3.50 pm – Speaker Scholes forwarded the supply bills to the governor-general for Assent – which was promptly provided.
- 4.30 pm – Kerr signed the proclamation dissolving both Houses.
- 4.45 pm – Smith read the proclamation on the steps of Parliament House, followed by Whitlam and his 'Kerr's cur' speech.

December 13 – The Liberal/Country Party coalition soundly won the federal election.

Chapter 1

The 1975 Dismissal

Misplaced Rage?

Figure 1.1 ALP Political Badges from the 1970s from the Collection of the Author. *Source*: Image taken by the author.

On November 11, 1975, just after 1.00 pm, the man who many consider Australia's greatest reforming prime pinister was dismissed from office. And that dismissal was undertaken by a man unknown to most Australians; a man whom they had not elected, who held an office considered by most as merely formal or ceremonial – the appointed governor-general. And that largely unknown ceremonial official dismissed the elected prime minister using a process that most had also never heard of or understood – the reserve powers. And when he did so, as many also came to believe, he used surprise, secrecy and duplicity to ambush the prime minister.

The dismissal became a national constitutional and political tragedy. It was described by Paul Kelly and Troy Bramston's factually excellent but oddly named book, *The Dismissal in the Queen's Name,*[1] as the 'most dramatic event in Australia's political history',[2] but it was more than that. To many Australians, the dismissal was nothing less than a coup or conspiracy; a destruction of democracy. It was an event that angered and divided the nation, and after almost fifty years, it still does.

It occurred when Prime Minister Gough Whitlam was dismissed, without any prior warning, by the Governor-General Sir John Kerr, who then appointed the leader of the Opposition, Malcolm Fraser, as prime minister, even though Fraser did not then have the confidence of the Lower House. An election was then called. The justification for this action was that the Whitlam government was unable to provide funding to support itself. It had the numbers in the Lower House, the House of Representatives, but the Upper House in Australia's Parliament, the Senate, controlled by the Opposition parties, deferred and would not pass the government's appropriation bills, known as the 'supply' bills.[3] As a result of that blockage of supply, the money was running out. Prime Minister Whitlam, however, refused to call another general election, considering that having just won two (one in 1972 and another two years later, in 1974), and as he still had the confidence of the Lower House, there was no justification for a third election. Whitlam, with the support of his majority in the Lower House, intended to 'tough it out'.[4]

The governor-general, however, took another view. He considered that when:

> an Upper House possesses the power to reject a money bill by denying supply, the principle that a government which has been denied supply by the Parliament should resign or go to an election must still apply.[5]

And that:

> The deadlock which arose was one which, in the interests of the nation, had to be resolved as promptly as possible and by means which are appropriate in our democratic system. In all the circumstances which have occurred the appropriate means is a dissolution of the Parliament and an election for both Houses.

As Whitlam refused to resign or call an election, Kerr felt it his 'duty as governor-general' to terminate his commission.

> If a Prime Minister refuses to resign or to advise an election, and this is the case with Mr Whitlam, my constitutional authority and duty require me to do what I have now done – to withdraw his commission – and invite the Leader of the Opposition to form a caretaker government.[6]

As a result of Whitlam's dismissal, an election was called, which the newly appointed government led by Fraser, easily won. It was a crisis that largely ended Whitlam's political career, but it also ruined the reputation of the governor-general, divided the nation, embittered its citizens, and compromised and confused its institutions.

But that national division has been intensified by subsequent disagreements and confusion as to what had occurred on November 11 and what its causes. And those confusions began on the day of the dismissal and can be seen from recollections of the speech that the dismissed prime minister gave on the steps of Parliament House.

Whitlam was, despite any weaknesses in his leadership style and effectiveness (which are discussed later in chapter 4), a remarkably formidable public speaker, combining his physical presence (Whitlam was then 6 ft 4 inches in height), his intellect, his arrogance and his dominance over his colleagues, to make him, even today for many, an idolized figure who had been executed by the combined duplicitous efforts of the governor-general, the leader of the Opposition and the chief justice. Others, however, minimized his grandeur of presence, referring to him, according to the most recent biographer of an earlier Prime Minister Harold Holt[7] as 'the brolga' due to Whitlam's supposed habit of displaying 'the grandeur of that native bird which danced and strutted imperiously'.[8]

After the governor-general's official secretary, David Smith, had read the governor-general's proclamation dissolving Parliament,[9] Whitlam then took control over the microphone and made what he then considered as nothing more than 'off-the-cuff remarks',[10] but remarks that he soon recognized as 'the best speech I even gave in this place, and it's not even in Hansard':[11]

> Ladies and gentleman, well may we say 'God Save the Queen' because nothing will save the Governor-General.
>
> The proclamation which you have just heard read by the Governor-General's official secretary was countersigned 'Malcolm Fraser' who will undoubtedly go down in Australian history from Remembrance Day 1975 as Kerr's cur.
>
> They won't silence the outskirts of Parliament House, even if the inside has been silenced for the next few weeks.
>
> The Governor-General's proclamation was signed after he already made an appointment to meet the Speaker at a quarter to five.
>
> The House of Representatives had requested the Speaker to give the Governor-General its decision that Mr Fraser did not have the confidence of the House and that the Governor-General should call me to form the Government.
>
> Maintain your rage and enthusiasm through the campaign for the election now to be held and until polling day.[12]

Those final words of those 'off-the-cuff remarks' have, however, been continually misquoted ever since, setting the tone of the disputes and arguments that have continued after the dismissal, after almost 50 years – with many Australians erroneously recalling that Gough Whitlam requested Australians to simply 'maintain your rage'! That contracted, but somewhat incorrect version of Whitlam's request, can be seen in many of the books and articles that have been written on the dismissal, including by his most recent biographer, Professor Jenny Hocking, who quotes the Whitlam speech but without its last fourteen words.[13] And the contraction can be seen in other sources, including those of the leading journalists who write on the subject, Kelly and Bramston.[14] Even the account written by the man who did the actual sacking, Sir John Kerr, made this error.[15]

However, Whitlam's 'maintenance of rage' request to the public, as he made clear in his own book on the subject, was much, much more limited. He was not seeking for us to keep and maintain any permanent preservation of our anger over his dismissal until all is righted. Instead, all he sought was for Australians to 'Maintain your rage and enthusiasm', and only to do so for a limited time period – 'for the campaign for the election now to be held and until polling day'.[16] But, for most Australians, those qualifications seem to have been forgotten.

That contraction might be thought to be largely unimportant – and if it was the only omission or confusion among the many complex issues involved in the events of November 11, 1975, it would hardly require recognition. But as the review of the events of the dismissal in this work will demonstrate, there were other, and more significant, confusions in the various retellings of the 1975 story.

Not only is there much that remains debatable as to what happened on that day in 1975, but it will be seen that the events leading up to the dismissal were based on poor understandings of what Australia's constitutional rules required. That confusion was caused to a large extent by the vagueness of those rules. As will be demonstrated, the dismissal in 1975 and its consequences were caused by the decision-makers on that day having different and conflicting ideas of what the constitutional rules required. As a result, as will be seen, they all just blundered in their application, confidently wandering into the actions taken by them, with little appreciation of the differing views of what the rules actually required.

This book will, like most others on the subject, discuss the decisions and errors made by the governor-general, those of the chief justice who had advised him immediately prior to the dismissal, and those of another High Court Justice Anthony Mason who had advised Kerr for a much longer period leading up to the dismissal. But it will also deal with the significant blunders made by the prime minister who was dismissed, errors that most commentators have since ignored. Whitlam's errors relate to what he could have, and in my view, should have done to save his government, had he appreciated the powers that he still controlled and could have taken. But as those were actions that Whitlam did not take or even consider, this work will argue that much of the rage maintained for Kerr's dismissal of the Whitlam government has been largely misplaced, as it should be directed, at least in part, towards Whitlam himself.

But before we can discuss those significant omissions, we need to address other matters:

- The competing theories or mythologies as to what occurred on November 11, 1975 – which are discussed in chapter 2;
- The constitutional rules that applied and governed the dismissal – discussed in chapter 3;
- The strengths and weaknesses of the Whitlam government – seen in chapter 4; and
- The events of the constitutional crisis that led up to the dismissal – chapter 5.

Then we will consider the decision taken by the governor-general to dismiss the Whitlam government (which is seen in chapters 6–9) and the causes of and errors in that dismissal (chapters 10–13).

While the events of November 11, 1975, on any construction, dealt badly with Gough Whitlam, subsequent history has considerably improved his treatment. He is now widely seen as a heroic, and to some, a virtually god-like, reformist political leader cut down in his prime by the deceptive, corrupt and weak vice-regal representative, and any arguments regarding steps that he could have taken to save himself have been largely airbrushed from the popular and academic memory of the event.

But as Whitlam himself said in 1973: 'The importance of an historical event lies not in what happened but in what later generations believe to have happened'.[17] And as he has certainly benefited from 'what later generations believe to have happened' in 1975, this work seeks to alter what people believe happened on November 11: from the various, but often rage-driven, popular but often erroneous accounts to what actually did happen and what could or should have happened on the day of Australia's most famous constitutional crisis, had Whitlam appreciated what he could have done to save his government.

NOTES

1. That inaccuracy is discussed in chapter 3.
2. Paul Kelly & Troy Bramston, *The Dismissal: In the Queen's Name* (Australia: Penguin, 2015), ix.

3. The Appropriation Bill (No. 1) 1975–1976 and the Appropriation Bill (No. 2) 1975–1976.

4. Kelly & Bramston, *The Dismissal*, 113.

5. John Kerr, "Statement by the Governor-General, November 11, 1975," 3. This statement can be seen in Kelly and Bramston, *The Dismissal*, 370 and these passages can be found at 372.

6. Kerr, "Statement," 1, which can be found in Kelly and Bramston, *The Dismissal,* 370.

7. Harold Holt was Australia's prime minister in 1966–1967.

8. Ross Walker, *Harold Holt, Always One Step Further* (Collingwood, Victoria: Latrobe University Press, Black Inc, 2022), 209. There is, however, no reference to this term in other biographies of Whitlam or in studies of the Whitlam government and I have not been able to locate any confirmation of the use of this term in relation to Whitlam.

9. See Kelly & Bramston, *The Dismissal*, 378–379.

10. Gough Whitlam, *The Truth of the Matter* (Carlton, Victoria: Melbourne University Press, 2005), 168.

11. Quoted in *The Wit of Whitlam*, ed. James Carleton (Carlton, Victoria: Melbourne University Press, 2015), 148.

12. Whitlam, *The Truth*, 167–168.

13. Jenny Hocking, *Gough Whitlam, His Time* (Carlton, Victoria: Miegunyah Press, 2012), 349.

14. Kelly & Bramston, *The Dismissal*, 302; Paul Kelly & Troy Bramston, *The Truth of the Palace Letters: Deceit, Ambush and Dismissal in 1975* (Carlton, Victoria: Melbourne University Press, 2020), 129.

15. John Kerr, *Matters for Judgment* (Melbourne, Victoria: Macmillan, 1979), 373.

16. Whitlam, *The Truth,* ix and 168.

17. EG Whitlam, "Speech By The Prime Minister Mr E G Whitlam, QC MP, At The Unveiling of The Eureka Flag, Ballarat Fine Art Gallery. Ballarat, 3 December 1973" (Australian Government, Department of Premier and Cabinet, PM Transcripts – https://pmtranscripts.pmc.gov.au/release/transcript-3092) 2. This passage is also quoted in Hocking, *His Time* (2014), 557.

Chapter 2

The 1975 Crisis

Conflicting Theories

Figure 2.1 ALP Political Badge from 1977, from the Collection of the Author. *Source*: Image taken by the author.

What made the impact of the 1975 dismissal and its causes so dramatic and long-term for Australia, its government, and its *Constitution* was not only its immediate political effect, which ended the short career of its long-awaited reformist ALP government. It has remained relevant and important to Australians after almost 50 years, for two other reasons.

First, the circumstances of the dismissal. A popularly elected government was removed by an appointed official, who was largely, if not completely, unknown to most Australians prior to November 11, 1975. And of those who had heard of him or his office, they also considered his role to be largely formal. So it was of some surprise to most Australians to find that that appointed and largely unknown ceremonial official had dismissed the popularly elected Whitlam using constitutional rules that few had heard of before, and when he did so, he provided no prior warning to the prime minister of his intention. This has led many to describe Kerr's actions as equivalent to both a coup and an ambush.

Second, the constitutional basis of the powers exercised to dismiss the Whitlam government, the 'reserve powers' of the governor-general, as there was little agreement as to what those powers actually were. That lack of agreement on what was constitutional and what was not is evidenced in a

CONSTITUTIONAL EXPERTS' SCOREBOARD

	Senate refusing to grant supply	Chief Justice advising Kerr	Governing without Supply when alternative money is raised legally	Dismissal of Prime Minister by Governor-General	Kerr limiting Fraser to caretaker role	Kerr's refusal to see Speaker before dissolution	Double dissolution of parliament by section 57
Sir John Kerr	OK	OK	Contrary to responsible government	Power exists	OK	OK	OK
Sir Garfield Barwick	OK	OK	Government impossible	Power exists	OK	?	Illegal
Maurice Byers, Solicitor-General	Against convention	?	?	Power exists	?	?	Illegal
Gough Whitlam	No power	Improper	OK	Power exists	?	Improper	?
Bob Ellicott, Attorney-General	OK	?	Constitutional anarchy	Power exists	?	?	?
Geoffrey Sawer, Prof Law, ANU	Against convention	Unwise	OK	Power exists	Undecided	Undecided	OK
Daniel O'Connell, Chichele Prof Law, Oxford	OK	Questionable	OK	Power exists	?	Speaker's message a charade	OK
Colin Howard, Hearn Prof Law, Melbourne Uni	Illegal	?	Serious blow to government	Power exists	Startling innovation	Against convention	Doubtful
Gareth Evans, Senior Lecturer Law, Melbourne Uni	Against convention	Improper	Undecided	Power exists	Bad thing	Outrageous	Doubtful
Paddy Lane, Prof Law, Sydney Uni	OK	OK	Illegal	Power exists	OK	OK	OK
Tony Blackshield, Assoc Prof Law, Uni NSW (1) Before Nov	Against convention	Illegal	OK	Power exists	Wrong	Discourteous	OK
(2) After Nov	OK	Illegal	OK	Power exists	OK	Discourteous	OK
Dr Paul Gerber, formerly Qld Uni	OK	OK if issue not in courts	Impossible	Power exists	Principle OK, but Whitlam not Fraser	Undecided	Legal, but a device
Leslie Katz, Lecturer Law, Sydney Uni	OK	Improper	Undecided	Power exists	Wrong	OK	Illegal

Figure 2.2 'Constitutional Experts Scoreboard'. From 'November 11 in Retrospect; Was Kerr Right?' The Bulletin, August 4, 1976, 36.

table that the *Bulletin* magazine produced within a year of the dismissal, on August 4, 1976, demonstrating the wide variety of the views and opinions taken by the country's senior lawyers and academics who should have known what the *Constitution* allows or prevents and why. (See figure 2.2).

This table reflects the differing views of the nation's senior legal experts on the Constitution, including three central participants in the 1975 story: Whitlam, Kerr and the Chief Justice Garfield Barwick about most of the issues relevant to 1975. And as can be seen, there was almost no agreement on almost any issue. The only question where there appeared any conformity was that all seem to have agreed that the governor-general did have the power to dismiss the prime minister. But now, as we will see in the next chapter, even that apparent agreement seems to have evaporated.

The dismissal has, however, been the subject of subsequent extensive arguments, accounts and analysis, both academic and popular. They include numerous journalistic works, including early, often both pained and angry works, the best of which was probably Donald Horne's 1976 *Death of the Lucky Country*, a book that was reprinted at least three times that year[1] but has not been printed again for decades. Paul Kelly has also written many works on the incident, beginning with his 1976 *The Unmaking of Gough*;[2] to his more recent works written with Troy Bramston, such as the 2015, *The Dismissal*[3] and their book on Kerr's correspondence with the Queen, *The Truth of the Palace Letters: Deceit, Ambush and Dismissal in 1975*. Other important works include the study by the New South Wales Solicitor-General, Michael Sexton SC, *The Great Crash*;[4] the now largely forgotten but still interesting earlier *Kerr's King Hit!* from 1976 from Clem Lloyd and Andrew Clark;[5] academic works, including the early works produced in the 1970s: Geoffrey Sawer's *Federation Under Strain,*[6] Gareth Evans' *Labor and the Constitution 1972–1975*,[7] Professor George Winterton's various works on the subject including his *Parliament, the Executive and the Governor-General*;[8] and the various later works, particularly from Professor Jenny Hocking, including her two-volume biography Gough Whitlam,[9] as well as her *Dismissal Dossier*[10] and her *The Palace Letters.*[11]

But the most important works on the dismissal are those who were there, particularly the memoirs and accounts from the man who did the sacking, Sir John Kerr, in his *Matters for Judgment*; the man who was thrown out, Gough Whitlam, in his *The Truth of the Matter;* and the man who advised Kerr, Garfield Barwick, in his short *Sir John Did His Duty*[12] from 1983 and his later 1995 autobiography *A Radical Tory.*[13]

Other accounts of those who were there include that of Whitlam's first biographer and excellent speech-writer, Graham Freudenberg;[14] not to forget the account of the one who benefited from Whitlam's dismissal, Malcolm Fraser[15] and that of the man who had read out the governor-general's proclamation on the steps of Parliament while Whitlam towered over him, the governor-general's official secretary, David Smith.[16] Other important accounts have also been provided by others involved, including the then head of the prime minister's department under Whitlam, John Menadue,[17] and the responsible Minister for the budget that was blocked, and future governor-general, Bill Hayden.[18]

This intensive attention to the subject should have clarified the uncertainties regarding the validity of the actions taken by Sir John Kerr in 1975, making this book, and other works on 1975, somewhat pointless. But they have not. And that is because, despite the various studies, the scope of the disagreements as to what is constitutional and what is not has not shrunk as one would have hoped, but has, it seems, grown even larger.

That can be seen because there are some who now disagree with the one area of agreement in the 1976 table, and instead now believe that the governor-general did not have the power to dismiss the prime minister. That can be seen from, for example, Whitlam's biographer, who has questioned, if not denied, those rules' existence regarding the 1975 dismissal as a 'falsification of democracy'.[19] Similar views were also expressed by a recent academic study by Dr David Long with his conclusion that 'the Governor-General does not possess a power, either prerogative or constitutional (statutory), with which to withdraw the commission of a government that has the confidence of the House of Representatives'.[20] The merits of Hocking's and Long's views are considered in chapter 3.

CONFLICTING THEORIES

Nonetheless, despite these disagreements, the various accounts have given rise to at least three conflicting theories of the dismissal and its causes. And those conflicting theories can be summarized as follows, that is, the dismissal was either:

- First, an unjustified political 'coup', ambushing the heroic Gough Whitlam by a weak and corrupt governor-general, working with the leader of the Opposition, to undermine the prime minister and his government; or
- Second, an ambush of a flawed prime minister by a weak and deceptive governor-general; or
- Third, it was the necessary termination of an incompetent and dangerous prime minister.

The first theory can be seen in the post-dismissal accounts and arguments of the dismissed Prime Minister Gough Whitlam[21] as well as those of his biographer, Professor Jenny Hocking, and the recent summary by Dr Harshan Kumerasingham. Dr Kumerasingham has regarded Kerr's actions as being 'extraordinary political acts'[22] taken in exercise of his 'right to rule'.[23] Hocking has also, in addition to her denial of the existence of the powers that the governor-general used to sack Whitlam, argued that the Queen and Buckingham Palace were intimately involved in the sacking. The elements in this monarchical conspiracy argument are discussed in chapter 11.

The second can be seen in most popular works on the dismissal, particularly those by Paul Kelly and Troy Bramston.[24]

And the third can be seen in fewer works now produced but can be seen in accounts of those responsible for the dismissal: the former governor-general, Sir John Kerr;[25] those of the chief justice who advised him, Sir Garfield Barwick[26] and the accounts made by the governor-general's official secretary, Sir David Smith.[27] It can also be seen in the more recent works and arguments of Professor Donald Markwell[28] and by Peter O'Brien.[29]

And the political justification, for the third theory at least, can be seen from the views of Whitlam's replacement, the newly appointed Prime Minister Malcolm Fraser, who considered that Kerr's actions were not only allowed by the *Constitution* but were necessary in view of the claimed recklessness, intransigence, and incompetence of the dismissed prime minister. As Fraser said to the Australian Broadcasting Commission's (ABC) *Four Corners* program, ten years after the dismissal, the Liberal Party should have looked at the events of November 11, 1975, 'as a matter of pride'.[30] As he argued, the supply blockage that led to Whitlam's dismissal was caused:

> because the whole record of the government over a considerable period was disgraceful; there had been scandal after scandal, there had been deception of the Executive Council, deception of the Governor-General himself.[31]

But that was toned down from his earlier views expressed prior to the dismissal – that the Whitlam government 'was a wretched government'[32] and was 'the most incompetent and disastrous Government in the history of Australia'.[33]

This book does not, however, accept any of those three competing theories. And that is because, as the central victim of that dismissal, Gough Whitlam said in 2001: 'The best history will always be based on the documents. . . . Go to the documents'.[34] And when one does go to the documents, it becomes apparent that those widely accepted but conflicting theories are better seen as popular mythologies of what occurred on November 11, 1975, rather than accurate accounts of what occurred on that day. And that is due to fundamental problems with each of the competing theories.

The *first of these problems* is that much of what has been written about 1975 and in presenting these theories, particularly in popular explanations, as well as in some academic literature about the 1975 dismissal and its causes,[35] while often very beneficial in locating primary sources, has been written by authors who have little understanding of the constitutional rules that applied in 1975. They simply do not appreciate what the concept of 'reserve power' or 'constitutional convention' means.

The former chief justice of Australia's High Court, Sir Harry Gibbs, in 1997, recognized this lack of understanding among popular commentators. In his view, many of the accounts of the dismissal of the Whitlam government are based on 'so little knowledge of the constitutional principles that they have expounded so confidently'. As a result, as he said: 'Much of the comment on the events of 11 November 1975 has been erroneous and distorted'.[36] In other words, much of what has been written about the events of November 11, 1975, particularly by popular authors, is often both misleading and valueless, as it is based on a lack of understanding of what the *Constitution* allows and requires. Such minimal appreciation will be demonstrated throughout this work, but one instance comparing the understanding of a basic question between two popular authors can serve as an example. The authors were giving their views as to the constitutional basis of the powers that Kerr used to sack Whitlam, the 'reserve powers' (which are discussed in more detail in chapter 3). Peter O'Brien, who favoured the third of the theories discussed above, said at the very beginning of his recent book on the supposed ills suffered by Sir John Kerr as a result of 1975, *Villain or Victim*?, that the reserve powers are 'listed in the Constitution' and that the concept of constitutional conventions is 'well understood'.[37] Meanwhile, Whitlam's biographer, Professor Hocking, who favours the first theory, has taken the opposite view, arguing that the reserve powers do not exist, or their 'very existence . . . was, at best, arguable'.[38] And her position relies, at least in part, on her view that the reserve powers are 'unspecified in the Constitution'.[39]

Now both of their understandings of the basic concept relevant to the 1975 dismissal, the reserve powers, and of their constitutional basis are poles apart and cannot both be accurate. They cannot be both 'listed in the Constitution' while also being 'unspecified in the Constitution'. Either only one of those understandings can be correct, or neither is.

The complexities of this issue we will examine in chapter 3. And from that examination, we will see that of these two popular authors, Hocking was more correct. That is because, although the powers used to dismiss Whitlam are specified in the *Constitution* (see s 64), there is also nothing expressed in the constitutional text that specifies which of the governor-general's powers are 'reserved'. That is, which of the powers specified in the *Constitution* must be exercised based on ministerial advice and those which are not, being 'reserved' from that obligation. But Hocking's conclusion is also insufficient as it tells us nothing about the constitutional existence of such 'reserved' powers. As we will see from chapter 3, the reservation of the governor-general's powers from ministerial advice is not a matter dependent on constitutional text.

The *second, and related problem*, is that the lack of understanding of what the *Constitution* allows and what it does not, was also held by those centrally involved in the 1975 events. As this account will demonstrate, each of the essential persons exercising power on November 11, 1975, made their various decisions and took their separate actions based on their own misunderstandings of what the *Constitution* requires, failing to appreciate the ambiguities and complexities of the applicable constitutional rules. Instead, each of those participants in the 1975 dismissal boldly reached their conclusions as to what their action should be, but did so based on their own problematic understandings of what the *Constitution* allows and does not allow, omitting salient factors from their individual considerations. It will be argued that the events that led to and caused the dismissal of the Whitlam government are better regarded as a blunder of classic dimensions; and those blunders were made by all involved, rather than any coup or conspiracy.

Blundering behaviour can be seen in the problematic actions of the governor-general, including his unnecessary secrecy in misleading the prime minister by failing to warn him of his intended actions and by exercising his powers before they needed to be exercised (as discussed in chapters 6, 7 and 9). This behaviour can be seen in the constitutional advice of the chief justice, which failed to appreciate the constitutional history of Australian states and earlier colonies, not understanding the long history of supply blockages in Australia that did not support his advice (as discussed in chapter 8).

But serious blunders were also made by the man dismissed, Prime Minister Whitlam. These include his arrogance over his colleagues and his lack of understanding of the man he had recommended to fill the role of governor-general. Additionally, they also include his basic flaws in his response to Kerr's actions, such as failing to include any senators in his planning meeting at the Lodge after his dismissal (as discussed in chapter 10). As will be demonstrated, Whitlam's errors in his actions were not confined to his omission of the Senate on November 11, 1975. He also failed to appreciate the constitutional powers that were still available to him from the Lower House. If appropriately used by him, these powers might still have allowed him to win the day in 1975. By utilizing what few powers Whitlam still had in the House of Representatives, as will be demonstrated in chapter 10, the governor-general would have found that he had few other choices but to reappoint Whitlam as prime minister, changing the result of the day from clear failure to, at least, the possibility of clear victory. However, Whitlam failed to even consider the Lower House powers that remained potentially in his hands, resulting in Kerr not being obliged to reappoint him, thus sealing the end of Whitlam.

Accordingly, Whitlam should not be regarded as the central victim of Kerr's actions, as he is presented in the three conflicting theories, but should also bear some responsibility for the outcome of those actions.

Some remaining rage for Whitlam's dismissal should, therefore, also be aimed at Whitlam himself for failing to save his government when he may have had the opportunity. But none of the competing theories has considered Whitlam's Lower House errors. Had they done so, as we will see in chapter 13, a different conclusion to November 11, 1975, may well have occurred.

The second problem, however, needs much more explanation. But before providing that explanation, the first thing to discuss is the misunderstood constitutional rules that were badly applied on November 11, 1975.

NOTES

1. Donald Horne, *Death of the Lucky Country* (Harmondsworth: Penguin Books, 1976), 4.
2. Paul Kelly, *The Unmaking of Gough* (Sydney, NSW: Angus & Robertson, 1976).
3. Kelly & Bramston, *The Dismissal.*
4. Michael Sexton, *The Great Crash* (Melbourne, Victoria: Scribe, 2005). This work had been earlier produced in 1979 under the title *Illusions of Power.*
5. Clem Lloyd & Andrew Clark, *Kerr's King Hit!* (Stanmore, NSW: Cassell, 1976).
6. Geoffrey Sawer, *Federation Under Strain* (Carlton, Victoria: Melbourne University Press, 1977).
7. *Labor and the Constitution: 1972–1975,* ed. Gareth Evans (Melbourne, Victoria: Heinemann, 1977).
8. George Winterton, *Parliament, the Executive and the Governor-General* (Carlton, Victoria: Melbourne University Press, 1983).
9. Hocking, *A Moment in History* (2008) and Hocking, *His Time* (2012 & 2014).
10. Jenny Hocking, *The Dismissal Dossier* (Carlton, Victoria: Melbourne University Press, 2015).
11. Jenny Hocking, *The Palace Letters* (Melbourne, Victoria: Scribe, 2020).
12. Garfield Barwick, *Sir John Did His Duty* (Wahroonga, NSW: Serendip Publications, 1983).
13. Garfield Barwick, *A Radical Tory* (Annandale, NSW: Federation Press, 1996).
14. See Freudenberg, *Certain Grandeur.*
15. Malcolm Fraser and Margaret Simons, *Malcolm Fraser, The Political Memoirs* (Carlton, Victoria: Miegunyah Press, 2010).
16. David Smith, *Head of State: The Governor-General, The Monarchy, The Republic and the Dismissal* (Sydney, NSW: Macleay, 2005).
17. John Menadue, *Things You Learn Along the Way* (Melbourne, Victoria: David Lovell Publishing, 1999).

18. Bill Hayden, *Hayden, An Autobiography* (Pymble, NSW: Angus & Robertson, 1996).

19. See the title of chapter 9 in Hocking's, *His Time.*

20. David Long, *Australia's American Constitution and the Dismissal* (Lanham, Maryland: Lexington, 2021), 33.

21. See his account in Whitlam, *The Truth.*

22. Harshan Kumerasingham, "Viceregalism," in *Viceregalism: The Crown as Head of State in Political Crises in Postwar Commonwealth*, ed. H Kumarasingham (Cham: Palgrave, Macmillan, 2020), 18, 37.

23. Kumerasingham, "Viceregalism," 37.

24. Most notably Kelly & Bramston, *The Dismissal*; Kelly & Bramston, *Truth, Palace Letters*; and Kelly, *Unmaking of Gough.*

25. Particularly in the account in his memoirs, Kerr, *Matters*; as well as his articles in the magazine *The Bulletin* – John Kerr, "Kerr Breaks his Silence: 'Why I was right to sack Whitlam,'" *The Bulletin,* September 3, 1985 and John Kerr, "Kerr Rejects 'ambush' Myth: 'PM knew I could sack him,'" *The Bulletin*, September 10, 1985; and in his 1987 interview with Geoffrey Robertson – John Kerr, "Sir John Kerr Speaks to Geoffrey Robertson," Interview by Geoffrey Robertson, *Talking Shop*, Australian Broadcasting Commission, 1987, https://www.youtube.com/watch?v=J_K0ljE_6Y8.

26. See Barwick, *Sir John* and Barwick, *Radical Tory.*

27. Smith, *Head of State.*

28. See Donald Markwell, *Constitutional Conventions and the Headship of State; Australian Experience* (Redland Bay, Queensland: Connor Court Publishing, 2016).

29. See Peter O'Brien, *Villain or Victim?* (Redland Bay, Queensland: Connor Court Publishing, 2022).

30. *Four Corners*, "The Dismissal of Gough Whitlam on the 11th of November 1975," Australian Broadcasting Commission, 1995, https://www.youtube.com/watch?v=09bb1uETzfE&list=PL18SxApCKfY6M9jrv3rNWXOQ7DV9rhzhF&index=10&t=1469s, 3.05-3.10, accessed July 8, 2022.

31. *Four Corners* (1995) 14.20-14.40.

32. Kelly & Bramston, *The Dismissal,* 186.

33. Quoted in "It's Government by Crisis. What they Said," *The Age*, October 16, 1975, 1.

34. E. G. Whitlam, "Go to the Documents," National Bi-annual Postgraduate History Conference, University of Melbourne, July 20 2001, *Whitlam Institute Collection*, 2, https://rosetta.westernsydney.edu.au/delivery/DeliveryManagerServlet?dps_pid=IE51463, accessed May 16, 2023; quoted in Hocking, *His Time* (2014), 561, Kindle.

35. See, for example, David Long's *Australia's American Constitution that* seeks to examine the dismissal but without considering the extensive range of works by most authors on the subject of conventions, such as the works of Professor Anne Twomey, Geoffrey Marshall or Andrew Heard, or the views of Sir Paul Hasluck. He made no reference to the circumstances in the 1932 dismissal of Jack Lang by the NSW governor, Sir Philip Game, or to the actions taken in 1952 by the Victorian

Governor when supply was blocked. Moreover, Long's book contains at least plain historical errors on page 5, when he asserted that:

- "five colonial referenda in 1898" were "inconclusive" – there were only four referenda in 1898, and there was a majority in each colony, but the size of the majority in NSW did not achieve the statutory amount; see John Quick and Robert Randolph Garran, *The Annotated Constitution of the Australian Commonwealth, 1901.* Reprinted with forewords by Maurice Byers (1994) and Geoffrey Sawyer (1976). (Sydney: Legal Books, 1995), 213.
- "further FEA's were enacted in 1899 by six colonies" – which is incorrect. Only two colonies enacted further FEA (Federation Enabling Act) in 1899, and WA passed its in 1900 – as can be seen from Long's bibliography on page 296.
- The colonial people approving a "slightly amended" constitution in 1899 is also incorrect. The nature of the amendments was not "slight" – see Ian Killey, *The Naked Australian Constitution* (Lexington: Lapham, 2022), 177–178. Additionally, that colonial approval did not all occur in 1899, as the WA referendum did not occur until July 31, 1900. See Quick and Garran, *Annotated Constitution*, 249–250.

36. Harry Gibbs, "The Dismissal and the Constitution," in *Power, Parliament and the People*, ed. Michael Coper and George Williams (Annadale, NSW: Federation Press, 1997), 146.
37. O'Brien, *Villain or Victim?*, 7 and 14.
38. Hocking, *His Time* (2014) 573, Kindle.
39. Hocking, *His Time* (2012) 307.

Chapter 3

The 1975 Crisis

The Rules

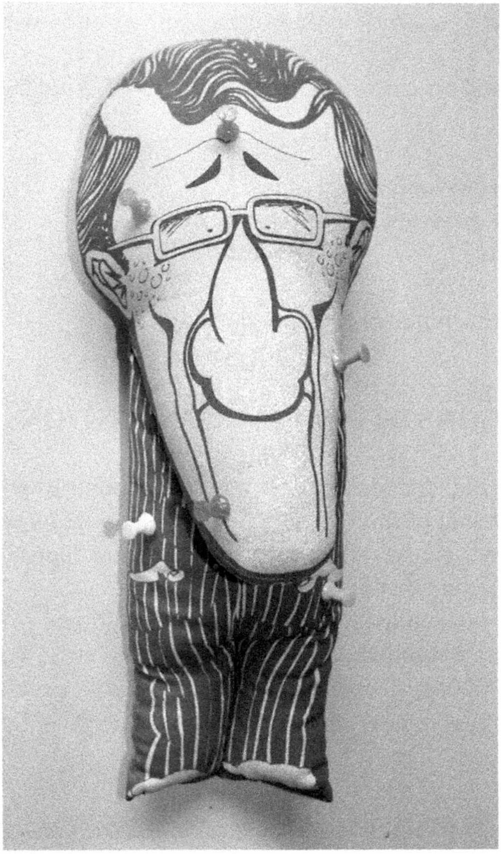

Figure 3.1 The Maladjusted Pin Cushion, a Toy Version of Malcolm Fraser, with Pins, Produced by Tomar in the Late 1970s and Early 1980s. *Source*: From the collection of the author. Image taken by the author.

Normally, when one is discussing technical errors in a law or in a Constitution, such defects would usually be based on what the law or the constitutional provisions states and means. But that is not the case with the constitutional issues involved with the 1975 dismissal. While the *Australian Constitution* is central to the events of 1975, the contested constitutional concepts that are relevant to what occurred on November 11, 1975, are both complex and obscure and are largely unrelated to the text of that *Constitution.*

It is, however, worth recognising that much of the popular commentary on the events of 1975 demonstrates little understanding of the *Australian Constitution* and how it works. Moreover, few commentators, particularly the popular commentators, have much idea of the constitutional concepts that are central to what occurred in 1975, concepts that are not included in the text of the *Constitution*, and often seem at odds with what is in the *Constitution.*

The complex and obscure elements relevant to 1975 are the related requirements of:

- constitutional conventions,
- the responsible government convention and
- reserved powers.

Each of those terms requires some explanation.

CONSTITUTIONAL CONVENTIONS

In Australia, like the United Kingdom and other countries with constitutional systems based on that of the United Kingdom, some of its essential constitutional requirements are based on what are known as 'constitutional conventions', rather than the text of constitutional provisions.

Constitutional conventions are rules for constitutional practices. But they are not laws that are applied and enforced by the courts. The courts' role in relation to conventions is very different from its role in relation to the law, including the common law. As the Canadian Supreme Court observed in 1981:

> The very nature of a convention, as political in inception and as depending on a consistent course of political recognition by those for whose benefit and to whose detriment (if any) the convention developed over a considerable period of

> time is inconsistent with its legal enforcement. The attempted assimilation of the growth of a convention to the growth of the common law is misconceived. . . . No such parental role is played by the courts with respect to conventions.[1]

Even though conventions are not laws, and even though, as Australia's current Solicitor-General Stephen Donaghue recently observed, 'departure from those conventions or practices does not result in invalidity',[2] but they also 'remain important as [they are] "part of the fabric on which the written words of the Constitution are superimposed"'[3] being considered as 'binding' on those to whom they apply.[4] If that was not mysterious enough, their existence and scope are determined not by courts (the role of which is confined to recognising the existence of conventions but not enforcing them) but by the participants in the field – persons described by Professor Jennings in 1947 as 'persons of authority',[5] and that includes both ministers and the governor-general. As Professor Twomey observed, 'what is "constitutionally proper" is not a matter for lawyers, academic or practising, but rather is "essentially a matter for statesmen"'.[6] Those who do not fall within the 'persons of authority' class, like courts as well as journalists and academic writers,[7] are nothing more than constitutional 'observers'.

These conventional binding practices serve an essential function of limiting the manner in which the legal powers provided to a participant in the scheme of government can or must be exercised. This is particularly important in Australia where its constitutions, both State and Federal, are silent on so many important issues (like the concepts of prime minister, cabinet or responsible government). Those constitutions require conventions to fill in those significant constitutional gaps, allowing the constitutions to operate effectively. But few understand conventions, and rarely are they extensively taught or studied in any university. As a result, as Professor Crommelin recently recognized, conventions are 'by nature . . . prone to controversy'.[8] All this is the stuff for a confused application. And that occurred in 1975.

THE RESPONSIBLE GOVERNMENT CONVENTION

One of the conventions that is central to the operation of the system of responsible government is the convention that a governor or governor-general acts in accordance with the advice of ministers. This convention is essential to the operation of the *Australian Constitution,* but it operates to counter a lot of what is actually said in the *Constitution.*

To understand why, one needs to examine Australia's *Constitution*. And when one does, it can be seen that the *Constitution* is a remarkably misleading document, particularly in relation to its provisions concerning the governor-general. An examination of the constitutional provisions relating to that office would make any reader believe that the governor-general has all the powers of a modern Henry VIII, as there are very few constitutional limitations on how the governor-general's extensive powers are to be exercised. That can be seen because Australia's governor-general:

- is head of the executive branch (s 61).[9]
- is, as the monarch's representative, one of the three arms of Australia's Parliament (ss 1 and 2).
- can determine the times for sessions of Parliament 'as he thinks fit' (s 5).
- may prorogue Parliament and dissolve the House of Representatives (s 5).
- may issue writs for the election of the House of Representatives (s 32).
- can assent to legislation passed by the other two elements of Parliament or can withhold that assent (s 58).
- may return to Parliament any presented proposed law and recommend amendments (s 58).
- appoints the members of the Executive Council who hold office 'during his pleasure' (s 62).
- may appoint 'the Queen's Minister of State' who holds office 'during the pleasure of the Governor-General' (s 64).
- is the 'commander in chief of the military and naval forces of the Commonwealth' (s 68).
- appoints, with the advice of the Executive Council, Commonwealth Justices (s 72).

Despite holding all of those extensive executive powers, we all know that Australia is not governed by a Monarch-appointed dictator. There are limitations on the exercise of powers by the governor-general, but those limitations are not found in any provision in the *Constitution*. They are due to the 'binding conventions' that oblige the governor-general to act solely on ministerial advice, subject to some exceptions. And those exceptions are known as the *reserve powers*. As Professor Twomey has recently observed:

> It is one of the basic principles of responsible government and constitutional monarchy that the Sovereign or his or her vice-regal representative, *except in the exercise of the reserve powers*, acts on the advice of responsible Ministers.[10]

RESERVE POWERS

Those exceptions, the reserve powers, are the third concept that is essential in understanding what occurred on November 11, 1975. It is the exception to the responsible government convention that otherwise obliges the governor-general to act on ministerial 'advice' (a subject that also has different meanings, which is explained later in this chapter).

There is, of course, a need for the governor-general to have some reserve powers – powers that he or she can exercise without or contrary to ministerial advice if the *Commonwealth Constitution* is to effectively operate. As an example, if an election is conducted and the governing party loses, the convention is that the prime minister resigns, and a new prime minister is appointed by the governor-general. But what if a losing prime minister simply refuses to resign? In the Commonwealth and most of the states, there is no statutory or constitutional rule that requires a prime minister who loses their election to resign, or one that limits his or her term to the term of the Lower House. It is only in Tasmania where there is a constitutional provision that ends a Minister's term seven days after the return of election writs.[11] In other Australian jurisdictions, a prime minister or a state premier remains in those offices until they resign, die or are dismissed. But if, as some popular experts on the subject would have it, the concept of reserve powers is a 'fiction', then it seems, a prime minister would be able to remain as prime minister for as long as he or she desires, considering that the governor-general cannot dismiss them, regardless, it seems, of the result of any election. Professor Hocking, who favours this fictional approach, oddly prefers the views of former Liberal Party prime minister Billy McMahon,[12] who 'acknowledged that he did not accept that the Governor-General had the power to dismiss a government'.[13] But if McMahon were correct, as this example demonstrates, it could and would lead to nonsensical and absurd results.

And what of an election where the losing prime minister is prepared to resign? How is the governor-general to choose the new prime minister? Is it based on some rule buried in some statute or the *Constitution*? The answer to that question is no. How then, is the governor-general to form his or her own view? Or, if we accept the fictional approach, must he accept the advice of the existing minister that remains, the losing prime minister? Given that we have no legal or constitutional provision that determines who a new prime minister is to be, the system of government requires that the formal head of the executive must have discretion to choose who the new prime minister will be. In most cases, it is unnecessary to exercise this discretion as the result of the election and the good sense of losing prime ministers makes the process automatic. But the efficiency and effectiveness of the system are based on the underlying power of the governor-general to make the system work if the political players won't – and to deprive the governor-general of that ability, as Hocking seems to argue, can only undermine the operation of the system of government.

The extent of the reserve powers exception is not, however, limited to those two circumstances. And there is disagreement, even among those with expertise in this concept, as to how far beyond the exception will go. Even Professor Twomey, who can now claim to be the leading Australian author on this subject due to her lengthy and excellent work on reserve powers, *The Veiled Sceptre,*[14] as well as her almost innumerable articles on the topic,[15] concedes that her approach to reserve powers varies from that taken by 'Most commentators'. As she said, they would 'deny that there are any other reserve powers beyond . . . three classic powers'. That is, most commentators would confine the scope of the governor-general's reserve powers to the power to appoint a prime minister, the power to dismiss a prime minister, and the power to refuse advice to dissolve the Lower House.[16] Beyond that, as Twomey accepts, most other commentators would 'see as mischievous, or even dangerous, any suggestion that there might be other circumstances in which a vice-regal officer could exercise a power without advice or contrary to advice, or refuse to exercise a power as advised'. And she is right. Most other commentators with expertise in the operation of constitutional law and conventions do confine, and have confined, the scope of the reserve powers to such limited areas. That can be seen from many works on the subject, including those of the late leading authority on the subject, Professor George Winterton, including his 1994 *Monarchy to Republic*, where he considered that: 'There are, at the most, four reserve powers: the power to appoint and (more dubiously) dismiss the prime minister or premier, and to refuse and (more dubiously) force a dissolution of the lower house of parliament'.[17] And it can be seen in the Australian scholar's Dr Brendan Lim work, *Australia's Constitution after Whitlam*, where he considered that the reserve powers 'are thought to include the power to dissolve or refuse to dissolve the Parliament, the power to appoint the Prime Minister, and the power to dismiss the government'.[18] Similarly, this confined scope of reserve powers can be seen in the studies of the Australian political scientist Professor Donald Markwell;[19] the recent survey by Mark McKenna;[20] the study of the subject by the former governor and Supreme Court justice of the State of Victoria, Richard McGarvie;[21] those of the Canadian experts in the field of constitutional conventions, Eugene Forsey[22] and Andrew Heard;[23] as well as that of the current author.[24]

The Australia's Constitutional Commission in 1988, which was comprised of not only the notable constitutional scholars, Professors Enid Campbell and Leslie Zines, but also the former solicitor-general Maurice Byers, the former prime minister Gough Whitlam, and the former Victorian premier Rupert (Dick) Hamer, also seems to have accepted the unanimous view of that Commission's Advisory Committee (a committee that included the constitutional academic and former governor-general, Sir Zelman Cowen,[25] as well as George Winterton,[26] the republican commentator Donald Horne and the future Federal Court judge Susan Kenny)[27] that the reserve powers exist and are limited to four subject matters. That is:

(1) the appointment of the prime minister,
(2) the dismissal of the prime minister,
(3) dissolution of the House of Representatives and
(4) a double dissolution pursuant to section 57 of the *Constitution*.[28]

A majority of that Commission, however, accepted that the governor-general 'should not have the power to terminate the appointment of a prime minister whose Government still has the confidence of the House of Representatives'[29] and recommended a number of changes to Chapter 2 of the *Constitution* to limit the governor-general's powers. Those proposed limiting provisions were, however, never put to a referendum, which seems to indicate that the then government (a Labor Government led by Prime Minister Bob Hawke)[30] was happy to remain with the *status quo* as described by the Constitutional Commission.

The view of the Constitutional Commission has also been accepted by the current Commonwealth solicitor-general, Stephen Donaghue KC, in his very recent opinion on the validity of secret ministerial appointments.[31] Even the former Prime Minister Paul Keating (not one of the great fans of the reserve powers, having been a very junior minister in Whitlam's dismissed government) defined the reserve powers in 1995 when debating what he was hoping for as the soon-to-be republic. He said, accepting the advice of the Republic Advisory Committee (which was led by Malcolm Turnbull (who would later himself be prime minister) and included the former NSW premier, Nick Greiner, and the constitutional scholar, George Winterton), that the reserve powers are limited to three types of power:

> the power to appoint the Prime Minister; the power to dismiss the Prime Minister and therefore the government; and the power to refuse a request by the Prime Minister to dissolve one or both Houses of the Parliament.[32]

Twomey, however, has taken a different and broader view. She considers that the reserve powers need to be defined 'from a different perspective, by identifying the principles that underlie them and how those principles intersect and conflict and support the reserve powers' and by doing so, she has sought to 'integrate them into the Constitution and identify their scope by reference to established constitutional principles'.[33] From her approach, she has recognized that 'this may open up the possibility of reserve powers being used in relation to other subjects, such as the operation of caretaker conventions or the prorogation or summoning of Parliament', although she was of the view that 'this should not be a matter of alarm as long as they are applied in accordance with the relevant constitutional principles to secure responsible constitutional governance'.[34]

Twomey's expansive view of the reserve powers, however, seems to be somewhat individual. This is not only because of the broader scope that she seems to have given to the reserve powers but she also seems to have taken a different view from that taken by most regarding the role of academics in the establishment of constitutional conventions. She seems to have now regarded academics, such as herself, as 'persons of authority' who have the capacity to determine the acceptance of a practice as a convention.[35] And she seems to have done so despite the earlier views of Professor Ivor Jennings expressed in his very influential *Cabinet Government* in 1947 regarding 'persons of authority'. Jennings specifically excluded 'text book writers' (presumably including himself) from this group, as, in his view, 'they are not persons of authority for this purpose'.[36]

Regardless of the apparent individuality of Professor Twomey's approach, she has accepted, in her notable and lengthy *The Veiled Sceptre,* that in her view, reserve powers are now classified in 'boxes' which she has divided into 'generally accepted' and those that are 'disputed' In her 'generally accepted box', she places the few clearly accepted powers discussed above; that is, 'the appointment of a chief minister; the removal of a chief minister; and the refusal of a dissolution'.[37] But into her 'disputed box' she has also included the problematic areas of 'the refusal of royal assent; the forcing of a dissolution; the summoning of Parliament; and the prorogation of Parliament'.[38]

A very different approach has also been taken by Dr David Long in his recent work.[39] Unlike Twomey or the majority of commentators, Long takes a very narrow interpretation of the reserve powers, arguing that Kerr did not hold any 'reserve power . . . with which to dismiss a government that had the confidence of the House of Representatives'. In his view, there is an 'unalienable right of a government to continue to govern while it has the confidence of the House of Representatives'[40] and that the governor-general holds no 'personal discretion'.[41] Long's view was based on his understanding of the original intent of the founders of Australia's *Constitution*, believing that the 'Founders did not support the view of either Kerr or Barwick'.[42] This view seems even more individual than that of Twomey and even more problematic. Moreover, his view was based on what appears to be a very selective use of resources. Not only did he assert that two authors who have demonstrated considerable expertise in examining the theory and effect of conventions, Winterton and Evatt, were 'reluctant to conclude that the reserve powers actually existed',[43] which seems, at least, a very questionable proposition, but Long's reasoning ignored much of the other published material regarding conventions, including making no reference at all to any of the many works of Professor Twomey on that subject.[44] His analysis also ignored many other instances of conventions being exercised – such as the 1932 dismissal of NSW Premier Jack Lang,[45] or the 1952 Victorian instance of the exercise of a refusal to accept advice to dissolve the Lower House when supply had been blocked.[46] Long's view seems a peculiar and individual interpretation of the operation of conventions, which does little to clarify the scope and effect of reserve powers.

All this still leads to confusion for most of today's readers as to the scope of reserve powers, which is made even worse when the supposed expertise of the popular commentators on the 1975 dismissal is taken into account. As an example, one can consider the otherwise informative 2020 seven-part podcast from the Australian Broadcasting Commission that discussed and sought to explain the 1975 dismissal, entitled *The Eleventh*, where the host Alex Mann seems to have ignored or simply misunderstood the rules of the game. Despite the purpose of the series, the terms 'convention' and 'reserve powers' were not even used, much less defined, in any of Mann's episodes, despite being essential to any understanding of 1975.

Misunderstandings on the 1975 events are also common in the widely quoted journalistic efforts written by Paul Kelly and Troy Bramston, as can be seen with their confused view of the basis of what occurred in 1975, which is apparent in the title of their very famous book on the dismissal: *The Dismissal in the Queen's Name*. Catchy, no doubt, but incorrect. All one needs to do is examine the documents covering that exercise of power (the important ones are in the back of their book) and, in particular, the letter from the governor-general to the prime minister of November 11 1975,[47] and the constitutional power that was exercised (s 64 of the *Australian Constitution*), to recognize their inaccuracy. While the governor-general was appointed by the Monarch, the powers under the *Constitution* to dismiss the prime minister are only exercisable by the governor-general. Moreover, Governor-General Kerr did not purport to sack the prime minister 'in the Queen's Name' but overtly exercised that power himself and made no reference to the Queen. To demonstrate, here are Kerr's words from his letter of dismissal to Whitlam of November 11, 1975:

> I hereby determine your appointment . . .
>
> I also hereby determine the appointment of all of the Ministers in your Government.
>
> I decided that, if you did, I would determine your commission and state my reasons for doing so.
>
> I have accordingly acted as indicated.
>
> I attach a statement of my reasons which I intend to publish immediately.
>
> I have taken this step . . .
>
> I propose to send for the Leader of the Opposition.[48]

Kelly and Bramston also take a very broad understanding of the scope of reserve powers, an understanding that will find little support from those with actual expertise in the field. For example, they consider that the doctrine includes: 'the Crown's discretion to deny royal assent to bills',[49] as well as the power to reject the prime minister's advice for a half-senate election 'because supply could not be guaranteed for the campaign'.[50]

Kelly and Bramston also have a somewhat confused understanding of what the concepts of conventions and reserve powers mean. That can be seen in their chapter in *The Truth of the Palace Letters*, which they confidently call 'The Truth of the Reserve Powers'. There, they describe their understanding of reserve powers, not by examining the basic nature of those powers but by listing a number of what they see as their method of operation and their historical origins. For them, it is 'a legacy from medieval times that permitted a king or queen to take discretionary action as guardian of the constitution' and that the reserve powers 'sit in a twilight land where politicians may disagree over whether or not they exist'. They also consider that they have 'evolved from the traditional operation of the monarchy' and that 'They are unwritten rules based on the discretion of the head of state'.[51] From this, it is still quite unclear what they consider reserve powers are. They do not explain what the nature of the governor-general's 'reserve power' is. But from their version of 'Truth', it seems that they consider that reserve powers are some form of unwritten legal power that they believe the governors-general, like the Monarch, can exercise without ministerial advice. If that is their view, it is simply unfounded.

The passages which Kelly and Bramston recite were, no doubt, based on Professor Twomey's book on the subject and, in particular, from her first chapter. But what Kelly and Bramston did not discuss in their chapter on the supposed 'Truth' regarding the reserve powers is the distinction between the powers being exercised, the legal or constitutional powers, and any conventions that limit the exercise of those powers,[52] a distinction which Twomey did recognize. As she said, in a passage that Kelly and Bramston did not refer to:

> 'Reserve powers', while not an ideal term, is still the more appropriate one to use for those powers that may be exercised at the head of state's discretion, but subject to convention.[53]

Had they done so, they would have recognized that, in Australia, there can be no doubt that the governor-general has the legal and constitutional power to, say, sack a head of government. That power is expressly provided by section 64 of the *Constitution*. The issue with reserve powers is not whether there is such a legal or constitutional power, but whether there is an unwritten but 'binding' convention that requires that legal or constitutional power to be exercised in accordance with ministerial advice. That constitutional power is a legal concept, being written or referred to in the *Constitution*, unlike any convention which controls the exercise of that power. Such a convention is not a law; it is not applied or enforced by the Courts[54] and it is not stated in the *Constitution*.

A better and more straightforward distinction between legal powers and conventions which constrain their exercise was made in the current author's earlier book on conventions, *Constitutional Conventions in Australia*:

> The name of the convention is in some ways misleading as it implies that the Governor has a 'reserve' of powers, in addition to the other powers that are exercised on the basis of advice. It is more accurate to say that all executive powers are vested in the Governor and he or she is required by law or convention to exercise the vast bulk of those powers in accordance with advice. However, by convention, some powers can be exercised without advice, and they are the 'reserve powers'.[55]

As to the views of Whitlam's biographer, Professor Hocking, her view is that the reserve powers either do not exist, or that their 'very existence . . . was, at best, arguable'.[56] Neither of those views is accurate. While she accurately considers that the reserve powers are 'unspecified in the Constitution';[57] but that tells you nothing about the existence of that convention, as conventions are, as we have seen, not listed in the *Constitution*. If they were there, that presence would lead to the risk of converting a 'binding' conventional practice, which the courts will not enforce, into a law enforceable by the courts.[58]

Hocking's views are also based on her questionable assessment that the existence of the reserve powers has been subject to 'intense debate'. But for that she has given little support other than the views of the former

Solicitor-General, Sir Maurice Byers, who has been quoted as later considering the reserve powers as 'a fiction'. She relied on his view that 'They don't exist . . . you can't have a reserve power because you are saying, "the Governor-General can override the people's choice." And that's nonsense'.[59] Gough Whitlam also had a similarly limited view of the reserve powers, at least prior to his dismissal. He told the Australian Broadcasting Corporation's *This Day Tonight,* on October 17, 1975, of his view of the respective powers of the governor-general and the prime minister, in an exchange that the governor-general recorded in his book on the dismissal:

> Q. Must Sir John Kerr accept your advice, whatever advice you give him?
> A. Unquestionably. The Governor-General takes advice from his Prime Minister and from no-one else.
> Q. And must he act on that advice?
> A. Unquestionably. The Governor-General must act on the advice of his Prime Minister.
> Q. There is no tolerance here? He must do . . .?
> A. None whatever . . . There is no question that the Queen or her viceroy must accept the advice of the Prime Minister.[60]

The difficulty with Hocking, and the early Whitlam and the late Byers 'fictional' view is that, as we have seen, most scholars and lawyers with extensive or even passing familiarity with government and the *Constitution* would not agree. There may be variations of opinion between these commentators and participants as to the scope of those powers and whether they agree with the actions of Sir John Kerr or not; but none of them would agree with the supposed view that the reserve powers are or were 'a fiction'.

Even Whitlam and Byers, as seen from their view when on the Constitutional Commission, as seen earlier in this chapter, have rejected such limited views. And that was not the only place where Byers accepted the existence of the reserve powers. Professor Twomey reviewed the opinions provided by Byers as solicitor-general between 1973 and 1983 for the purpose of the Maurice Byers Lecture in 2020 and has pointed out that his formal legal advice accepted the existence of the reserve powers. She made reference to the draft opinion delivered November 6, 1975, discussed later in chapter 8, and to another opinion from Byers from November 1983. As Professor Twomey put it:

> This draft opinion is often mischaracterised as saying that the Governor-General did not have the power to dismiss Whitlam or that the reserve powers did not exist. This is untrue. It recognised that such a power existed, but argued that Kerr did not have a duty to exercise it and was not compelled to do so in the circumstances. That, in itself, is a perfectly reasonable view to take, with which most would agree. The Governor-General had a discretion, but not an obligation,

to act, and how he exercised that discretion remains a subject of genuine and heated debate. But that is ultimately a political issue, not a question of law.

In a later opinion, given in 1983, Sir Maurice confirmed his view that the constitutional power of Sir John Kerr to dismiss the Whitlam Government existed, that the Governor-General possessed this power in his own right, and that it was his alone and not the Queen's to exercise. But in his view there was no duty to exercise the power.[61]

Moreover, Byers, in a letter to the *Australian Financial Review* of November 19, 1975, also accepted the existence of the reserve powers. As that letter said, the governor-general has:

> asserted a reserve power to dismiss Mr Whitlam's Ministry and to appoint Mr Fraser as Prime Minister. The exercise of this power was assented to, as of course, it must be. *The question can never be the existence of that power.* It is always whether the power should have been exercised. Such I take to be the present question under debate. [Emphasis added][62]

None of this supports Hocking's fictional or imaginary view regarding the reserve powers, a view that became more confused when she seems to have changed her conclusion later in her book, even if she did not seem to recognize that change. In the Epilogue that she added to the second volume of Whitlam's biography in 2014, she discussed her view of what should have happened after the House of Representatives had passed its no-confidence motion on the newly appointed Fraser Government, as it did on the afternoon of November 11, 1975 (see chapter 10). Then, according to Hocking, 'Kerr's actions in dismissing Whitlam would have, and should have, unravelled' and that, as a result, 'Kerr would reinstate Whitlam as Prime Minister'.[63] But how could Kerr have done that unless Fraser had ceased to be Prime Minister? That could only have occurred if either Fraser had resigned (something which Kerr cannot control) or if Kerr had sacked Fraser. So, if Hocking believes that Kerr should have 'reinstated' Whitlam as prime minister, it seems that she must also now accept that the governor-general did have the power to sack a prime minister. As such, although she may not have realized it, she now seems to have accepted that the reserve powers cannot be a 'fiction'.

RESERVE POWERS AND 'ADVICE'

It does, however, appear that much of the confusion regarding the operation of the reserve powers, particularly by the various 'popular' experts on 1975 has been caused by their apparent lack of appreciation of what the apparently simple word 'advice' actually means when conventions apply, and what it means when they do not. That can be seen from, for example, Paul Kelly's inaccurate observation as to the constitutional role of the governor-general: 'By convention and tradition, the Governor-General always acted on the advice of his Ministers and not without that advice'.[64] Similarly, Professor Hocking expressed the incorrect view that 'the very basis of the Governor-General's role in the Australian system of government' necessitated 'the central requirement that he act on the advice of his elected ministers';[65] and a decision of a governor-general to obtain 'formal advice' from the chief justice regarding the reserve powers was 'perverse' if it was 'against the Prime Minister's direction'.[66]

Both of those and similar observations of popular experts fail to recognize the difference between the nature of the advice which the governor-general receives when he or she is conventionally obliged to act in accordance with that advice, when the advice is *formal constitutional advice* that is binding on the governor-general; and any *informal and non-binding advice* that the governor-general can seek when conventions do not require compliance with that advice – when the reserve powers operate. As Professor Twomey has observed:

> Much of the controversy about the legitimacy of the Sovereign or a vice-regal officer consulting constitutional experts arises from confusion about the different types of 'advice' sought and relied upon.[67]

Popular 'experts' have demonstrated that confusion arises from failing to recognize both the differences between the two types of 'advice' and also failing to recognize that when the reserve powers apply, the governor-general is free to seek informal advice from any source that will assist him in exercising his powers.

Twomey described the two types of advice, binding and informal, in the following two paragraphs:

> The constitutional convention binding the Sovereign and her vice-regal representatives is that except in the exercise of reserve powers, he or she acts upon the advice of responsible Ministers. 'Advice', in this context, is conventionally binding advice. Responsibility for the actions taken pursuant to such advice is transferred from the person who takes the advice to the person responsible for giving the advice. Ministers are responsible to the people through Parliament for the advice that they give the Sovereign or her vice-regal representatives. This type of advice will be described here as 'formal constitutional advice'.
>
> When, however, the Sovereign or a vice-regal officer is contemplating the exercise of a reserve power, he or she might wish to have advice about the extent of his or her reserve powers and the application of conventions and precedents to their exercise. That advice may be legal or political in nature. There is no

> conventional requirement that the advice be acted upon. Nor is there any transfer of responsibility from the person acting pursuant to the advice to the person who gave it. The advice is given simply to inform the Sovereign or vice-regal officer, aiding the formation of his or her own decision about how to act. In this article, it will be described as informal advice.[68]

As a result, as Twomey has also observed:

> while it is true to state that 'the Governor-General cannot act on the advice of anyone other than responsible ministers', when what is meant by advice is formal constitutional advice, it is also true that the Queen and her vice-regal representatives are entitled to seek and receive informal advice from others, including constitutional and political science experts, to aid them in the formation of their own independent judgement when it comes to exercising the reserve powers.[69]

As to the source of advice, when the governor-general is conventionally bound to comply with advice, the advice must come from Ministers. But when reserve powers apply, the governor-general is responsible for their exercise, so the governor-general is, as Professor Twomey has recently observed, 'entitled to act according to his or her discretion, without the advice of responsible ministers or contrary to such advice'[70] and that 'an actual decision to exercise a reserve power is one that only the head of state can make'.[71] And in relation to such 'non-formal advice', the governor-general can seek whatever advice he or she seeks. That is apparent from the views of Professor Don Markwell, relying on the words of Sir John Kerr's predecessor as governor-general, Sir Paul Hasluck, who had expressed the view that a governor-general, when considering the exercise of the reserve powers, must be 'free to consult "eminent authorities *of his own choosing*"'.[72] Accordingly, as Markwell also said in 1999, the governor-general can seek 'opinions and information from *all sources*' as determined by the governor-general to assist 'in helping to determine how to exercise his or her powers'.[73]

Professor Twomey has reached the same view. As she said, in 2015, a governor-general may receive advice regarding the scope of the reserve powers and:

> this advice is sought or received for the purposes of informing and aiding the Governor-General in making his or her own determination about the exercise of his or her powers. *The decision is that of the Governor-General.* Any advice that he or she receives does not shift responsibility for the exercise of a power from the Governor-General to the person giving the advice. It is not conventionally binding. The Governor-General may receive advice from many quarters as a means of developing an informed opinion. Such advice, which is described in this article as 'informal advice', is necessary to support the Governor-General

> in the performance of his or her functions. It is commonly given and received. It is neither unprecedented nor unconstitutional.[74]

The Canadian expert on reserve powers, Eugene Forsey, also put it in his 1990 review of the reserve powers (when referring to the Monarch's use of those powers):

> If she is to use her discretion wisely, she is entitled to all the information and informed opinion she can get. She is therefore free to consult whom she chooses. The opinions she may receive are, of course, not in the least binding.[75]

These, then, were the rules that governed the 1975 dismissal. And, as can be seen, they were everything that good government does not require, being obscure, vague and complex. As a result, those obscure, vague and complex rules have served to confuse not only most subsequent attempted explanations of 1975 and its causes, particularly those of popular authors, but also the understandings of most Australians, whether lawyers, politicians or anyone else.

Whether those actually involved in the 1975 supply crisis and the dismissal of the Whitlam government had any better understanding of what they were doing, we will consider in the later chapters.

NOTES

1. *Re Resolution to Amend the Constitution* [1981] 1 SCR 753, 774–5.
2. Stephen Donaghue, "In the Matter of the Validity of the Appointment of Mr Morrison to Administer the Department of Industry, Science, Energy and Resources," August 22, 2022, 16; https://www.pmc.gov.au/news/solicitor-general-opinion-matter-validity-appointment-mr-morrison-administer-department.
3. Donaghue, "In the Matter of The Validity" 16, quoting Isaacs J in *Commonwealth v Kreglinger & Fernau Ltd* (1926) 37 CLR 393 at 413.
4. See Anne Twomey, *The Veiled Sceptre* (Cambridge: Cambridge University Press, 2018), 26; Ian Killey, *Constitutional Conventions in Australia* (North Melbourne, Victoria: Australian Scholarly Publishing, 2009 & 2012), 20–24.
5. W. Ivor Jennings, *Cabinet Government* (Cambridge: Cambridge University Press, 1947), 7. He specifically excluded "text book writers" (presumably including himself) from this group as "they are not persons of authority for this purpose."
6. Anne Twomey, "Constitutional Convention and Constitutional Reality" (2004) 78 *Australian Law Journal* 798, 810.
7. See Killey, *Constitutional Conventions*, 25.

8. Michael Crommelin, "Book Review – Constitutional Conventions and the Headship of State by Donald Markwell" (2017) 40 *Melbourne University Law Review* 1132, 1133.

9. The executive power of the Commonwealth is vested in the monarch, but "is exercisable by the Governor-General as the Queen's representative."

10. Anne Twomey, "Advice to Vice-regal Officers by Crown Law Officers and Others" (2015) 26 *Public Law Review* 193, 194, emphasis added.

11. *Constitution Act 1934* (Tas) s 8B.

12. Prime minister between 1971 and 1972.

13. Hocking, *His Time* (2012), 308.

14. Anne Twomey, *The Veiled Sceptre* (Cambridge: Cambridge University Press, 2018).

15. Which includes: Anne Twomey, "Advice to the Governor-General on the Appointment of Kevin Rudd as Prime Minister" (2013) 24 *Public Law Review* 289; Anne Twomey, "Advice to Vice-regal Officers by Crown Law Officers and Others" (2015) 26 *Public Law Review* 193; Anne Twomey, "Changing the Leader – The Constitutional Conventions Concerning the Resignation of Prime Ministers and Premiers" (2011) 39(3) *Federal Law Review* 329; Anne Twomey, "Constitutional Convention and Constitutional Reality" (2004) 78 *Australian Law Journal* 798; Anne Twomey, "From Bagehot to Brexit: The Monarch's Rights to be Consulted, to Encourage and Warn" (2018) 107(4) *The Round Table* 417; Anne Twomey, "Legal Advice by Judges on the Exercise of Reserve Powers" [2016] *Public Law* 285; Anne Twomey, "Sir Maurice Byers Lecture 2020: 'Maurice Byers – Legal Advice in the Constitutional Maelstrom of the Whitlam Era'" [2020] (Summer) *Bar News* 36; Anne Twomey, "The Exercise of Reserve Powers in Victoria from 1912–1955" (2014) 39 *Australian Bar Review* 198; Anne Twomey, "The Governor-General's Role in the Formation of Government in a Hung Parliament" (2011) 22 *Pubic Law Review* 52; Anne Twomey, "The Reserve Powers in Times of Political Crisis: The Dutton/Turnbull Leadership Challenge and Royal Assent to the Medevac Bill and Brexit Bills" (2021) 49(1) *Federal Law Review* 96.

16. Anne Twomey, "The Unrecognised Reserve Powers" *High Court Public Lecture* (2012) 1.

17. George Winterton, *Monarchy to Republic, Australian Republican Government* (Melbourne: Oxford University Press, 1994), 32. Also see Winterton, *Parliament, Executive, Governor-General*, 16–17.

18. Brendan Lim, *Australia's Constitution after Whitlam* (Cambridge: Cambridge University Press, 2017), 40.

19. See Markwell, *Australian Experience*, 61.

20. Mark McKenna, "Kerr's Ghost: The Office of Governor-General in Australia After 1975," in *Viceregalism: The Crown as Head of State in Political Crises in Postwar Commonwealth*, ed. H. Kumarasingham (Cham: Palgrave, Macmillan, 2020), 412, 418.

21. Richard E. McGarvie, *Democracy, Choosing Australia's Republic* (Carlton, Victoria: Melbourne University Press, 1999), 146.

22. See his discussions in Eugene Forsey, "Introduction – The Present Position of the Reserve Powers of the Crown," in *Evatt and Forsey on the Reserve Powers* (Sydney, New South Wales: Legal Books, 1990).

23. Andrew Heard, *Canadian Constitutional Conventions, The Marriage of Law and Politics* (Ontario: Oxford University Press, 2nd edition, 2014), ch 2.

24. Killey, *Constitutional Conventions*, ch 7.

25. Governor-General between 1977 and 1982.

26. See Winterton's writings, which include:

- Winterton, *Parliament, Executive, Governor-General*;
- Winterton, *Monarchy to Republic*;
- George Winterton, "1975: The Dismissal of the Whitlam Government," in *Australian Constitutional Landmarks*, ed. H. P. Lee and George Winterton (Cambridge: Cambridge University Press, 2003).

27. Appointed to the Federal Court in 1998.

28. *Final Report of the Constitutional Commission* (Canberra: Australian Government Publishing Service, 1988), Vol 1, 327 [5.71].

29. *Final Report Constitutional Commission*, Vol 1, 326 [5.67].

30. Prime minister between 1983 and 1991.

31. Donaghue, "In the Matter of The Validity," 7.

32. Commonwealth of Australia, *Parliamentary Debates*, House of Representatives, June 7, 1995, 1434.

33. Twomey, "Unrecognised Reserve Powers," 1. The principles that she has used that underlie her view of what the reserve powers are – are Responsibility, the rule of law and Necessity.

34. Twomey, "Unrecognised Reserve Powers," 13.

35. Jennings, *Cabinet Government*, 7.

36. Jennings, *Cabinet Government*, 1, fnote 1.

37. Twomey, *Veiled Sceptre*, 10.

38. Twomey, *Veiled Sceptre*, 10.

39. Long, *Australia's American Constitution.*

40. Long, *Australia's American Constitution*, 261.

41. Long, *Australia's American Constitution*, 237.

42. Long, *Australia's American Constitution*, 4.

43. Long, *Australia's American Constitution*, 260.

44. He did, however, rely on Twomey, but only in relation to different and unrelated subjects, such as the Commonwealth being subject to Imperial sovereignty, despite s 128 (see Long, *Australia's American Constitution*, 23–25 & 44.

45. This dismissal is discussed in Anne Twomey, "The Dismissal of the Lang Government," in *State Constitutional Landmarks*, ed. George Winterton (Annandale, NSW: Federation, 2006), 129.

46. See Killey, *Constitutional Conventions*, 169–171.

47. Kelly & Bramston, *The Dismissal*, 369. Sadly, the pages in this book where the documents are pictured are not numbered – but are between the unnumbered pages 331 and 398.

48. Passages from the letter from Sir John Kerr to the Hon E G Whitlam QC MP of November 11, 1975, found in Kelly & Bramston, *The Dismissal*, 369.

49. Kelly & Bramston, *Truth, Palace Letters,* 35.

50. Paul Kelly & Bramston, *The Dismissal*, 175.

51. See Kelly & Bramston, *Truth, Palace Letters,* 35 and see Kelly & Bramston, *The Dismissal,* 76.

52. In the "Truth" chapter itself, Kelly and Bramston used the word "convention" only once, and in a quotation from Twomey. See Kelly & Bramston, *Truth, Palace Letters,* 41.

53. See, for example, Twomey, *Veiled Sceptre*, 7.

54. See *Re Resolution to Amend the Constitution* [1981] 1 SCR 753, 774–5.

55. Killey, *Constitutional Conventions,* 130.

56. Hocking, *His Time* (2014) 573.

57. Hocking, *His Time* (2012) 307.

58. Unless there is some form of limiting provision, as was attempted in the 1999 Establishment of Republic Bill, which is discussed in Killey, *Naked Constitution,* 51.

59. Byers' views are quoted by Whitlam, "Go to the Documents," 6, and were used by Hocking in *His Time* (2014), 573 and *Palace Letters,* 204.

60. Kerr, *Matters,* 279; See also Kelly, *Unmaking,* 274 and Kelly & Bramston, *The Dismissal,* 137.

61. Twomey, "Sir Maurice Byers Lecture 2020," 40.

62. "Solicitor General Explains Opinion: Did Not Deny Crown's Power," *Sydney Morning Herald*, November 19, 1975, 10.

63. Hocking, *His Time* (2014), 571.

64. Kelly, *Unmaking*, 328.

65. Hocking, *His Time* (2014), 309

66. Hocking, *His Time* (2014), 361.

67. Twomey, "Legal Advice by Judges," 286.

68. Twomey, "Legal Advice by Judges," 286.

69. Twomey, "Legal Advice by Judges," 286.

70. Twomey, *Veiled Sceptre*, 19.

71. Twomey, *Veiled Sceptre*, 23.

72. Don Markwell, "On Advice from the Chief Justice: A Reply to Gareth Evan' Challenge," *Quadrant,* July 1985, 38, 38. The words in inverted commas are those of the former governor-general, Paul Hasluck from *The Office of Governor-General* (Carlton, Victoria: Melbourne University Press, 1979), 21. The emphasis was added by Markwell.

73. Don Markwell, "Griffith, Barton and the Early Governor-Generals: Aspects of Australia's Constitutional Development" (1999) 10 *Public Law Review* 280, 282, emphasis added.

74. Twomey, "Advice by Crown Law Officers," 195, emphasis added.

75. Forsey, "The Present Position," lxxvii and quoted in Killey, *Constitutional Conventions,* 136. Also see Twomey, *Veiled Sceptre*, 206 & 257 and Markwell, *Australian Experience*, 41.

Chapter 4

1975

And the ALP

Figure 4.1 ALP Political Badge from the 1972 Election. From the collection of the author. Image taken by the author.

The supply crisis, the underlying cause of the dismissal of the Whitlam government, occurred when the Australian Senate, which the government did not control, deferred passage of appropriation legislation (supply bills). Without money, the governor-general took the view that the prime minister must call an election. As Prime Minister Whitlam refused to do that, the governor-general felt he had no other option but to terminate Whitlam's commission and appoint someone else who could both provide supply and advise him to call an election. For that to occur, the dismissal needed to occur weeks before the money actually ran out, without giving any indication to the prime minister of the likelihood that he would be dismissed.

That is the John Kerr version of what occurred on November 11. The issue is, however, a bit more complex than that. But to understand that, we need to first examine and explain the nature of the government that was dismissed on that day – a government that has been left with a variety of conflicting descriptions ranging from being the most significant reformist government that Australia has seen to one that was scandal-ridden, chaotic and shambolic. As Malcolm Fraser then put it, Whitlam's government was 'the most incompetent and disastrous Government in the history of Australia'.[1]

THE ALP AND THE WHITLAM GOVERNMENT

The election in 1972 of the Whitlam Labor government was a long-awaited return of a reform administration. The Australian Labor Party (the ALP) had, in the first half of the twentieth century, a long and central role in Australian government. Indeed, Australia was the first country with a national government devoted to the Labor cause when the ALP's federal parliamentary leader, Chris Watson, became Australia's third prime minister in 1904.[2] Even though Watson's government did not last long, less than four months, he and his government demonstrated that the ALP had the capacity to run a country. This capacity was accepted by the Australian electorate, as can be seen from the successes of Watson's successors as head of the ALP (Fisher and Hughes), who went on to lead Australia for much of the country's first two decades.[3] Later leaders of the ALP (Curtin and Chifley) were also in office for the bulk of World War II and in its following years, with a Labor government lasting from 1941 until 1949. But despite Labor's early successes, by 1972, the ALP had not been in government for almost 23 years.[4] The conservative coalition of the Liberal Party and the Country Party, now called the National Party, had won all subsequent national elections since December 1949, even though in three of those elections (1954, 1961 and 1969) the ALP had actually won more votes than the Liberal/Country Party coalition government. This has led Donald Horne, with some justification, to argue that Australia's electoral system has an 'entirely false emphasis'. It is Australia's version of the perversions of the United States' electoral college system that, in 2016, allowed Hillary Clinton to lose the presidential election to Donald Trump, even though she had won more votes from the electorate.[5] Although Australia's electoral oddity can sometimes operate in Labor's favour, as it did in

1990,[6] it normally does not. As a result, Horne's conclusion seems justified; that is, 'A democratic Constitution should guard against such injustice'.[7] But Australia's *Constitution*, like that of the United States, clearly does not.

But the electoral advantages that had previously assisted the conservative coalition were not sufficient to keep Labor from office in the 1972 election. The conservative parties had become less electable, less popular and were remarkably enfeebled. And that was largely because the Liberal Party had suffered from many leadership changes in the previous six years since 1966 – from Menzies, to Holt, to Gorton and then to the leader whom the Liberal Party's coalition partner, the Country Party, did not trust – the very unappealing and non-charismatic Billy McMahon.[8] And when that enfeeblement was combined with the reformist energies of the Labor leader, Gough Whitlam, and his 'It's Time' electoral campaign, Australians were prepared to finally change the direction of the country and bring Labor back into power after its very long absence.

Paul Hasluck, the governor-general when Whitlam came into office in 1972, was an astute political observer. And he predicted, despite his Liberal Party background, that Whitlam 'would be one of our great prime ministers and certainly the first leader of distinction and capacity since Menzies'. But he also considered that Whitlam's 1972 election success was assisted by 'some good fortune', occurring 'at a time when the government was sadly discredited and when the contrast between him and McMahon' (a man who Hasluck also disliked, considering him a 'mean little figure') 'was the most favourable contrast for which any party leader could have hoped'.[9]

It's Time. That was the election slogan used by the ALP in 1972 to regain power after decades in opposition (see figure 4.1). It was the first developed use of modern media techniques in selling political messages in election campaigning in Australia.[10] And it was remarkably successful.

The election campaign sold the Labor message with a very catchy and emotive tune, one composed by an advertising executive and a jingle writer.[11] This process was so central to Labor's plan that it released the slogan, the song and its central television advertisement used in its media campaign in August 1972, well prior to the election being called, taking the initiative from the McMahon coalition government. That advertisement that we can see now in its colour version was then seen by Australian voters on their black and white televisions, as colour television did not become Australia's form of television broadcasting until March 1975. But that monochrome presentation did not impact the song, the 'It's Time' slogan or the advertisement. The campaign theme was sung by the young singer, Alison MacCallum, and that song is probably the most famous of her recordings. The opening words of 'It's

Time' reflect the theme of changes that the Whitlam government intended to introduce:

It's Time
It's time for freedom,
It's time for moving, It's time to begin,
Yes It's time
It's time Australia,
It's time for moving, It's time for proving,
Yes It's time.

And when the election occurred on December 2, the electorate agreed with the slogan, and Labor's time had finally and eventually begun. Labor's victory was clear. The party that had not been in federal government since 1949 had now won 67 Lower House seats in comparison with the 58 seats of the coalition. Labor had swept all seats in Tasmania and the Australian Capital Territory (ACT) and was the dominant party in the states of New South Wales and South Australia. Voting was closer in the rest of the country, but the overall result was clear, if not substantial. Labor had an overall vote of 52.8%, with a nine seat majority in the Lower House.

Gough Whitlam was, however, not prepared to wait before he got into action. As he had earlier told Freudenberg on the evening of his policy speech: 'It's been a long road, comrade, but we're there'.[12] The new government began its reforming approach immediately, with all Ministerial portfolios initially divided between Whitlam and his deputy, Lance Barnard. This new, two-man government, known as the 'duumvirate' government, operated for the first fortnight of the new Labor government, between December 5 and 19. This was, as observed by Whitlam, 'the smallest administration having jurisdiction over Australia since the Wellington-Lyndhurst Government in 1834'.[13] But as Bill Hayden has also recalled, Whitlam demonstrated both his eagerness, his ego as well his hubris, when he had said that the 'duumvirate' government was 'the best government he had ever had, except it was twice as large as it needed to be'.[14]

This two-man government was an unorthodox but constitutional basis for government. And it was the one that allowed rapid decision-making regarding government decisions that did not require legislative change, enabling decisions to be made on a considerable range of important issues. Significant decisions were made by the duumvirate, including:

- withdrawing Australian troops from the Vietnam War;
- freeing conscientious objectors to that war;
- banning racially selected sporting teams visiting Australia;

- purchasing new F-111 planes from the US;
- commencing the independence of Papua New Guinea;
- removing the ban on the advertisement of contraceptives;
- instructing the internal government-owned airline, TAA, to lower fares;
- closing the Rhodesian Information Centre in Sydney;
- restoring the passport of the communist journalist Wilfred Burchett, who had been deprived of an Australian passport since 1955;[15]
- recalling the Australian ambassadors to the UN, Washington and Taiwan;
- announcing a judicial inquiry into Aboriginal Land rights and
- beginning talks leading to the diplomatic recognition of China.[16]

This form of decision-making was concerning to many in the public service as it was considered rushed. But to others, it may well have been the best time of the Whitlam government as it allowed decisions to be made promptly, reflecting Labor values and policy objectives. As Bramston observes, the decisions made by the Whitlam government in its first 40 days 'were among the most ground-breaking decisions of any government since Federation'.[17] There were concerns that there were no Cabinet meetings during the duumvirate period, but Whitlam apparently saw no difficulty with this, considering that every decision was based on 'our unmistaken mandate'.[18]

The duumvirate, however, could not be a permanent approach, and so, from December 19, 1972, a full Cabinet was appointed, and the pace of government decisions slowed down considerably. This does not mean that Labor had lost its reformist drive, as later decisions that have impacted Australia included:

- abolishment of tertiary fees in 1973;[19]
- the introduction of a universal health care scheme, then known as Medicare – a scheme that, although it has changed since the 1970s, is now so well established and so well accepted by the Australian community that no conservative government would ever want to remove it;
- Senate representation for the Territories;
- the introduction of the *Family Law Act 1975*, which replaced dissolution of marriage due to guilt with 'irretrievable breakdown of marriage'[20] and
- the purchase, for the then extraordinary price of $A1.3 million, of the abstract artwork of the artist Jackson Pollock, *Blue Poles*. Whitlam himself approved the purchase price and required that that sum be made public, generating much debate and furore. Whitlam became the subject of numerous aggressive denunciations following this purchase as it brought out, as Hocking put it, 'the essential Philistine in his opponents'.[21] The value of the painting, however, has subsequently risen considerably and has recently been reported as 'now worth a whopping $500 million, according to a new

valuation by its keeper, the National Gallery of Australia'.[22] As a result, Whitlam's investment in this abstract work seems to have become representative of the Whitlam government at its best, being both his finest economic as well as his best cultural achievement.[23]

SCANDALS IN THE WHITLAM GOVERNMENT – MURPHY AND ASIO

Things, however, did not always go so well for the Whitlam government. The first serious decision made by the Whitlam government was one made by its Attorney-General Lionel Murphy as early as March 1973, when he 'raided' the nation's security organization, the Australian Security Intelligence Organisation (ASIO).

The relationship between ASIO and the ALP has never been good, and it was not assisted by the growing number of protests against the Vietnam War, which centrally involved some key ALP leaders, particularly the future deputy prime minister, Dr Jim Cairns, who was very suspicious of the methods and intent of the ASIO.[24] For example, in July 1968, Cairns argued that ASIO had spies working for it in every Australian university, with information tabulated and provided to government officials.[25] Lionel Murphy also had, as Blaxland put it, a 'deep concern over the practices of ASIO and reluctance to take on trust what ASIO officers told him'.[26] The result was that when the ALP finally returned to government in December 1972, it replaced what Blaxland also refers to as 'A cosy relationship of apparently studied indifference to the detailed workings of ASIO' under the conservative coalition, with what most ASIO officers considered to be Labor's 'unduly intrusive approach to the day-to-day running' of the organization.[27] And that strained relationship was not assisted by what, even today, seems as absurd – the Murphy ASIO ministerial 'raid'.

That 'raid' happened three months into the new government, on March 16, 1973[28] when Murphy was seeking information regarding an assassination plan of Whitlam and other senior officials by a right-wing Croatian organization, a threat that ASIO had not raised with the attorney-general.[29] But the decision to 'raid' ASIO was also based on two other related factors that seem more rooted in the attorney-general's lack of experience and his limited understanding of ASIO. According to ASIO's historian, John Blaxland, Murphy had little knowledge 'as to how ASIO functioned', and what understanding that he did have of the organisation was 'largely politically driven'.[30]

Although there have been attempts to minimize Murphy's ASIO foray as being merely a 'ministerial visit',[31] it seems pointless to deny that ASIO was 'raided' on the early morning of March 16 when 27 Commonwealth Police

Officers, under the direct control of Police Commissioner, Jack Davis, seized control of the ASIO headquarters. They sealed its safes and stairwells, preventing ASIO staff from going to their offices or even to the toilet. As Blaxland records, 'A subsequent report on the incident noted that "for practical purposes the staff were under house arrest and this had a chilling effect on morale"'.[32]

The raid (or visit) was also pointless, as it achieved nothing of interest to the Minister or damaging to ASIO. But what it did achieve was to further increase the already high tensions between the attorney-general and ASIO. What was even worse was that it was also made without Whitlam being informed or advised.[33] As he would later concede to Bramston, 'the ASIO raid was the biggest mistake of his government's first year'.[34] However, its greatest external effect may well have been, as Freudenberg pointed out, 'the end of the honeymoon period normally enjoyed between a new government and the press'.[35] The latter was of particular importance as, to the press, 'The ASIO visit smacked of that authoritarian tendency which had been the most unattractive characteristic of the [earlier] Chifley Labor Government'.[36]

This incident also had other effects of more significance to Whitlam's new government and its supporters, as that hastily arranged, badly advised and ineffectual 'ASIO visit' became, as Freudenberg has observed, 'the first serious blow to the self confidence of the Labor Government and the first serious check to the unqualified enthusiasm of its supporters'.[37] Sadly for the new government, more would follow.

PROBLEMS WITH JIM CAIRNS

The second area of concern for the Whitlam government was the prime minister's relationship with another senior Labor minister, Jim Cairns. Cairns was not close to Whitlam. However, he was very popular in the Party due to both charisma and intellect, being a central hero and leader of anti-Vietnam War protest marches during the late 1960s and early 1970s, including leading one with a crowd of 70,000 in Melbourne in May 1970.[38] He was a former Victorian policeman who became an academic with expertise in economic history, a very odd background for any Labor politician, much less one from the left of that Party. It was also a remarkable achievement, particularly in the 1940s and the 1950s[39] when Australian university education was not for the man in the street.

Cairns was one of those who, as Freudenberg puts it, both 'distrusted power and wanted power'. He was noted for delivering his 'speeches of burning passion' but in his 'cold monotone'.[40] As Sexton puts it, Cairns was 'A fluent, lucid and compelling speaker who could, unlike, the majority of

Australian politicians, appeal unselfconsciously to the broad ideals of morality and justice'.[41] And he was one of the few in the Party who could effectively challenge Whitlam for Party leadership. Although Whitlam had clearly won the Party leadership when that office fell vacant in 1967, easily beating off all other potential Party leaders,[42] the new leader seemed to have undermined that victory in the following year when he made what many believed a highly questionable decision: resigning his leadership due to his dispute with the Party Executive. Whitlam sought re-election from Caucus,[43] a step that many in the Party consider as petulant.[44] But it also made his domination of the Party far less clear as he was now only able to defeat his sole challenger, Cairns, by the relatively narrow margin of six votes, 38 to 32.[45] And that minority included Whitlam's predecessor as Party leader, Arthur Calwell,[46] who had never trusted Whitlam, considering him both 'a careerist and opportunist'.[47] Calwell openly supported Cairns and opposed the continuation of Whitlam's leadership, considering that Whitlam was 'not a true Labor man'.[48]

Cairns also failed to obtain the Party's deputy leadership in 1967, but by an even closer margin when Whitlam's 'closest confidant', Lance Barnard, held on to that office by just two votes, 35 to 33.[49] After the 1974 election, however, the Labor Caucus replaced the second element in Labor's duumvirate with Cairns, and it did so with some emphasis – 54 to 42.[50] According to a Cairns' ally, Tom Uren, 'There was a strong feeling in Caucus that Cairns would be a break on Whitlam's arrogance'.[51] This was, however, as we will see, a flawed hope.

This advancement of Cairns also led to Barnard's resignation from Parliament when he became Australia's Ambassador to Sweden. That resignation, however, as we will see, was one that Labor would have been much better without (see chapter 5). The promotion of Cairns also brought some other dangers for the Labor Government, but not until December 1974, when Cairns was made Treasurer. Cairns' handling of this portfolio attracted criticism for a variety of reasons, including his hiring and relationship with his Office Co-ordinator[52] or private secretary,[53] the young, female and Asian, Junie Morosi. As Cairns later said, in 1998, Morosi was: 'always too sexually dangerous for anyone to have around'.[54] But Cairns did. He seemed more willing to accentuate and publicize this risk when he and Junie provided a lengthy interview to the press during the February 1975 ALP National Conference regarding their personal lives, which led to what Kelly described as 'banner headlines' in the Sydney *Sun*: 'My Love for Junie'.[55]

Another Cairns-related danger for the government came from allegations regarding Cairns' stepson, Phillip[56] once Cairns had promoted him to the role of 'project manager'. As Laurie Oakes observed, this gave Phillip 'a grand title', but with 'few official responsibilities'.[57] In 1998, Cairns described his stepson as 'successful as a human being but he was never successful in business'.[58] This may well be related to the allegations made in mid-1975 that Phillip had been using his newly inflated official position in Cairns' office to obtain business success and private profit. This led to an auditor-general report critical of Phillip's activities[59] and to a front-page story in the Melbourne *Age* on Tuesday, July 1, 1975, 'Cairns' Son in Arab Plan; Philip Cairns involved in scheme to sub-divide Point Cook land'.[60] In remarkably convoluted articles on that and the following day, the issue of concern was that Phillip had used his position with Cairns to gain significant private financial benefit. According to those allegations, Phillip had been a director of a company that had sought a loan of $US250 million from a Saudi Arabian prince, which would have allowed that company to develop land in Point Cook. And if that story was accurate and the loan was made, the loan would also have benefited Phillip, as his use of his official position with Dr Cairns to negotiate this loan would have allowed him to receive a commission of $600,000 (as the *Age* reported on July 2).[61] How accurate this story was remains unclear, as Phillip has denied that he would have received any commission,[62] and the source of much of what was asserted in the *Age* (another of the directors of the relevant company) also agreed that his earlier statements were both 'untrue and a fabrication by me'.[63]

That may have been enough to save Jim and his political career but for the third, Cairns-related, danger to the Whitlam government. It was an even bigger story, and one that directly affected Cairns. This arose from Cairns' relationship with a Melbourne businessman and former dentist, George Harris;[64] and may not have occurred at all had Cairns not been a supporter of the Carlton Australian Rules Football Club.

Harris was the president of that club and a very successful one. Under his presidency (between 1964 and 1974, and later from 1978 to 1980), he converted the team from one with no success for decades into one of the most powerful clubs in the league, with Carlton winning four more premierships.[65] Australian Rules Football, for any twentieth-century Melbournian, was a very passionate and personal activity based on territorial allegiances that crossed boundaries of class, religion and politics, each with its own team, generally based on the place of birth or early life. Cairns' Carlton allegiance seems based on having been born in that suburb in 1914. Although Harris and Cairns had little else in common, football drew them together. Harris recognized Cairns' football passion and arranged for him to attend football finals and meals with other prominent Carlton supporters, even ones with whom the reformist anti-Vietnam War protester would otherwise have had no common interest (such as Sir Robert Menzies).[66] But Harris also sought to make use of Cairns for business reasons.

In late 1974, he wrote to Cairns regarding loan raising from overseas sources.[67] Despite Treasury warnings regarding the dangers of using non-traditional methods,[68] Cairns met with Harris in a series of meetings in March and April 1975.[69] He provided Harris with four letters or notes empowering him to locate overseas loans. Cairns, however, it seems, was unaware of the effect of those documents and was of the incorrect view that they did not create any legal agency between Harris and the government.[70] This was an example, as Kelly observes, of both Cairns' 'unilateral administrative style . . . and his naivety in dealing with people whom he believed were respectable business men and consequently beyond reproach'.[71]

The dates of the notes or letters provided were: March 7, March 10 and two of April 15, and their content is set out in Kelly's *The Unmaking of Gough.*[72] What makes Cairns' actions odder is that he never told Treasury or anyone else about the notes. And, as Kelly also recognized, he had 'no government authority to seek overseas loan funds through intermediaries'.[73] Treasury did, however, more by accident than design, discover the March 10 and the two April 15 documents,[74] and as Treasury was most suspicious of Harris, the head of the Department, Sir Frederick Wheeler, decided to seek a legal opinion regarding the consequences and the government's obligations under the April 15 documents. And he did so without telling his Minister.[75] Legal advice was provided on Wednesday, May 28 from the head of the attorney-general department, Clarrie Harders, and it confirmed the Treasury concerns.[76] Cairns was then in Paris, and in his absence, Bill Hayden was acting treasurer. Wheeler provided Harders' advice to both Hayden and the prime minister, and, as Kelly observes, 'Whitlam was furious that Cairns had taken this action and consulted no one about it'.[77] The political danger of those letters was, to Whitlam, as Kelly puts it, 'an irrefutable basis' for his decision to dismiss Cairns from Treasury.

Whitlam wrote to Cairns requiring all overseas loan borrowing activities be stayed and that Cairns provide 'urgently copies of the documentation you have'.[78] He also rang him and asked him to return to Australia immediately.[79] Cairns returned on the following Sunday and saw the prime minister on Monday morning. As Kelly recounts it, Whitlam was in a 'resolute and blunt mood', requiring Cairns' resignation if he had signed the two April 15 notes.[80]

Cairns initially refused. But after recognising that he had lost much of the political support that had, one year earlier, enabled him to become the deputy prime minister, he now accepted his transfer and demotion to the lesser Environment portfolio on June 6.[81]

This was, however, not the end of Cairns' problems, as the text of the March 7 letter to Harris was not then known to Treasury or the prime minister. And when the letter became known, that occurred first to the Opposition, led by Malcolm Fraser, rather than the prime minister.[82] The Opposition recognized the opportunities that letter provided, and used it as the basis for a parliamentary question from the then deputy leader of the Liberal Party, Phil Lynch, on June 4. Lynch asked whether Cairns, 'in a letter dated on or about 5

March, offer[ed] a commission of two and a half percent on any loan money'. And in his response, Cairns was specific in his denial:

> The answer is no. At no stage did I offer a commission of two and half percent or any other amount or give any authority whatever to any person to do anything to any person to do anything other than make inquiries.[83]

He went on to explicitly reject offering any 'brokerage fee' to anyone.[84] The difficulty with this answer is not in its clarity but in its accuracy, as the letter of March 7, which the Opposition held, contained the promise to George Harris that:

> we would be prepared to pay a once only brokerage fee of 2½% deducted at the source to you and/or your nominees.[85]

Not only had Cairns misled Parliament, but he also went on to mislead the prime minister. Whitlam required confirmation of the location of any overseas borrowing letters later in the month, and Cairns wrote to the head of the prime minister's department, John Menadue, on June 25, stating that 'Each of the letters given to Mr Harris have [*sic*] been returned to me and have (sic) been destroyed to prevent any possible misuse'.[86] Another inaccurate statement as Cairns had at no point recovered or destroyed the March 7 letter.

Cairns presented this error as being one of memory rather than deception. In 1998, his recollection was that:

> Some short time later George Harris turned up at the Treasurer's Office in the city here, Melbourne, saying he was going overseas, and he'd like to make enquiries about what's been going on in these loans dealings. . . . And I said, 'Yes all right. I don't mind if you make enquiries, and let me know'. . . . So he said, 'Will you give me a letter of introduction?' and I said, 'Yes, I'll give you a letter of introduction'. There's about three lines in it.

As to how he came to provide the March 7 note to Harris, which was much longer and did much more than his three-line letter of introduction, he said:

> I came back upstairs and there were about fifty letters on the table. I signed them fairly quickly, and I signed one to George Harris, completely unaware that I had, so when I was asked in parliament had I ever signed a letter to George Harris I said, 'No'.[87]

In his earlier letter to the prime minister, he claimed that he rejected the Harris request for a 2.5% brokerage fee. He claimed that he:

> answered the [parliamentary] question as I did, believing that I spoke the truth. I have no recollection at all of having signed the letter . . . and I have a clear recollection that I rejected it because I found it unacceptable.[88]

He also claimed that once he had rejected the Harris draft of the March 7 letter, he had 'replaced this letter with another letter with another one which I dictated and later signed'.

However, his secretary, Karen Stegmar, made a statutory declaration regarding how the March 7 letter was prepared and signed. Her recollection was that she had prepared the letter, which had been dictated by both Cairns and Harris, and then provided the letter to Cairns with five or six other letters for signature. She asked Cairns to sign what became the March 7 letter first as Harris was waiting for it. According to Kelly, Stegmar said that Cairns 'looked at the letter for a few seconds, appeared to read it, and then signed it'.[89] She later confirmed to Cairns that he signed the March 7 letter.[90]

There are, therefore, three possible explanations of how the March 7 letter was signed, and none are to Dr Cairns' credit. The first is that he did sign it and understood its effect, and that his denials are simply not to be believed. The second is that he did not sign it, but in some manner, unexplained, the March 7 letter with his signature was provided by his office to Harris. And the last is that he signed it, but without understanding what he had signed. In any of those versions, Cairns has been duplicitous or incompetent, or both.

Not surprisingly, Whitlam was not satisfied with Cairns' explanation. This, however, is not the end of the Cairns scandal as the recently demoted minister was not prepared to resign from his ministerial post, as Whitlam now required.[91] Cairns, like Minister Clyde Cameron who Whitlam intended to demote in his ministerial reshuffle of June 1975, refused to accept the prime ministerial decision. As such, Whitlam advised the governor-general to withdraw the ministers' commissions.[92] That is, to sack them.

Both Cameron and Cairns sought, most unwisely, to meet with the governor-general to contest the prime minister's advice. Kerr, sensibly, refused to meet with them.[93] He took the view that he should not receive such ministerial arguments 'because I could not put myself in the position of being at the same time the recipient of conflicting political advice from the two Ministers'. Unless the decision falls within the scope of the reserve powers (discussed in chapter 3), the governor-general's role is not to decide the issue but to accept the advice from the prime minister, as Kerr did in relation to both Cameron and Cairns.[94] Nonetheless, the approaches to the governor-general by two experienced senior ministers to challenge advice given by the prime minister to the governor-general can only emphasize, first, the growing shambolic nature of Whitlam's lack of control over his ministry and, second, indicate to the governor-general the extent of his constitutional powers, powers that may need to be used at some stage in the future to deal with such a shambolic ministry. This was not a good combination for Prime Minister Whitlam.

REX CONNOR AND KHEMLANI

But the final scandal that impacted on the Whitlam government was the most significant. It involved the Minister for Minerals and Energy, Rex Connor, an unlikely supporter of Whitlam. He was, as Freudenberg observes, 'a massive shambling hulk of a man . . . who had spent years of frustration and resentment on the backbench of the New South Wales Legislative Assembly', out of sympathy with the right-wing control of the State Party. He was a man regarded as the unwavering 'lion of the left', and was known as 'the Strangler'[95] with his approach to Australian politics, which was 'rooted in the bitterness of the thirties and the Great Depression'.[96] Accordingly, his promise for advancement in federal politics also appeared unlikely, particularly after his transition to Canberra had been opposed by the then-Federal Labor leader, Arthur Calwell, who regarded the transfer of Connor from Sydney to Canberra as transferring 'the thorn in your side by putting it in mine'.[97] But such a transfer occurred when the Labor member for the federal seat of Cunningham, Victor Kearney, retired in 1963.[98] Connor won ALP preselection for that seat and became a formidable backbencher in the Canberra Parliament.

Connor's form of left-wing philosophy, as Kelly puts it, was 'dominated by his commitment to the cause of Australian nationalism, forged in the early part of the century before the death of Henry Lawson, whose poems he read as a boy'. And of those Lawson poems that Connor must have read and absorbed are likely to have included one of Lawson's then[99] most famous early poems, *Freedom on the Wallaby*. That poem was first published in 1891 in *The Worker*, the Journal of the Associated Workers of Queensland, and it closes with the following call for a rebellious, even a revolutionary call for Australian workers:

> So we must fly a rebel flag,
> As others did before us,
> And we must sing a rebel song
> And join in rebel chorus.
> We'll make the tyrants feel the sting
> O' those that they would throttle;
> They needn't say the fault is ours,
> If blood should stain the wattle.[100]

This may have been, as Kelly observes, a call 'of a bygone generation'; but it was still an approach that 'always carried immense weight with the ranks of the ALP'. And by this form of nationalism, Connor sought to convert it 'into a ruthless and long-range policy to maximise Australian ownership and control of the country's mineral and energy wealth'.[101] Connor, as he told Parliament on July 9, 1975, through his years as a Minister of the Crown, had 'stood in the path of those who would have grabbed the mineral resources of Australia'. And he had 'no apologies whatever to make for what' he had done. 'It has been done in good faith; it has been done in honesty'. As a result, 'I fling in the face of the little men of the Opposition the words of' what he regarded, inaccurately, as another 'old Australian poem':

> Give me men to match my mountains, Give me men to match my plains, Men with freedom in their vision, And creation in their brains.[102]

Unfortunately, this reference was not to an old Australian poem, but was an adopted and adjusted version of the American poem from 1894 by Sam Walter Foss, named 'The Coming American'.[103]

Whatever defects Connor had in his knowledge of the origins of poetry, he had other skills. One that he developed was an encyclopaedic understanding of the minutiae of the requirements of the mining and resources industry. This enabled him to become the most well-prepared Minister for Minerals and Energy whenever that office became available. And it did when he was elected by Caucus to the first post-duumvirate government, commencing from December 19, 1972. He was then one of the oldest of Whitlam's ministers (aged just under 65), but he was still very junior in the ministry: Connor was the twentieth of the twenty-seven ministers elected that day. However, his understanding of the technicalities of his portfolio, combined with his 'strangler' approach, turned him into one of the most influential and important members of the Whitlam ministry. He became the first minister elected by Caucus after the 1974 election, ranking him third after Whitlam and his new deputy, Jim Cairns.[104]

Connor saw himself as a visionary with the goal of a national minerals and energy policy, with the Australian government deciding the pace and direction of Australia's mining development. But his version of Australia's development was to be largely controlled by the government rather than the private sector.

And his public sector development program was both ambitious and extravagant. It included remarkably large and very expensive projects, such as the completion of natural gas pipelines; uranium mining, milling and enrichment plants; the electrification of heavy freight rail areas in NSW and Victoria; the upgrade of coal exporting harbours; research on coal conversion and solar energy and the development of the North-West Shelf.[105] To achieve all of that, Connor required funding that would be, on any assessment, massive. This made Connor's planning for his objective difficult, and it was also not assisted by, as Sexton observes, 'Connor's consistent refusal to take others into his confidence'.[106]

Connor first raised the massive loan issue in late 1974, initially with Lionel Bowen, the Special Minister of State, in September 1974, when the size of his proposed loan was only $A240 million.[107] And then he raised it with the minister of labour, Clyde Cameron, and through him, an Adelaide builder, Gerry Karidis, became involved. Through Karidis and a number of other middlemen, Connor then made contact with a Pakistani financial trader, Tirath Khemlani, a man who promised the world but delivered little. By that stage, in October 1974, the size of Connor's proposed loan had more than doubled to $A500 million.[108]

Khemlani met with Connor and his head of department on November 11, 1974 (one year before Whitlam's sacking), and Khemlani was provided with a letter confirming that Australia was seeking a loan of an even greater amount, having grown by a factor of eight into the astronomical figure of: '$US4,000m in blocks of $US500m, repayable at the end of twenty years'.[109]

That process was brought to its formal culmination one month later when, on Friday, December 13, 1974 (one year prior to the national election that disposed of the Whitlam government), the Executive Council gave Connor the authority to borrow $US4000 million.[110] There were, however, two other oddities regarding that meeting and that authority.

The first was that the loan was expressed to be for '"temporary' purposes. This is remarkable and problematic, being done to avoid a constitutional requirement to advise the States. Section 105A of the *Australian Constitution*, which was added to the *Constitution* in 1928, allows the Commonwealth to make agreements with the States 'with respect to the public debts of the States, including: . . . (f) the borrowing of money by the States or by the Commonwealth'. And section 105A(5) gives these agreements superior constitutional status:

> (5) Every such agreement and any such variation thereof shall be binding upon the Commonwealth and the States parties thereto *notwithstanding anything contained in this Constitution* or the Constitution of the several States or in any law of the Parliament of the Commonwealth or of any State.[111]

The agreement that was relevant in 1974 was the 1927 Financial Agreement, as varied in 1934 and 1944 and as specified in the schedule to the *Financial Agreement Act 1944* (Cth). In that Agreement, clause 3 established a body, the Loan Council, comprised of the prime minister and the State Premiers. Clause 3(8) required that:

> The Commonwealth and each State will from time to time, . . . submit to the Loan Council a programme setting forth the amount it desires to raise by loans during each financial year for purposes.

But excluded from that obligation are loans for 'the conversion, renewal or redemption of existing loans *or temporary purposes*'.[112]

As Sexton records, the head of the attorney-general's department, Clarrie Harders, was 'very uncomfortable' that such a large loan would be one for 'temporary purposes'. Similarly, the solicitor-general, Maurice Byers, was 'not confident' and the senior lawyer from the attorney-general's department, Dennis Rose (whom Sexton described as 'probably the best mind in the Department' and who later became the Commonwealth's first Chief General Counsel),[113] 'expressed flat disagreement'.[114]

However, the Attorney-General Lionel Murphy who was shortly to become a High Court justice, together with the prime minister, took a very different view, and that view prevailed. It is noted, however, that a subsequent Labor attorney-general under Prime Minister Bob Hawke (in 1983 and 1984), Gareth Evans, in his 1977 study with Professor Michael Crommelin of the Whitlam Government and its use of its constitutional powers, was forced to accept that 'It appears, then that the Labor Government's proposed loan raising without consultation with the States may indeed have been in breach of the Financial Agreement'.[115]

The second oddity of this approval is that it was done without the governor-general being present. Although s 62 of the *Constitution* refers to the functions of the Executive Council as being 'to advise the governor-general in the government of the Commonwealth', the *Constitution* also says nothing as to who is to preside over its meetings. As a result, a practice developed in Australia for a vice president of the Executive Council, usually a senior minister, to chair its meetings in the absence of the governor-general.[116] But under Whitlam, the vice president was Frank Stewart, the Minister for Tourism and Recreation,[117] which was hardly a senior portfolio – and he wasn't even at this meeting of the Executive Council. That meeting was comprised of the prime minister, Gough Whitlam; the deputy prime minister and treasurer, Jim Cairns; the attorney-general, Lionel Murphy; and Rex Connor.[118] The practice in 1974, as Whitlam made clear, was that 'If neither the governor-general nor the vice-president attends, the senior minister in attendance presides'.[119] The governor-general's function, if unable to attend, is to endorse by signature the minutes of the meeting of the Executive Council. And so, for the meeting of the Executive Council held on December 13, 1974, which allowed the Labor

Government, as Crommelin and Evans have described it, to embark 'on the biggest loan-raising enterprise in Australian history, an enterprise huge by international standards and one which if carried through to fruition would have tripled the country's total overseas debt',[120] the governor-general was not present. The reason for that was that he was at the ballet in Sydney – to see *Romeo and Juliet*.[121] Kerr was not even aware of the meeting and was not aware until the following day when Whitlam advised him by telephone at 8.00 am.[122] This seems a remarkably odd procedure, and fortunately one that can no longer operate, as para 16 of the Federal Executive Council Handbook now states that: 'The Vice-President . . . may only summon executive councillors and preside at a Council meeting with the agreement of the governor-general'.

What makes this bizarre meeting even odder is that Kerr formed the view that the meeting of December 14 was 'invalid'.[123] And if that was not enough, as Kelly and Bramston make clear, despite his negative view, Kerr 'conveyed no such concerns to Whitlam'![124] This seems indicative of Kerr's later secretive behaviour and his unwillingness to frankly express his concerns to the prime minister (which is discussed in more detail in chapter 6).

The December 13 authority to Connor was never acted upon and was later reduced to $US 2000 million (on January 28, 1975), at a meeting where the governor-general was present.[125] Connor was, however, keen to finalize this loan, and Khemlani kept promising that the loan was soon to be finalized. For example, according to Kelly, he told Connor by telex on December 3, 1974, that the loan would be completed by December 9.[126] But it never was. Connor's hopes, however, remained – and on March 22, he provided Khemlani with a further letter 'which referred to funds totalling $US 8000 million, which would come in two batches of $US 4000 each'.[127] What authority Connor had for this letter is not apparent.

Connor's loan authority was finally revoked on May 20. Nonetheless, Connor remained in contact with Khemlani. Moreover, a journalist from the Melbourne *Herald*, Peter Game, had extensively interviewed Khemlani, who revealed, as late as October 8, that he still had approval from Connor to raise $US8000 million, despite the May 20 revocation.[128] Connor had earlier denied similar allegations in Parliament on July 9;[129] and on October 8 he issued a further statement with greater precision:

> Specifically I have had only one telephone discussion with Mr Khemlani since 20 May which was initiated by him, about 11 June. I indicated to him then that I was in no way authorised to discuss loan matters with him, and such matters were under the control of the Treasurer.[130]

This prompted Khemlani and the *Herald* to defend their positions. Khemlani came to Australia on October 10 and released a statutory declaration that began:

> I have read a copy of the statement of Mr Connor of October 8. Much of what Mr Connor said in this statement is not correct.
>
> In his statement, Mr Connor has said that he had only one telephone conversation with me after May 20. I say that I had at least twenty telephone conversations with Mr Connor between May 20 and the middle of June about problems I had run into with the negotiations for loans for the Australian government.

Khemlani's statutory declaration went on to say:

> I have not received from Mr Connor either directly or indirectly any notification that my authority to negotiate loans for the Australian government had been revoked. On the contrary, it has been clear from my dealings with Mr Connor since May 20 that he personally has continued to work for the raising of loan monies.[131]

On October 14, the *Herald* administered what Sexton has described as the 'coup de grace to Connor's career with the reprint of an otherwise innocuous telex' of May 23, 1975, three days after Connor's authority had been withdrawn:

> Attention Mr T H Khemlani: Response your telex of 0310 of today. I await further specific communication from your principals for consideration. From RFX Connor.[132]

What this telex indicated was that Connor was still engaging Khemlani to obtain funds; and that he had not advised him that his authority had been withdrawn. Moreover, this telex had not been provided to the prime minister, which led him, as he accepted, to mislead Parliament, even if unknowingly, on October 9, 1975, when he told the House of Representatives that:

> I am assured by the Minister for Minerals and Energy that all communications of substance between him and Mr Khemlani were tabled by him on 9 July 1975.[133]

Misleading Parliament is one of the few ministerial errors for which 'there seems no comeback'.[134] Certainly, Whitlam regarded it as such. In his view, he was faced with this choice: 'to stick to the first principle of ministerial answerability to Parliament, dismissing a senior and respected colleague and provoking, obviously, a first class crisis, or run away from the principle and try to gloss over its breach'.[135]

Whitlam chose the first course, persuading Connor to resign on October 14, after a 90-minute meeting with the Minister.[136] But that led to, as we will see, the next step in the dismissal story – the blockage of the 1975 budget.

NOTES

1. Quoted in "It's Government by Crisis. What they Said," *The Age*, October 16, 1975, 1.

2. See Ross McMullin, *So Monstrous a Travesty* (Melbourne: Scribe Publications, 2004).

3. Scott Brodie, *Statesmen, Leaders and Losers, The Twenty-three Prime Ministers of Australia* (Sydney, NSW: Dreamweaver, 1984), 62–66; 126–135.

4. The 1949 election was conducted on December 12, 1949, and the 1972 election was conducted on December 2, 1972.

5. See Federal Election Commission, *Federal Elections 2016, Election Results for the US President, the US Senate and the US House of Representatives* (Washington: Federal Election Commission, 2017), 6.

6. See the result of the 1990 federal election, which Labor prime minister Bob Hawke won with a two-party preferred vote of 49.9%. See the table in Richard Farmer, "Gough Whitlam: The Campaigner," in *The Whitlam Legacy,* ed. Troy Bramston (Leichardt, NSW: Federation, 2015), 58, 59.

7. Horne, *Death of the Lucky Country,* 42–43.

8. Robert Menzies, Australia's twelfth prime minister, who had been prime minister since 1949, retired on January 26, 1966, and was replaced by Harold Holt, Australia's seventeenth prime minister, who served until he drowned on December 17, 1967. There was some delay in replacing Holt, as the Country Party leader, John McEwan (Australia's eighteenth prime minister), made it clear that his Party would not serve in the coalition if the Liberal Party was led by its then Deputy Leader, Bill McMahon. As a result, Senator John Gorton became leader of the Liberal Party and Australia's nineteenth prime minister, leading it from January 10, 1968, until March 10, 1971, when Billy McMahon became Australia's twentieth prime minister.

9. Paul Hasluck, *The Chance of Politics* (Melbourne: Text Publishing, 1997), 202.

10. "It's Time: Audio, Video and Lyrics," November 13, 1972, WhitlamDismissal.com, https://whitlamdismissal.com/1972/11/13/its-time-audio-video-lyrics.html/.

11. Paul Jones and Mike Shirley.

12. Quoted in Freudenberg, *Certain Grandeur*, 229.

13. Whitlam, *The Truth,* 23.

14. *Whitlam: The Power & the Passion*, directed by Paul Clarke (Australian Broadcasting Corporation, 2013) DVD, Chapter Five, 0.55-0.56. Hayden also added that Whitlam had denied making that observation, but Hayden was clear that he had.

15. Tom Heenan, "Burchett, Wilfred Graham (1911–1983)," in National Centre of Biography, *Australian Dictionary of Biography* (Canberra: Australian National University, published first in hardcopy 2007), Vol 17, https://adb.anu.edu.au/biography/burchett-wilfred-graham-12265/text22015, accessed online May 12, 2023.

16. Troy Bramston, "The Whitlam Government Through the Cabinet Papers," in *Whitlam Legacy,* 96, 98.

17. Bramston, "Cabinet Papers," 99.

18. Quoted in Bramston, "Cabinet Papers," 99.
19. Michael Hogen, "Education Policy," in *Whitlam Legacy,* 186, 190 – a decision for which I am eternally grateful.
20. George Williams, "Law Reform and the Constitution," in *Whitlam Legacy,* 280, 286.
21. Hocking, *His Time* (2012), 123.
22. Linda Morris, "Jackson Pollock's Controversial Blue Poles Valued at $500 million," *Sydney Morning Herald,* January 30, 2023.
23. Siobhan Heanue, "Stroke of Genius: The Legacy of Blue Poles," *ABC News,* August 29, 2012, https://web.archive.org/web/20121101101757/http://www.abc.net.au/news/2012-08-28/stroke-of-genius-the-legacy-of-blue-poles/4228672, viewed August 23, 2022.
24. See, for example, Blaxland, *Protest Years*, 178.
25. Blaxland, *Protest Years,* 172.
26. Blaxland, *Protest Years,* 349.
27. Blaxland, *Protest Years,* 457.
28. Blaxland, *Protest Years,* 330–333.
29. Blaxland, *Protest Years,* 329.
30. Blaxland, *Protest Years,* 329.
31. See for example, Hocking, *His Time* (2012), 66.
32. Blaxland, *Protest Years,* 333.
33. Blaxland, *Protest Years,* 337.
34. Bramston, "Cabinet Papers," 102.
35. Freudenberg, *Certain Grandeur,* 263.
36. Freudenberg, *Certain Grandeur,* 263.
37. Freudenberg, *Certain Grandeur*, 263.
38. Freudenberg, *Certain Grandeur*, 169.
39. Sexton, *Great Crash*, 49.
40. Freudenberg, *Certain Grandeur*, 136.
41. Sexton, *Great Crash*, 44–45.
42. See Freudenberg, *Certain Grandeur*, 86.
43. Freudenberg, *Certain Grandeur*, 129.
44. Freudenberg, *Certain Grandeur*, 129.
45. Freudenberg, *Certain Grandeur*, 136; Hocking, *A Moment in History,* 319.
46. Troy Bramston, "Prologue, The Whitlam Ascendency," in *Whitlam Legacy*, 1, 9.
47. Hocking, *A Moment in History,* 318.
48. Quoted in Hasluck, *Chance of Politics,* 199.
49. Freudenberg, *Certain Grandeur*, 86.
50. Bramston, "Prologue," 9.
51. Quoted in Bramston, "Prologue," 9.
52. Freudenberg, *Certain Grandeur*, 318.
53. Paul Strangio, *Keeper of the Faith, A Biography of Jim Cairns* (Carlton South, Victoria: Melbourne University Press, 2002), 310, 318.

54. Robin Hughes, "Australian Biography: Jim Cairns – Transcript," NFSA ID: 420890, recorded May 22, 1998, https://www.nfsa.gov.au/collection/curated/australian-biography-jim-cairns#field-file-transcript.
55. Kelly, *Unmaking,* 219.
56. There is much written on this "scandal" including in Kelly, *Unmaking,* ch 16. Kelly has spelled the Christian name with one "L" as has Freudenberg (see Freudenberg, *Certain Grandeur,* 356) and Strangio, *Keeper,* 31. Other works have used the double L spelling (see Sexton, *Great Crash,* 75 and Rodney Tiffen, "Scandals," in *Whitlam Legacy,* 158). Ben Hills, "Cairns' Son in Arab Plan," *The Age,* July 1, 1975, used both spellings. I have used the double L spelling as that is the spelling used by both Dr Cairns and Mr Whitlam in their letters of July 2, 1975, that were reprinted in *The Age* on July 3, 1975, on page 1.
57. Laurie Oakes, *Crash Through or Crash* (Richmond, Victoria: Drummond, 1976), 89.
58. See Hughes/Cairns transcript.
59. Kelly, *Unmaking,* 260.
60. Ben Hills, "Cairns' Son in Arab Plan," *The Age,* July 1, 1975, 1.
61. Peter Cole-Adams and Ben Hills, "Cairns, the Full Story," *The Age,* July 2, 1975, 1.
62. "Son: No Profit for Me," *The Age,* July 3, 1975, 3.
63. Ben Hills and Staff Reporters, "I Made up $4m Story: Cowls," *The Age,* July 3, 1975, 1.
64. Kelly, *Unmaking,* 199.
65. Under Harris's presidency, Carlton recruited the successful captain of the Melbourne Club, Ron Barrasi, under whose leadership Carlton returned to winning its first premiership since 1947. While Harris was president of the Club, it won four more premierships (1968, 1970, 1972 and 1979) and is now the equal winner of the greatest number of premierships in the League.
66. Kelly, *Unmaking,* 200.
67. Kelly, *Unmaking,* 200.
68. Kelly, *Unmaking,* 200.
69. Kelly, *Unmaking,* 202.
70. Kelly, *Unmaking,* 203.
71. Kelly, *Unmaking,* 201.
72. Kelly, *Unmaking,* 202 (March 10 & April 15 letters) and 256 (March 7 letter).
73. Kelly, *Unmaking,* 203.
74. Kelly, *Unmaking,* 204 and 205.
75. Kelly, *Unmaking,* 205.
76. Kelly, *Unmaking,* 207.
77. Kelly, *Unmaking,* 208.
78. Kelly, *Unmaking,* 207.
79. Kelly, *Unmaking,* 221.
80. Kelly, *Unmaking,* 222.
81. See the Table in Appendix 3 to *Whitlam Legacy,* 446, 451.
82. Kelly, *Unmaking,* 257.

83. Commonwealth of Australia, *Parliamentary Debates*, House of Representatives, June 4, 1975, 3294. Also see Kelly, *Unmaking,* 257.

84. Kelly, *Unmaking,* 257.

85. Quoted in Kelly, *Unmaking,* 257.

86. As quoted in Kelly, *Unmaking,* 259.

87. Hughes/Cairns transcript.

88. Quoted in "The Cairns Letters," *The Age,* July 3, 1975, 1. A variation is quoted in Kelly, *Unmaking,* 263.

89. Kelly, *Unmaking,* 265.

90. Kelly, *Unmaking,* 266. Also see Strangio, *Keeper,* 327.

91. See Cairns' letter to the prime minister dated July 2, 1975, in "The Cairns Letters," *The Age*, July 3, 1975, 1.

92. See letters between Whitlam and Cairns in "The Cairns Letters," *The Age,* July 3, 1975, 1.

93. Kerr, *Matters,* 241–244.

94. Kerr, *Matters,* 243.

95. Kelly, *Unmaking,* 180.

96. Freudenberg, *Certain Grandeur*, 134.

97. Quoted in Freudenberg, *Certain Grandeur*, 134.

98. Kelly, *Unmaking,* 181.

99. Lawson is now better known for his short stories, such as the poignant *Drover's Wife* and the amusing *The Loaded Dog*, as well as his bush poetry, such as *Faces in the Street*. His more overt political works are now much less known.

100. Henry Lawson, "Freedom on the Wallaby," *The Worker*, May 16, 1891, 8.

101. Kelly, *Unmaking*, 179.

102. Commonwealth of Australia, *Parliamentary Debates*, House of Representatives, July 9, 1975, 3625.

103. Foss' poem, which began with:

> *Bring me men to match my mountains,*
> *Bring me men to match my plains,*
> *Men with empires in their purpose*
> *And new eras in their brains.*

104. Kelly, *Unmaking,* 181.

105. Kelly, *Unmaking,* 184.

106. Sexton, *Great Crash*, 125.

107. Kelly, *Unmaking,* 184–185.

108. Kelly, *Unmaking,* 185–186.

109. Commonwealth of Australia, *Parliamentary Debates*, House of Representatives, July 9, 1975, 3613. Also see Kelly, *Unmaking,* 187.

110. Commonwealth of Australia, *Parliamentary Debates*, House of Representatives, July 9, 1975, 3618. Also see Sexton, *Great Crash*, 190.

111. Emphasis added.

112. Emphasis added.

113. See Stephen Gageler, "Australian Government Solicitor, No 1: What is it to be a Government Lawyer," Australian Government Solicitor, https://www.ags.gov.au/publications/agsmagazine/issue-1/guest-case-studies, accessed May 27, 2023.

114. Sexton, *Great Crash*, 180–181.

115. Michael Crommelin and Gareth Evans, "The Exploration and Adventures with Commonwealth Powers," in *Labor and the Constitution*, ed. Evans 24, 61.

116. See *Federal Executive Council Handbook, 2021* (Canberra: Commonwealth of Australia, Department of Prime Minister and Cabinet, 2021), para 16, https://www.pmc.gov.au/sites/default/files/resource/download/executive-council-handbook-2021.pdf, accessed May 12, 2023. Also see Matt Harvey et al., *Australian Constitutional Law and Government* (Chatswood, NSW: LexisNexis, 2021), 184.

117. See the Table in Appendix 3 to *Whitlam Legacy*, 446, 454.

118. Commonwealth of Australia, *Parliamentary Debates*, House of Representatives, July 9, 1975, 3618. Also see Crommelin and Evans, "Exploration and Adventures," 57.

119. Whitlam, *The Truth,* 68.

120. Crommelin and Evans, "Exploration and Adventures," 58.

121. Whitlam, *The Truth*, 70.

122. Kelly, *Unmaking,* 192.

123. Kerr, *Matters,* 225.

124. Kelly & Bramston, *The Dismissal,* 107 & 109.

125. Whitlam, *The Truth,* 95. Also see Commonwealth of Australia, *Parliamentary Debates*, House of Representatives, July 9, 1975, 3620.

126. Kelly, *Unmaking,* 187.

127. Kelly, *Unmaking*, 194.

128. Kelly, *Unmaking,* 312.

129. Commonwealth of Australia, *Parliamentary Debates*, House of Representatives, July 9, 1975, 3610 and following pages.

130. John Jost, "Connor Denied Loan Charges," *The Age*, October 9, 1975, 3 and Kelly, *Unmaking,* 314.

131. Kelly, *Unmaking,* 316.

132. Sexton, *Great Crash*, 203; Kelly, *Unmaking,* 317.

133. Whitlam, *The Truth,* 92.

134. David Hamer, quoted in Killey, *Constitutional Conventions*, 102.

135. Whitlam, *The Truth,* 92.

136. Kelly, *Unmaking,* 318. Also see Whitlam, *The Truth,* 92–93.

Chapter 5

1975

The Supply Crisis

Figure 5.1 A Political Badge from the 1970s; from the Collection of the Author. *Source*: Image taken by the author.

The blockage of supply in 1975 was the fundamental cause of the dismissal of the Labor government. But it is not the first time that an Upper House in a Westminster system has rejected a government's funding. As will be discussed later in chapter 8, there have been many occasions in the Australian States, both before and after federation, when supply has been blocked by an Upper House. Probably the most famous instance of Upper House supply blockage occurred in the United Kingdom in 1909 when there was a constitutional battle between the Peers and the People, discussed and explained in the dramatically named book on that dispute, *Mr Balfour's Poodle*[1] from 1954 by the then British Labour politician and author, Roy Jenkins.[2] And to Jenkins, the answer to a government facing a supply blockage from the Upper House was clear and simple:

> Any course other than immediate dissolution was out of the question. The legislature had refused Supply, and in these circumstances no government could carry on. It was this, most of all, which gave the full measure of what the Lords had done. They had not merely confronted the Government with the choice of an immediate election or of acceptance of the loss of a particular measure, as they had frequently done before. They had left the Government with no choice, and had taken upon themselves the right of deciding when a Government could carry on and when it could not, when a Parliament should end and when it should not. It was a claim which, if allowed, would have made the Government as much the creature of the hereditary assembly as of the elective assembly.[3]

But to Australia's prime minister in 1975, a very different approach was to be taken. Gough Whitlam's intention of not resigning or calling an election, but 'toughing it out' was a contrary approach to Jenkins' one course of an 'immediate dissolution'. Indeed, that was precisely what Whitlam did not want. But to Governor-General Kerr, Jenkins' conclusion for a government in such a position seems highly influential, even definitive. Although Kerr made no reference to either Jenkins or to *Balfour's Poodle* in his accounts of 1975, or in his correspondence with the Palace, the importance that he gave to Jenkins' approach can be seen from the steps that he took when he ensured that Jenkins' salient passage of words quoted earlier was retained in the National Archives[4] as part of the significant material that Kerr considered when making his dismissal decision that he had not otherwise made public or included in his public account.

But for a governor-general to hold fundamentally different positions from his prime minister on such an important constitutional question can be a recipe for disaster. How Kerr and Whitlam dealt with those two different and contradictory approaches held by the head of state and the head of government will be seen in subsequent chapters, particularly in chapters 8 and 9, regarding any warnings or advice that Kerr gave or should have given to Whitlam before he dismissed him.

But before we get to that, we need to consider how the 1975 crisis arose – and to understand that, we first need to examine the role of another member of Parliament, Senator Reg 'Toe-cutter' Withers.

THE INFLUENCE OF SENATOR WITHERS

Despite the changed direction of the country under Whitlam, the conservative parties, in their new and, at that time, unusual opposition position, were quick to plan their return to government. This can be seen by examining the leadership of the Liberal Party in the Senate, under Senator Reg Withers. Like Rex Connor, Withers was a very hard man in politics, but from the other side. And, just like Connor, he had a very colourful and fearsome nickname: Withers was known as the 'Toe-cutter'.[5]

As early as March 8, 1973, three months into the term of the newly elected Labor government, Withers, the Leader of the Opposition in the Senate, set out the Opposition's method of regaining power. And it was to use the Senate.

Withers was prepared to accept, but with no great joy, that Labor was entitled to form a government after the 1972 election. But he also maintained that whatever victory had occurred, it did not bring with it any 'mandate'.

> It is true that the Australian Labor Party received 49.6 per cent of the first preference vote and 52.7 per cent of the vote under the Mackerras preferred party vote allocation system, and is therefore entitled to form a Government. With this we do not quarrel, but what is also true is that a very large proportion of the electorate did not give the Labor Party a so-called 'mandate'.[6]

Moreover, he argued that any electoral victory gained by Labor in 1972 was also undermined by what he disdainfully referred to as 'the temporary electoral insanity of the 2 most populous Australian States'. And he gave the first indication of the methods that would later be used to save Australia from that 'insanity' when he predicted, three months into Whitlam's first year as prime minister, that:

> the Senate may well be called upon to protect the national interest by exercising its undoubted constitutional rights and powers.[7]

Withers seems to be the founder of the supply crisis concept that was later successfully put into place in November 1975, a concept that he provided in more detail in October 1973, in a memorandum to the then Leader of the Opposition, Billy Snedden. As Whitlam summarized that memorandum: 'the key element in the strategy was to defer a vote on Supply, rather than reject it; this would have the dual effect of keeping the Appropriation Bills under the Opposition's control while the whole process of delay could bring increasing pressure on the Governor-General to resolve the deadlock'.[8] Senator Withers' press secretary at the time, Russell Schneider, recalled in 2015 Withers' original scenario:

> it was that if the Senate did wish to force an election . . . it should do it on money bills, but it should not reject the . . . supply bills, but hold them in the Senate . . . because if the bills were rejected it was then the province of the prime minister and the Lower House to determine whether to re-restore them and send them up to the Senate again. If they were held in the Upper House . . . and if you had numbers, a simple majority would get the legislation through. And what that meant . . . – the leader of the party which controlled the numbers in the Senate could – would be the only person who could guarantee the governor-general that his money bills would be passed.[9]

Withers seemed to have had, like most of the other members of the Opposition, as Labor Senator John Button put it, an 'oleaginous and born to rule'[10] approach to Australian politics. And Withers was unprepared to accept any period of not being in government after more than twenty years of uninterrupted Menzies-led and inspired Liberal/Country Party rule. The coalition was, however, not prepared to block Labor's first national budget since 1949. Not so with the next budget in 1974. But that may not have occurred without a piece of Whitlam's adventurous political planning – what became known as '*the Gair affair*'.[11]

On March 21, 1974, Whitlam advised the House of Representatives that the Governor-General Paul Hasluck had accepted his advice to hold a half-Senate election on May 18 for senators whose term was to expire on July 1.[12] Whitlam attempted to make use of this half-Senate election to also include an election for a 'casual vacancy', a vacancy caused by the resignation or death of a senator whose term did not expire on July 1. The vacancy on this occasion would have been caused by the resignation of Queensland's Senator Vince Gair.

To understand this, it is necessary to appreciate the arrangements for Senate representation and the requirements for 'casual vacancies' then applicable. In Australia, the Senate then (in 1974) had 60 members, 10 from each state.[13] And each senator had a six-year term; but they were elected on a staggered basis, so half of the Senate members' terms expired every three years. An exception to this was for 'casual vacancies' in the Senate. Any casual vacancy, caused by the death or resignation of a senator before their term had expired, would be filled by a replacement nominated by the Parliament of the relevant state. But the term of such a state-nominated replacement senator would end at the next election when the voters would elect a senator for the remainder of the resigning/deceased member's term. That can be seen from section 15 of the *Australian Constitution* which then included the following passages:

> If the place of a senator becomes vacant before the expiration of his term of service, the Houses of Parliament of the State for which he was chosen shall,

> sitting and voting together, choose a person to hold the place until the expiration of the term, or until the election of a successor as hereinafter provided, whichever first happens.

And

> At the next general election of members of the House of Representatives, or at the next election of senators for the State, whichever first happens, a successor shall, if the term has not then expired, be chosen to hold the place from the date of his election until the expiration of the term.[14]

Prime Minister Whitlam attempted to take advantage of this provision by appointing the Democratic Labour Party (DLP) senator and former premier of Queensland, Vince Gair, to be the Ambassador to Ireland. The DLP was a party that had broken with the ALP and split that party in the 1950s. It was a very conservative and very Catholic labour party which had operated to oppose the ALP in parliaments around the country, keeping it in opposition federally until the early 1970s.

Gair, although having been the Parliamentary leader of the DLP for many years (since 1964), had become, as Costar observes, alienated from his DLP colleagues due to his 'earthy humour and coarse language' as well as his 'aggressiveness and heavy drinking'. Moreover, Gair had 'compounded his problems by regularly criticizing the Liberal Party's leader, Billy Snedden who, he alleged, was incapable of leading a "flock of homing pigeons"'.[15] Gair's lengthy political career had appeared to be at an end when he succumbed to intense pressure from his colleagues and resigned as DLP's Parliamentary leader on October 10, 1973, declaring that he would retire and leave Parliament when his Senate term expired in June 1977.[16] But by obtaining his earlier resignation from the Senate and then holding a half Senate election, Whitlam had hoped that the ALP would then win Gair's casual vacancy when it was filled by the electorate in 1974. But to achieve that, Gair needed to resign from the Senate before the writs for the election were issued.

The news of the Whitlam/Gair proposal, however, became publicly known on April 2, 1974, and before Gair had actually resigned. The Opposition was able to delay Gair from resigning by (an evening of Country Party delivered beer and prawns) until after the writ for the half-senate election had been issued.[17]

While that defeated any preference to the ALP for the Gair Plan, the Opposition was still, as Whitlam recalled, 'incensed at such a wicked political appointment'.[18] The leader of the Opposition announced that 'I'll take the bastard to the country', considering the Gair appointment as 'the most shameful act ever perpetrated' by government.[19] Accordingly, Withers attempted his supply blockage strategy in the Senate on April 10, 1974, arguing that 'because of its mal-administration, the Government should not be granted funds until it agrees to submit itself to the people'.[20] The Labor leader in the Senate, Lionel Murphy, promptly responded by roundly rejecting what he described as Withers' 'absurd amendment' recognising it for what it was, a denial of supply. Murphy moved that the question of the passage of the supply bills be now put. If that motion was lost, as it was (31 to 26), the prime minister would then advise the governor-general with a view to calling an election.[21]

And that is what occurred. Whitlam advised Governor-General Hasluck to call a double dissolution of both Houses of Parliament, a process that the *Australian Constitution* allows when legislation is repeatedly not passed by the Senate.[22] Hasluck was a former Liberal Party front bencher and his earlier relationship with Whitlam was not particularly friendly as it included one incident, nine years earlier, when Whitlam threw a glass of water over Minister Hasluck in an unusual fit of pique and frustration during a parliamentary debate.[23] This is one of the few incidents approaching physical violence in the Australian Parliament, a much more pacific place than the United States Congress has been.[24] But despite this watery episode and the taunts that Whitlam subsequently received as a result, the relationship between Whitlam and Hasluck had significantly improved to the point that Whitlam's first choice when Hasluck's five-year appointment as governor-general was to expire in 1974,[25] was for the governor-general to extend his appointment for another two years.[26] Life may well have been very different for Whitlam had he been able to secure his first preference.

Hasluck dissolved both Houses on April 11, and at the following election that was conducted on May 18, 1974, the result was not what Withers or Snedden had hoped for. Whitlam became the first Australian Labor leader to win two consecutive federal elections[27] when the ALP won 66 of the 127 seats in the House of Representatives. In addition, no doubt to Labor's joy, its old adversary from the 1950s, the DLP, lost all of its five Senate seats and was destroyed as a parliamentary force. Labor, however, did not win control of the Senate, with both Labor and the Liberal/Country Party coalition winning 29 seats, while two seats were held by independents.[28] Whitlam's majority in the Lower House had also shrunk from nine seats to five. But things were not going any better for the Leader of the Opposition, particularly following his relatively silly statement after the 1974 election: 'We were not defeated. We just didn't win enough seats to form a government'.[29]

FRASER'S LEADERSHIP

Whitlam's victory in 1974, however, was not the end of the Withers' supply deferral plan. This became apparent on March 21, 1975, when the leadership of the Liberal Party changed. A new leader of the Opposition was elected when John Malcolm Fraser, known by his middle name of Malcolm, challenged and then defeated the leader of the Opposition. Fraser defeated Billy Snedden by ten votes.[30]

Fraser was from a very wealthy Victorian Western District sheep grazing family, a family known in Australia as part of its 'squattocracy'. That is, a family who had occupied and used large areas of Crown land in the nineteenth century for the grazing of livestock and used that land and that livestock to become fabulously wealthy and, as a result, to be among the most influential and powerful in the colony. Like many sons of such well-off squatting families, Malcolm was born in the most expensive part of Victoria's capital, Melbourne, in the suburb of Toorak; he had been educated at the most private and most exclusive of Melbourne's secondary schools, Melbourne Grammar, before his tertiary education, where the local institution, Melbourne University, was not considered sufficient. Young Malcolm was packed off to Magdalen College (his father's college) at Oxford for three years, graduating in 1952 with a pretty ordinary third-class honours degree in Philosophy, Politics and Economics. His fairly average academic skills, however, did not hamper Malcolm's entry into politics, with him winning the House of Representatives' District of Wannon seat in the State of Victoria in 1955.

Wannon is a large electoral province covering much of the Western District of the State of Victoria. It has an area, in 2022, of 33,595 sq km, making it larger than many of the states in the United States. For example, Wannon is just larger than the states of Maryland (32,134 sq km) and Massachusetts (27,363 sq km) and much larger than the area of New Jersey (22,591 sq km), not to mention, by Australian standards, tiny states such as Delaware (5,133 sq km), Connecticut (14,357 sq km) and Rhode Island (3,144 sq km). Malcolm won that seat at the young age of 25 and remained Wannon's member until his retirement from Parliament in 1983.

Fraser was, like Whitlam, a tall man, standing at 6 feet and four inches. He was a strong, if not subtle, speaker, but he had little appreciation for irony. Possibly his most famous speech before he became prime minister was his 1971 Alfred Deakin Lecture speech, where he adopted as his own, George Bernard Shaw's line from the play (or series of plays) *Back to Methuselah*: that 'life is not meant to be easy' as part of his gloomy paternalistic prediction of Australia's future path.[31] But he omitted the following words which Shaw added after the words that Fraser adopted: 'but take courage: it can be delightful'.[32] And for Fraser, with his 'squattocracy' background, his inherited wealth, his very privileged education and his easy and early pathway to a political life, it was delightful. All material things came easily to him, with the result that his actions regarding the supply crisis and the dismissal were also easy steps – steps that one might have taken in a game, thoughtless of any damage they could do to others or to the system they were part of. And by taking those steps, Fraser seems to have ignored words that he included in that same 1971 speech:

> If a man has not known adversity, if in his lifetime his country has not been subject to attack, it is harder for him to understand that there are some things for which we must always struggle. Thus people or leaders can be trapped to take the easy path. This is the high road to national disaster.

For Fraser, a man who had not 'known adversity' in any manner known to the rest of the Australian community, the path that he forcefully adopted regarding 1975 was an 'easy path'. And while it benefited him for some years, for many others it did have all the elements of a 'national disaster'.

Fraser, at that stage of his career, was also a very divisive man and was then very conservative. He was, as Kelly and Bramston observed, a manipulator of internal party disputes, being instrumental in the downfall of Prime Minister Gorton in 1971 and in the downfall of Billy Snedden in 1975. His 'personal aloofness and proclivity as a manipulator . . . made him a polarising figure'. Indeed, in Henderson's view, 'there was an air of a bully about Fraser – so much that most of his staff, and many of his parliamentary colleagues, were literally scared of him'.[33] However, as Kelly and Bramston observed, 'his strength of purpose, policy grasp, political aggression and dedication meant nobody in the relatively weak Liberal Party of the 1970s could match his leadership ability'.[34] And those abilities allowed Fraser to gain the support of former Prime Minister Bob Menzies in his challenge to Snedden, who considered that 'Fraser's the only one with any hint of statesmanship about him'.[35]

Efforts had been made before March 1975 to replace Snedden with Fraser. The first attempt was made in November 1974, which failed by eleven votes. But with the majority of the Liberals in the House of Representatives having supported Fraser (and an early election),[36] it did not take long before a second and more effective challenge was made to Snedden. And here we also see another instance of Senator Withers' effect on the future of the Liberal Party. As Whitlam notes, in the March 21, 1975, challenge, 'Senator Withers had swapped sides bringing enough senators with him to topple Mr Snedden'.[37]

Fraser's initial position on the supply bills, however, did not appear to be different from that of Snedden. In his first press conference as Leader of the Opposition, Fraser made it apparent that:

> I generally believe if a Government is elected to power in the lower House and has the numbers and can maintain the numbers in the lower House, it is entitled to expect that it will govern for the three-year term *unless extraordinary events intervene.*[38]

Precisely what Fraser meant by 'extraordinary events' he did not make clear. But he did add, as both a form of threat and a prediction of what later occurred on November 11, 1975, the following:

> If we do make up our minds at some stage that the Government is so reprehensible that an opposition must use whatever power is available to it, then I'd want to find a situation in which we made that decision and Mr Whitlam woke up one morning finding the decision had been made and finding that he had been caught with his pants well and truly down.[39]

Fraser did have numerous instances of crisis, or claimed crisis, that he might have acted on as 'extraordinary events', including the Cairns/Morosi 'affair', the Cairns' misleading of Parliament, and the loans affair and the activities of Tirath Khemlani. But the required element for Fraser's approach was the electorate and its growing disenchantment with Whitlam. And Whitlam unnecessarily provided evidence of that to Fraser on June 28, 1975, when a by-election was held in the Tasmania seat of Bass, caused by the resignation of the former deputy prime minister, Lance Barnard (mentioned in chapter 4), to allow him to take up an ambassadorial role after Cairns had replaced him as deputy leader. This by-election was described by the psephologist, Malcolm Mackerras, as a 'foolish move' by Whitlam, as it not only caused Labor to lose a relatively safe seat in the House of Representatives but also did so with a massive swing against it of 13.8%.[40] However, it was not until October 14, 1975, and the enforced resignation of Rex Connor, discussed in the last chapter, that Fraser considered the circumstances sufficiently 'extraordinary' and the government to be 'so reprehensible' that supply must be blocked.

On the following day (October 15), the Coalition leadership group decided unanimously to block the budget.[41] Fraser announced at a press conference that the objective of this activity was to force an election – 'The House of Representatives must go to an election'.[42] And Fraser's reasoning was clear:

> The Labor Government 1972–1975 has been the most incompetent and disastrous Government in the history of Australia. Although Australia has basically one of the strongest and healthiest economies in the world, in three years this has been brought to the brink of disaster by incompetence of the worst kind . . .
>
> From the Parliament and from the people I now call on the Prime Minister, if he has a shred of decency left, to put an end this whole sorry episode and place himself and his Government before the ultimate tribunal of the people.
>
> We will use all the constitutional opportunities available to us to ensure this occurs.[43]

The Fraser method was to adopt the Withers' approach – to not reject the budget, but to defer it. The benefit of deferral over rejection was control, as rejection meant that the Opposition lost control over the money bills.[44]

But unlike 1974, Whitlam's response to the 1975 blockage of supply was not to advise the governor-general to call another election. Nor would he resign. His intention was to 'tough it out'.

WHY DID FRASER DO IT?

But before discussing the consequences of these decisions, which include the dismissal of the Whitlam government, one question needs to be addressed. Why did Fraser choose to adopt Withers' blocking supply plan and not just wait until the next election?

As Kelly and Bramston point out, 'By late 1975, there was near universal agreement that Whitlam would be defeated at the next election whenever it was held'.[45] The impact of the Connor and Cairns loan affairs, combined with what seemed Labor's inability to govern effectively under Whitlam's peculiar style of leadership, seemed to indicate that a third electoral win for Whitlam was never a possibility. Indeed, as the conservative analyst Gerard Henderson observes, 'From the moment that Fraser became Opposition Leader, there was a sense that the Whitlam Government was doomed' and 'all Fraser had to do was to be patient and a landslide election victory would be achieved in the first half of 1977'.[46] So why did Fraser act in 1975, and not wait until, at most, May 1977?

There are two reasons. The first is the one that Fraser has consistently presented: that he considered the Whitlam government was such a disaster, damaging to Australia, which needed to be removed in the nation's interest. As he said in a press conference on October 23, 1975, 'The action we have taken is right to remove from Australia the worst government since the beginning of Australia'.[47] This view was again recalled much later in his life in 2010, and in more detail, in an interview with Kerry O'Brien of the Australian Broadcasting Commission:

> There was one sort of trauma in having an election forced, but there would have been another sort of trauma in having that government staying in power for six or seven months. Most people are unaware of it, but 1975 was the only year since the migration programme began when more people left Australia than came to Australia. I had people from Eastern Europe saying we sat around watching our countries decay, we are not going to sit around and watch Australia decay. We are not going to go through it again, a second time. And we had made a decision, after a long series of scandals and alarms, and a lot of talk about the loans affair and Khemlani and all the rest; we had made the decision,

> early in the Spring of 75 to allow the budget to go through on proviso that there wasn't one more major scandal. Then it became evident that poor old Rex Connor had deceived everyone, including his own Prime Minister, his own government, and was still sitting up at night waiting for that call that, obviously, never came. And so Gough had to get rid of him; and, you know, that I really believed that we would have been held in contempt as an Opposition, if we had not given Australians the opportunity to have a vote. I never thought that it was a terrible thing trying to create the circumstances where people could exercise a vote.[48]

It is, however, difficult to accept the accuracy of Fraser's assessment of the expectations on the Opposition, particularly given the views of Sir Robert Menzies, the founder of the Liberal Party and former long-standing prime minister. Doug Anthony, the then head of the Country Party (the rural conservative party that regularly governs in coalition with the Liberal Party), had regular conversations with Menzies during the period when supply was blocked. And according to Anthony, Menzies 'was totally up with what was happening and didn't like it at all. He was against our tactics'.[49] Menzies had also lectured Anthony that 'we shouldn't be acting as we were. It wasn't the job of the Senate to dismiss the government'.[50]

Similarly, a group of Australia's leading academic constitutional lawyers (including Leslie Zines,[51] Geoffrey Sawer[52] and Colin Howard[53])[54] had, on October 11, issued a public letter which declared:

> The rejection of the budget by the senate in the present circumstances would be a constitutional impropriety of the first order. It would be likely to do irreparable damage to the parliamentary system as we have known it. . . . The reduction of an ultimate constitutional sanction – if indeed it should be used at all – to the level of a routine political tactic is a debasing of our constitutional system and the democratic values it is supposed to protect.[55]

But there was also a second reason, and one that Fraser did not discuss. That is, if Whitlam had conducted a half-Senate election, the Labor Party may well have gained control over the Senate as well as the House of Representatives. And this would not only allow Labor to complete its many reforms, but with control over both Houses, it may also have removed certain electoral advantages of the conservative coalition.

One of the many reforms of the Whitlam government was to expand the representation of the Senate to include Australia's territories – the Australian Capital Territory (the ACT) and the Northern Territory (the NT). Many of the States considered this move inconsistent with the basis of the Senate as that House had been established as a States House (s 7 *Australian Constitution*). Whitlam, however, relied on s 122 of that Constitution, which allows the Parliament to 'allow the representation of such territory in ether House of Parliament to the extent and on the terms which it thinks fit'. Using s 122, new legislation had been passed, increasing the size of the Senate by four seats: two for each of the two territories. Those senators were to be elected for the first time at the proposed half-Senate election. But unlike most other senators elected at a half-Senate election who would not take their places until July 1, 1976, the newly elected territory senators would take their positions immediately. The Senate territory legislation had been challenged in the High Court by non-Labor State governments, but the High Court, on October 17, 1975, found the legislation valid. [56]

There was also one other class of senator elected at a half-Senate election who would take their positions immediately. That is, senators elected to fill 'casual vacancies'. As section 15 of the *Constitution* then provided, those vacancies were to be filled, initially by the Parliament of the relevant State, but only until 'the next general election of members of the House of Representatives, or at the next election of senators for the State', at which time the remainder of the term will be filled by elected senators.

And there were two casual vacancies in the Senate caused by the death[57] or resignation,[58] of labor senators. There were significant problems with the senators appointed by states to fill those vacancies (which we will discuss more below). But it is clear that the term of the two state-appointed senators would end when the half-Senate election was held. And when that occurred, it was likely that most of the territory and the elected replacement senators at that election would be filled by Labor candidates. According to Sexton:

> It was theoretically possible for Labor to win the two causal vacancies and one seat in each of the ACT and the Northern Territory. In addition, former Liberal prime minister John Gorton[59] had announced his intention to stand for the Senate in the ACT as an Independent. If Gorton were to poll well enough to snatch the second ACT seat from the Liberal candidate, the numbers in the Senate from December 1975 until June 1976 could be Labor 31, LCP 31, with Steele Hall[60] and Gorton holding the balance of power. While there were many measures on which these two would not vote with Labor, the blocking of the budget was not one of them.[61]

And the effects of such a half-Senate election are likely to have been significant, giving the Labor Party control of both Houses, if only for a limited period of up to six or seven months. But that was a period that was long enough for more extensive Labor reforms that had been blocked by the Senate to be passed. And that includes removing some of the electoral inequalities between city and country Lower House electorates that have provided significant over-representation of the Country Party. [62]

BUT HOW WAS SUPPLY BLOCKED?

To understand how the Opposition was able to adopt the Withers' approach to defer, rather than reject supply in 1975, it is first necessary to appreciate how the casual vacancy conventions regarding Senate vacancies were ignored by the Premiers of New South Wales and Queensland.

The Senate in Australia, as a States House, has equal representation for each State. Prior to the 1975 election, each state had ten senators, regardless of population differences.[63] The Territories were not then represented. At the beginning of 1975, the number and political affiliation of Australian senators was:

- Opposition (the Liberal/Country Party Coalition) – 29
- Government (ALP) – 29
- Independent – 2

The independent senators were Senator Steele Hall, a former member of the Liberal Party but now an independent liberal in his own Liberal Movement Party, and Senator Michael Townley from Tasmania, another former Liberal. Townley, however, re-joined the parliamentary Liberal Party in February 1975, reducing the number of independents in that House to one – Steele Hall. And while Steele Hall disagreed with Labor on many things, he consistently supported them on budget or supply issues.

Accordingly, on any disputes on supply, both the Government and the Opposition would have had 30 votes, and that was sufficient to reject supply bills but not to defer them. This is clear from s 23 of the *Constitution*, which has two important requirements on the voting in the Senate. First, the Senate president has no casting vote. He or she has a vote like other senators. And second, 'when the votes are equal the question shall pass in the negative'.

However, things went awry in the Australian Senate in 1975 as a result of two casual vacancies and the willingness of two State Premiers to ignore the established convention for filling such vacancies. Casual vacancies (that is, vacancies that arise between elections) were, as s 15 of the *Constitution* then provided, initially filled by the Parliament of the State from which the former Senator was elected. But the accepted convention or practice dictated that those State Parliaments that were to exercise that power did so by appointing a person to fill a casual vacancy who had been nominated by the same political party as the resigned or deceased senator. However, all of that changed when two casual vacancies arose in early 1975.

First, Labor's attorney-general Lionel Murphy resigned from the Senate when he was appointed to the High Court in February 1975. But, contrary to the established convention, his vacancy was not filled by the person named by the ALP. Instead, on 27 February 1975, the Liberal Party Premier of New South Wales, Tom Lewis, nominated an independent, the long-time mayor of Albury, Cleaver Bunton, who was then appointed. Although Bunton was not nominated by the ALP and was not a member of that party, his appointment was not as damaging to the ALP as Premier Lewis probably hoped, as Bunton did not support the Coalition during the supply crisis.

The second casual vacancy had the potential to be, however, more damaging to the ALP.

On 30 June 1975, Senator Bertie Milliner from Queensland, a member of the ALP, died. The Queensland Parliament did not follow the established convention when it did not appoint the person nominated by the ALP. Instead, on September 3, it appointed a government-employed French polisher, Albert Field. Whitlam described Field as 'an individual of the utmost obscurity, from which he rose and to which he sank with equal speed'.[64] But until he sank, he had a significant impact on both the Senate and the government.

Field had been a long-term ALP member, but that party did not nominate him to fill this Senate vacancy. He was also openly critical of Whitlam and he was immediately expelled from the party for accepting the Senate appointment. Nonetheless, Field took his seat in the Senate but never gave his maiden speech. Labor was able to take advantage of the eligibility requirements in s 44 of the *Constitution*, challenging Field's capacity to sit at all. Although Field had resigned from the Education Department immediately before his Senate appointment, he may still have breached s 44(iv) if it was found that he still held an office of profit under the Crown, as he had not provided the statutory notice period before his resignation. Despite the apparent weakness of this argument, Field did take leave from the Senate from October 1, taking no part in the voting over the deferral of supply. Nonetheless, Field's appointment had deprived the government of one vote; and due to his leave, his vote was also not available to the opposition. This was, however, not sufficient to prevent the opposition from implementing the Withers' supply blockage plan.

During the supply dispute between the Government and the Opposition in October and November 1975, the numbers in the Senate were:

- Opposition – 30
- ALP – 27
- Independents – 2
- Absent – 1

And while both Independents, Bunton and Steele Hall, voted consistently with the Government on supply issues,[65] the Opposition now had a small one-seat advantage in the altered Senate, over both the Government and the independents. And with their casual vacancy-based majority of one in the

Senate, the Liberal/Country Party Opposition was able to defer supply bills – which it did, on October 16, 1975.

On that day, Liberal Senator Bob Cotton from NSW moved the Senate deferral amendment of the supply bills. That:

> this Bill be not further proceeded with until the Government agrees to submit itself to the judgment of the people, the Senate being of the opinion that the Prime Minister and his Government no longer have the trust and confidence of the Australian people because of
>
> (a) the continuing incompetence, evasion, deceit and duplicity of the Prime Minister and his Ministers as exemplified in the overseas loan scandal which was an attempt by the Government to subvert the Constitution, to by-pass Parliament and to evade its responsibilities to the States and the Loan Council;
> (b) the Prime Minister's failure to maintain proper control over the activities of his Ministers and Government to the detriment of the Australian nation and people; and
> (c) the continuing mismanagement of the Australian economy by the Prime Minister and this Government with policies which have caused a lack of confidence in this nation's potential and created inflation and unemployment not experienced for 40 years.[66]

This motion won by a single vote: 29 to 28 and supply was deferred,[67] with the supply bills remaining under the control of the Senate. This had no immediate effect on the government, but the money now started running out. And as the *Age* newspaper said on October 16, reminiscent of President Truman, 'The buck stops when the money runs out'.[68]

WHITLAM'S REACTION – HALF-SENATE ELECTION?

Whitlam, however, remained confident that he could tough the situation out, and that the Opposition would crack. And this confidence seems supported by the polls. As Kelly observes, a Herald-Age poll on October 30 showed that 70% of people in capital cities (where most Australian voters live) believed that the budget should pass.[69]

The Labor Parliamentary Caucus met at 7 pm on the day of Fraser's press conference (October 15) and Whitlam won overwhelming support for his defiant stance. In addition, he won approval for the calling of a half Senate election, at a time of his choosing.[70]

Nonetheless, certain of Whitlam's tactics and methods seem questionable, if not flawed. And that starts with a statement made in the House of Representatives on October 16 in the course of a debate on a motion that Whitlam moved expressing confidence in his government. In his address to the House, he made the following comment:

> The convention has been clearly established that the Senate, which has no power to originate or amend money Bills, shall not block or reject them either.[71]

This comment is correct insofar as the Senate is unable to originate or amend money bills, as this is based on the language of s 53 of the *Australian Constitution*:

> Proposed laws appropriating revenue or moneys, or imposing taxation shall not originate in the Senate.

And further on:

> The Senate may not amend proposed laws imposing taxation, or proposed laws appropriating revenue or moneys for the ordinary annual services of the Government.

Otherwise, the Senate has the same legal powers as the House of Representatives – as the closing words of s 53 make clear:

> Except as provided in this section, the Senate shall have equal power with the House of Representatives in respect of all proposed laws.

But as to the convention that Whitlam now claimed, his view seems directly contrary to the approach he adopted five years earlier when he was challenging the supply bill of the Liberal/Country Party government led by John Gorton in 1970. As Whitlam then told the House of Representatives, he intended 'to press our opposition by all available means on all related measures *in both Houses*'. His purpose was '*to destroy this Budget and to destroy the Government which has sponsored it*'.[72] Whitlam's intent in 1970 seems to have been to attempt the tactic that Fraser successfully implemented in 1975.

Kelly and Bramston also consider that Whitlam's primary methods to counter the Senate's blockage of supply were also examples of what they refer to as 'Whitlam's folly'.[73] Those methods were:

- to call a half-senate election on November 11; and
- alternate financial arrangements.

The alternate financial method was a speculative and unpredictable arrangement that relied on the unlikelihood of banks agreeing to provide credit to the Commonwealth until the crisis was resolved.[74] While the government had secured the approval of the Law Officers regarding its legality, it still relied on banks agreeing to lend the funds, which seemed unlikely. Moreover, Whitlam's Treasurer, Bill Hayden, had 'large doubts' and felt that the system 'could only function briefly and not happily and would have broken down early in the New Year'.[75]

As to the concept of holding a half Senate election, Kelly and Bramston consider that advising the governor-general on November 11 to call a half Senate election was 'not a tenable proposition', and that was because 'supply would expire during the campaign'.[76] In their view:

> No responsible governor-general, Kerr or anyone else, would have accepted his advice on 11 November, because supply could not be guaranteed for the campaign.[77]

This assessment, however, relies on an extremely broad understanding of the scope of the governor-general's reserve powers. And as discussed in chapter 3, that very broad understanding is not accepted by any Australian constitutional law expert. There is simply no precedent or any accepted convention that governors-general can or should refuse the prime minister's advice for a half Senate election. And there is no reason that such advice must be supported by any 'guarantee' of supply during the campaign. This does not mean that supply for elections is not relevant, as the refusal of a dissolution of the Lower House of the Victorian Parliament in 1952 because there was insufficient supply for the whole campaign, demonstrates.[78] But a half Senate election is not the same as the dissolution of the Lower House or the Parliament. Once Parliament or the Lower House is dissolved, there is no means of obtaining supply. But the Senate is not dissolved when a half Senate election is to occur. The Senate is a continuing House,[79] and can only be dissolved when there is a double dissolution under s 57. It could still, then, provide any missing supply, something that a Lower House or the Parliament that has been dissolved cannot do. Kelly and Bramston, however, seem not to have appreciated this distinction.

There is, therefore, no reason why the political process in 1975 could not have been allowed to continue while there were still some funds; and for any decision to dismiss Whitlam to await such time, if it ever arose, when supply had expired or was much closer to expiring. As Kerr expected that supply would last until November 30[80] there was simply no justification for:

- an expansion of the scope of reserve powers into new and unconventional areas – to include refusing advice for half Senate elections;[81] or for
- the dismissal of Whitlam well before supply expired.

NOTES

1. Roy Jenkins, *Mr Balfour's Poodle* (London: Collins, 1968).

2. Jenkins was a member of Parliament in the House of Commons between 1948 and 1977 and between 1982 and 1987, before being appointed to the House of Lords. He held senior ministerial offices as a Labour MP, serving as the UK's home secretary between 1965 and 1967 and between 1974 and 1976, and Chancellor of the Exchequer between 1967 and 1970. He later left the Labour Party for the Social Democratic Party (between 1981 and 1987) and then the Liberal Democrats.

3. Jenkins, *Balfour's Poodle*, 107.

4. See NAA, *Miscellaneous Handwritten Notes*, M4523, 1 Part 16, 5.

5. Hocking, *His Time* (2012), 61.

6. Commonwealth of Australia, *Parliamentary Debates*, *Senate,* March 8, 1973, 290.

7. Commonwealth of Australia, *Parliamentary Debates*, *Senate,* March 8, 1973, 291.

8. Whitlam, *The Truth,* 11.

9. Russell Schneider, "Oral History," interview with Barry York, *Museum of Australian Democracy at Old Parliament House,* April 1, 2015, https://oralhistories.moadoph.gov.au/russell-schneider.

10. John Button, "Out of the Blue," in *The Dismissal: Where Were You on November 11, 1975?,* ed. Sybil Nolan (Carlton, Victoria: Melbourne University Press, 2015), 31.

11. The full details of the "Gair Affair" and its other ramifications are fully explained and explored in Paul Davey, *Ninety Not Out: The Nationals 1920–2010* (Sydney, NSW: UNSW Press, 2010) in its chapter 11, entitled "The Night of the Long Prawns" at 149–162, and by Professor Twomey in her recent YouTube program, Constitutional Clarion, "The Night of the Long Prawns – Senate Manipulation during the Whitlam Era," *YouTube*, May 20, 2024, https://www.youtube.com/watch?v=Ofjuyl82IXM.

12. Whitlam, *The Truth,* 13.

13. The Senate now has 76 members: 12 from each original state and 2 from each territory (the Australian Capital Territory and the Northern Territory).

14. Section 15 of the *Constitution* was extensively altered in 1977, making the device that Whitlam attempted no longer possible.

15. B. J. Costar, "Gair, Vincent Clare (1901–1980)," in National Centre of Biography, *Australian Dictionary of Biography* (Canberra: published first in hardcopy 1996), Vol 14, https://adb.anu.edu.au/biography/gair-vincent-clare-vince-10267, accessed online May 12, 2023.

16. Whitlam, *The Truth,* 13.

17. Davey, *Ninety Not Out,* 155–156.

18. Whitlam, *The Truth,* 13.

19. Quoted in Kelly and Bramston, *The Dismissal,* 91.

20. Commonwealth of Australia, *Parliamentary Debates*, *Senate,* April 10, 1974, 884; quoted in Hocking, *His Time*, 147.

21. Commonwealth of Australia, *Parliamentary Debates*, *Senate,* April 10, 1974, 893.

22. *Australian Constitution*, s 57. Six government bills that had been rejected by the Senate since 1972 were used as the basis for this double dissolution. See Leslie Zines, "The Double Dissolution and Joint Sitting," in *Labor and the Constitution*, ed. Evans, 217.

23. Hocking, *A Moment in History,* 243.

24. As can be seen in Joanne Freeman, *Field of Blood* (New York: Picador, 2018).

25. Appointments as governor-general are not for a fixed period, but the practice is that they end after five years.

26. Whitlam, *The Truth,* xxii.

27. In earlier national elections, Labor had won consecutive elections in 1943 and 1946, but under different leaders (John Curtin and Ben Chifley). In later elections, Labor won five consecutive elections between 1983 and 1993, the first four of which were under the leadership of Bob Hawke, while the last was under the leadership of Paul Keating. It also won consecutive elections in 2007 and 2010, but under two different leaders (Kevin Rudd and Julia Gillard).

28. The two independents were Michael Townley from Tasmania and Raymond Steele Hall from South Australia. In February 1975, Townley re-joined the parliamentary Liberal Party, reducing the independents to one.

29. Quoted in Jenny Hocking, "Introduction: History by Numbers," in *The Dismissal: Where Were You on November 11, 1975?,* ed. Sybil Nolan (Carlton, Victoria: Melbourne University Press, 2015), 14, 21.

30. Hocking, *His Time*, 216; Whitlam, *The Truth,* 57; Gerard Henderson, "Whitlam's Opposition," in *Whitlam Legacy,* 83, 90.

31. Malcolm Fraser, "Towards 2000: Challenge to Australia" (The Fifth Alfred Deakin Lecture – July 20, 1971). The *Malcolm Fraser Collection,* University of Melbourne.

https://library.unimelb.edu.au/asc/collections/highlights/collections/malcolm-fraser/resources/postparliamentspeeches/towards-2000-challenge-to-australia.

32. These lines are spoken by The He-Ancient, in the final play in the *Back to Methuselah* series*: As Far as Thought Can Reach: A.D. 31,920*:

> Life is not meant to be easy, my child; but take courage: it can be delightful. What I wanted to tell you is that ever since men existed, children have played with dolls.

33. Henderson, "Whitlam's Opposition," 90.

34. Kelly and Bramston, *The Dismissal*, 88.

35. Quoted in Henderson, "Whitlam's Opposition," 89.

36. Whitlam, *The Truth,* 57.

37. Whitlam, *The Truth,* 57.

38. Quoted in Whitlam, *The Truth,* 58; emphasis added.

39. Quoted in Whitlam, *The Truth,* 59. See *Four Corners* (1995) 6.00-6.20.

40. Malcolm Mackerras, "Victories, Defeats and Electoral Politics," in *Whitlam Legacy*, 64, 73 & 81.

41. Kelly & Bramston, *The Dismissal,* 96.

42. Kelly, *Unmaking,* 323.
43. "It's Government by Crisis. What they Said," *The Age*, October 16, 1975, 1.
44. Kelly, *Unmaking,* 320.
45. Kelly & Bramston, *The Dismissal,* 87.
46. Henderson, "Whitlam's Opposition," 90–91.
47. Quoted in Kelly, *Unmaking,* 339.
48. ABC News, "Malcolm Fraser on his Legacy and Modern Politics," YouTube, filmed in 2010, https://www.youtube.com/watch?v=V21t-wJrXgE.
49. Quoted in Davey, *Ninety Not Out*, 185.
50. Quoted in Kelly & Bramston, *The Dismissal,* 96. Menzies was, however, pleased with the strength of Fraser's approach to defeating the Whitlam government.
51. Then Dean of the ANU Faculty of Law and Professor of Constitutional Law, "Zines, Leslie Ronald (1930–2014)," Obituaries Australia, in National Centre of Biography, Australian National University, https://oa.anu.edu.au/obituary/zines-leslie-ronald-17895/text29475, accessed May 12, 2023.
52. Then Professor of Law, Australian National University, "Geoffrey Sawer – Emeritus Professor, Lawyer and University Administrator," ANU Emeritus Faculty Oral History Project, The Australian National University, Emeritus Faculty Inc, https://openresearch-repository.anu.edu.au/handle/1885/13027, accessed September 17, 2022.
53. Then Hearn Professor of Law and later Dean of the Faculty of Law, University of Melbourne, and later appointed a Queen's counsel. "Vale Professor Emeritus Colin Howard QC," University of Melbourne, Melbourne Law School, *MLS News*, Issue 6, October 2011, https://law.unimelb.edu.au/alumni/mls-news/issue-6-october-2011/vale-professor-emeritus-colin-howard-qc.
54. The full list of the authors is – G Sawer, L Zines, A Castles, C Howard, J Stone, R Sackville, I Shearer and G Nettheim.
55. Quoted in Kelly, *Unmaking,* 325.
56. *Western Australia v Commonwealth* (First Territory Senators' Case) (1975) 134 CLR 201. The States had a second go two years later, but with no greater success. (See *Queensland v Commonwealth* (Second Territory Senators' Case) (1977) 139 CLR 585).
57. Senator Bert Milliner from Queensland.
58. Senator Lionel Murphy from New South Wales resigned to allow him to become a High Court Justice.
59. Gorton was prime minister from 1968 to 1971.
60. Raymond Steele Hall had been the Premier of South Australia (1968–1970) as a member of the Liberal Party. He had, however, been elected to the Senate in 1974 as a Liberal independent or with the Liberal Movement. He re-joined the Liberal Party in 1976. He was, however, overtly opposed to the Fraser blockage of supply.
61. Sexton, *Great Crash*, 212.
62. See Mackerras, "Victories, Defeats and Electoral Politics," in *Whitlam Legacy*, 64, 78.

63. *Constitution* s 7, which provided six senators for each state until the Parliament varied that amount. In 1948, the number was increased to 10. In 1984, that number was further increased to 12.

64. Quoted in Geoffrey Hawker, "Field, Albert Patrick (1910–1990)," Parliament of Australia, *Biographical Dictionary of the Australian Senate (online)* – https://biography.senate.gov.au/field-albert-patrick/. First published in *The Biographical Dictionary of the Australian Senate*, 1962–1983, vol 3 (Sydney: University of New South Wales Press Ltd, 2010), 371–375.

65. J. R. Odgers, *Australian Senate Practice* (Canberra: Royal Australian Institute of Public Administration (ACT Division) 6th edition, 1991), 79.

66. Commonwealth of Australia, *Parliamentary Debates, Senate,* October 16, 1975, 1221 & 1241. Kelly and Bramston are not entirely correct when they state that the supply bills deferral began on October 15 (see Kelly & Bramston, *Dismissal*, 97). It is true that the Loan Bill was deferred on that day as Senator Withers considered it "inextricably linked" with the supply bills. See Commonwealth of Australia, *Parliamentary Debates, Senate,* October 15, 1975, 1152 & 1160. But the Supply Bills were not deferred until the following day.

67. Commonwealth of Australia, *Parliamentary Debates, Senate,* October 16, 1975, 1241.

68. John Jost, "It's Government by Crisis. Comment: The Buck Stops when the Money Runs Out," *The Age,* October 16, 1975, 1.

69. Kelly, *Unmaking,* 340.

70. Kelly, *Unmaking,* 326.

71. Commonwealth of Australia, *Parliamentary Debates, House of Representatives*, October 16, 1975, 2201.

72. Commonwealth of Australia, *Parliamentary Debates, House of Representatives*, August 25, 1970, 463. Emphasis added.

73. Kelly & Bramston, *The Dismissal,* 174.

74. See Sawer, *Federation Under Strain,* Appendix 3, 212–217.

75. Quoted in Kelly & Bramston, *The Dismissal,* 177.

76. Kelly & Bramston, *The Dismissal*, 174.

77. Paul Kelly & Bramston, *The Dismissal*, 175.

78. See Killey, *Constitutional Conventions,* 169; and Twomey, *Veiled Sceptre*, 195.

79. See Rosemary Laing, ed., *Odgers' Australian Senate Practice as Revised by Harry Evans* (Canberra: Department of the Senate, 14th edition, 2016), chap. 1.

80. Kerr, *Matters,* 297.

81. Even Anne Twomey, whose view of the scope of the reserve powers is broader than most, does not seem to accept that they include half-Senate elections. See Twomey, *Veiled Sceptre*, 10.

Chapter 6

The Governor-General

And His Decision

Figure 6.1 ALP Political Badge from the 1975 Election. From the collection of the author. Image taken by the author.

Whitlam was dismissed by the Governor-General John Kerr shortly after 1.00 pm on November 11, when the prime minister had arrived at Government House with the intention of advising that a half-Senate election be called. That dismissal was done with no warning. To appreciate that remarkable action and its impact, it is first necessary to understand who the governor-general was, as well as what that office did and why. To do that, it is necessary to unpick Kerr's background, what he did leading up to November 11, as well as the various events of that very dramatic day.

THE GOVERNOR-GENERAL AND HIS APPOINTMENT

Kerr was from the working class. He was born in 1914 to what he describes as an 'unambitious' Balmain boilermaker father and a 'stronger' dressmaker mother.[1] He was remarkably clever and hardworking; and like other clever boys from the less well-off classes, such as the High Court's youngest justice, and later Australia's attorney-general and then Labor leader, Dr Bert Evatt, Kerr went to the academically demanding public school, Fort Street High School. And he did very well there. Indeed, he went to Fort Street because Evatt, who was then commencing his political career, had also been there. According to Kerr, at the age of eleven: 'I concluded that I would have to go to Fort Street too'.[2] From there, and with some financial assistance of Dr Evatt,[3] he then went to Sydney University to study law. Then, again with the benefit of Dr Evatt's advice, he went on to the Sydney Bar[4] where his hard work and successful progression continued, becoming a Queen's counsel in 1953[5] and a judge of the Industrial Court in 1966 before becoming the chief justice of New South Wales in 1972.[6]

Although Kerr had formed a close relationship with Dr Evatt in his early career, with Evatt financing much of Kerr's early tertiary studies, offering him employment as his associate,[7] and according to Kerr, proposing that he 'collaborate' on the preparation of Evatt's work on the prerogative powers,[8] Kerr progressively moved away from both Evatt and the ALP. Kerr recalls that he became 'less and less admirer of Evatt the man' who he grew to regard as 'in many respects a strange person'.[9] As Kerr also records, eventually 'Evatt wanted no more co-operation with me nor I with him'.[10] And that seems to be because of Kerr's politics, which are somewhat of a puzzle. Although Kerr had been an ALP candidate for the unwinnable seat of Lowe in 1951,[11] he was then approached to be the Leader of the DLP later in that decade.[12] And by the late fifties and early sixties, he then considered Liberal Party candidature both federally and in New South Wales.[13] Despite Kerr's movement away from the ALP, Whitlam still selected him to replace Sir Paul Hasluck as governor-general in 1974. This was, as we will see, a very bad decision.

Hasluck's term ended in 1974, and in June 1973 he had provided Whitlam with a handwritten list of eight potential replacements.[14] Despite Hasluck having been a senior Liberal Party minister, and one who had often been at odds with Whitlam and Labor, he was still Whitlam's first choice to continue as governor-general. Whitlam wanted Hasluck to extend his appointment for another two years.[15] When that proved not possible due to Mrs Hasluck's health,[16] Whitlam chose from the Hasluck list. Kerr, however, was not Whitlam's first choice from that list.

The list of persons Hasluck provided to Whitlam fell into four groups. First, those experienced and with ALP seniority: Frank Crean,[17] Kim Beazley[18] and the less well-known Harold Souter.[19] Second, senior legal academic scholars, David Derham[20] and Kenneth Wheare.[21] Third, those experienced in both business and philanthropy, Kenneth Myer[22] and Vincent Fairfax.[23] And the last group, the judiciary, recommended by Hasluck, contained only one member, Sir John Kerr. It is also possible that a few others may also have been considered including, as Kelly records,[24] Cardinal Norman Gilroy[25] and Sir Richard Eggleston.[26]

Had Whitlam chosen anyone from those names, other than Kerr, his 1975 problems are unlikely to have occurred. Clearly, Crean, Beazley and Souter would have been more compliant with the objectives of the prime minister and not Fraser. And Eggleston also seems unlikely to be willing to sack Whitlam, with or without a warning, particularly as he was clearly of the view, as he demonstrated in December 1975, that the Senate did not have the power to reject supply.[27] As to Derham and Wheare, both were experts in constitutional law, and Derham seems one of the few with that expertise who has not expressed a public view on the validity of Whitlam's dismissal or the circumstances that led to it. Wheare, however, did provide some support to Kerr, and as such he was extensively quoted by Kerr.[28] But his support seems more limited than Kerr would have liked and it really comes down to his opinion: 'for what it is worth, . . . the course of action taken by the Governor-General was one of the several options open to him'.[29] Whether Wheare, himself, would have adopted that course, if he was in the job, and would have done so in secrecy, as did Kerr, we will never know.

Whitlam, however, did not choose from either of those Labor-based or academic groups, but his first preference was from those with business and philanthropy experience, seeking the appointment of Ken Myer. Myer, evidently, had publicly supported Labor in 1972; but when Myer was not prepared to become governor-general,[30] Whitlam then went to another group – the one member of the judiciary on Hasluck's list, John Kerr. And he chose him, despite the prescient, if blunt, warning from the then trade union leader[31] and later Labor prime minister Bob Hawke: 'What are you doing appointing this bastard. He's just a DLP stooge'.[32]

Whitlam, however, took a different view. He had known Kerr at the bar, if not closely, and felt that as Kerr was now the chief justice of Australia's most populous state, the appointment would be, as Kelly puts it, 'orthodox and impeccable'. Whitlam, moreover, had an arrogant attitude towards his colleagues; and, as his private secretary John Mant put it, in Gough's view 'everyone else . . . were pissants'.[33] And, as Mant has also observed, he now treated Kerr as if he had 'joined the pissant group . . . and the assumption was that he would do what Gough told him'.[34] But nothing could be further from the truth. As Kerr said, shortly before he began his new office:

> What I will do as governor-general is to pursue my interest in law and politics. There are plenty of issues, many things I will have the opportunity to express an opinion about.[35]

JOHN KERR: HIS MEETINGS, THE DECISIVE DAY AND HIS DECISION

Kerr recognized the significance of the blockage of supply even before it had occurred. As he recalled in his memoirs, he raised with the prime minister, on October 13 or 14, 1975, the proposition of having 'a talk with Mr Fraser with a view to ascertaining how serious things were'. Whitlam, however, initially refused. But at a dinner with the then prime minister of Malaysia on October 16, he changed his position, accepting that an official chat would be appropriate.[36] Kerr, however, had already closed himself off from providing effective advice to Whitlam. He had formed the view, prior to October 14, that Whitlam had become 'implacable' regarding the supply crisis, and that 'He made it clear that my suggestion was not discussable and never would be'.[37] And after Whitlam had, on October 14, rejected 'out of hand and very forcibly' some views of Kerr regarding potential actions if supply were blocked, Kerr decided that he would then keep his views to himself and those that he chose he would communicate with – and that did not include Whitlam.

> From that time forward my opinion was that he was beyond the reach of any argument of mine or even discussion. Everything he said publicly, or privately to me, thereafter, strengthened me in that view.[38]

This position was further reinforced for Kerr once the prime minister also began, in Kerr's words, to 'publicly hammer the theme that I had no choice but to adopt his advice'. That can be dated from, at least, October 17 and Whitlam's *This Day Tonight* interview and his 'unquestionably' responses (as discussed in chapter 3). But this did not prompt Kerr to question or debate those views. Instead, he took the view that Whitlam had 'disqualified himself from being offered a running account of the development of my thinking, until such time as it had crystallized in a way which might affect him positively'.[39]

What Kerr considered the phrase 'affect him positively' meant is far from clear as Whitlam never found anything from Kerr about the governor-general's thinking until he was sacked on November 11, and only after that action had taken effect (see the discussion in the next chapter of Kerr's four varying versions of what occurred on November 11). This closed approach is a markedly ineffective and confusing method of any relationship between senior officers in government – and seems more based on the desires of the governor-general to avoid any debate or disagreement with the prime minister, rather than the needs of good government.

But despite his growing secrecy from the prime minister, Kerr was prepared, as Hocking makes clear, to take other and even more proactive actions, although not ones known to the prime minister. She records that Kerr had his earliest discussions with Justice Anthony Mason of the High Court, and a personal friend of Kerr's, in August 1975, well before the supply crisis began.[40] We will discuss Mason and his interrelationship with the governor-general more in chapter 8. But here, it is worth noting that Kerr subsequently recorded that Mason was 'historically important' in reaching his decision to dismiss Whitlam, as he was not aware of any other person who 'could better, by conversation, help me to sort out my own thoughts on the constitutional powers of the governor-general'.[41]

In their conversations, Kerr and Mason discussed 'probabilities, options and timing' regarding a crisis that might or might not arise. But those early discussions and conclusions were largely academic as there was then 'no conceivable ground for action on my part'. However, by October 17, after supply had been blocked, Kerr was recording that 'the real question at this time is whether I should act before the money runs out and whilst the Senate is still only deferring'.[42]

His concerns should have been apparent to the prime minster as on October 19, Kerr had asked Whitlam for his approval for him to confer with the Chief Justice Garfield Barwick.[43] Whitlam, however, refused that permission. Kerr considered that the prime minister's instruction was contrary to both Paul Hasluck's earlier view (see chapter 3) and 'despite what Sir Samuel Griffith did early in the century'. Yet he accepted, at least for the time being, that 'I was not entitled ever to ask for the advice of the Chief Justice'.[44]

Kerr also asked Whitlam on October 20 to meet with Fraser so as to allow him to 'ascertain the likely course of future events', a meeting that occurred on October 21.[45] On that day, he also asked Whitlam for an opinion of the Law Officers (the attorney-general, Kep Enderby, and the solicitor-general, Maurice Byers).[46] But regardless of that opinion, whatever it said, Kerr had already decided that he would act if he considered it necessary. As he wrote on that day: 'a joint opinion of the Law Officers to the contrary would certainly not deter me if the moment arrives for action'.[47] It took, however, some time before anything approaching a joint opinion from the Law Officers was received. As will be discussed in the next chapter, what can only be described as a draft joint opinion did not arrive until November 6.[48] And for Kerr, that day, November 6, became the 'decisive day';[49] the day when he knew that 'I must make up my mind as to the actions to be taken by me, and follow that decision through'.[50]

In addition to Kerr having received the draft Law Officers' opinion on November 6, the Senate also repeated its deferral of the supply bills.[51] Kerr also had a short but informative meeting on that day with the Treasurer, Bill Hayden, who advised that the existing supply would last until about November 27.[52] After that, the nation would be without funds unless different financial arrangements were put in place. This reflects the serious economic consequences of the course of action initiated by the Opposition, combined with the government's chosen response of 'toughing it out'. As Hayden had explained to the House of Representatives on the day that supply was deferred, October 16:

> The course of action which the Opposition has now set before this Parliament and this nation involves the gravest consequences for the country. It represents the most reprehensible conduct imaginable. The present course the Opposition is setting will grind this nation to a halt.

And:

> the economy of this country, if the present course of action which the Opposition has set in train is pursued, will get out of hand, that there will be a major economic collapse, that a substantial number of enterprises in the corporate sector will fail, that there will be an upsurge in unemployment and generally that there will be the worst deepening of the recession that we have seen at any time since the great Depression of the 1930's.[53]

This was the consequence that Kerr's actions against Whitlam were designed to avoid.[54] And on the decisive day, November 6, Kerr had decided that the action he chose to undertake to avoid those serious economic effects was, as Kelly recognized, 'to dismiss Gough Whitlam'. But he had also decided that he needed to keep his reasoning and that decision an absolute secret from the prime minister.[55] In Kerr's view, he considered that 'the only neutral and intelligent course to follow, [was] that I should keep silence about my thinking unless and until I decided I must act'.[56] This is a remarkably odd conclusion, as his memoirs have omitted to record other advice that he had received regarding the reserve powers from very experienced sources that took a very different view as to the course that he should follow (as will be discussed in chapter 9).

Kerr's secretive approach has been criticized by many as neither neutral nor intelligent, but as ambushing his head of government. He, however, considered it to be his 'proper behaviour in the circumstances to stay at my post and not invite dismissal'.[57] That is, the reason for his secret non-communicative approach was Kerr's fear that Whitlam would sack him first.

Kerr's decision to take this very reticent approach seems to have predated the 'decisive day' and may have developed from the day that supply was first deferred. On that day, October 16, at a formal dinner at Government House in honour of the Malaysian prime minister Tun Abdul Razak, Whitlam made what he later described as a 'passing'[58] and 'flippant'[59] remark, but one that, in Whitlam's words, 'had a traumatic effect on Sir John Kerr and entered profoundly into his calculations throughout the crisis'.[60] And that comment was made in response to Razak's query about the role of the governor-general in the current supply deferral, to which Whitlam responded, 'it all depends who gets to the phone first, he to dismiss me or I to have him recalled'.[61] While this led, as Kerr accepted, to laughter from those present,[62] Whitlam's 'flippant' comment seems to have created a serious concern in the mind of Kerr. This is apparent from his comments and reaction to the NSW governor, Sir Roden Cutler VC, four days later, on the 20th. Cutler had advised Kerr that if he considered dismissing Whitlam, he should first discuss that possibility with Whitlam, a course that Kerr made 'fairly clear' he did not want to do. When Cutler also referred to Whitlam's power to have Kerr's commission withdrawn, in Cutler's words, Kerr became 'quite animated and said: "I know, I know!"'[63]

It also seems that Kerr later wanted to spread some of the responsibility or blame for his secrecy to his wife. This seems apparent from a conversation that he held with his old friend, the poet Jim McAuley, in February 1976. According to Kelly, Kerr told McAuley that he had been 'seriously thinking of telling Whitlam that he may have to dismiss him' until his wife Anne had said, 'No don't do that. If you tell him, he'll sack you first'. [64]

Kerr also took other steps in his preparation for the dismissal on the decisive day, some of which were unknown to the prime minister. Of most concern have been Kerr's conversations with the Leader of the Opposition. In addition to the approval provided for Kerr to have unofficial discussions with Fraser on October 16,[65] on October 30 Whitlam also approved of Kerr having further meetings with Fraser, the first of which occurred later that day.[66] They also met on November 3 when Fraser told the governor-general that he was now prepared to pass supply, but only if Whitlam also agreed to a House of Representatives election at the same time as the Senate poll.[67] As Kelly and Bramston have argued, this was a significant concession on Fraser's part, and 'one of the most overlooked yet most decisive events in the crisis'.[68] It indicated that Fraser was 'retreating', making him 'look weak'. But Whitlam ignored it, rejecting Fraser's idea 'out of hand'.[69]

Whitlam was, however, not told of other important aspects of the Kerr/Fraser conversation of November 3. What he did not know, as Kelly and Bramston record, was that Kerr had advised Fraser of his doubts as to the validity of Labor's proposed alternate financial arrangements[70] mentioned in the last chapter. Kerr, however, had never expressed any of those concerns to the prime minister.

Whitlam did, however, know and approve of the meeting the governor-general had with Fraser on the 'decisive day', November 6. But that meeting did little or nothing to resolve the constitutional crisis, as Fraser was not prepared to take any further steps to resolve the crisis.[71] 'He said the terms he had already announced were final'.[72] As Fraser later said, 'I repeated the only thing the Opposition was asking for was an election' and 'I told him frankly that this was a wretched government' and 'that Australians want to vote'.[73] Whatever else was discussed at that meeting is unclear. But as Kelly and Bramston record, on the evening of November 6, Kelly met with Fraser, who told him, in what was supposed to be an 'off-the record discussion', that 'the issue would be resolved by Christmas' and that 'the governor-general would "do the right thing"'. To Fraser, the 'right thing' meant that by the decisive day, November 6, he believed that 'the Governor-General . . . will sack the Prime Minister'.[74]

Meanwhile, none of that was known to Whitlam. As Kelly records, he was still believing, on that same decisive day, that 'Kerr is the best appointment we've made'.[75] And that he maintained that inaccurate view even though, in one incident that most accounts have ignored, he had been warned, and on that day, of Kerr's possible intention. That warning came from the treasurer, Bill Hayden, who had met Kerr on that day and, as his memoirs record, 'My old coppers instincts tell me that he's going to sack us'. He advised Whitlam at Parliament House of that suspicion, but it was rejected.

> He stood outside his office, pressed against the corridor wall, twirling his spectacles thoughtfully between thumb and finger of one hand. After a few seconds reflection he pronounced with finality. 'No Comrade, he wouldn't have the guts to do it'. With that decisiveness one of the great moments of our history went unanticipated.[76]

Three days later, on the evening of November 9, Kerr 'had made up my mind as to what I must do if the two leaders were still in a deadlock when 11 November came up, inexorably, on the calendar'.[77] And that action was to sack Whitlam, which he confirmed to both his wife[78] and in a further private talk with Justice Mason.[79] In Kerr's notes of his conversation with Mason, he recalls that he asked Mason for his opinion on the draft advice of the Law Officers, and Mason rejected their conclusions.[80] But more importantly, Kerr attempted to transfer at least part of the responsibility for his eventual sacking decision to Mason, who Kerr records as saying:

> quite spontaneously and with genuine relief, 'I am glad of that. I thought that I might this afternoon have to urge that course upon you'.[81]

And on that day, Kerr also decided to take a position clearly contrary to the advice of the prime minister and without telling him. Contrary to the advice of the prime minister given on October 19, Kerr decided to seek the advice of Chief Justice Barwick.[82] They met on the following day, and as a result, Barwick produced his two-page letter dated November 10, 1975, which fully supported Kerr's decision. It has the following conclusion:

> Accordingly, my opinion is that, if Your Excellency is satisfied in the current situation that the present Government is unable to secure supply, the course upon which Your Excellency has determined is consistent with your constitutional authority and duty.[83]

But Whitlam knew nothing of that. As Hayden later recalled, 'If the Prime Minister believed Kerr to be a man of putty, this was a regrettable miscalculation'.[84]

NOTES

1. Kerr, *Matters,* 25–26 & 33.
2. Kerr, *Matters,* 32.
3. Kerr, *Matters,* 40–41.
4. Kerr, *Matters,* 46.
5. Sexton, *Great Crash*, 134.
6. Sexton, *Great Crash*, 138 & 140.
7. Kerr, *Matters*, 42.
8. Kerr, *Matters,* 52.
9. Kerr, *Matters,* 145.
10. Kerr, *Matters,* 151.
11. Kerr, *Matters,* 134.
12. Kerr, *Matters*, 148.
13. Kerr, *Matters,* 186–187.
14. Which can be seen in Kelly & Bramston, *The Dismissal,* 331 and in Whitlam, *The Truth,* xxiii.
15. Whitlam, *The Truth,* xxii.
16. Kelly, *Unmaking,* 21.
17. Crean had been Whitlam's first post-duumvirate treasurer, and then minister for overseas trade (from December 12, 1974) and deputy prime minister from July 14,

1975. He had been in Parliament for the Victorian seat of Melbourne Ports between 1951 and 1977, and before that, a member of the Victorian Parliament since 1945.

18. Beazley had been Whitlam's minister of education. A former teacher, who had been responsible for the abolition of tertiary fees. He was a member of Parliament for the Western Australian seat of Fremantle between 1945 and 1977. Like Frank Crean, his family is well entrenched in Labor Party politics as both had sons who went on to become senior federal Ministers in later ALP governments and to lead the federal ALP. That is, Kim Beazley Jr who led the ALP between 1996 and 2001 and 2005 and 2006. After he left politics, he became the Ambassador to the United States and then the Governor of Western Australia; and Simon Crean, who led the ALP between 2001 and 2003.

19. A man who Hasluck probably knew little of, as his note identifies him as "HJ Souter" rather than Harold. But his prominence would be because he had been the Secretary to the federal unions body, the Australian Council of Trade Unions (the ACTU), for a very long time, holding that influential post for two decades – 1956–1977.

20. Derham was a legal scholar from Melbourne who had been the foundation Dean of the Law School at Victoria's second university, Monash University, from 1963 (the Law School is now called the David Derham School of Law) and then the Vice Chancellor of Melbourne University between 1968 and 1982.

21. Wheare was another legal scholar, born in the country town of Warragul, the son of a grocer's assistant, but who progressed through hard work and scholarship to become, among other things, the Gladstone professor of government at Oxford and the vice chancellor of that University between 1964 and 1966. He was an expert in the constitution of the then Empire and then the Commonwealth, but he may have been a little too old for this office as he had been born in 1907 and died in 1979. See J. R. Poynter, "Where, Sir Kenneth Clinton (1907–1979)," in National Centre of Biography, *Australian Dictionary of Biography* (Canberra: Australian National University, published first in hardcopy 2002) Vol 16, https://adb.anu.edu.au/biography/wheare-sir-kenneth-clinton-12005, accessed online May 12, 2023.

22. The American-born son of the founder of the Melbourne-based Myer Emporium, the company that revolutionized retail trade in Australia. In addition to his business interest, Ken Myer, with the rest of the Myer family, was one of the most dedicated and generous arts patrons in the country, and he had served on or chaired the National Library Council, the Sidney Myer Fund, the National Gallery of Australia and the National Gallery Society of Victoria.

23. Fairfax had been a leading member of the business community, holding numerous directorships and official positions with some of Australia's major financial firms, organizations with interests in rural Australia and the Anglican Church. He had been the Chairman of the AMP and a Director of John Fairfax Limited, publishers of *The Sydney Morning Herald*, *The Age* and other newspapers.

24. Kelly, *Unmaking,* 21.

25. The first Australian-born Cardinal of the Catholic Church, having held that office since 1946, was probably too old for the office of governor-general, having been born in 1896 and having died in 1977.

26. Legal scholar, Judge of the Australian Industrial Court, who became Chancellor of Monash University in 1975.
27. See Colin Howard & Cheryl Saunders, "The Blocking of the Budget and Dismissal of the Government," in *Labor and the Constitution,* ed., Evans, 251, 263.
28. See Kerr, *Matters,* 393–395.
29. Kerr, *Matters,* 393.
30. Kelly, *Unmaking*, 21.
31. He was then president of the Australian Council of Trade Unions.
32. Kelly & Bramston, *The Dismissal,* 286.
33. Kelly & Bramston, *The Dismissal,* 136.
34. Kelly & Bramston, *The Dismissal,* 136.
35. Quoted in Kelly, *Unmaking,* 3.
36. Kerr, *Matters,* 264.
37. Kerr, *Matters,* 254.
38. Kerr, *Matters,* 254.
39. Kerr, *Matters,* 310.
40. Hocking, *His Time* (2014), 565.
41. As recorded in 1981 and quoted in Kelly & Bramston, *The Dismissal*, 43.
42. Hocking, *His Time* (2012), 308.
43. Kelly & Bramston, *The Dismissal,* 159.
44. Kelly & Bramston, *The Dismissal*, 160.
45. Kerr, *Matters,* 266–267.
46. Kerr, *Matters,* 271.
47. National Archives of Australia, *The Kerr Palace Letters*, M4523, 1 Part 12, 11[2]. Quoted in Kelly & Bramston, *The Dismissal,* 161.
48. Kerr, *Matters,* 272.
49. Kerr, *Matters*, 298.
50. Kerr, *Matters*, 308.
51. See Commonwealth of Australia, *Parliamentary Debates, Senate*, November 6, 1975, 1836 and Kerr, *Matters*, 296.
52. Kelly, *Unmaking,* 14.
53. Commonwealth of Australia, *Parliamentary Debates, House of Representatives*, October 16, 1975, 2206.
54. Kerr, *Matters,* 276.
55. Kelly, *Unmaking,* 4 and Kelly & Bramston, *The Dismissal,* 28 which were based on Kerr, *Matters*, 298, 308–311.
56. Kerr, *Matters,* 310.
57. Kerr, *Matters,* 310.
58. Whitlam, *The Truth,* 89.
59. Whitlam, *The Truth,* 130.
60. Whitlam, *The Truth,* 89.
61. Whitlam, *The Truth,* 130.
62. Kerr, *Matters,* 258 & Whitlam, *The Truth,* 130.
63. *Four Corners* (1995), 22.50-23.10.
64. Kelly, *Unmaking,* 5.

65. Kerr, *Matters,* 264.
66. Kelly & Bramston, *The Dismissal,* 172.
67. Kerr, *Matters,* 291 & 297; Kelly & Bramston, *The Dismissal,* 179 & 180.
68. Kelly & Bramston, *The Dismissal,* 179.
69. Kelly & Bramston, *The Dismissal,* 180.
70. Kelly & Bramston, *The Dismissal,* 180.
71. Kelly & Bramston, *The Dismissal,* 185.
72. Kerr, *Matters,* 297.
73. Kelly & Bramston, *The Dismissal,* 186.
74. Kelly & Bramston, *The Dismissal,* 186.
75. Kelly, *Unmaking,* 5.
76. Hayden, *Hayden,* 278.
77. Kerr, *Matters,* 308.
78. Hocking, *His Time* (2012), 320.
79. Kelly & Bramston, *The Dismissal,* 42; Hocking, *His Time* (2012), 320–321.
80. Kelly & Bramston, *The Dismissal,* 42.
81. John Kerr, *Conversation with Sir Anthony Mason during October-November 1975.* NAA, M4523, 1 Part 14, 12. Also see 16; also quoted in Hocking, *His Time* (2012), 321. As will be seen in chapter 8, Mason has rejected that he encouraged Kerr to dismiss Whitlam.
82. Hocking, *His Time* (2012), 321 & Barwick, *Sir John,* 78.
83. See Kelly & Bramston, *The Dismissal,* 366.
84. Hayden, *Hayden*, 278.

Chapter 7

The Dismissal

And November 11

Figure 7.1 ALP Political Badge from the 1975 Election. From the collection of the author. Image taken by the author.

November 11 is Remembrance Day. That is, it is the day when Australians, just like many across the world, pause at the 11th hour of the 11th day of the 11th month to commemorate those who died or suffered for their countries in all wars and armed conflicts. It is a day that marks the anniversary of the end of World War I, a war which was, as the Australian War Memorial reminds us, the 'first modern world conflict', a war that 'had brought about the mobilisation of over 70 million people and left between 9 and 13 million dead, perhaps as many as one-third of them with no known grave'. But on November 11, 1975, in Australia, all of that had to play second fiddle to another drama. November 11, 1975, was the day of the government's dismissal.

That day, for those who became involved in that dismissal, began with a range of meetings. The first meeting relevant to the constitutional crisis was between the two sides of politics at 9 am, when the prime minister, his deputy, Frank Crean, and the leader of the Lower House, Fred Daly, met with the coalition leadership group (Fraser, Doug Anthony and Phillip Lynch).[1] The purpose of that meeting was to ascertain if there was any potential for resolution of the dispute, but as the meeting quickly recognized, none was possible. This was confirmed in a telephone call between Fraser and Whitlam at 10:05, which, as Kelly records, ended with the one thing that the two were prepared to agree on: 'There'll be no deal'.[2] The furthest that Whitlam was prepared to go was to delay a half Senate election to the end of June 1976 so the Senate before July 1 would not include territory senators. Fraser, however, wanted another Lower House election. He was, however, prepared, according to Kelly and Bramston, to repeat his earlier compromise – passing supply if there was a double dissolution election in May or June 1976, which Whitlam rejected, as he had before.[3]

Both sides had their terms, and neither was moving. Nonetheless, at a coalition joint party meeting held later that morning, according to Kelly, Fraser and Lynch decided to take a course that seems to indicate how tentative they considered their position. They 'decided not to report to the party on their talks with Whitlam or even tell the party that the prime minister was seeking a 13 December half-Senate election'. Their objective was to prevent any 'crack in the party room'. Their concern was that if any news of Whitlam's half-Senate election plan was known to the party members, it might provoke an internal party debate, a concept that Fraser was keen to avoid. Such a debate, particularly if known to the press, had the potential, in Kelly's view, to 'shatter the fabric of their unity'.[4] However, taking steps to avoid an internal party examination and debate, particularly regarding the problematic elements of a novel and adventurous constitutional course of action favoured by party leadership, seems quite odd for any political party, much less one that purports to follow a liberal philosophy.

The telephone call between Fraser and Whitlam has also been claimed to contain another element highly relevant to the constitutional crisis, as Fraser has maintained that he provided a warning to Whitlam regarding the governor-general's freedom to act outside of ministerial advice: 'You know, Prime Minister, the Governor-General can make up his own mind what to do. You can't necessarily assume he will do just as you advise'. According to Fraser, this was dismissed by Whitlam as 'Nonsense'.[5] Whether this limited warning was ever made is unknown, as other reports of this discussion do not seem to include any accounts of such a warning. However, whether it was made or not, this recognition by Fraser, at least, seems to indicate that he accepted that some form of warning should have been given to the prime minister. The question of the relevance of warnings to prime ministers is discussed in more detail in the next two chapters.

After that Whitlam/Fraser discussion, Prime Minister Whitlam then spoke to Kerr by phone, advising of the result of his discussions with Fraser and seeking an early meeting to recommend a December 13 half-Senate election. Kerr, however, seemingly using his Remembrance Day obligations as well as his granddaughter's illness,[6] delayed that meeting until the House of Representatives' lunch adjournment period, commencing at 1.00 pm.

As to what was to happen at that meeting, Whitlam advised Kerr that supply was still not available, but that his plan was 'to govern without it'.[7] And that, according to Kerr, seemed decisive and led him to the conclusion that, if he was to intervene, it needed to be at that 1.00 pm meeting. To Kerr, his options for that meeting were limited to two:

> I had either to let him have that election without supply, with consequential financial chaos, or to act, so as to ensure full elections for both Houses with full supply produced at the last realistic moment before supply ran out.[8]

But limiting his options to those two courses is simply not correct. Allowing a half-Senate election on November 11 would not have prevented the Senate from subsequently granting supply before the existing funds expired. Neither would it have prevented Kerr from dismissing Whitlam later that month and closer to when supply would have run out. As Kerr had accepted that supply would last until November 30,[9] so his assessment of November 11 as the 'last realistic moment before supply ran out' as the basis for the timing of his dismissal actions seems far too early and unjustifiable. His reason for choosing November 11 for his decision to dismiss Whitlam, however, seems based on other, very questionable factors regarding caretaker periods, the merits of which are discussed in chapter 9.

Kerr also had two other discussions prior to his telephone conversation with Whitlam, both of which indicate his secretive approach to his role.

The first was with Chief Justice Barwick (which was not referred to in his published account). Its purpose, according to Kelly and Bramston, was 'tactical issues'.[10] It is not clear what those tactical issues were, but the call seems more designed to ensure that the chief justice remained supportive of Kerr's approach. And he was.

The second was another telephone conversation, this time between Kerr and Fraser, that occurred at 9.55 am, initiated by the governor-general.[11] Kelly and Bramston have considered the meeting a matter of 'high dispute'.[12]

Kerr maintains that this conversation was limited to Fraser confirming the result of his meeting with Whitlam and that he 'said nothing else to him about the situation'.[13] However, in Fraser's account, he made notes of that conversation on the back of the agenda of the joint party meeting that he was shortly to attend. Those notes, which still exist, indicate the promises that Kerr required of Fraser 'If Whitlam was dismissed and Fraser was made Prime Minister'.[14]

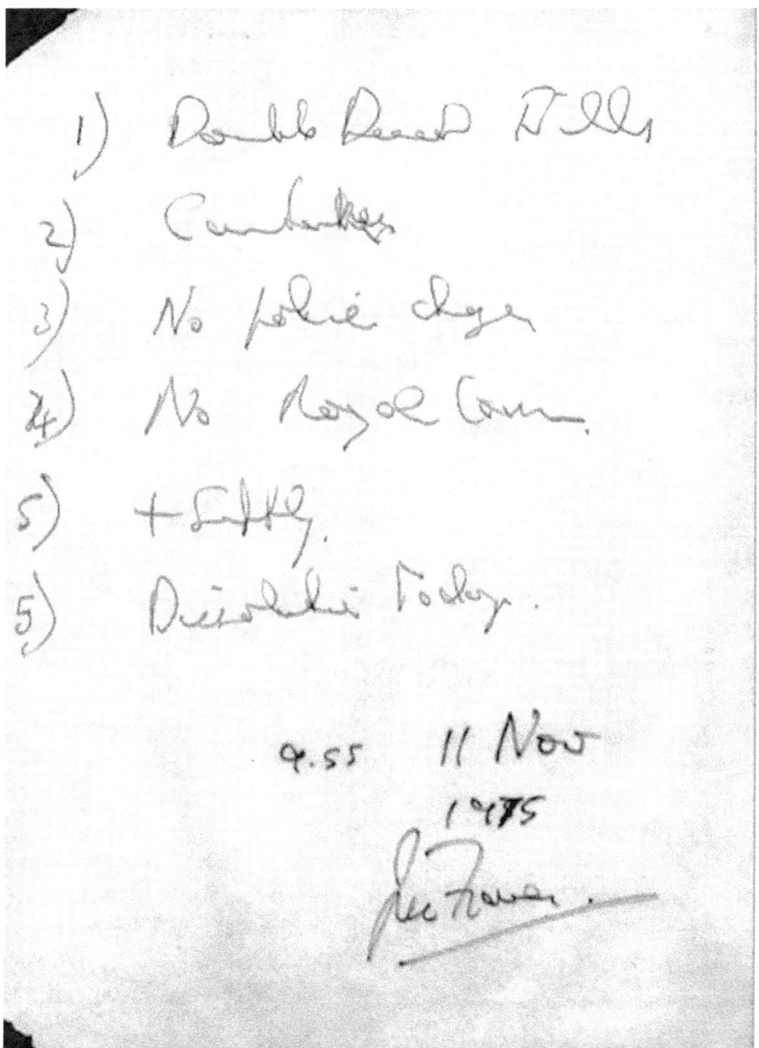

Figure 7.2 Notes of Phone Call between John Kerr and Malcolm Fraser, November 11, 1975. From Papers of Malcolm Fraser, University of Melbourne.

Fraser noted in six short points (see figure 7.2) recording the following questions posed by Kerr:[15] 'would he agree to call a double dissolution? Would he agree to run a caretaker administration, making no policy changes? Would he obtain supply straightaway? Would he advise a dissolution on that very day?' and that 'there no action would be taken against the ministers of the Whitlam government over the loans affair, and that there would be no royal commission'.[16] And Fraser agreed to them all.

Henderson, however, has challenged the Fraser account – in that Fraser's document went missing until it was located in the early 2000s, and because of the different pen apparently used in Fraser's signature and what appears to be an alteration to its date. As Henderson later wrote:

> the writing at the top of the note is dramatically different from that at the bottom of the note. Indeed it seems that when dating the note Fraser wrote a '7' over an '8' – suggesting that he first dated the note '1985' but corrected it to '1975'. It's quite possible that Fraser dated the note in 1985, ten years after the event. Fraser was certainly capable of back-dating a document.[17]

But if one accepts Fraser's version of events, is the heavy criticism that others have made of it correct? Kelly and Bramston have regarded the call as 'tantamount to a tip-off'[18] to Fraser and as 'collusion',[19] while Hocking has held similar views: 'A greater conflict of interest for both parties to this arrangement to remove the elected government would be difficult to conjecture'.[20] To her, the meeting was 'scandalous, even treacherous'[21] with the governor-general acting 'in contravention of the Constitutional requirement that the Governor-General act on the advice of his ministers'.[22]

Those concerns, however, seem another example of those authors' limited understanding of the basis and operation of the governor-general's reserve powers (see chapter 3). Fraser, however, seems to have had a much better appreciation of those powers and how they operate. Fraser considered that Kerr did nothing improper – 'he merely checked to be sure Fraser would accept the terms of the commission'[23] if such an offer was ever made. Fraser, as his memoirs made clear, 'knew now that today was the day Kerr intended to act' but that he 'still wasn't certain that, once faced with an ultimatum, Whitlam would not back down and choose to go to an election as Prime Minister'.[24] This is not what Kelly and Bramston assert as mere 'wordplay on Fraser's part',[25] but was a reflection of what Fraser knew and what he did not know.

It also reflects that the responsibility for the exercise of the reserve powers. As pointed out in chapter 3, the responsibility is taken by the person who exercises those powers, the governor-general, not by his or her informal advisers. To repeat what Professor Twomey said regarding advice given to the governor-general regarding reserve powers:

> There is no conventional requirement that the advice be acted upon. Nor is there any transfer of responsibility from the person acting pursuant to the advice to the person who gave it.[26]

That responsibility rule, however, seems not apparent to many popular experts on 1975. That apparent misunderstanding can be seen from Kelly's recent views expressed to the ABC when he discussed the Kerr/Fraser 'collusion' telephone call, saying that:

> The Governor-General is not a referee. The Governor-General acts on the advice of the Prime Minister. He does not act on the advice of the Opposition leader.[27]

But in this telephone call, Kerr was not acting on, nor seeking, the formal advice of the Opposition Leader. He was seeking informal advice from Fraser so as to give him what he considered necessary before considering exercising the reserve powers. He was ascertaining, if he exercised those powers in the manner he intended, whether he still would have a government. And only Malcolm Fraser could have given Kerr that information. Kerr did not need the consent of the prime minister before he sought that type of information from Fraser, as the governor-general was not under any constitutional requirement to require the approval of his constitutional advisers when the governor-general was considering the exercise of the reserve powers, powers for which the governor-general has sole responsibility. As to the content of that conversation, so long as the decision on the reserve powers remained that of the governor-general, and so long as he had not conveyed any decision regarding the exercise of the power before it had been exercised, Kerr's conversation with Fraser on the morning of November 11 cannot be, and should not be, regarded as either wrong or, as Kelly has incorrectly asserted, 'collusion'.

After all of those exchanges, the dismissal occurred. The following summarizes what happened over the next few hours leading up to that event, including the appointment of Fraser as prime minister and the double dissolution of both Houses prior to the next election:

- 11.00 am – The governor-general attended the Remembrance Day ceremony in Canberra.[28] The attorney-general, Kep Enderby, also attended but was avoided by the governor-general during the short ceremony.[29]
- 11.46 am – A censure motion of the government moved by Fraser in the House of Representatives[30] became, by amendment moved by Whitlam, a censure motion of the Opposition.[31]

- Whitlam addressed the Lower House between 12.09 and 12.35,[32] and then left the House prior to its lunchtime adjournment, which began at 12.55 pm,[33] so as to allow him to meet with the governor-general at 1.00 pm. He arrived at Yarralumla, Government House, at around 12.50 pm[34] (although the governor-general's official secretary, David Smith, puts it at 12.45 pm).[35] Fraser also left the House before its adjournment. However, he was keener than Whitlam. Indeed, Whitlam's contemporary account, made on November 13, was that Fraser left the House while Whitlam was still speaking.[36] As a result, Fraser arrived at Yarralumla before Whitlam. Fraser minimizes this as 'a mix-up',[37] which it certainly was. But to Whitlam, 'had I known Mr Fraser's car was there, I could have at once have instructed my driver . . . to turn round and drive me back to Parliament House. Had I known Mr. Fraser was already there, I would not have set foot in Yarralumla'.[38] As a result of Fraser's eagerness and early arrival, there has been much talk of Fraser being conspiratorially hidden in a 'closeted room, blinds draw', and his car, 'around the back out of site'.[39] David Smith, with whom Fraser sat while he waited, however, has rejected this as 'the figment of a vivid journalistic imagination'.[40]
- 1.01 pm (approximately).[41] Whitlam was taken to the governor-general's study, but before he could make his recommendation for a half Senate election, Kerr interrupted, handing Whitlam his one-page letter of November 11, 1975, together with the attached statement of reasons.[42]
- There is, however, a dispute between Whitlam and Kerr as to what Kerr's interruption was. Moreover, Kerr himself has given at least four different versions of his discussions with Whitlam on that day, with the differences growing with each variation, each of which needs to be examined and compared.
  - *Kerr version 1* was provided in his letter to the Queen's Private Secretary, Sir Martin Charteris, of November 11, 1975.[43] In that letter, Kerr's version was:

    > When Whitlam came to see me before he had said anything about his proposal for a Half Senate election I told him that I had decided to terminate his commission. He said, 'I shall have to get in touch with the Palace immediately'. To this I replied that this would be pointless as he was at the time no longer Prime Minister. I had already signed the document terminating his commission.[44]

    In this version, Kerr's intervention and termination occurred 'before he had said anything about his proposal for a half-Senate election'.
  - *Kerr version 2* was provided in a lengthy handwritten letter from Kerr to Charteris a few months later, on January 22, 1976 (also discussed in chapter 12). In this difficult-to-read letter, Kerr now said that Whitlam

had not been advised that he was to be sacked until 'I was about to do it'. This, Kerr did not regard or describe as a 'warning'. He gave such minimal notice of his actions because 'I believed he would seek to have me dismissed on the instant if I gave him any foreknowledge'.

◦ *Kerr version 3* was provided in his memoirs, *Matters for Judgment*, first published three years after the dismissal, in 1978. In this version, Kerr still did not argue that Whitlam had been warned, even though he further altered the account. He now maintained that he had first asked Whitlam if he intended to govern without supply, and when Whitlam confirmed his intention, Kerr's version is that he advised Whitlam of his intended action. In this version, Kerr advised Whitlam that he 'had to have parliamentary supply to govern and as he had failed to obtain it and was not prepared to go to the people, I had decided to withdraw his commission'.[45] But according to Kerr, he still had not dismissed Whitlam.

> He could still say, 'Let us talk about this. If you are determined to have an election, I would rather go to the people as Prime Minister'. Had he done so I would have agreed, provided he committed himself by action there and then. I was not prepared to run any further risks.[46]

Kerr's statement to Whitlam became, to Professor Markwell, what he later described as Kerr having 'warned him that, since he proposed to govern without parliamentary Supply, it would be necessary to dismiss him'.[47] Kerr, however, did not express his statement to Whitlam as a 'warning'. That needed to await ten years until his last account, version 4, which we will get to shortly.

Kerr, in version 3, did not exercise the power to dismiss until Whitlam responded to his 'decided to withdraw his commission' statement. And that response, according to Kerr, was that 'I must get in touch with the Palace at once'. Kerr now knew, so he said in 1978, that 'there would be no changed advice, only the certainty of constitutional disruption if any time were allowed to elapse'.[48] As a result, 'I therefore made my final decision to withdraw his commission and hand him the signed documents'. Kerr then, according to this version, told Whitlam that it was 'now too late' to contact the Palace.[49] And when Whitlam asked, 'Why?' Kerr 'told him, "Because you are no longer Prime Minister. These documents [which had still not been delivered to Whitlam] tell you so and why"'.[50]

Kerr, in this version, seems to have altered the time that Whitlam had ceased to be prime minister. In version 1, Whitlam seems to have ceased to be prime minister, as far as Kerr was concerned, when he had signed his dismissal documents, even before they had been delivered to Whitlam. That seems apparent from Kerr's view that he expressed when Whitlam spoke of contacting the Palace. To Kerr, Whitlam was 'at that time no longer Prime Minister. I had already signed the document terminating his commission'.[51] That might sound like an odd way to terminate a commission. But according to the 1978 version 3, an even more bizarre construction is presented as Kerr now seems to have considered that Whitlam ceased to be prime minister, not when the documents terminating his commission were signed by Kerr, or even when they were delivered to Whitlam (which would be the normal expectation for a document terminating an appointment), but at some stage solely based on some mental decision of the governor-general that did not need to be communicated to its subject (other than, possibly, in the past tense – 'you are no longer prime minister'). As Kerr said in his memoirs, that he then 'made my final decision to withdraw his commission and hand him the signed documents'.[52]

- *Kerr Version 4* was provided in the *Bulletin* magazine[53] almost ten years after the dismissal, in September 1985,[54] and is largely consistent with his 1978 account. But he now removed any subtleties from his 1978 account and began to blame Whitlam directly for his dismissal, interpreting Whitlam's supposed desire to contact the Palace not merely as an indication of 'no changed advice' from Whitlam and 'the certainty of constitutional disruption' as it was in 1978. It now became (as it had been in version 2, in 1976) a threat to Kerr – that 'he would try to have me dismissed by the Queen'. As a result, in this version, he now considered that Whitlam 'forced my hand' by that supposed threat, and as a result 'I dismissed him immediately'.[55]

The other variation in this 1985 version is that Kerr also now fully adopted the 'warning' construction, even though it was absent from his 1975 advice to the Palace and was not described as such in 1976 or 1978. But he told the *Bulletin* on September 10, 1985, 'I did warn Mr Whitlam on November 11 that I would dismiss him'.[56] The difficulty with this new warning element in Kerr's 1985 argument (and that of Professor Markwell) is in language used. That is, in Kerr's 1975 and 1978 versions, Kerr's 1975 statement to Whitlam, according to Kerr, was not in the future sense, as would be appropriate for an action that he may or may not exercise, as Kerr's 1985 version now has it (i.e., 'I would dismiss him').[57] But in his earlier statements, the tense was, at best, ambiguous or was in the past tense (i.e., 'I had decided to withdraw your commission')[58] indicating that the governor-general's reserved power had already been exercised when the statement was made.

The 1985 warning argument seems, however, to be nothing more than a reconstruction of events, and one that would now allow it to be argued that Kerr had given Whitlam a warning of some limited sort prior to the powers being exercised. But the 1985 version should be rejected. And that is not only because of the problematic basis for the timing of the ending of Whitlam's commission that seems necessary under versions 3 and 4 but also because that supposed warning is inconsistent with his earlier versions and, in particular, Kerr's letter to Buckingham Palace of November 11, 1975, which made no reference to any limited warning to Whitlam or any final chance that Whitlam may have had had changed direction. Kerr's 1985 supposed 'warning' advice to Whitlam seems a clear invention.

The November 11 letter to the Palace indicates that no warning was ever provided. Not only was there no reference to such a 'warning' in the letter, but the words that Kerr used when communicating to the Palace were clear – that Whitlam's commission had already ended before Whitlam responded to Kerr. Whitlam was 'at that time no longer Prime Minister' and that was because 'I had already signed the document terminating his commission'.

This indicates that, according to Kerr's earliest account after the dismissal on November 11, 1975, Kerr considered that Whitlam's appointment was not ended based on any uncommunicated mental conclusion, or on the basis of delivered documents to Whitlam, but on the signing of those documents. This makes any statement Kerr may have made to Whitlam when he interrupted Whitlam's half-Senate election advice not a pre-exercise of powers warning, as Markwell (and Kerr, at least in 1985) suggest, but a statement of what had happened. That is, when he told Whitlam that 'I had decided to terminate his commission'[59] he meant what he said: Whitlam had been sacked.

That is also consistent with Whitlam's version. In his accounts, he denied making any reference to him approaching the Palace. In the press conference given by Whitlam after his dismissal and the dissolution of Parliament, he said that: 'The Governor-General prevented me from getting in touch with the Queen by just withdrawing the Commission immediately'.[60] And in his later version in *The Truth of the Matter,* Whitlam did ask, after he received the documents from Kerr, whether Kerr had discussed this course with the Palace, to which Kerr responded: 'I don't have to and it's too late for you. I have terminated your commission'.[61] In both Whitlam variations, there was also no warning, direct or indirect, from the governor-general and no question about Whitlam's intention regarding governing without supply, as Kerr had immediately interrupted Whitlam in his presentation regarding a half-Senate election, advising that 'I have decided to terminate your commission' (in the past tense) and 'I have a letter for you giving my reasons'.[62]

- At some point between 1.10 (according to Kelly and Bramston)[63] and 1.30 pm (according to Whitlam),[64] Fraser was sworn in as 'caretaker' prime minister. But the question of Fraser's new status and responsibility needs some examination in relation to three issues.

First, Kerr required Fraser to assume *retrospective responsibility* for his decisions to dismiss Whitlam and dissolve parliament, which Fraser purported to do on November 11, and his other Ministers did on the following day.[65] Although Kerr considered this necessary 'In accordance with constitutional principle', this seems an incorrect understanding of the constitutional rules. As Kerr has accepted, his decisions were exercises of powers reserved to him and were taken without consulting Fraser – with the result that any responsibility accepted by Fraser can only have been taken retrospectively. Leading constitutional authorities have rejected the viability of retrospective ministerial justifications. For example, Ivor Jennings has disposed of the concept of retrospective responsibility as nothing other than a 'fiction' or 'nonsense'. In his view, any retrospective responsibility is unable to protect a monarch or a vice-regal decision maker from being provided with any protection from their own actions.

> Nor can the fiction protect the King from attack. A king who insists on dissolution or, what is really the same thing, compels the resignation of Ministers, will be attacked as partisan in the house and in the country.[66]

As Twomey has said more recently:

> Ultimately, the actual decision to exercise a reserve power is one that only the head of state can make, no matter how many desperate attempts are made after the event to pin responsibility onto someone else. In practice, the head of state will be held responsible by the public for the exercise of a reserve power and attempts to sheet home responsibility to ministers who had no role in making or advising upon the decision will be seen as no more than a fig leaf.[67]

The second element was that Fraser's appointment was founded on his ability to *provide supply*, and he was able to satisfy that requirement later in the day. Fraser's compliance, however, as we will see in chapter 10, could have been delayed or possibly prevented had Whitlam appreciated the powers that he still possessed, even after his dismissal. This issue, and what Whitlam could have done to save his government, will be closely examined later in this work.

The final element is that Fraser was appointed as a 'caretaker' prime minister. This has led many to consider that Fraser's powers were limited to those of a prime minister who could only exercise 'caretaker' powers (whatever that means). Even Barwick has stated, inaccurately, in relation to Fraser: 'Before the polls were declared he was merely a caretaker *without authority to put policies into force*'.[68] And Kelly and Bramston have gone so far as to repeatedly, and incorrectly, refer to Fraser's 'caretaker commission'[69] including referring to 'one of the conditions of his caretaker commission'.[70] Indeed, Kelly had earlier referred to his inaccurate understanding of caretaker government arrangements as 'a caretaker government would receive a commission on limited terms'.[71] These statements are, however, simply incorrect.

So, to clarify this issue: Fraser did not receive any 'caretaker commission' and was not appointed as prime minister with any limited powers. His commission was not subject to any conditions or limitations aside from the ones that Fraser agreed to comply with, as the text of the Commission that Kerr issued on November 11 makes patently clear.[72] It appoints:

> The Honourable JOHN MALCOLM FRASER, M.P.
> to be Prime Minister and to administer the Department of the Prime Minister and Cabinet.

That Commission provided Fraser with all of the powers and authorities of a normally appointed prime minister. Fraser's caretaker status arose not from any limited terms of his appointment, but from the undertakings Fraser made when he was appointed. He signed a letter on November 11, no doubt prepared by Kerr in advance, which accepted appointment as the governor-general's 'Chief Adviser and Head of Government'. And in that letter, Fraser stated:

> My government will act as a caretaker government and will make no appointments or dismissals or initiate new policies before a general election is held.[73]

The result is that if Fraser had breached those caretaker undertakings, those actions would still have been valid and he would still have remained prime minister, capable of more activities inconsistent with his undertaking. If that had occurred, the governor-general would then have had but one choice – to either dismiss Fraser, a course he was highly unlikely to take (if only because of a shortage of any further replacement prime minister), or to live with it. Fortunately for Kerr, this issue was never put to a test as Fraser apparently lived with his undertakings.[74]

After Whitlam was dismissed and Fraser was appointed, the following summarizes what then occurred.

- 1.15–1.30 pm (approx.) – First, Whitlam did not return to Parliament House. Instead, he went back to the prime minister's residence, the Lodge, for lunch, which was a steak, and then for a meeting with his central advisers to work out how to respond to his dismissal. This meeting is discussed in some detail below, in chapter 10. But what is important here to note is that in that meeting Whitlam did not include any senators, even though the provision of supply was an essential element of Fraser's appointment, and supply was currently being held up in the Senate. As a result, when Parliament resumed at 2.00 and Fraser's first priority was to secure the passage of the supply legislation that his Party had been blocking since October 16, those who should have had an interest in preventing him from fulfilling that objective were left in the dark.
- 2.00 pm – Both Houses of Parliament resumed. This is examined in more detail in chapter 10 below, but the following summarizes what then occurred:
    - In the House of Representatives:
        - between 2.00 and 2.34 pm, the House completed its debate on the no-confidence motion in the Opposition – a pointless exercise given that Fraser had been appointed prime minister an hour earlier.[75]
        - At 2.34 pm – Fraser then told the House that he was now the prime minister and moved his first motion as head of government: that the House adjourn, which he lost 55 to 64.[76]
        - At 3.00 pm, Whitlam moved a no-confidence motion in the new prime minister, which was passed promptly, 64 to 54, and the House was then suspended at 3.15.[77]
    - Meanwhile, in the Senate, no one on the Labor side of that House knew that Fraser was now prime minister. But the Liberals did. (See chapter 10). What occurred in the Senate was:
        - At 2.00 pm – the Senate resumed;[78]
        - At 2.20 pm – ALP Senator Wriedt, leader of the government in the Senate, being unaware that he was no longer a minister, moved that the appropriation bills 'be now passed – which question shall not be open to debate or amendment', and the Liberal/Country Party senators now readily agreed. So, without a division, and within four minutes, supply had been passed by the Senate, and that House was then suspended.[79] Labor senators believed that the battle was over and that they had won. But that was not the case.
- 2.23–3.50 pm – *The Provision of Royal Assent* – Although some commentators have expressed the view that all Fraser needed to do to fulfill his obligation to provide Supply was to pass the bills through the Senate,[80] the

position was much more complex. As the Standing Orders of the House and the Senate made clear,[81] (and this is explained in more detail in chapter 10), a bill that originated in the Lower House and which has been passed by both Houses is then to be returned to the Lower House. After being certified by the Clerk of that House, it is the responsibility of the Speaker to present the bill to the governor-general for Assent. Had the Speaker of the House Gordon Scholes or the recently dismissed former prime minister Gough Whitlam appreciated the significance of this requirement, or had referred the matter to the Lower House for its direction, the Labor Party and the Lower House would arguably have remained in control over the supply bills, and Fraser would not have been able to fulfill one of the essential elements of his appointment. Sadly for the ALP, however, that did not occur. As a result, after the supply bills were passed by the Senate at 2.23 pm, they were then returned to the Lower House. This seems to have been known to Whitlam shortly after 2.34 pm when he intervened during Prime Minister Fraser's first speech in the House of Representatives as prime minister. After Fraser had read from his letter to the governor-general the phrase 'the Appropriation Bills which are at present before the Senate', Whitlam then intervened: 'They have been passed'.

Scholes, the Speaker of the Lower House, like Whitlam, seems then not to have recognized the extent of the powers that were still in his hands. Instead of making use of those powers, he signed the necessary documentation for the governor-general and sent the bills off to Government House at around 3.40 pm,[82] with the bills arriving there at around 3.50 pm. The governor-general then promptly provided Royal Assent.[83] That was the end of Labor's chance of holding onto office, and there was nothing it could do to prevent the dissolution of the Lower House. That can be seen from the remaining events of November 11, 1975.

- 4.30 pm – The governor-general signed the proclamation dissolving both Houses of Parliament;[84]
- 4.35 pm – The Speaker arrives at Government House for a pointless meeting with the governor-general (at 4.40 pm);[85] and
- 4.45 pm – The governor-general's Official Secretary David Smith on the steps of Parliament House, read out the governor-general's lengthy proclamation dissolving both Houses. Smith, towered over by the much taller Gough Whitlam, was faced by both the questioning press and a growing crowd of angry demonstrators, who often drowned him out with loud chants of 'We want Gough'.[86] Once Smith completed reading the dismissal proclamation, Whitlam then took over the microphone and gave his most famous 'Kerr's cur' speech (see chapter 1), which was both stirring and unforgettable. But it was also electorally ineffective. As Kelly has said, 'the campaign proved to be a mere formality'.[87]

NOTES

1. Kelly & Bramston, *The Dismissal,* 212.
2. Kelly, *Unmaking,* 353.
3. Kelly & Bramston, *The Dismissal,* 212.
4. Kelly, *Unmaking*, 354.
5. Fraser & Simons, *Malcolm Fraser,* 356.
6. See Kelly & Bramston, *The Dismissal,* 215.
7. Kerr, *Matters,* 355.
8. Kerr, *Matters,* 355.
9. Kerr, *Matters*, 297.
10. Kelly & Bramston, *The Dismissal,* 217.
11. Fraser & Simons, *Malcolm Fraser,* 356; David Kemp, "Red Felt on Green Paper," in *Where Were You?,* ed. Sybil Nolan, 55, 61 – Kemp gives the time of the call as being at "around 9.45am."
12. Kelly & Bramston, *The Dismissal,* 217.
13. Kerr, *Matters,* 355.
14. Fraser & Simons, *Malcolm Fraser,* 356.
15. This note can also be seen in Kelly & Bramston, *The Dismissal,* 367 & 368 and in *Whitlam Legacy,* Appendix 1, 425.
16. See Fraser & Simons, *Malcolm Fraser,* 356; Hocking, *His Time*, 336; Kelly & Bramston, *The Dismissal,* 19.
17. Gerard Henderson, "Evidence, Memory and The Dismissal," review of *The Dismissal* by Kelly and Bramston, *Where Were You*? edited by Nolan and *Dismissal Dossier* by Hocking, *The Sydney Institute*, February 2, 2016, https://thesydneyinstitute.com.au/blog/evidence-memory-and-the-dismissal/.
18. Kelly & Bramston, *The Dismissal,* 217.
19. Kelly & Bramston, *The Dismissal,* 17.
20. Hocking, *His Time*, 337.
21. Hocking, *Dismissal Dossier*, 4.
22. Hocking, *Dismissal Dossier*, 4.
23. Kelly & Bramston, *The Dismissal,* 21.
24. Fraser & Simons, *Malcolm Fraser,* 357.
25. Kelly & Bramston, *The Dismissal,* 18.
26. Twomey, "Legal Advice by Judges," 286.
27. Alex Mann, "State Secrets," 24 March 2020, Episode 7 in the Australian Broadcasting Corporation podcast series *The Eleventh*, podcast audio, 24.40-24.50.
28. Kerr, *Matters,* 354.
29. Kelly, *Unmaking,* 353; Freudenberg, *Certain Grandeur*, 391.
30. Commonwealth of Australia, *Parliamentary Debates, House of Representatives*, November 11, 1975, 2913.
31. Commonwealth of Australia, *Parliamentary Debates, House of Representatives*, November 11, 1975, 2921.
32. Commonwealth of Australia, *Parliamentary Debates, House of Representatives*, November 11, 1975, 2917 & 2921.

33. Commonwealth of Australia, *Parliamentary Debates, House of Representatives*, November 11, 1975, 2924.

34. Whitlam, *The Truth,* 277.

35. Smith, *Head of State,* 245.

36. Quoted in Freudenberg, *Certain Grandeur*, Loc 393.

37. Fraser & Simons, *Malcolm Fraser,* 358.

38. Whitlam, *The Truth,* 153.

39. Peter Bowers from the *Sydney Morning Herald*, quoted in Whitlam, *The Truth,* 153.

40. Smith, *Head of State,* 260 and see 261 relating to Fraser's car.

41. Whitlam, *The Truth*, 277. Smith maintains that it occurred earlier at around 12.45 – see Smith, *Head of State,* 245.

42. The text of these two documents can be seen in Kelly & Bramston, *The Dismissal,* 369–373 & in Kerr, *Matters,* 359–364.

43. This letter can be found in Kelly & Bramston, *Truth, Palace Letters,* 214.

44. Kelly & Bramston, *Truth, Palace Letters,* 214.

45. Kerr, *Matters,* 358.

46. Kerr, *Matters,* 358.

47. Markwell, *Australian Experience*, 153.

48. Kerr, *Matters*, 358.

49. Kerr, *Matters,* 359.

50. Kerr, *Matters,* 359.

51. See the letter of November 11, 1975, from Kerr to Charteris, in Kelly & Bramston, *Truth, Palace Letters*, 214.

52. Kerr, *Matters,* 358.

53. An Australian magazine focused on politics and business that was published between 1880 and 2008.

54. John Kerr, "Kerr Breaks his Silence: 'Why I was right to sack Whitlam,'" *The Bulletin*, September 3, 1985, 66 & John Kerr, "Kerr Rejects 'ambush' Myth: 'PM knew I could sack him,'" *The Bulletin,* September 10, 1985, 72.

55. Kerr, "Kerr Rejects 'ambush' Myth," 75.

56. Kerr, "Kerr Rejects 'ambush' Myth," 75.

57. Kerr, "Kerr Rejects 'ambush' Myth," 75*; and see* Markwell, *Australian Experience*, 153.

58. That is the phrase that Kerr used in both his memoirs and in his letter to the Palace signed on November 11, 1975. See Kerr, *Matters,* 358 and Kelly & Bramston, *Truth, Palace Letters*, 214.

59. See Kelly & Bramston, *Truth, Palace Letters*, 214.

60. "Gough Whitlam's Post-Dismissal Press Conference," November 11, 1975, WhitlamDismissal.com, https://whitlamdismissal.com/1975/11/11/whitlam-post-dismissal-press-conference.html/ 4.

61. Whitlam, *The Truth,* 155.

62. Whitlam, *The Truth,* 155.

63. Kelly & Bramston, *The Dismissal,* 224.

64. Whitlam, *The Truth,* 277.

65. Kerr, *Matters,* 364.
66. Jennings, *Cabinet Government,* 340.
67. Twomey, *Veiled Sceptre*, 23.
68. Barwick, *Sir John,* 96 [emphasis added].
69. Kelly & Bramston, *The Dismissal,* 18, 19 and 238.
70. Kelly & Bramston, *The Dismissal*, 228.
71. Kelly, *Unmaking,* 17.
72. An image of Fraser's commission can be seen in *Whitlam Legacy,* Appendix 1, 426.
73. Kerr, *Matters,* 367.
74. Hocking does, however, maintain that Fraser had breached the caretaker undertaking regarding East Timor (see Hocking, *His Time* (2012) 378–386). Yet her view that the "notional 'caretaker' arrangements had been immediately breached with the proclamations final words, 'God save the Queen'" also demonstrates a clear misunderstanding of caretaker conventions, as their purpose is to prevent a government from instituting, during a caretaker period, policy changes that will bind an incoming government. And the formulation of the form of words on a proclamation, even if Fraser had made that change (which is most unlikely as it seems more likely based on a decision of the Official Secretary [as Hocking seems to accept]), is procedural and is not a change that will bind any future action of an incoming government. See Hocking, *His Time* (2012), 348 & 378 and Killey, *Constitutional Conventions,* 242.
75. Commonwealth of Australia, *Parliamentary Debates, House of Representatives*, November 11, 1975, 2924–2927.
76. Commonwealth of Australia, *Parliamentary Debates, House of Representatives*, November 11, 1975, 2928–2932.
77. Commonwealth of Australia, *Parliamentary Debates, House of Representatives*, November 11, 1975, 2930–2932.
78. Commonwealth of Australia, *Parliamentary Debates, Senate*, November 11, 1975, 1880.
79. Commonwealth of Australia, *Parliamentary Debates, Senate*, November 11, 1975, 1885.
80. See, for example, Kelly & Bramston, *Truth, Palace Letters,* 50.
81. See, for example, the then applicable Standing Order, SO 265 of the House of Representatives.
82. Whitlam, *The Truth,* 161.
83. See Whitlam, *The Truth,* 278.
84. Whitlam, *The Truth,* 278.
85. Whitlam, *The Truth,* 278.
86. Kelly, *Unmaking,* 360.
87. Kelly, *Unmaking,* 362.

Chapter 8

1975

And the Errors of Legal Advisers

Figure 8.1 A Rydalmere Bowling Club Trophy from 1977 Donated by, and Named after, the Then Chief Justice of the High Court, Sir Garfield Barwick. From the collection of the author. Image taken by the author.

Having described the circumstances that led to the dismissal of the Whitlam Labor government in 1975, we need to now explain the basis of that decision and how those involved got it all so very wrong. So, in this chapter, we will commence with the central legal advice provided in 1975.

There were four separate sources of legal advice. First, was that provided by the nation's former solicitor-general and later Fraser's attorney-general,

Robert Ellicott. The second was the opinion of the government Law Officers (the attorney-general, Kep Enderby, and the solicitor-general, Sir Maurice Byers). The final two sources of legal advice for the governor-general were from the chief justice of the High Court, Sir Garfield Barwick, and from another justice of the high court, Anthony Mason.

THE ELLICOTT OPINION

The first was the legal opinion that an opposition shadow minister, Robert Ellicott, released on October 16.

Robert Ellicott was then the Shadow Minister for Aboriginal Affairs and for Tasmania,[1] and not Fraser's Shadow Attorney-General, despite the incorrect views of some who really should have known better, such as Hocking, Peter O'Brien and Whitlam himself.[2] That shadow attorney-general role was then filled by Senator Ivor Greenwood QC.[3]

Ellicott was, however, a significant lawyer, having been solicitor-general between 1969 and 1973, and as such, had been Whitlam's first Solicitor-General. However, his political views were not those of the Labor Party, so he chose to leave that office, becoming a Liberal Party MP and later Fraser's second attorney-general between December 1975 and 1977. He later became a judge of the Federal Court between 1981 and 1983. He was also Chief Justice Barwick's cousin.

The form of Ellicott's opinion was unusual as it was released as part of a press release on October 16, the day the process for the supply blockage began. In that press release, Ellicott stated[4] that the governor-general's reserve powers are only to 'be exercised on the rarest occasions'. But he also then asserted that the concept of 'rarest occasions' includes failure to obtain supply, regardless of its cause. In his view, 'A Government without supply cannot govern' and that 'The refusal by Parliament of supply, whether through the House or the Senate, is a clear signal to the Governor-General that his chosen Ministers may not be able to carry on'. If the governor-general was not satisfied that a prime minister's anticipated course would resolve a disagreement between the Houses, leaving 'the Government without funds to carry on', in Ellicott's view it would be the governor-general's '*duty to dismiss his Ministers* and appoint others' [emphasis added].

He also considered that, in the circumstances in 1975, the governor-general was entitled to know from the prime minister 'immediately what steps the Government proposes to take in order to avert the problem'. He considered that the governor-general 'is entitled to know':

(1) when it is that the government will or is likely to run out of funds under the current Supply Acts; and
(2) how the government proposes to carry on after those funds run out; and
(3) how the government proposes that the disagreement between the two Houses should be resolved.

Ellicott also considered that, if the prime minister proposes that a half-Senate election be held in the hope that this will provide his government with a majority in the Senate, the governor-general would then, according to Ellicott, need to be satisfied of two factors: that 'the Government will have sufficient supply to carry on until the result of that election has been ascertained' and that 'the election is likely to resolve the difference between the two Houses by giving the Government a majority in the Senate'.

In addition, in Ellicott's view, the governor-general also needs to 'have information which justifies' the conclusion that the difference between the Houses will then be resolved, and that he should 'consider, how those who will be in the Senate after the election are likely to vote if the Appropriation Bills were re-submitted'. But if the 'Governor General was not satisfied that the Government would have supply until the election result in the Territories was known he would only have one option open to him in the interests of good government'. That is 'He is entitled to and should ask the Prime Minister if the government is prepared to advise him to dissolve the House of Representatives and the Senate or the House of Representatives alone as a means of ensuring that the disagreement between the two Houses is resolved'. And 'If the Prime Minister refuses to do either it is then open to the Governor General to dismiss his present Ministers and seek others who are prepared to give him the only proper advice open'. In Ellicott's view, the 'proper advice in the circumstances is to dissolve both Houses of the Parliament or the House of Representatives alone with or without a half Senate election'.

Ellicott also drew attention to what he considered the prime minister's inaccurate appreciation of the role of the Governor-General. In his view, 'The Prime Minister is treating the Governor-General as a mere automaton with no public will of his own, sitting at Yarralumla waiting to do his bidding. Nothing could be further from the truth'.

From those passages, whatever else may be said of Ellicott and his opinion, it was clear that he was not in favour of keeping the prime minister in the dark as to the governor-general's thinking. But, as we will see, this is not the course that the governor-general took.

This opinion made it clear what the Opposition's plan was to be and what it expected from the governor-general. Some of its expectations, however, seem clearly excessive. Why, for example, are the governor-general's options as limited as Ellicott proposed if a governor-general is not satisfied that there is insufficient supply for a half-Senate election? Why could not the governor-general not wait until such time when the supply is exhausted before exercising his power of dismissal? Ellicott did not explain.

Kerr queried the accuracy of Ellicott's opinion, at least in relation to his 'immediate obligations',[5] which he considered a 'constitutional absurdity'.[6] And on October 21, he seems to have further pacified any government concerns regarding Ellicott and his advice, with his blunt question, according to Whitlam, that 'it's all bullshit, isn't it?'[7]

THE LAW OFFICERS DRAFT OPINION

Kerr did, however (and as mentioned in chapter 6), ask the prime minister, on October 21, for an opinion from the Law Officers, the Attorney-General (Kep Enderby QC) and the Solicitor-General (Maurice Byers QC)[8] and Whitlam agreed. But it took until November 6 before anything arrived. And when it did arrive, it was far from complete.[9]

On that day, Kep Enderby gave the governor-general a document headed 'Opinion' dated November 4 dealing with the reserve powers and the Ellicott opinion. It had been signed by the Solicitor-General and was to be a joint opinion with the Attorney-General. However, Enderby, in front of Kerr, scratched out Byers' signature and also added the word 'Draft' to the title of the document.[10] He advised the governor-general that the document contained 'Byers' own views subject to final discussions between him and the Attorney-General'.[11] According to Kelly, the governor-general was also told that he could 'regard this as background but it shows the line of advice which the Prime Minister will be giving you'.[12] But a final advice was never provided.

It is unclear whether Kerr was aware of the changes that Enderby wanted made, but to Kelly, at least, there seems no doubt as to the direction of the changes that Enderby wanted made. According to Kelly, Enderby wanted to both 'improve the style of document', and that he did not agree with Byers' view that s 53 allowed the Senate to refuse supply. The latter point, however, may be incorrect, being inconsistent with Kerr's understanding of the private advice that the Attorney-General had given to him on September 30 (discussed in chapter 12), when Enderby, according to Kerr, 'was of the clear view that under Section 53 of the Constitution, the Senate has the legal power to reject the Appropriation Bills'. But the most significant area of disagreement between Enderby and Byers was, according to Kelly, that Enderby also did not agree with Byers' view that 'conceded the existence of the reserve powers'.[13]

Nonetheless, the conclusion of this 28-page document was clear. It was 'firmly of opinion that Ellicott's expressed views are wrong'.[14] However, this opinion did not say what was right, despite the length of the now 'Draft' opinion. All Kerr knew from the draft opinion was that, as Ellicott's opinion had 'disregard[ed] or ignore[d] constitutional practices hitherto apparently governing the exercise of those powers', the governor-general 'requires, we venture to think, the gravest consideration before its adoption could even be contemplated'.[15]

Moreover, as the Attorney-General had never signed that opinion, and as he had removed the Solicitor-General's signature, and as no final advice was ever provided, the governor-general was left, as he wrote, with the conclusion that he 'could not know what might be the content of any final joint opinion should one ever emerge; and none ever did'.[16] That conclusion may be somewhat evasive, depending on what Enderby had told Kerr, but it is also incorrect for both Professor Hocking and Whitlam to omit the adjusted title of the documents or its lack of signature from their accounts and to pretend, as Hocking has claimed, that:

> The government's chief law officers and formal legal advisers to the Governor-General – the solicitor-general, Maurice Byers, and the Attorney-General, Kep Enderby – [had] firmly rejected Ellicott's approach.[17]

That, they had clearly not done. An unsigned draft opinion is not a "firm rejection." It is, at most, an indication of the direction that one of the authors of the document may well take.

Nonetheless, this lack of a clear Law Officers' opinion served to assist what became the governor-general's duplicitous approach. He had already decided (as discussed in chapter 6), to ignore any contrary Law Officers' opinion, having decided that he had 'no escape from the duty to assert that the Reserve Powers of dismissal and dissolution still exist' and that he was not to be limited in the exercise of those powers by any opinion of the Law Officers. As he wrote, 'a joint opinion of the Law Officers to the contrary would certainly not deter me if the moment arrives for action'.[18] But as an unsigned draft document was no clear Law Officers' opinion, there was nothing that could have deterred the governor-general.

THE HIGH COURT JUSTICES' ADVICES

On October 19, Kerr's concerns about the Ellicott advice, as well as some press commentary that it had caused, led him to ask Whitlam if he could confer with the Chief Justice. This request, the prime minister, as he has accepted, was 'at once' refused.[19] But in doing so, Whitlam had made two apparent errors. First, he failed to appreciate or accept that Kerr was seeking advice regarding the reserve powers, and as such (as pointed out in chapter 3), he did not need the prime minister's approval. And Whitlam's assessment of past history, the basis for his advice to Kerr, was also limited. He considered that there had been 'Only one Governor-General, Sir Ronald Munro Ferguson, [who] had consulted with the chief justice' and that was done with the prime minister's approval.[20] But he failed to recognize that there are many other instances of judicial advice to the governor-general which, as we will later see in this chapter, have been identified by Professor Twomey and others.

Despite the prime minister's refusal on October 19, the governor-general ignored that advice and did discuss this matter with two members of the High Court: its chief justice, Garfield Barwick, and another high court justice who would later become its chief justice, Anthony Mason.

Garfield Barwick was born in 1903 and was educated, like many other notable Sydney lawyers from modest backgrounds, such as his cousin Bob Ellicott, Kerr himself, and Dr Evatt, at Fort Street Boys High School and then the University of Sydney. He was a very clever, diligent and hardworking student and then lawyer, going to the bar in 1927; and by the 1940s, he became one of Sydney's leading barristers. He was a forceful advocate, playing significant roles in a number of notable constitutional cases, and was knighted in 1953. Barwick, however, also had politics in mind and in 1958, at the relatively late age of 54, he became a member of the House of Representatives. He was immediately made a minister in the Menzies government, becoming its attorney-general, and after 1961, the Minister for External Affairs. However, Barwick's political career was also short as he was appointed, on the retirement of Owen Dixon from the High Court in 1964, as Australia's seventh Chief Justice. He remained in that office until 1981, dying in 1997 at the age of 94.

Barwick's approach to the law was literal, conservative and powerful. He was also no fan of the Whitlam Government, regarding it in his memoirs, as 'an amateur as far as government administration went' while also being both 'arrogant and dictatorial in manner'.[21]

The governor-general did consult with Chief Justice Barwick, despite Whitlam's earlier advice to Kerr. But Barwick's involvement in the 1975 events came quite late. As pointed out in chapter 6, Barwick's advice was not sought by Kerr until two days prior to the dismissal, with Kerr and Barwick meeting and discussing the matter on the morning of the following day, November 10. On that day, the Chief Justice, despite sitting in Court, composed and provided to the governor-general his two-page supportive letter, which Kerr received at around 4.00pm.[22] Barwick provided that very important advice in what seems to be a very short timeline because, as Barwick wrote in 1983: 'I had gathered that the Governor-General intended to carry out his decision during the following day'.[23]

In that advice, Barwick advised Kerr that if Whitlam was not able to secure supply, 'the course upon which Your Excellency has determined is consistent with your constitutional authority and duty'.[24] That advice was, in substance, similar to that of Ellicott. The only variation was that there was nothing in the Barwick advice that indicated any obligation of the governor-general to advise the prime minister of his course of action before that course was taken.

Barwick has been described by Professor Hocking as having been 'long cast as the secret force' in the dismissal,[25] but with no good reason. Not only was Barwick's written advice to the governor-general dated November 10, 1975, made public shortly after the dismissal (on November 18)[26] and is quoted and discussed at some length in Kerr's book,[27] but Barwick also wrote and discussed the dismissal and his role in it in his short book on the subject, *Sir John Did His Duty*[28] in 1983 and in his later 1995 autobiography, *A Radical Tory.*[29] This is not the stuff of any 'secret force'.

A more interesting source of informal advice to Kerr came from another High Court Justice, Anthony Mason, and over a much longer period of time. Barwick was unaware of those discussions.

Anthony Mason was born in 1925 and is one of the few remaining participants in the 1975 who is still alive (as of 2024). He was always a talented lawyer, and at the relatively young age of 39, in 1964, he was both appointed Queen's counsel and made NSW solicitor-general. Five years later, he had been appointed to the NSW Supreme Court, where he remained for a short period of three years until 1972, when he was appointed to the high court. Following the retirement of Harry Gibbs from the Court in 1987, Mason was further promoted to the office of Chief Justice, an office that he held until 1995, when he retired in accordance with s 72 of the *Commonwealth Constitution.*

In John Kerr's *Matters for Judgment*, he made no direct reference to his discussions with Mason. He did, however, discuss conversations he had held with 'only one person other than the Chief Justice', a person whom Kerr did not name. Although the conversations with that unnamed person 'did not include advice as to what I should do', they 'sustained me in my own thinking as to the imperatives within which I had to act, and in my conclusions, already reached, as to what I could and should do'.[30] This person was Anthony Mason, and his identity remained largely unknown until Professor Hocking published the second volume of her biography of Whitlam in 2012, *Gough Whitlam, His Time* – when Mason's involvement in 1975 was detailed in chapter 10 – 'The Third Man'. This was not, however, completely new information, despite what Hocking asserts. As Gerald Henderson wrote in 2016:

> Sir Garfield Barwick . . . first revealed Mason had a role in the dismissal in an interview with Bruce Donald on the ABC in January 1994. Gerard Henderson soon after disclosed that Kerr had told him some years earlier than he had sought Mason's advice prior to the dismissal, and that they had engaged directly.
>
> Sir Anthony Mason's involvement in The Dismissal was first revealed by Gerard Henderson in an article in the *Sydney Morning Herald* on 8 January 1994 – over two decades ago. It is true that full details were not exposed until Jenny Hocking reported in detail on the Kerr Papers, which were deposited in the National Archives of Australia. But Henderson did point out in his SMH column that Kerr regarded Mason's advice as more significant than that professed by Barwick. So Hocking's claim in *The Dismissal Dossier* that in 1994 Mason's role was still seen as 'relatively minor' before the publication of her book *Gough Whitlam: His Time* simply does not stand up.[31]

Regardless of the somewhat inflated role of Hocking in revealing the contribution of Mason to the dismissal, it is true, as she later said in the 'Epilogue' that she added to *His Time* in 2014, that:

> Barely two days after these revelations were published in this book, Mason broke his silence with a written statement in response, acknowledging for the first time his role in the dismissal of the Whitlam government, and adding further to it.[32]

Mason's 2012 statement, which he somewhat inelegantly named *CONVERSATIONS WITH SIR JOHN KERR RELATING TO HIS TERMINATION OF THE COMMISSION OF THE PRIME MINISTER (THE HON E G WHITLAM AC QC) ON 11 NOVEMBER 1975,* dated 23 August 2012,[33] described his relationship with Kerr and their discussions prior to the 1975 dismissal. In that statement, Mason agreed that he had been a close friend of John Kerr, having known him since first appearing as junior counsel in cases led by Kerr in the 1950s.[34] He had, however, preceded him in his judicial career, being appointed to the NSW Supreme Court three years before Kerr was appointed as chief justice of that Court in 1972. There was, however, little overlap in their judicial careers in that Court; Kerr was appointed as chief justice in May 1972, shortly before Mason left that Court for the high court in August. Nonetheless, Kerr and Mason remained good friends, and Kerr had sought Mason's views as to whether he should accept the office of governor-general.[35] As a result, Mason:

> was willing to talk to him about the issues that were to confront him in October-November 1975 and to give him my views on the exercise of the Governor-General's reserve powers to dismiss a Prime Minister.[36]

Mason's advice to Kerr seems largely similar to that of Barwick, but with one significant distinction. In Mason's then view, in sacking Whitlam, Kerr had 'acted consistently with his duty'. But he disagreed with Kerr's decision not to warn the prime minister of his intended action.[37] As Mason perceptively advised Kerr: 'if he did not warn the prime minister, he would run the risk that people would accuse him of being deceptive'.[38]

Hocking, however, has rejected Mason's views and has decided to redefine him and his 1975 role. In her view, his legal career, other than 1975, was now merely 'anodyne'.[39] But with his dismissal advice role now being revealed, largely as a result of her work, she now regarded Mason as the critical player in the events of 1975 with 'proximity and influence, behind Sir John Kerr's deception'.[40] In her view, Mason used his influence over Kerr in 1975 to the point that he not only provided advice and reassurance to the governor-general, but he also provided 'instruction'[41] to Kerr regarding the actions that he took on November 11, 1975. To Hocking, Mason's 'instruction' can be seen in the telephone call Kerr made after the House of Representatives passed its no-confidence motion in the new Fraser government, when the governor-general 'rang the ubiquitous "third man" seeking *instruction* and reassurance, and received both'.[42] In her view, Mason, rather than Barwick, was the 'secret force' behind Kerr, with Mason being the 'secret confidant and guide',[43] playing 'the immensely significant role'[44] in the dismissal, and in doing so, 'deceived' both the Whitlam[45] as well as the Chief Justice.[46] Mason was 'not only Kerr's *eminence grise*[47] in the dismissal, but also . . . carefully and insistently kept his role secret, allowing a false historical narrative of the dismissal to take hold'.[48] He had, according to Hocking, arrogantly assumed 'personal power in public office'[49] but with the secrecy of his advice and 'instruction' to Kerr, he had also rejected 'the essential respect between the arms of government, without which democratic institutions cannot function'.[50]

These are, however, very questionable conclusions and seem based on Hocking's incorrect view that Kerr had said that 'he had consulted no one, received no advice'.[51] But Kerr never said that. He recognized that he had discussed the supply problem with at least one other,[52] and that person has turned out to be Mason; but the final decision itself was one for Kerr alone. As he said clearly in *Matters for Judgment,* a distinction needs to be drawn between consultation with others prior to a decision, and the decision itself for which Kerr had sole responsibility:

> The loneliness of the decision I was engaged in making in these final days was one of the most burdensome experiences I have known. Most policy or executive decisions are made with the aid of advisers or colleagues, both as to what

> can and what should be done. There are others to consult and to offer counsel. But the decision to dismiss the Prime Minister could only be made by me. It was a time of intense mental solitude.[53]

Hocking also formed an incorrect view of what she said was a 'fundamental and irredeemable inconsistency in Mason's account'.[54] In her view, Mason 'strongly argues that he did not advise Kerr' while also claiming 'in this instance, to have done just that'.[55] This claim, however, indicates that Hocking has either not read Mason's statement or has simply ignored what it said. This can be seen as, in Mason's statement, he did not 'strongly argue that he did not advise Kerr'. Mason made it clear that:

- His 'first conversation in 1975 with Sir John with reference to the reserve powers was at Yarralumla in August, not 12 October'.[56]
- He specifically states that he could not advise what Kerr should do regarding accepting the appointment of governor-general 'and that he would have to make up his own mind whether or not to accept the appointment'.[57]
- He did 'not volunteer or agree to give a written opinion on Mr R J Elliott QC's press statement or document of 16 October 1975 and the draft Law Officers' opinion and allow my opinion to be made public' and 'played no part at all in the preparation of Sir John's statement of decision'.[58]
- He suggested to Kerr 'that he should ask the Prime Minister to obtain the Law Officers [*sic*] opinion on the Governor-General's power to terminate the commission of the Prime Minister'. Mason 'did not receive a copy of the Ellicott document, despite Sir John's claim to the contrary'.[59]
- But that he prepared, at Kerr's request, 'a draft letter terminating Mr Whitlam's commission (which Sir John did not adopt)'.[60]
- In October, he also 'said to Sir John that, if he considered it legitimate or necessary to consult the Chief Justice, it would be unwise to do so at that time as the Chief Justice might agree with Mr Ellicott's view that immediate action be taken'.[61]
- That Kerr's statement that 'The conversation(s) did not include advice as to what I should do but sustained me in my own thinking as to the imperatives within which I had to act, and in my conclusions, already reached as to what I could and should do' was an 'accurate description of the substance of our conversations on 9 November and on other occasions, except' for Mason's advice that Kerr should warn Whitlam.[62]
- On November 9, Mason had had two conversations with Kerr, and in the course of those conversations:
    - Mason read the 'Draft' Opinion of the Attorney-General and the Solicitor-General and disagreed with it. However, he also refused to provide a written opinion without first consulting with Barwick.

Additionally, he stated that it would not be appropriate for him, rather than the Chief Justice, to give such a written opinion.[63]

  - Mason also read the Law Officers' Opinion on alternative financing, but 'was not prepared to express a view as to its legal efficacy'. However, he also said that he 'thought that the private banks would be unlikely to act on it'.[64]
  - Kerr advised him that:
    - 'he had decided that he had no alternative but to dismiss Mr Whitlam and to commission Mr Fraser to form a caretaker government'.
    - If the election were to be held before Christmas, the Electoral Commission had advised that 'it had to be held on 13 December'.
    - And 'To enable such an election to take place instructions for it must be given no later than the next Wednesday'.[65]
- He also states that 'At the end of our first conversation [on November 9] I expressed my relief that Sir John had made a final decision to resolve the crisis by dismissing the Prime Minister because I thought that the crisis should be resolved by a general election'. But he also clarified that statement when he said:

> My comment was not, and should not have been understood as, encouragement to dismiss the Prime Minister as Sir John had already announced his decision to take that step.[66]

- As to the supposed November 11 'instruction' that Mason is said to have given to Kerr, Mason's words are clear as to the effect of the conversation, if not its timing:

> On 11 November 1975 Sir John telephoned me to say that the Speaker and others wished to see him to present a resolution of the House of Representatives expressing no confidence in the Fraser government. I said that the resolution was irrelevant as he had commissioned Mr Fraser to form a caretaker government for the limited purposes to hold a general election.[67]

This is not, however, an 'instruction' to Kerr, but an expression of Mason's informal legal advice. As to the correctness of that advice, that seems dependent on when that call was made. If it was made after Royal Assent had been given to the supply bills, that is after 3.50 pm (see chapter 7), his advice was clearly correct. By that stage (see chapter 10), Whitlam had lost the few opportunities that he had to use the powers of the Senate and the House of Representatives that would have delayed and possibly defeated Fraser's provision of supply and, therefore, the basis for Kerr's dismissal of Whitlam. If, however, the call was made before the governor-general had received the bills from Speaker Scholes for Assent, then

Mason's conclusion that the House's resolution was 'irrelevant' seems, at least, precipitous. But regardless of the accuracy of Mason's advice, it was not an 'instruction' to Kerr; and there is nothing to indicate that Mason ever intended it to be an instruction, or that Kerr believed himself to be bound by any of Mason's views.

All this seems not indicative of any strong argument that Mason did not advise Kerr, but a statement of what informal, non-binding advice Mason did provide to Kerr, and what he did not. Moreover, Mason's account, in line with what Kerr said in his book and in his correspondence with the Palace, clearly demonstrates that Kerr was not acting under any instructions from Mason or anyone else. There is also nothing in Mason's statement to support Hocking's argument that Mason was assuming any secretive 'personal power in public office'.[68] He was simply informing his friend and colleague of his own views. And that friend received those views, accepting the parts that convinced him – and took full responsibility for any actions that were then taken.

Accordingly, despite Hocking's elaborate allegations, there simply is nothing to support her argument that Mason 'instructed' Kerr. As a result, if there has been any 'flawed history of the dismissal'[69] regarding Mason's advisory involvement, it is of much less significance than Hocking's inflated conclusions regarding the significance of the role that Mason played with his advice and suggestions he provided to Kerr. Mason's discussions with and advice to Kerr should not confuse or detract from Kerr's fundamental responsibility for the actions he took on November 11, 1975.

Did Mason mislead Barwick? Hocking also takes the view that Mason played a much more significant role than Chief Justice Barwick. Barwick, in her view, has been 'badly served by history'[70] to be now seen as just a 'historically maligned side-kick' to Kerr.[71] In Hocking's view, Barwick himself had been 'deceived in his own minor role in Mason and Kerr's planning and remained oblivious to the far more extensive role that Mason had already played'[72] while Kerr and Mason had 'between themselves determined at what point to bring the apparently unsuspecting Chief Justice of the High Court, Sir Garfield Barwick, into their planning'.[73] This is a puzzling interpretation and seems one that can only be accepted if Barwick's objective (as well as Mason's) was to influence and strengthen any waning spirits of the governor-general to dispose of Whitlam's government. That is, Hocking's conclusion can only be correct if Mason had sought to be, as Hocking asserts, 'Kerr's *eminence grise*'; and if Barwick had also believed that that was his role – that he was to be the 'secret force'[74] behind Kerr and his decision. There is nothing to support either position. Kerr was an experienced lawyer, having been the Chief Justice of New South Wales and, in his book on 1975, whether one agrees with his approach regarding the dismissal or not, demonstrates both a considerable understanding of the *Australian Constitution* and its history, as well as the responsibility for the actions that he took as governor-general. There is no reason to consider that Kerr needed any strengthening of his will from either Mason or Barwick. As we have seen, there is nothing to suggest that either Mason or Barwick needed to reinforce Kerr's will or desire or considered that either was manipulating or instructing Kerr.

Hocking has also failed to appreciate that Mason and Barwick played very different roles in the 1975 events and in their relationships with Kerr. What Kerr wanted from Mason, as he said himself, was someone he could trust to 'temper his solitude' when dealing with the 1975 issues and to 'sustain . . . me in my own thinking', which seems to mean someone with whom he could debate and test options.[75] And that Mason provided. Barwick, however, played a different role – which was to provide an official judicial assessment of Kerr's position. What Barwick provided to Kerr was not found in his one discussion with the governor-general prior to the dismissal but instead, and in line with a fairly consistent line of history, it was his documented independent legal advice regarding the exercise of Kerr's constitutional reserve powers. Barwick did not need to be aware of any other informal advice that Kerr had received from any other source when he provided his own legal and historical analysis of Kerr's powers. Indeed, any advice that Mason or anyone else provided to Kerr seems irrelevant to Barwick's independent constitutional assessment.

As a result, it is incorrect to consider that Barwick was deceived when he provided his written advice by being unaware of any informal advice that Mason had provided. In addition, Hocking's description of Barwick being Kerr's 'historically maligned side-kick' misunderstands or misrepresents not only the role that the Chief Justice played in the 1975 events, but also the Chief Justice himself. As anyone with any familiarity with the life of the late Chief Justice should know, Barwick was never anyone's 'side-kick'.

Why didn't Mason own up? The other important issue regarding Mason and his role in Whitlam's dismissal is why he didn't reveal the part he played. As Kelly and Bramston observe, Mason 'offered no explanation of how his confidential "running" dialogue with Kerr . . . was consistent with his role as a High Court judge'.[76] They conclude, but with no explanation, that both Barwick and Whitlam would have been 'unimpressed, even shocked'[77] had they known of the role played by Mason. And they ask the question: if there was no impropriety, whose interests were served by keeping these meetings between Kerr and Mason 'secret from the entire public for so long'?[78]

They assume that the government needed to be made aware of all the sources of advice to Kerr, and they seem to accept the view of the former Prime Minister Paul Keating, that Mason had some form of obligation to dissociate from his discussions with Kerr 'the moment the conversation turned on the use of the reserve powers in a really serious way'.[79] Keating, however, with clearly no appreciation of the historical interrelationship (discussed below) between chief justices and governors-general, also thought that Barwick should have dissociated himself from such discussions.[80] For Keating, and it seems Kelly and Bramston, when the conversation reached this issue, 'Mason crossed the line'.

What the basis was for that 'line', however, is somewhat difficult to determine. Kelly and Bramston did interview a number of former Labor politicians, including former prime ministers Bob Hawke[81] and Paul Keating,[82] as well as Bill Hayden,[83] Gareth Evans[84] Michael Duffy[85] and Ralph Willis[86] and found a 'uniform theme in their responses – anger at Mason's failure to disclose his role'. As those authors have observed, those former Ministers all 'drew a distinction between Mason's competence as a chief justice' (which none of them would criticize) and with what Kelly and Bramston described as 'the fact', and that 'fact' was 'that his behaviour in 1975 would have ruled him ineligible for appointment had a disclosure been made'.[87] And that is despite Mason's excellent reputation as Chief Justice, particularly by the Labor Party. Even Whitlam considered, as Hocking tells us, that Mason was 'the first adequate Chief Justice in Australia for more than seventy years'.[88] That is, Mason was regarded as a better Chief Justice, at least in Whitlam's assessment, than all previous Chief Justices aside from the first, Samuel Griffith, who held the office between 1903 and 1919. That is, he was regarded as better than:

- Harry Gibbs (1981–87)
- Garfield Barwick (1964–1981)
- Owen Dixon (1952–1964)
- John Latham (1935–1952)
- Frank Gavan Duffy (1931–1935)
- Isaac Isaacs (1930–1931) and
- Adrian Knox (1919–1930).

Nonetheless, Mason's behaviour that the former Ministers found so objectionable, 'extraordinary' and 'scandalous'[89] was in advising Kerr. As former prime minister Bob Hawke said, 'In terms of his acceptability to a Labor government, it would have brought him undone'.[90] In other words, the Labor Ministers were not concerned with Mason's fitness for the office of Chief Justice, or for his performance in that office once appointed, as his 8 years as chief justice[91] have demonstrated. They would have disqualified him, not because of his skills, knowledge or expertise, but because they disapproved of something he had done that they did not approve of for political reasons. But that objectionable something was, as we will see, consistent with the standard practices of judges up until then – in advising the head of the executive regarding constitutional conventions on a confidential basis. As Professor Twomey said in 2012: 'it is actually quite hard to find an occasion when judges have not been involved in advising upon the exercise of reserve powers'.[92]

This maintenance of the prevailing political bias of Labor Ministers to keep a highly skilled person from promotion, despite the views of Kelly and Bramston, should not have raised any 'serious questions about his judgement'.[93] Instead, it actually seems a very good and sensible reason why Mason kept very quiet regarding his confidential dialogue with and advice that he provided to his friend and colleague, the governor-general in 1975.

ISSUES WITH THE HIGH COURT JUSTICES ADVICE

A number of other issues have also been raised concerning the advice provided by Barwick and Mason, and they fall into two categories:

- The propriety of the judicial advice to the governor-general; and
- Were those pieces of advice correct?

PROPRIETY?

There are a number of arguments that have been raised that the Justices of the Court in 1975 should not have advised the governor-general, and each of those arguments is wrong.

The first of those arguments was that Barwick and Mason should not have advised Kerr, as the governor-general should only act on the government's advice and is constrained to receive only the government's advice or advice from persons known by and approved by the government. This was the view then expressed by Whitlam. As Whitlam told the press on October 17, 1975, the governor-general must 'take[] advice from his Prime Minister and from no-one else'. That was clearly Whitlam's view, 'Unquestionably'.[94]

It also was the view of both Professor Hocking, who seems to have accepted that Kerr acted erroneously when he acted 'in defiance of him [Whitlam] and his explicit and unqualified advice to the Governor-General weeks earlier that he not meet with the chief justice'.[95] Kelly and Bramston also seem to hold a similar view.[96] These views, however, fail to recognize the nature of the reserve powers, which was the reason for the advice, and they seem not to recognize the distinction discussed in chapter 3: the difference between binding advice provided when a governor-general is acting in accordance with conventions, and non-binding informal advice that the governor-general can seek when exercising reserve powers.

The governor-general takes personal responsibility for the exercise of the reserve powers, and accordingly, the governor-general can seek non-binding advice regarding those powers from any source. As such, as pointed out in chapter 3, in the words of the Canadian expert on reserve powers, Eugene Forsey, when referring to the Monarch: 'If she is to use her discretion wisely, she is entitled to all the information and informed opinion she can get'. Accordingly, 'She is . . . free to consult whom she chooses'.[97]

And that is what Kerr did. Kerr was not seeking advice that he was conventionally bound to accept, but he sought and received from both Barwick and Mason non-binding advice from persons with considerable experience in the vice-regal role. As will be discussed later in chapter 9, Kerr had also received informal and non-binding advice from the then Governors of both the States of New South Wales, Sir Roden Cutler VC, and of Victoria, Sir Henry Winneke. Both of them had advised Kerr that Whitlam should be warned before the power to dismiss was used, advice that Kerr rejected. No one has ever suggested that it was inappropriate for those State Governors to informally advise Kerr or that they were under any obligation to advise Whitlam of what Kerr indicated to them. That is because it was entirely appropriate for Kerr to seek non-binding advice regarding the exercise of Kerr's reserve powers from beyond those who Whitlam approved. If he could confer with Governors Cutler or Winneke, why then would Kerr be confined to the advice of State Governors? Why could Kerr not also seek the views of High Court Justices, Barwick or Mason, particularly if history supports that approach?

There is, however, an argument that if the governor-general can seek his own advice separate from those whom the government approves, that advice cannot come from High Court members because such advice is inconsistent with the role of judges and is a breach of the doctrine of separation of powers.[98] But that argument is also flawed.

Kelly and Bramston, however, continue to maintain that it has some merit and use their interviews with subsequent high court chief justices, including the late Gerard Brennan[99] and Robert French[100] in support. They quote former chief justice Brennan, who had said that:

> The reaction to the events of that date demonstrates that there is now a public expectation that the Chief Justice will not participate, whether by advice or otherwise, in the exercise of a prerogative or reserve power.[101]

And they consider French as concluding that Barwick's standards are 'now so obsolete that would no longer pass the tests of judicial impartiality and proper behaviour for a chief justice'.[102] As a result, in Kelly and Bramston's opinion, 'This is an unqualified repudiation, if not of Barwick's action, then of the so called Barwick rules'.[103] But if this 'unqualified repudiation' was intended to indicate that what Barwick and Mason had done in advising the governor-general was then wrong, this is simply incorrect.

As Professor Twomey said in 2016, allegations that Barwick's and Mason's roles in 1975 as having been 'thoroughly objectionable', 'unprecedented' or 'unconventional' were unsound, having been 'made, in part, because of public ignorance of the long historical role of judges in advising vice-regal officers on such matters'.[104] From her study of the problem, she has concluded that, in Australia:

> Judges have given advice to vice-regal officers in relation to constitutional matters on at least 20 documented occasions in the period 1904 to 1985, with instances occurring in every decade.[105]

As a result, criticisms of Barwick's and Mason's advice to Kerr were 'ill-informed' and that 'Prior to November 1975, it was uncontroversial for the Governor-General or a Governor to consult with the Chief Justice, and there was often an expectation that he should do so'.[106] She has also quoted the views of a former Official Secretary to the governor-general, Sir Murray Tyrrell, who said, in October 1975, that he had requested advice for the governor-general 'many times in the past', recalling himself having done so, as Twomey said, 'on half a dozen occasions'.[107]

And a lengthy early history of the interrelationship between governors-general and the high court has also been provided by Professor Markwell, who found that Australia's early governors-general:

> regarded themselves as entitled to seek advice from High Court judges and from other individuals on the exercise of their discretions. They thought themselves entitled to seek advice without seeking the approval of the Prime Minister. In return, the High Court judges who were consulted – Griffith and Barton – regarded themselves as entitled to offer advice, both when it was sought by the Governor-General and when it was not.[108]

He, like Professor Twomey, has traced the use by governors-general of chief justice advice, starting from that provided to Governors-General Northcote and Dudley from Australia's first chief justice, Sir Samuel Griffith, regarding the refusal of prime ministerial advice for a dissolution of the Lower House. And as Twomey has observed, both Chief Justice Griffith and Justice Barton had also:

> freely advised the Governor-General Sir Ronald Munro Ferguson on many constitutional issues, including the extent of his discretion in relation to the grant of a double dissolution in 1914; how to deal with the resignation of Prime Minister Fisher in 1915; whether a referendum could be held over conscription; and how to deal with Prime Minister Hughes' resignation after the second conscription referendum failed in 1917.[109]

Later High Court justice's advice that have been identified also includes that of Sir John Latham, who was the chief justice between 1935 and 1952. During that period, as Professor Fiona Wheeler recounts in her study of the extra-judicial activities of Latham, the Chief Justice:

> clandestinely advised several conservative political figures, notably Robert Menzies, Richard Casey and Harold Holt, on a range of controversial matters. Most astoundingly, after *Australian Communist Party v Commonwealth* ('*Communist Party Case*')[110] in 1951 – in which the High Court held that the Menzies government's ban on communism was invalid – Latham, the only dissentient in the case, appears, by his own admission, to have secretly advised Prime Minister Menzies on alterations to the Constitution to overcome the effect of the Court's ruling.[111]

As Wheeler also observed,

> Almost from the beginning of his time as Chief Justice, Latham volunteered advice to government and actively communicated with political contacts about sensitive and partisan issues. Significantly, his 'politicking' was not confined to the conservative Lyons (1932–39) and Menzies (1939–41, 1949–66) governments but . . . extended – though in a more subdued fashion – to his former political adversaries in the Curtin Labor government (1941–45).[112]

In her view: 'The sheer volume of Latham's policy advising suggests that he was not troubled by the consistency of his actions with his independence as a judge.'[113] As such, she considers that if those activities were undertaken by a Justice today, 'such conduct on the part of a serving High Court justice would lead to calls for that person to be removed from office under s 72 of the Constitution'.[114] Yet she accepts that:

> today's standards of judicial behaviour are not necessarily the same as those in previous periods. In particular, judicial independence is a value that varies in its demands over different eras and between legal systems. Even at a single point in time, the boundary between 'acceptable' and 'unacceptable' judicial involvement in activity outside the courtroom is liable to be contested.[115]

The practice of the Chief Justice advising the head of the executive was, in fact, the norm in 1975. In addition to the examples already discussed, Barwick himself had earlier given advice to the executive in other circumstances, including in 1967 when Governor-General Casey took his advice before appointing John McEwan as prime minister to replace the then-missing prime minister, Harold Holt.[116]

Twomey has also identified instances when chief justices (State or Federal) have regularly advised State Governors on the exercise of the reserve powers. And that included advice from the NSW Chief Justice to the NSW Governor in:

- 1927, on reserve powers concerning the dissolution of Parliament and the 'swamping' of the Upper House;
- 1932, on the dismissal of the Lang Government; and
- 1939, about a constitutional crisis involving the defeat of the government on a financial measure.[117]

And she also observed that in Tasmania, as late as 1972, the expectation was that the Chief Justice had a central role to play when the reserve powers were being considered. And that went as far as, as she observed, the then Governor being 'criticised for failing to consult the Chief Justice on whether to grant or refuse a dissolution'.[118]

In addition, Twomey also identified High Court chief justice Sir Owen Dixon, who actively provided advice to the State Governors regarding reserve powers. The instances that she cites include Victoria, in 1952 and 1955;[119] and Western Australia, in 1956 and 1960.[120]

As a result, from all of this fairly active judicial role in assisting the vice regal representatives of the Monarch, Professor Twomey concludes that much of the recent press and other commentary regarding Justice Mason's advice to Kerr is best described as 'hyperbole'[121] based on 'Ignorance of the common practice of consultation'.[122]

Nonetheless, Twomey did accept that since 1975 there have been 'significant changes' preventing judges from advising the executive, even when they are acting in a non-judicial capacity. As a result, in her view: 'While it would be unwise for a judge today to take on such a role, it is much harder to make that assessment in relation to actions taken in 1975.'

Kelly and Bramston, however, did argue that the Mason advice was very unusual in that 'as far as the authors can establish, there is no precedent for a High Court judge, who was not chief justice, extensively advising a governor-general without the knowledge of the chief justice'.[123] However, that seems not the case with, at least, the early High Court. As Markwell has observed, in May 1914, Lord Denman, whose term was then ending, wrote to his successor, Sir Ronald Munro Ferguson, advising who he should consult if expert advice was needed:

> I suppose Griffith and Barton the most reliable authorities, should you want advice. Isaacs is a judge who I believe is well thought of by the Labor Party . . . but perhaps Griffith and Barton might hardly like a third opinion being sought. . . . [B]ut Barton particularly should be sound, as he has political as well as legal knowledge.[124]

Both Barton and Isaacs were then ordinary (puisne) High Court Justices. And from the information that remains, Munro Ferguson did not consider that he needed anyone's permission to consult with them. As an example, Markwell refers to the advice that Barton gave to Munro Ferguson in January 1917, that he consult Griffith, but 'without telling Griffith of Barton's opinion', advice which Munro Ferguson accepted.[125]

But even assuming that Kelly and Bramston's doubtful historical views regarding puisne judges are correct, they still did not explain why the permission or knowledge of the Chief Justice would or should be relevant to a non-judicial function of an ordinary judge of the High Court. And no relevance seems apparent. As Chief Justice Malcolm of the Western Australian Supreme Court said in 2004 in his address on the role of the Chief Justice:

> The powers of a Chief Justice are in fact, quite limited. Each Judge holds a commission which authorises and requires the Judge to exercise judicial office and which entitles the Judge to do so *without interference from the others,* while the Judge acts according to law [emphasis added].[126]

Kelly and Bramston did refer to the evidence and arguments of Twomey,[127] but they seem to be of the view that the precedents relied on by Professor Twomey are largely 'colonial', developed at a time when, in their view, the doctrine of separation of powers 'was not developed to the extent it is today'.[128] In Kelly and Bramston's view, the 'doctrine has become stronger since 1975'.[129] This proposition was put most forcefully by the late Sir Gerard Brennan when he told Kelly and Bramston:

> In recent years the concept of the separation of powers has been popularly understood to require not only that judges should be immune from political bias and political influence in making decisions but should themselves avoid conduct that may give rise to a reasonable apprehension of political bias (or any other form of bias) that might affect judicial impartiality . . . In earlier times, popular understanding did not insist on such a rigorous standard.[130]

There are, however, two observations in relation to this. First, if it is true that the separation of powers has become 'stronger since 1975', this does not mean that Barwick or Mason had done anything wrong in 1975 in acting in accordance with the practice that was then, in 1975, the accepted function of a High Court Justice. As even Kelly and Bramston seem to accept, the criticisms made by Brennan, Gleeson and French would mean that Barwick's intervention is now 'behaviour no longer acceptable',[131] not that it was unacceptable in 1975.

As to the supposed 'strengthening' of the doctrine since 1975, it needs to be remembered that the development of the separation of powers doctrine in Australia can hardly be based on developments post-1975 but relies on the work of Dixon CJ, particularly on his very famous judgment from 1956 in the *Boilermakers case.*[132] That decision, which all Australian law students have implanted in their memories, has become the essential Australian decision on this doctrine, and it has confirmed that the doctrine has two elements. The first is the principle derived from earlier cases such as the *Wheat Case*[133] – that the judicial powers of the Commonwealth may only be exercised by Ch III courts.[134] And the second is that federal courts may not exercise non-judicial power.[135] This judgment was largely the product of the pen of the then Chief Justice, Owen Dixon. His biographer, Philip Ayers, considers the judgment was 'written by Dixon in his finest style, with an authority derived from his profound interest in federalism in Australia and the United States, replete with [in Ayer's view] compelling legal argument, acute analysis of the Constitution and rhetorical conclusion'.[136] Whether one accepts Ayers' highly praiseworthy assessment of the content of the *Boilermaker* judgment, there seems no reason to reject his assessment of its authorship or that the judgment required that the 'federal constitution must be rigid'.[137] But Dixon, the great proponent (and advancer) of the rigidity of the judicial arm of the *Constitution,* was also prepared, while holding a judicial office, to advise State Governors on their reserve powers, as well as prime ministers on other matters, such as who should be appointed as Australia's High Commissioner in London.[138] And he was also prepared to act as Australia's minister to the United States for two years during World War II.[139] Like his predecessor as Chief Justice, John Latham, they had both taken 'leave from the Court to serve in a full-time executive post with wide-ranging diplomatic and administrative responsibilities'.[140] So was Dixon, during his 35 years on the High Court, operating in a 'colonial' or in a 'different constitutional context' [141] where the doctrine of separation of powers had little application, as Kelly and Bramston seem to consider? And the answer is clearly no.

The better view is that while Australian judges are no longer expected to advise regarding the reserve powers, the reason has little to do with the doctrine of separation of power or any strengthening of the doctrine since 1975.

And to establish that, one only needs to look to the relatively newly discovered exception to the doctrine – the *persona designata* rule, a concept that was first applied by the High Court, not during Dixon's lengthy term, but ten years after Whitlam's dismissal, in 1985. In that year, in *Hilton v Wells*,[142] the Court accepted that the power to issue warrants for telecommunications was not a judicial power, and as such, it cannot be exercised by a Ch III court. But the majority (Gibbs CJ, Wilson and Dawson JJ) also accepted such a power can be provided to a judge, but only if it is provided to the recipient, not as a judge, but as a designated person or *persona designata.* And they did so by a puzzling (if not absurd) process which virtually guarantees the validity of the provision of non-judicial powers to judges, despite the second of the *Boilermakers*' tests.

> the nature of the power conferred is of importance in deciding whether the judge on whom it is conferred is intended to exercise it in his capacity as a judge or as a designated person. If the power is judicial, it is likely that it is intended to be exercisable by the judge by virtue of that character; if it is purely administrative, and not incidental to the exercise of judicial power, it is likely that it is intended to be exercised by the judge as a designated person.[143]

The minority (Mason and Deane JJ), however, recognized the silliness of the majority position:

> One may ask: what is the point of our insisting, in conformity with the dictates of the *Boilermakers*' *Case*, that non-judicial functions shall not be given to a Ch III court, if it is legitimate for Parliament to adopt the expedient of entrusting these functions to judges personally in lieu of pursuing the proscribed alternative of giving the functions to the court to which the judges belong? [144]

They also said:

> To the intelligent observer, unversed in what Dixon J accurately described – and emphatically rejected – as 'distinctions without differences'[145] . . . it would come as a surprise to learn that a judge, who is appointed to carry out a function by reference to his judicial office and who carries it out in his court with the assistance of its staff, services and facilities, is not acting as a judge at all, but as a private individual. *Such an observer might well think, with some degree of justification, that it is all an elaborate charade* [emphasis added].[146]

Despite that well-constructed dissent, two years later, in 1987, the Court in *Jones v Commonwealth*,[147] by a majority of 6:1, affirmed *Hilton v Wells* – and both Mason and Deane had now moved into the majority.[148] In *Jones*, the Court refused to reconsider the 1985 decision, largely, it seems, due to the doctrine of *stare decisis.*[149] Subsequent decisions have also continued to apply the *persona designata* principle, most notably *Grollo v Palmer*[150] in 1995 and in *Wilson*[151] in the following year. And that exception has provided a basis to allow federal judges to preside at Royal Commissions and administrative tribunals and be ambassadors.

Despite this acceptance, there remains some occasional expressions of judicial rationality, such as the observations of two former Chief Justices in *Wainohu v NSW*[152] that:

> so long as that function is conferred upon the judge by virtue of his or her office as a judge, the distinction is difficult to grasp and the fact that the function is conferred *persona designata* should not be given great weight.[153]

And they also quote, with apparent approval, the views expressed by Mason in 1996, after his retirement from the court:

> The concept of *persona designata* has a distinctly artificial flavour about it. The concept, which would have appealed to mediaeval schoolmen, has been criticised on the ground that it contemplates the judge acting in his character at large, detached from the court of which he is a member. The concept has little to commend it. Rationality would be advanced if the concept were jettisoned and replaced by the incompatibility test.[154]

All this seems to indicate that since 1985 the Court has adopted a convenient conclusion supported by a fictional justification in an effort to avoid the natural requirements of the strict separation of powers doctrine as defined by Dixon in 1956. This is not the stuff of a more robustly applied doctrine since 1975, or a doctrine strengthened to 'avoid conduct that may give rise to a reasonable apprehension of political bias (or any other form of bias) that might affect judicial impartiality', despite the views of Brennan, Kelly and Bramston. It is, in fact, a doctrine not strengthened but watered down by an 'elaborate charade' to avoid the consequences of the Dixon 1956 test.[155]

The separation of powers argument also seems to have ignored the position of the Australian States – where there is no strict separation between the branches of government.[156] In at least four of the Australian States, the judiciary is not only not separate from the executive, but has been built into that branch. That can be seen from an examination of the position in the State of Victoria where the head of the executive is the Governor. But in the Governor's absence, his or her role is filled by the Lieutenant Governor or, if that person is not available, then by the Administrator.[157] And in that state, the Administrator is either the Chief Justice of the Supreme Court or, if he or she is unable to act, the most senior judge of that Court who is available.[158]

Moreover, there has been a long history of Victoria's Chief Justice also holding the office of Lieutenant Governor. That can be seen from the appointments of the following Chief Justices to that office:

- Marilyn Warren CJ – between 2006 and 2017;
- John Young CJ – between 1974 and 1991;
- Henry Winneke CJ – between 1972 and 1974;
- Edmund Herring CJ – between 1945 and 1972;
- Frederick Mann CJ – between 1936 and 1945;
- William Irving CJ – between 1918 and 1936; and
- John Madden CJ – between 1899 and 1918.

A similar, but simpler, joinder of the State judiciary with the State executive can also be seen in most other States, such as both Western Australia and Tasmania, where the current Chief Justice has also been appointed the Lieutenant Governor of those States.[159] And in New South Wales, it is also clear that its Chief Justice has been appointed as Lieutenant Governor for many years. Indeed, it can be seen that, at least for the last 50 years, all Chief Justices of NSW have also been its Lieutenant Governor:

- Andrew Bell CJ – since 2022;
- Thomas Bathurst CJ– 2012–2022;
- James Spigelman CJ – 1998–2012;
- Murray Gleeson CJ – 1989–1998;
- Laurence Street CJ – 1974–1989; and
- John Kerr CJ – 1972–1974.

That list includes both the man central to the 1975 dismissal, John Kerr, as well as a Chief Justice who later went on to be the High Court's Chief Justice between 1998 and 2008, Murray Gleeson. And Gleeson has made some observations that seem to indicate that the reasons why judges no longer provide advice to the executive after 1975 are unconnected with the doctrine of separation of powers. As he said:

> I was twenty years the chief justice (in NSW and in Australia) and I was never asked any incumbent governor or governor-general on the exercise of any power. Now maybe one reason I wasn't asked was because of the public reaction to what Barwick did.[160]

Now, during the first nine of those twenty years referred to by Gleeson, he was also the Lieutenant Governor of the State of NSW. As a result, if Gleeson was not asked during those nine years, the justification seems to have little to do with any separation of powers. And that can be seen, not only from the overlap of the judiciary and the executive in that State as shown by the two offices Gleeson held, but also because, as the High Court has made clear, there is no strict separation of powers in Australian States. As McHugh J said in *Kable v DPP*, the *NSW Constitution* 'is not predicated on any separation of legislative, executive and judicial power. . . . I can see nothing in the constitutional history of the State that would preclude the State legislature from vesting legislative or executive power in the New South Wales judiciary or judicial power in the legislature or the executive'.[161]

There is, however, an argument that since 1996 and the decision in *Kable,* State Courts are now subject to the Commonwealth separation of powers restrictions, and the result must be that, whatever had occurred before, State Judges should not now be holding vice-regal roles or be advising State Governors on reserve powers. But in *Kable*, McHugh J also accepted that the appointment of Chief Justices as Lieutenant Governors was likely to be a valid extra-judicial appointment, and, therefore, an exception to the *Kable* doctrine. In his view:

> Given the long history of such appointments, it is impossible to conclude that such appointments compromise the independence of the Supreme Courts or suggest that they are not impartial.[162]

And those views were accepted by French CJ and Kiefel J in *Wainohu*. As they said:

> It is, however, important that the requirement of compatibility within the *Kable* doctrine, . . . be approached with restraint. . . . Allowance must be made in assessing incompatibility for the long history in the States of the appointments of judges to extra-judicial roles, a history which predates Federation.[163]

As a result, State Judges seem able to hold the Lieutenant Governor or Administrator offices without being contrary to the *Kable* doctrine. And if that is the case, it seems difficult, if not impossible to see any justification why any holder of both a State judicial office and an executive office (the office of Lieutenant Governor (or Administrator)) would, should, or even could be hampered in advising another executive office holder (a State Governor) regarding reserve powers based on separation of powers.

It is suggested that the reason why judges do not now get involved in advising state governors or the Commonwealth governors-general is not related to the doctrine of separation of powers or any questionable strengthening of that doctrine, but it is based on two other reasons. The first is, as Gleeson earlier indicated, to avoid criticism similar to that aimed at Barwick as a result of his 1975 advice to Kerr, which unnecessarily damaged the Court in the minds of the public by aligning it with one side of politics. As another of the High Court's former chief justices, Robert French (2008–2017), has said in his agreement with what one of his predecessors, Gerald Brennan (1995–1998), had previously said regarding Barwick's advice to Kerr – 'It was, and remains, a controversial matter but, if only on that account, will not happen again'.[164] That is, the first reason why the Barwick approach will now not be followed is based on the reputation of the Court in the mind of the public, not with any connection to the constitutional law concept of separation of powers.

But the second reason may be the deciding factor. That is, judges really have little knowledge of constitutional conventions, so they have little understanding or expertise in the subject of their advice. As we will see, many of the items in Barwick's advice to Kerr were problematic, if not simply flawed. But this criticism is not confined to Barwick alone. Owen Dixon, the judge often praised as Australia's best legal mind, provided very questionable advice when he advised State Governors on reserve powers. This can be seen from the advice he provided to the Victorian governor, Dallas Brooks, in 1952 in relation to a fairly complex arrangement involving three political leaders and three political parties: John Cain (ALP), John McDonald (Country Party) and Thomas Holloway. The intricate details of that event are not necessary here to explain,[165] but the basis of Dixon's advice demonstrates his questionable understanding of the conventions involved. His advice, as his diary recorded, was that: 'Holloway should not go to the country as Premier because (1) he could not be returned (2) his project had failed',[166] advice that Professor Winterton later correctly queried. In Winterton's view, any 'assessment of the electors' likely judgment is not only foolhardy, but both irrelevant and politically controversial'. In his view, such a consideration would be: 'an inappropriate consideration for a Governor who must maintain (in Dixon's apt phrase) "Rhadamanthine impartiality"',[167] criticism that seems clearly correct. Fortunately for Governor Dallas Brooks, he had an alternate source of advice from the Victorian Solicitor-General (and later Governor, Henry Winneke), which seems to have avoided the problems of Dixon's advice.

Both instances (1952 and 1975) seem to demonstrate that Chief Justices, while they know a lot about constitutional law, their understanding of constitutional conventions and how they operate in a difficult political environment can be both simplistic and erroneous. As a result, Governors and Governors-General can be better off without the assistance of the judiciary.

From this discussion, it seems clear that the conclusions of Professor Twomey are correct – that the actions of Barwick and Mason were 'neither unprecedented, unusual, nor unconventional' and that their actions were 'consistent with those of his predecessors or his colleagues'.[168] The judiciary's willingness to provide advice to the governor-general may not be acceptable today, but there was no constitutional problem in what Barwick and Mason did in 1975.

ACCURACY?

The second issue regarding the legal advice from the High Court Justices concerns their accuracy. This is particularly so because Kerr seems to have accepted the bulk of that advice. As Kerr made clear in his account of Whitlam's dismissal in his *Matters for Judgment*, his view of the legal and constitutional position regarding supply in Australia was based on the following observation:

> Just as in the United Kingdom a Government which cannot get supply from the House of Commons because of, say, a crossing of the floor by some members, must recommend an election or resign, so in Australia there could be no question, in the case of denial of funds by the Representatives, of governing without supply to force House rebels to break and recross the floor. Where two Houses hold the purse strings, the same is true in the Upper House. In neither case can it be appropriate or necessary to wait until the money runs out on the chance that someone may break. Supply must be secured before this dire result occurs.[169]

Kerr, therefore, considered the provision of supply a particular form of confidence to be provided by both Houses before a government can continue. Mallory noted this, observing that Kerr seemed to have 'introduced a novel and hitherto unheard convention in the Australian constitution, namely that responsible government involves a government having the confidence of both Houses'.[170] While this suggestion was rejected by Forsey as a 'complete misconception',[171] Barwick seems not to have agreed. In his autobiography, when discussing 1975, he acknowledged that 'the ministry was supported by a majority of members of the House of Representatives. But that Chamber is only part of the Parliament'.[172] This he had earlier expanded in his 1983 justification for his actions and those of Kerr, *Sir John Did His Duty*, when he wrote:

> whilst it may be said that the government does not need in general to have the confidence of the Senate in the sense that it must retain the confidence of the House, it must so far have that confidence as to obtain the Senate's concurrence to the annual grant of supply.[173]

Accordingly, in his view: 'When the Prime Minister was unable to secure supply from Parliament' (not just the Lower House), 'his ministry lost any claim it had to be the government of the country'.[174] And in his advice to Kerr of November 10, 1975, Barwick put the issue plainly:

> there is an analogy between the situation of a Prime Minister who has lost the confidence of the House of Commons and a Prime Minister who does not have the confidence of the Parliament, i.e., of the House of Representatives and of the Senate. The duty and responsibility of the Prime Minister to the Crown in each case is the same: if unable to secure supply to the Crown, to resign or to advise an election.[175]

As Mason subsequently said, the requirement of the prime minister to have the confidence of the Senate 'was, after all, the keystone of the advice which Sir Garfield Barwick famously gave to Sir John Kerr in 1975'.[176]

The correct constitutional position in Australia regarding the 'confidence' power of the Senate was, however, left unclear by the 1975 events as the debate on that issue was 'cut short in 1975 by the Governor-General's intervention'.[177] Nonetheless, Barwick's position does seem remarkably odd. It seems to reflect a conclusion based on both his political preference (he had been the Attorney-General to the Robert Menzies Liberal/Country Party government) and his sparse knowledge of political/constitutional practice and history, as distinct from his extensive appreciation of constitutional law. That can be seen, for example, from his remarkably confident, but remarkably incorrect, assertion in his 1983 book, that there is 'a universal practice under which a Prime Minister when unable to secure supply from the Parliament immediately resigns for himself and the members of the ministry'.[178] And later on that page, he stated, again completely inaccurately, that 'until 1975, no Prime Minister in any Westminster system, including the United Kingdom, has refused to resign or advise dissolution if unable to secure supply'.[179] There are, however, numerous instances of supply blockages by Upper Houses that have not led to ministerial resignations or elections that have occurred in Australian States. As John Waugh points out in his 2002 article,[180] supply had been rejected in Victoria on a number of occasions in the nineteenth and twentieth centuries – 1865, 1867 (three times), 1877, 1947 (three times again) and 1952. Supply has also been blocked in Tasmania in 1924 and 1948 and in South Australia in 1911–12. None of these events led to a dismissal of government and the general result was either dissolution of, or resolution between, the Houses. But few can be regarded as instances requiring 'immediate' resignation or dissolution, as Barwick asserted, as some governments attempted to use creative alternative sources of finance (of doubtful or no legality)[181] and harsh savings methods to allow government to continue.

For example, the first supply blockage in the State of Victoria in 1867 occurred on July 25; but that did not lead to any immediate dissolution of the Lower House, as the dissolution needed to await almost six months, occurring on December 11. And the most severe example of the use of creative financial arrangements to avoid Lower House dissolution is Premier Berry's 'Black Wednesday' in Victoria in January 1878, when a range of public officials, including County Court judges, senior public servants, police, magistrates, coroners and many others were dismissed, a step considered necessary to allow the government to survive a supply blockage that occurred in December 1877.[182] This and other devices allowed Graham Berry and his government to survive. Berry's government was not required to resign and neither was it dismissed by the 1877 supply blockage, but it remained in power until March 5, 1880. The Tasmanian incident of 1924 is also informative. There the government dealt with Upper House amendments to an appropriation bill, which that State's Constitution allowed, but with which the government did not agree,[183] not by any government resignation or being dismissed, but as Waugh puts it, 'by the original, if plainly illegal, expedient of ignoring the Council and obtaining royal assent to the Bill regardless'.[184]

It might be thought that Barwick was not referring to non-national governments in that his reference was to the 'Prime Minister' rather than to 'Premiers', the title used for the head of government in Australian States. But as he said later in his short book, his assertion was that 'no Prime Minister *or Premier* in a Westminster system of government has ever failed to resign or to advise a dissolution',[185] he did not have that limitation in mind. In fact, it seems that it was not until he wrote his biography, much later in his life and twenty years after the dismissal, in 1995, that he became aware of other supply blockage instances. But even then, he was still only aware of 'instances in the colony of Victoria', which he attempted, somewhat unconvincingly, to diminish as instances from its 'frontier days'.[186]

Barwick also had some unusual views as to the timing of Kerr's dismissal of Whitlam. In his view, expressed in 1995:

> it may be that Sir John delayed too long in taking action. I incline to the view that he ought to have acted, at the latest, by 25 October. I think this is because by the delay after that date, the Prime Minister had a party-political advantage enabling him to indulge in brinkmanship to coerce some, no doubt weaker, of the senators to break ranks.[187]

Not only was this view at odds with the position of Kerr and his very supportive Official Secretary, Sir David Smith,[188] Barwick's assessment seems based on an ahistorical and asymmetrical view as to the 'acceptability' of

Whitlam's proposed course of 'toughing it out'. He asked if that course of conduct was 'acceptable', then:

> Is it acceptable in a parliamentary democracy where the members are expected to do their parliamentary duties honourably and free of coercion of any kind? Brinkmanship of this kind might be acceptable in the factional infighting in a political or industrial group, but to my mind not in an assembly of honourable representatives of the people.[189]

These may be sensible questions if they also applied to the other side of politics or of this crisis. That, however, was not considered by Barwick. For example, Barwick did not consider how the apparent brinkmanship of Fraser fits in with this analysis. That is, as pointed out in chapter 5, Fraser's ideal method of contesting Whitlam was:

> to find a situation in which we made that decision and Mr Whitlam woke up one morning finding the decision had been made and finding that he had been caught with his pants well and truly down.[190]

And what of the approach of a governor-general whose course of action was, as Kelly and Bramston record it, to sack Whitlam, but with 'the guiding principle . . . to keep this decision secret from the prime minister'.[191] Of those views, Barwick expressed no view.

DIFFERENCES – THE NEED TO WARN

The final issue is the differences in the positions taken by Barwick and Mason. In essence, this arises from Mason's assertion that his advice to Kerr included his view that Whitlam should be warned that the governor-general may terminate his commission, a position that Barwick rejected and Kerr did not accept. As Hocking has observed:

> Had Kerr taken Mason's advice on this and warned the Prime Minister, the sense of 'ambush' expressed by Whitlam, the polarisation and the continuing controversy over the dismissal, may well have abated.[192]

The basis of Mason's warning advice to Kerr was found in one of the most important works on the nineteenth-century Westminster Constitution by Walter Bagehot, *The English Constitution*.[193] In that work, written in 1867 and reviewed in 1872, Bagehot wrote of what he described as the 'three rights' of a Monarch in their dealings with their Ministers – the right to be consulted, the right to encourage and the right of most relevance to 1975, the right to warn.[194] Bagehot considered that a Monarch, when exercising the right to warn:

> would say to his Ministers: 'The responsibility of these measures is upon you. Whatever you think best must be done. Whatever you think best shall have my full and effectual support. *But* you will observe that for this reason and that reason what you propose is bad; for this reason and that reason what you do not propose is better. I do not oppose, it is my duty not to oppose; but observe that I *warn*.'[195]

Mason considers that Kerr 'acted consistently with his duty' in sacking Whitlam, but with one exception. That is, Mason considered that Kerr 'had a duty to warn the Prime Minister of his intended action [to dismiss] and he did not do so'.[196] Mason states that he had advised Kerr that an 'incumbent Prime Minister should, as a matter of fairness, first be offered the option of holding a general election to resolve any dispute over supply between the two Houses and informed that if he did not agree to do so his commission would be withdrawn'.[197]

Hocking spent some time considering this difference – that Kerr made no reference to that element of the advice from Mason. As she said: 'Kerr's notes on their meetings, written in late October 1975, with additional comments made in 1981, make no mention of this caution'.[198] And for once, she prefers Kerr's views. To her, Mason's views do 'not sit comfortably with the fact that he continued to meet with Kerr knowing that Kerr had not in fact so warned Whitlam'.[199] This is a puzzling observation, as it seems to assume that a person will only advise a friend, a colleague or a client if that advice is accepted. This seems to indicate little appreciation of the nature of a professional relationship, or the trust between friends.

There are, however, reasons why Kerr may not have included a reference to any Mason warning advice in his papers, although not reasons that serve Kerr's reputation. It seems that Kerr may well have wanted his records to support his position as much as possible – and Mason's warning advice would not have served that purpose. Kerr was selective in relation to other aspects of the 1975 story and that can be seen from other notable omissions from *Matters for Judgment.* Those omitted matters included Bagehot and his 'right to warn'.[200] This is a notable and odd omission from Kerr's account, particularly given the many other legal and constitutional authorities that Kerr did cite. Kerr also omitted the advice that he received from both the Governors of New South Wales and Victoria who each advised that Whitlam should be warned (and will be discussed in more depth in chapter 9) Again, that information, like Bagehot's 'right to warn', would not be consistent with the course of action that Kerr adopted. We will, however, never be sure what Kerr's justification was for the omission of Bagehot, Cutler or Winneke from his account. But as to Mason, his omission by Kerr was probably because Mason did not wish to be publicly recorded as conferring with and advising Kerr; and given the negative reaction of Labor Ministers to that news (as discussed above), maintaining that privacy was, for Mason at least, a wise and sensible course of action.

Mason has also taken a broader view of his role in the historical record of the 1975 dismissal, with his view that 'I owe history nothing',[201] a position that Hocking strongly rejected, regarding it as 'a marvellous and dreadful response'.[202] But whether Mason's reasons for maintaining his privacy were in the long-term public interest or not, there seems no reason to conclude that Mason's advice to Kerr or his reasons for not advising the public of his role were in any way based on any desire to want Whitlam's government dismissed, or to misuse his advice to his friend to manipulate that friend and colleague.

There is, however, one other interesting and possibly damaging element in the Mason statement, with his acknowledgement that his discussions with Kerr relating to the dismissal of Whitlam commenced in August, not October. As Mason said:

> My first conversation in 1975 with Sir John with reference to the reserve powers was at Yarralumla in August, not 12 October, as Sir John says. In that conversation he mentioned that an occasion might arise for him to exercise the reserve powers, dismiss Mr Whitlam and commission Mr Fraser to form a caretaker government for the purpose of securing supply and holding an election.[203]

Hocking makes the point that this conversation began 'three months before the dismissal and two months before there was even a Supply "crisis" to precipitate it'.[204] As such, to her, this seems to indicate a long-term plan of both Kerr and Mason to both deceive and dispose of the Whitlam government. This conclusion, however, is not accurate. Although the supply crisis did not actually begin until October 16 when the Opposition Parties in the Senate first deferred the supply bills (see chapter 5) and the Opposition's Robert Ellicott issued his Press Statement (see earlier in this chapter), there had been earlier discussion of a potential supply crisis and its constitutional consequences as early as July 1975. As Kerr observes, on July 4 the *Canberra Times* included a lengthy editorial[205] discussing the role of the governor-general as the 'ultimate guardian of the Constitution' with the power to 'revoke the commissions of a Prime Minister or of other Ministers'. That editorial concluded that the governor-general has the power 'to take steps that could lead to a dissolution of the Parliament and to a general election' and that 'The good government of Australia, especially at a time of grave economic disruption, is the only thing that counts'.[206] Kerr was also aware of a possible future supply crisis arising from other sources, and that includes, according to Kerr, Whitlam's August 25 advice of his intention to call an election in December 'if supply were denied'.[207] As such, it seems that a possible future supply crisis and the potential use of the reserve powers were not surprise issues when supply was first blocked in October, but had been raised as early as July when the governor-general considered them as matters that he needed to anticipate and plan for. As such, Kerr's consultation with Mason in August can only be seen as consistent with Kerr's planning to avoid or deal with a possible constitutional crisis – and nothing more.

NOTES

1. Parliament of Australia, *Biography for Ellicott, the Hon Robert James, AC, KC,* https://parlinfo.aph.gov.au/parlInfo/search/display/display.w3p;query=Id%3A%22handbook%2Fallmps%2FYF6%22. Parliamentary Library, *Parliamentary Handbook*, "Shadow Ministers in the Fraser Shadow Ministry from 21.03.1975 to 11.11.1975," https://handbook.aph.gov.au/ShadowMinistry/25.
2. See Whitlam, *The Truth*, 80; Hocking, *His Time* (2012), 262; and O'Brien, *Villain or Victim?*, 46.
3. Greenwood had been Attorney-General in the McMahon government between 1971 and 1972 and went on to be Fraser's first Attorney-General for a short period between November and December 1975. See Drew Cottle, "Greenwood, Ivor John (1926–1976)," Parliament of Australia, The Biographical Dictionary of the Senate (online) – https://biography.senate.gov.au/greenwood-ivor-john/. First published in *The Biographical Dictionary of the Australian Senate*, 1962–1983, vol 3 (Sydney: University of New South Wales Press Ltd, 2010), 77–82. Parliamentary Library, *Fraser's Shadow Ministry*, https://handbook.aph.gov.au/ShadowMinistry/25.
4. The text of the Ellicott opinion can be found in Kelly & Bramston, *The Dismissal,* 332–336.
5. Kerr, *Matters*, 271.
6. John Kerr, *Conversation with Sir Anthony Mason during October-November 1975,* NAA M4523, 1 Part 14, 6 & 10–11.
7. Whitlam, *The Truth,* 115.
8. Kerr, *Matters*, 271.
9. Kerr, *Matters,* 272.
10. Kerr, *Matters,* 303.
11. Kerr, *Matters,* 302.
12. Kelly, *Unmaking,* 346.
13. Kelly, *Unmaking,* 345.
14. This opinion can be found in Kelly & Bramston, *The Dismissal,* 337–364.

15. Law Officers' Draft opinion para 38 – see Kelly & Bramston, *The Dismissal,* 364.
16. Kerr, *Matters,* 303.
17. Hocking, *His Time* (2012), 308.
18. Quoted in Kelly & Bramston, *The Dismissal,* 161.
19. Whitlam, *The Truth,* 125–126.
20. Whitlam, *The Truth,* 126.
21. Barwick, *Radical Tory*, 200.
22. Which can be found in Kelly & Bramston, *The Dismissal,* 365–366.
23. Barwick, *Sir John,* 80.
24. See Kelly & Bramston, *The Dismissal,* 366 and Barwick, *Sir John,* 82.
25. Hocking, *His Time* (2014) 569.
26. Whitlam, *The Truth,* 192.
27. Kerr, *Matters,* 340–345.
28. Barwick, *Sir John.*
29. Barwick, *Radical Tory.*
30. Kerr, *Matters,* 341.
31. Henderson, "Evidence, Memory and Dismissal."
32. Hocking, *His Time* (2014), 565.
33. Which can be seen in Kelly & Bramston, *The Dismissal,* 390–398.
34. Hocking, *His Time* (2012), 304.
35. Anthony Mason, *Conversations With Sir John Kerr Relating To His Termination of The Commission of The Prime Minister (The Hon E G Whitlam AC QC) on 11 November 1975* (2012) [3] – See Kelly & Bramston, *The Dismissal,* 390.
36. Mason, *Conversations with Kerr* [3] – See Kelly & Bramston, *The Dismissal,* 390.
37. Mason, *Conversations with Kerr* [34] – See Kelly & Bramston, *The Dismissal*, 390, 398.
38. Mason, *Conversations with Kerr* [26] – See Kelly & Bramston, *The Dismissal,* 390, 396.
39. Hocking, *His Time* (2014), 568.
40. Hocking, *His Time* (2014), 569.
41. Hocking, *His Time* (2014), 572.
42. Hocking, *His Time* (2014), 572 – Emphasis added.
43. Hocking, *Palace Letters,* 8.
44. Hocking, *His Time* (2014), 564.
45. Hocking, *His Time* (2014), 566.
46. Hocking, *His Time* (2014), 564.
47. "a confidential agent, esp one who exercises power unofficially." *The Concise Oxford Dictionary of Current English* (Oxford: Clarendon Press, seventh edition, 1982), 315.
48. Hocking, *Palace Letters,* 8.
49. Hocking, *His Time* (2014), 575.
50. Hocking, *His Time* (2014), 575.
51. Hocking, *Palace Letters,* 9.

52. See Kerr, *Matters,* 341.
53. Kerr, *Matters,* 347–348.
54. Hocking, *His Time* (2014), 567.
55. Hocking, *His Time* (2014), 567.
56. Mason, *Conversations with Kerr* [8] – See Kelly & Bramston, *The Dismissal,* 390, 392.
57. Mason, *Conversations with Kerr* [4] – See Kelly & Bramston, *The Dismissal,* 390, 390–391.
58. Mason, *Conversations with Kerr* [7] – See Kelly & Bramston, *The Dismissal,* 390, 391–392.
59. Mason, *Conversations with Kerr* [14] – See Kelly & Bramston, *The Dismissal,* 390, 393.
60. Mason, *Conversations with Kerr* [7] – See Kelly & Bramston, *The Dismissal,* 390, 391–392.
61. Mason, *Conversations with Kerr* [13] – See Kelly & Bramston, *The Dismissal,* 390, 393.
62. Mason, *Conversations with Kerr* [6] – See Kelly & Bramston, *The Dismissal,* 390, 391.
63. Mason, *Conversations with Kerr* [21] – See Kelly & Bramston, *The Dismissal,* 390, 397.
64. Mason, *Conversations with Kerr* [22] – See Kelly & Bramston, *The Dismissal,* 390, 395.
65. Mason, *Conversations with Kerr* [19] – See Kelly & Bramston, *The Dismissal,* 390, 394.
66. Mason, *Conversations with Kerr* [23] – See Kelly & Bramston, *The Dismissal,* 390, 395.
67. Mason, *Conversations with Kerr* [30] – See Kelly & Bramston, *The Dismissal,* 390, 397.
68. Hocking, *His Time* (2014), 575.
69. Hocking, *Palace Letters,* 8.
70. Hocking, *His Time* (2014), 569.
71. Hocking, *His Time* (2014), 564.
72. Hocking, *His Time* (2014), 564.
73. Hocking, *His Time* (2014), 563.
74. Hocking, *His Time* (2014), 569.
75. Kerr, *Matters*, 341.
76. Kelly & Bramston, *The Dismissal*, 43.
77. Kelly & Bramston, *The Dismissal,* 43.
78. Kelly & Bramston, *The Dismissal,* 43.
79. Kelly & Bramston, *The Dismissal,* 44.
80. Kelly & Bramston, *The Dismissal,* 44.
81. Prime Minister, 1983–1991.
82. Prime Minister, 1991–1996.
83. Leader of the Opposition, 1977–1983. Governor-General 1989–1996.

84. Evans held a number of ministerial offices including attorney-general 1983–1984, minister of Foreign Affairs 1988–1996; leader of the govt in the Senate, 1993–1996; deputy leader of the Labor Party 1996–1998.

85. Duffy held a number of ministerial offices including attorney-general 1990–1993.

86. Willis held a number of ministerial offices including treasurer in 1991 and 1993–1996.

87. Kelly & Bramston, *The Dismissal,* 45.

88. Hocking, *His Time* (2014), 574.

89. Kep Enderby quoted by Hocking, *His Time* (2014), 569.

90. Quoted in Kelly & Bramston, *The Dismissal,* 44.

91. Between February 6, 1987 and April 20, 1995.

92. Anne Twomey, "Mason's Role in the 1975 Dismissal 'unprecedented'? Hardly," *Conversation,* August 31, 2012.

93. Kelly & Bramston, *The Dismissal,* 45.

94. See Kelly & Bramston, *The Dismissal,* 137.

95. Hocking, *His Time* (2012) 304.

96. Kelly & Bramston, *The Dismissal,* 53.

97. Forsey, "The Present Position," lxxvii and quoted in Killey, *Constitutional Conventions,* 136.

98. See Kelly & Bramston, *The Dismissal,* 50–53 and Hocking, *Palace Letters,* 9.

99. Chief Justice between 1995 and 1998, and before that, Justice of the Court between 1981 and 1995.

100. Chief Justice between 2008 and 2017.

101. Kelly & Bramston, *The Dismissal,* 39.

102. Kelly & Bramston, *The Dismissal,* 40.

103. Kelly & Bramston, *The Dismissal,* 39.

104. Twomey, "Legal Advice," 293.

105. Twomey, *Veiled Sceptre,* 68.

106. Twomey, *Veiled Sceptre,* 69.

107. Twomey, "Legal Advice," 294; and Twomey, *Veiled Sceptre*, 69.

108. Markwell, "Griffith, Barton," 282.

109. Twomey, "Mason's Role" and see Markwell, "Griffith, Barton," 288.

110. (1951) 83 CLR 1.

111. Fiona Wheeler, "Sir John Latham's Extra Judicial Advising" (2011) 35 *Melbourne University Law Review* 651, 652–653.

112. Wheeler, "Latham's Extra Judicial Advising," 653.

113. Wheeler, "Latham's Extra Judicial Advising," 653.

114. Wheeler, "Latham's Extra Judicial Advising," 672.

115. Wheeler, "Latham's Extra Judicial Advising," 673.

116. Markwell, "Griffith, Barton," 294.

117. Twomey, "Mason's Role."

118. Twomey, *Veiled Sceptre*, 69.

119. Also see Philip Ayers, *Owen Dixon* (Carlton, Victoria: Miegunyah Press, 2003), 235–237 (in relation to 1952) and 249 (in relation to 1955)1955), and Killey, *Constitutional Conventions,* 170–171 (in relation to 1952).

120. See Ayers, *Owen Dixon,* 255 (in relation to 1956) and 275 (in relation to 1960). Twomey states the second issue arose in 1961, but, based on Ayers, it should have been 1960.

121. Twomey, "Mason's Role."

122. Twomey, *Veiled Sceptre*, 68.

123. Kelly & Bramston, *The Dismissal,* 164.

124. Markwell, "On Advice from the Chief Justice," 39.

125. Markwell, *Australian Experience*, 85–86.

126. David K. Malcolm, "Role of the Chief Justice," Law Society of Western Australia, Lunch with the Press, May 5, 2004, https://www.supremecourt.wa.gov.au/_files/Law%20Society%20Press%20Lunch%205%20May%2004.pdf.

127. Kelly & Bramston, *The Dismissal,* 52.

128. Kelly & Bramston, *The Dismissal,* 53.

129. Kelly & Bramston, *The Dismissal,* 53.

130. Quoted in Kelly & Bramston, *The Dismissal*, 50.

131. Kelly & Bramston, *The Dismissal*, 50.

132. *R v Kirby; Ex parte Boilermakers Society of Australia* (1956) 94 CLR 254. The majority judgment was made by Dixon CJ, McTiernan, Fullagar and Kitto JJ.

133. *NSW v Commonwealth* (1915) 20 CLR 54 ('*The Wheat Case*').

134. (1956) 94 CLR 254, 270 (Dixon CJ, McTiernan, Fullagar and Kitto JJ).

135. (1956) 94 CLR 254, 271–272 (Dixon CJ, McTiernan, Fullagar and Kitto JJ).

136. Ayers, *Owen Dixon*, 255.

137. (1956) 94 CLR 254, 267 (Dixon CJ, McTiernan, Fullagar and Kitto JJ).

138. Ayers, *Owen Dixon*, 134.

139. 1942–1944 – see Ayers, *Owen Dixon*, 134–175.

140. Wheeler, "Latham's Extra Judicial Advising," 662. Latham had been Australian Minister to Japan from 1940 to 1941.

141. Kelly & Bramston, *The Dismissal,* 53.

142. (1985) 157 CLR 57.

143. (1985) 157 CLR 57, 73.

144. (1985) 157 CLR 57, 83.

145. *Medical Board of Victoria v Meyer* (1937) 58 CLR 62, 97.

146. (1985) 157 CLR 57, 84.

147. (1987) 61 ALJR 348.

148. The rest of the majority were Wilson, Brennan, Dawson and Toohey JJ.

149. (1987) 61 ALJR 348, 349. *Stare decisis* means "to stand by decided matters" – see John Gray, *Lawyer' Latin: A Vade Mecum* (London: Robert Hale, 2002), 130.

150. (1995) 184 CLR 348.

151. *Wilson v Minister for Aboriginal and Torres Strait Affairs* (1996) 189 CLR 1.

152. (2011) 243 CLR 181 (French CJ and Kiefel J). Kiefel was later promoted to the office of Chief Justice, holding that office between 2017 and 2023. French was Chief Justice between 2008 and 2017.

153. (2011) 243 CLR 181, 211[50].

154. Anthony Mason, "A New Perspective on Separation of Powers" (1996) 82 *Canberra Bulletin of Public Administration,* 1, 5; quoted at (2011) 243 CLR 181, 211[50].

155. Winterton, however, has suggested that the *persona designata* doctrine has been "considerably narrowed in recent years," but the only support for this non-expanded argument is *Wilson v Minister for Aboriginal and Torres Strait Affairs* (1996) 189 CLR 1. See George Winterton, "1975: The Dismissal of the Whitlam Government," in *Australian Constitutional Landmarks,* ed. H. P. Lee & George Winterton (Cambridge: Cambridge University Press, 2003), 229, 249.

156. See the discussion in Matthew Stubbs, "The Constitutional Validity of State Chief Justices acting as Governor." (2014) 25 PLR 197 and the cases cited in Killey, *Naked Australian Constitution*, 138–139.

157. *Constitution Act 1975* (Vic) s 6A.

158. *Constitution Act 1975* (Vic) s 6A(3).

159. In Tasmania, the Chief Justice and Lt Governor has been Alan Blow since 2013. In Western Australia, the Chief Justice, Peter Quinlan, has been Lt Governor since 2019. And as Stubbs observed, in Queensland "the Chief Justice as Administrator serves as acting Governor." See Stubbs, "State Chief Justices," 199.

160. Quoted in Kelly & Bramston, *The Dismissal,* 40. Also see the conclusion of former Chief Justice, Robert French, "The Chief Justice and the Governor-General" (2009) 33 *Melbourne University Law Review* 647, 656.

161. (1996) 189 CLR 51, 109. Other cases reaching the same conclusion regarding other States and Territories are listed in Killey, *Naked Constitution*, 138.

162. (1996) 189 CLR 51, 118.

163. *Wainohu v NSW* (2011) 243 CLR 181, 197. Also see Rebecca Ananian Welsh & George Williams, "Judges in Vice Regal Roles" (2015) 43 *Federal Law Review* 119, 142–146.

164. Robert French, "The Chief Justice," 656.

165. The details of this instance are discussed in Killey, *Constitutional Conventions,* 169–171.

166. From Dixon's diary of October 30, 1952, and is quoted in Ayers, *Owen Dixon*, 237.

167. Quoted in Killey, *Constitutional Conventions,* 170.

168. Twomey, "Mason's Role."

169. Kerr, *Matters,* 328.

170. Quoted in Forsey, "The Present Position," lv.

171. Forsey, "The Present Position," lv.

172. Barwick, *Radical Tory,* 292.

173. Barwick, *Sir John,* 42.

174. Barwick, *Sir John,* 5.

175. Which can be seen in Kelly & Bramston, *The Dismissal,* 366 and Barwick, *Radical Tory,* 292.

176. Anthony Mason, "The Convention Model for a Republic" (1999) 10 *Public Law Review* 147.

177. Lim, *After Whitlam*, 90.
178. Barwick, *Sir John,* 55.
179. Barwick, *Sir John*, 55. He also repeated this conclusion on page 115.
180. John Waugh, "Blocking Supply in Victoria" (2002) 13 *Public Law Review* 241, 242–243.
181. This is discussed in Killey, *Constitutional Conventions,* 149.
182. Raymond Wright, *A People's Counsel* (Melbourne, Victoria: Oxford University Press Australia, 1992), 86.
183. The Tasmanian *Constitution Act*, s 33 (18 Vic, No 17) allowed appropriation bills to be amended by the Upper House. See H. V. Evatt, *The King and Dominion Governors* (Oxford: Oxford University Press, 1936 (1st edition) & London: Frank Cass, 1967 (2nd edition), reprinted in *Evatt and Forsey on the Reserve Powers* (Sydney: Legal Books, 1990), 178.
184. Waugh, "Blocking Supply," 243 and see Evatt, *Dominion Governors,* 178–184.
185. Barwick, *Sir John*, 115, emphasis added.
186. Barwick, *Radical Tory,* 282.
187. Barwick, *Radical Tory,* 297.
188. Sir David Smith's views on the timing of the dismissal are discussed in chapter 9.
189. Barwick, *Radical Tory,* 293.
190. Quoted in Whitlam, *The Truth,* 59.
191. Kelly & Bramston, *The Dismissal,* 28.
192. Hocking, *His Time* (2014), 567.
193. Walter Bagehot, *The English Constitution* (Glasgow: Fontana/William Collins, 1983, reprint of the 2nd 1872 edition).
194. Bagehot, *English Constitution*, 111.
195. Bagehot, *English Constitution*, 111. Emphasis is original.
196. Mason, *Conversations with Kerr* [34] that can be found in Kelly & Bramston, *The Dismissal,* 398.
197. Mason, *Conversations with Kerr* [9] that can be found in Kelly & Bramston, *The Dismissal,* 392.
198. Hocking, *His Time* (2014), 567.
199. Hocking, *His Time* (2014), 567.
200. Bagehot, *English Constitution,* 111.
201. Hocking, *His Time* (2014), 359 & 575.
202. Hocking, *His Time* (2014), 575.
203. Mason, *Conversations with Kerr* [8] that can be found in Kelly & Bramston, *The Dismissal,* 392.
204. Hocking, *His Time* (2014), 566.
205. "An Arrogant Silence," *Canberra Times,* July 4, 1975.
206. Kerr, *Matters,* 244.
207. Kerr, *Matters,* 246.

Chapter 9

1975

And the Errors of Kerr

Figure 9.1 ALP Political Badge from the 1975 Election. From the collection of the author. Image taken by the author.

A number of criticisms have been made regarding Sir John Kerr's actions and planning leading up to the dismissal of the Whitlam Government in 1975. Most of those criticisms are, however, either baseless or doubtful, such as the arguments that:

- the reserve powers themselves actually do not exist (discussed in chapter 3),
- the reserve powers included the power to reject advice for a half-Senate election (also discussed in chapter 3),
- Kerr should not have had discussions with Fraser on the morning of November 11 (discussed in chapter 7),
- Kerr should not have conferred with Barwick and Mason (discussed in chapter 8) and that
- Kerr should have acted much earlier than he did (also discussed in chapter 8).

There are, however, other criticisms of the actions of the governor-general that have much more substance, and they are examined in this chapter. They are:

- that Kerr acted well before he needed to, and
- that that he acted in secrecy, providing no warning to Whitlam of his intended actions. That is, that he 'ambushed' Whitlam.

THAT KERR ACTED TOO EARLY

On November 6, Kerr advised the prime minister of the effect of his meeting with Fraser. As a result, Whitlam indicated that he would 'probably . . . advise a half-Senate election on 13 December, which was the last practical day on which an election could be held before Christmas'. This seems to be the salient factor in convincing Kerr that he needed to exercise the reserve powers. In his view:

> It was clear that if the Prime Minister so advised and I acquiesced, and if the Senate stood firm – there was no guarantee of temporary supply for a half-Senate election – the election would be held after the money had run out, as it would by 30 November.[1]

And as to the date when Kerr needed to act, he considered that if 'the reserve powers were to be exercised and a general election produced before Christmas, 11 November would be the last day for decision'.[2] Kerr had decided that he was going to sack Whitlam on that day unless the prime minister first advised a general election.

This was well before supply had expired, which the governor-general believed would not occur until the end of the month. And that decision was taken not only because the half-Senate election that Whitlam sought would necessarily be held without supply, but because, as Kerr has recorded:

> To wait longer would mean having a caretaker Government until probably February at least, which because of the conditions in which such a Government operates would mean virtually interrupting the government of the country for a period of two months or so, and must obviously be avoided.[3]

In Australia, as in the United Kingdom, an election period usually runs from the date of the dissolution or expiry of the Lower House until the election result is clear. During that election period, the government operates under what is known as the 'caretaker conventions'. This conventional arrangement limits the nature of the business of government, so a 'caretaker government' avoids taking significant decisions likely to commit any incoming government. Its justification is that every election brings with it the possibility of change of government; and with the dissolution of a Lower House, there is no Parliament to which ministers making decisions can be accountable.

Caretaker conventions are a relatively newly formed constitutional development and can be dated to the caretaker arrangements entered into by the UK prime minister Sir Winston Churchill in 1945 once the then deputy prime minister, Clement Attlee, and the Labour Party of the United Kingdom left the British National Government after VE Day.[4] Subsequently, Australia has largely followed the United Kingdom practice, but our caretaker conventions were largely undocumented until 1987,[5] after which each Australian jurisdiction has closely documented its caretaker convention requirements.[6]

Kerr's approach in 1975 seems based on the advice he had received that if an election was not held in December 1975, it would need to wait until mid-February. Nonetheless, Kerr's belief that the caretaker period 'virtually interrupts government' is clearly not correct as the caretaker convention arrangements always ensure that all government decisions that must be taken can be taken, even if the government is to undertake more consultation with the Opposition than would be the norm. For example, in the current arrangements for the Commonwealth Caretaker Conventions, it provides that:

> If circumstances require the Government to make a major policy decision during the caretaker period that would bind an incoming government, the minister would usually consult the Opposition spokesperson beforehand.[7]

Moreover, Kerr's view that a caretaker period of two months or so should be avoided also seems odd, particularly as the first of the modern caretaker governments (i.e., that of Winston Churchill in 1945) was one that went for more than two months (from May 23, 1945, to July 26, 1945); and it was also one conducted while the United Kingdom was still at war. Given that this was much more serious than those facing Australia, even in 1975, it would seem that a longer-than-usual caretaker period would have been an eventuality of much less significance than an exercise of the reserve powers by the governor-general when there was no immediate need in that supply had not then run out.

There is also one other timing-related argument that has been presented that also needs consideration. Sir John Kerr's Official Secretary David Smith has claimed in his 2005 book *Head of State* that the sacking of November 11 was all Whitlam's fault. Smith has argued:

> Had Whitlam not decided to go to Government House on that day to ask the Governor-General for a half-Senate election, the events of 11 November simply would not have occurred. If Whitlam had needed more time, he could have had it. Instead, he chose to present the wrong advice at the wrong time. Whitlam was the architect of his own misfortune; he was hoist with his own petard.[8]

This argument is simply incorrect and is one that can only be made by ignoring Sir John Kerr's own writings. As Kerr has made it clear in his memoirs[9] and in his correspondence with the Palace,[10] he had determined that if there was going to be a general election before Christmas, '11 November would be the last day for decision'.[11] He was not prepared to have a later election date, as that would lead to what he expected to be a caretaker period of 'two months or so, and must obviously be avoided'.[12] Kerr had made up his mind, and he had done so 'conclusively' by November 9.[13] November 11 was the decision day. Either Whitlam advised an election on that day, or he would be sacked. Despite Smith's reformulation of the story, there was, for Kerr, no future time for Whitlam on November 11.[14]

THAT KERR 'AMBUSHED' WHITLAM

On November 11, 1975, Sir John Kerr dismissed Prime Minister Whitlam and did so in great secrecy. As seen in chapters 7 and 8, no warning to Whitlam was provided.[15]

And according to many, this was an ambush of the prime minister. As the former governor of Victoria, Richard McGarvie (between 1992 and 1997) and former Victorian Supreme Court justice, was very clear on this point:

> It is a cardinal principle that a Governor should never 'ambush' a Premier – should never exercise the reserve power without having given the Premier adequate warning that it may be exercised.[16]

Kerr, however, took that secretive approach, as Kelly and Bramston argue, because he 'felt threatened by both leaders'. He was concerned that 'if I had said anything to Mr Whitlam about the possibility that I might take away his commission I would no longer have been there',[17] but by saying that, he also seems to have had no appreciation that the dismissal of a governor-general is more than a simple process of a telephone call to the Palace. He seems to have given more emphasis to the 'flippant' comments made by the prime minister on October 16 discussed in chapter 6 ('it all depends who gets to the phone first, he to dismiss me or I to have him recalled')[18] rather than the advice that he received from the Palace. But if a prime minister wants to remove a governor-general, as a later private secretary to the Queen, Sir William Heseltine, made clear in 1982, the process was neither quick nor automatic:

> I can say that, while a telephone call from the Prime Minister might have frozen the situation, Her Majesty certainly could not, and would not have acted on the basis merely of a telephone conversation to dismiss her Governor-General. Some formal instrument, whether transmitted by mail or cable would most certainly have been required.[19]

This was made obvious to Kerr in his correspondence with the Palace prior to the dismissal.

In the letter of October 2, 1975, to Kerr, the Queen's private secretary Sir Martin Charteris made the complexity of the process of the removal of a governor-general very clear: 'If such an approach was made you may be sure that The Queen would take most unkindly to it. There would be considerable comings and goings'. However, he also said: 'at the end of the road The Queen, as a Constitutional Sovereign, would have no option but to follow the advice of her prime minister'.[20]

It would seem that Sir John gave more attention to Charteris' second sentence, rather than the first. Moreover, by the time Kerr was writing to Charteris in the following month on November 20, it seems that he had also forgotten what Charteris had earlier advised him when he wrote:

> The issue has arisen here as to whether I should have given him say twenty-four hours to consider whether, after being told of my intention to dismiss him, he would advise a dissolution of the House of Representatives or a double dissolution and go to the people himself. History will doubtless provide an answer to this question but I was in a position where, in my opinion, *I simply could not risk the outcome for the sake of the Monarchy.* If in the period of say twenty-four hours, during which he was considering his position, he advised The Queen in the strongest of terms that I would be immediately dismissed, the position would then have been that either I would in fact be trying to dismiss him whilst he was trying to dismiss me, an impossible position for The Queen, or someone totally

> inexperienced in the developments of the crisis up to that point, be it a new Governor-General or an Administrator who would have to be a State Governor, would be confronted by the same implacable Prime Minister.[21]

This is, however, a remarkable and misleading passage. In it, Kerr had expanded his task beyond what it should have been, as his decisions, which should have been founded on what is best and most appropriate for Australia and its citizens, seem to have based his decisions regarding the reserve powers on what he considered the interests of the Monarchy. But even that misplaced direction of his decision not to warn Whitlam, supposedly in an effort to protect the Monarchy, was also both unjustified and misleading. And that is not only because Kerr had not asked the Crown whether it wished to be protected from exercising one of the Queen's few constitutional roles in Australia but also because there is nothing in the extensive correspondence between Kerr and the Palace (discussed below) that indicates any desire from the Queen or the Palace for the governor-general to play such a prophylactic role.

The other misleading view expressed by Kerr in that quoted passage from November 20 was that state governors taking over his role were 'totally inexperienced' in dealing with the 'same implacable Prime Minister'. Kerr would have known that that view was clearly incorrect in that he had already discussed the developing supply crisis with the two most qualified and expert State Governors at the time (Cutler and Winneke), both of whom had considerable experience in dealing with their own politicians, some of whom would have been very implacable. And they had both advised Kerr that he should have warned Whitlam.

The then New South Wales Governor, Roden Cutler VC, who served in that office between 1966 and 1981, told the ABC's *Four Corners* program in 1995 that Kerr had raised the issue with both him and the Victorian governor, Sir Henry Winneke. Precisely what Winneke advised Kerr was not entirely clear to Cutler, as his recollection was largely confined to Kerr's comment on November 3, 1975, that: 'Henry Winneke does not understand the problem'.[22] But this is a very odd observation for the man who, in addition to having been Victoria's Chief Justice for a decade, between 1964 and 1974, then became the State's Governor for almost another decade, between 1974 and 1982. Winneke had also been Victoria's Solicitor-General in 1952, the last occasion when supply had been rejected in Australia by an Upper House, and when a Governor had refused advice for a general election because of that insufficient supply.[23] It would seem that if anyone had understood Kerr's position, Winneke would have had (and did have), a greater appreciation of what was required. In Winneke's biography, his biographer, Robert Coleman, records that Winneke 'remembered having a long discussion with Sir John Kerr on the constitutional implications of the crisis' and that he had 'no doubt in his mind that Sir John Kerr had power to act as he did and that he was justified in doing so'. But according to Coleman, Winneke was also 'astonished that Sir John had not discussed his proposed action in advance with Mr Whitlam, which . . . he would have done had he been placed in the same situation'. Furthermore, 'It never occurred to him from their discussion . . . that the Governor-General would not do this'.[24]

As to Cutler, his views match those of Winneke. From his account to *Four Corners* in 1995, he had told Kerr as early as October 20, 1975, that he should warn Whitlam: 'I did say that I thought that he should talk to Whitlam and that, after all, is the requirement'.[25] Cutler had also told Kerr on the morning of November 11, according to Whitlam, that 'he thought his proposed action was wrong' as well as his highly accurate and prospective view, that it 'would prove damaging to the Crown and the office of Governor-General'.[26] Sadly, for Kerr (as well as for Whitlam and the Australian community), having sought and received advice from those with expertise and experience in the vice-regal role, Kerr ignored it. And Kerr never mentioned any of that advice to the Palace.

Other governors-general and governors have also recognized Sir John's error in operating in secrecy due to any perceived fear of potential action by Whitlam. Indeed, Bill Hayden, who had been a senior minister in the Whitlam government before being his successor as leader of the ALP and then governor-general for a longer period than Kerr, between 1989 and 1996, expressed the view in 1998 that if Whitlam had sought to have Kerr's commission withdrawn, it 'would not have been proceeded with. There would have been prudent delays and we would have been forced . . . to sort these sorts of matters out ourselves'.[27] Similar views were expressed by Sir William McKell (a former Labor premier of NSW who had been Australia's governor-general between 1947 and 1953), who considered that 'Kerr's problem was he lacked the political nous to handle the situation'.[28]

Both Hayden[29] and McKell were also critical of Kerr's secrecy in not informing and warning Whitlam of his intention. McKell, whom Kerr regarded as having been an 'excellent Governor-General', was clear that he would have openly warned of his intentions. He has expressed his view that he 'would have called both Mr Whitlam and Mr Fraser to Yarralumla and warned them I would have to intervene unless the crisis was resolved by a specific date'.[30] Their views reflect those of Mason (discussed earlier in chapter 8) but also those of the former governor of Victoria, Richard McGarvie quoted earlier.

The views of Hayden, McKell and McGarvie might, however, be countered by their own preferences, based on their own ALP backgrounds. That, however, cannot be said of the views of Sir John Kerr's predecessor as

Governor-General Sir Paul Hasluck. Hasluck had been a senior Liberal Party minister between 1951 and 1969 before serving as governor-general between 1969 and 1974. He wrote a memorandum on August 10, 1977, which concerned the activities of Sir John Kerr. Hasluck's observation was that 'in a constitutional monarchy the wisdom is to avoid confrontation and never let an issue come to a crisis in a political sense'.[31] In Hasluck's view, as summarized by Professor Twomey, he 'saw the 1975 dismissal as a failure by Kerr to exercise his functions of counselling and warning when needed'.[32] And by that failure, Hasluck considered, as Twomey put it, that Kerr had allowed 'the crisis to build until such time as it had to be resolved'.[33]

Kerr's approach also fails to assess the reality of Whitlam taking any action to remove Kerr. Although Whitlam did say, immediately after his sacking, at his press conference, that he would have communicated with the Queen had Kerr warned him of his intentions,[34] with his objective having been, as one of the participants in the Lodge meeting, Fred Daly, recalls, to 'sack Kerr',[35] those views seem to have been their instinctive and immediate reaction to the dismissal. And like most of the other items discussed in that short and stunned Lodge meeting, as seen in the next chapter, were ill-considered reactions to Kerr's actions. Whitlam's more thoughtful reaction was made much later. As he said in the ABC's *Four Corners* program in 1995: 'If I had removed the Governor-General, surreptitiously, I'd be as popular and respected as Kerr became for removing me surreptitiously'.[36] This seems to reflect the earlier views of Sir Paul Hasluck of Whitlam; as a leader, he was both 'conscious of the judgement of history as well as immediate advantage', being 'very responsive to a question or a cautionary word'.[37] But Kerr was not willing to provide Whitlam with any of his cautionary words as his main priority seems to have been to maintain his own vice-regal office, rather than to advise his prime minister.

Kerr has minimized his role to warn Whitlam, and it is remarkable how little attention was given to the right to warn in the documents that supported the dismissal. Neither Barwick's letter of advice to Kerr of November 10 nor Kerr's *Statement of Reasons for the dismissal of Gough Whitlam* mentioned Bagehot (discussed in chapter 8) and his 'right to warn'. As to Kerr's, *Matters for Judgment*, there was also no mention of Bagehot, but he did include one isolated reference to the right to 'advise and warn', but only by minimising that right to what was 'prudent' to the governor-general. To understand how he had limited his 'right' to warn, it is necessary to repeat what Kerr had said. Making reference to his discussion with Whitlam on, or shortly before[38] October 14, when he questioned the wisdom of governing without supply, Kerr had said:

> 'Wouldn't it be better to go to an election even if you lose. . . . You are still young and, even if you lose now, if you play your cards right you could easily

have a second term as Prime Minister'. In saying this I was going as far, as Governor-General, as I could prudently go in the exercise of my right to 'advise and warn'.[39]

Three arguments have been made to minimize the relevance of Bagehot's right to warn in relation to 1975. The first was that it was not necessary as Whitlam was already aware of Kerr's power to dismiss. That can be seen from his apparently 'flippant' comments at the dinner with the Malaysian prime minister on October 16 discussed in chapter 6. Kerr also relied on what Whitlam told him on November 3, to support his no-warning position:

> Mr Whitlam told me that the only way for an election for the House could occur would be if I dismissed him. The expression he used was: if I were willing 'to do a Philip Game'.[40] This revealed him to be taking into account the possibility that I might exercise the reserve power.[41]

Whitlam has denied making such comments to Kerr.[42] But even if he made it, an understanding that a power to sack exists is not the same as being aware that such a power is being contemplated for potential exercise.

Barwick has also provided two other minimization arguments: that the three Bagehot rights do not constitute an obligation and that they have no relevance to the exercise of the reserve power to dismiss.[43] The last argument seems to have ignored the only other Australian precedent of the dismissal of a head of government by a governor, when the governor of NSW, Sir Philip Game, sacked the premier, Jack Lang, in 1932. When that power was exercised, it was preceded by the right of warning when Governor Game advised Lang that 'If Ministers are not prepared to abide by the law, then I must state without any hesitation that it is their bounden duty under the law and practice of the Constitution to tender their resignations'.[44]

Kerr seems not to have adopted that 'no relevance' argument, but relied on the other Barwick, 'no obligation' view judging from his only publicly available[45] interview on the 1975 dismissal, which occurred in 1987 to Geoffrey Robertson[46] and in his 1985 *Bulletin* article.[47] There he expressly denied that the Bagehot right to warn was an obligation when he strongly expressed the view that 'There is no convention that the Governor-General must advise and must warn'. His view was that there was no obligation or duty to warn, but that he had an option or discretion to do so.[48] He considered that his actions were consistent with Bagehot, who, as he understood it, 'does *not say* that the Crown has a duty to warn in such circumstances'.[49]

But by saying that, Kerr has ignored or rejected or forgotten the advice that he had been provided by Anthony Mason and by Governors Cutler and Winneke discussed above. Each of them advised that a warning should have been made. As Governor Cutler has said: 'that, after all, is the requirement'.[50]

Anthony Mason, in the statement that he released on August 23, 2012, was also specific about what he claims that he had advised Kerr regarding the need to provide a warning to Whitlam:

- he should warn the prime minister that he would terminate his commission if he did not agree to hold a general election;[51]
- if he did not warn the prime minister, he would run the risk that people would accuse him of being deceptive;[52]
- if he were to publish our discussions, he would need to record that I had said that he should warn the prime minister and give him the option of calling a general election;[53] and
- the advice concerning the provision of a warning [by Mason to Kerr] was not heeded.[54]

Mason importantly also referred to the function of providing a warning to the prime minister as more than just an option, but as 'a duty',[55] advice that Kerr clearly also did not accept.

In *Matters for Judgment*, Kerr said nothing else about his power to warn and did not express a view as to whether it is a right or a duty. His view was that he considered his 'proper behaviour . . . [was] to stay at my post and not invite dismissal' and that he 'should keep silence about my thinking unless and until I decided I must act'.[56] In other words, he seems of the view that his right to warn is only to be exercised if it would not place his post at risk. In his view, as he told Geoffrey Robertson in 1987, 'it would have been impossible to have done it more openly and stay there. . . . But there was much more at stake in that decision that you seem to realise'.[57]

But for Kerr to have taken the 'stay at my post' position in preference to warning his prime minister, in addition to ignoring the advice that he had received from Mason as well as Governors Cutler and Winneke, he also seems to have taken a very different position to that taken by Cutler and Winneke as to the nature of the post that he was so desperate to maintain. As Cutler told the ABC *Four Corners* program in 1995:

> a Governor-General or a Governor, should never be worried about the security of their job. I think it's always on the line. And I think Sir John Kerr was not really prepared to put it on the line. I think that he intentionally meant to deceive Mr Whitlam and not give any intention of what he might do.[58]

Similarly, Governor Winneke of Victoria, according to the former Liberal Party Premier of that State, the late Dick Hamer, told *Four Corners* that 'he made it clear to me that he [Sir John Kerr] had not acted correctly; that he should have consulted with Mr Whitlam, even presumably at the cost of Mr Whitlam trying to get him dismissed'.[59]

NOTES

1. Kerr, *Matters,* 297.
2. Kerr, *Matters,* 297–298.
3. Kerr, *Matters,* 298.
4. See Killey, *Constitutional Conventions,* 238.
5. See Department of Prime Minister and Cabinet, "Special Article, Caretaker and Other Pre-Election Practices," in *Department of Prime Minister and Cabinet, Annual Report, 1986–87* (Canberra: Australian Government Publishing Service, 1987), 39.
6. Caretaker arrangements are discussed in detail in Twomey, *Veiled Sceptre*, chap. 6 and Killey, *Constitutional Conventions,* chap. 10.
7. Australian Government, Department of Prime Minister and Government, *Guidance on Caretaker Conventions, 2021*, 3.4. Also see 3.5. As to the convention consultation requirements in earlier elections, see "Caretaker Conventions and Other Pre-Election Practices," *Department of Prime Minister and Cabinet*, Annual Report, 1986–87, 39, 41. See, for example, the discussion of consultation with the Opposition.
8. Smith, *Head of State,* 272. Also see Smith, "Whitlam Could have had More Time," 11.
9. Kerr, *Matters,* 296–298.
10. Letter from John Kerr to Martin Charteris, November 17, 1975, available in Kelly & Bramston, *Truth, Palace Letters,* 218–220, where Kerr said, at 218, "November 11 was the last day for action if an election of any kind was to be held before Christmas."
11. Kerr, *Matters*, 298.
12. Kerr, *Matters,* 298.
13. Kerr, *Matters*, 341.
14. This issue was raised by Ian Killey, "Letters: The Whitlam Shambles," *Quadrant*, July–August 2005, 7–8. David Smith attempted to respond to this letter but ignored the caretaker issue in his response – see David Smith, "Letters: Whitlam Could Have Had More Time," *Quadrant,* September 2005, 11.
15. Markwell has argued that Kerr had given Whitlam a very limited warning on November 11, 1975. This seems a reconstruction, inconsistent with Kerr's letter of that day to the Palace made that day, and to be not correct. This is discussed in Ch 7. See Markwell, *Australian Experience*, 153 and Kerr, *Matters,* 358–359.
16. Quoted in Killey, *Constitutional Conventions,* 205.
17. Kerr, *Matters,* 309.
18. Whitlam, *The Truth,* 130.
19. Quoted in Killey, *Constitutional Conventions,* 208, from V. Bogdanor and G. Marshall, "Dismissing Governor-Generals" [1996] *Public Law* 205, 208.
20. Letter from Sir Martin Charteris to Sir John Kerr, October 2, 1975, a copy of which can be found in Kelly & Bramston, *Truth, Palace Letters,* 200–201.
21. Which can be found in National Archives of Australia, *The Kerr Palace Letters,* AA1984/609, Part 2. Emphasis added.
22. *Four Corners* (1995) 33.25.

23. This incident is summarised in chapter 9 and in Killey, *Constitutional Conventions,* 170–171.

24. Robert Coleman, *Above Renown* (South Melbourne, Victoria: Macmillan, 1988), 340.

25. *Four Corners* (1995), 22.40-22.46. It is, however, to be noted that these discussions are not included in his biography – see Colleen McCullough, *The Courage and the Will* (London: Weidenfeld and Nicolson, 1999).

26. Whitlam, *The Truth,* 158.

27. Quoted in Killey, *Constitutional Conventions,* 209.

28. Quoted in McGarvie, *Democracy,* 170. McKell's preferred approach, however, also seems problematic as it would have required the Queen to refuse to exercise her constitutional role. That is, McKell "would have alerted the Queen not to take any call from Gough if he tried to involve her."

29. Hayden's views can be found in Hayden, *Hayden,* 238 & 294, and are discussed in more detail in chapter 12.

30. Quoted in Kerr, "Kerr Rejects 'ambush' Myth," 79.

31. Quoted in Twomey, "From Bagehot to Brexit," 421.

32. Twomey, "From Bagehot to Brexit," 421.

33. Twomey, "From Bagehot to Brexit," 42.

34. "Whitlam's Post-Dismissal Press Conference," 4.

35. Quoted in Fred Daly, *From Curtin to Hawke* (Sun Books, South Melbourne, 1984), 231.

36. *Four Corners* (1995), 39.25-39.42.

37. Quoted in Twomey, "From Bagehot to Brexit," 421.

38. Kerr, *Matters,* 254.

39. Kerr, *Matters,* 254.

40. A reference to the NSW Governor in 1932 who dismissed Premier Lang.

41. Kerr, *Matters,* 292.

42. *Four Corners* (1995), 31.40-31.45.

43. Barwick, *Sir John,* 113–114 and Barwick, *Radical Tory,* 295; see Killey, *Constitutional Conventions,* 206.

44. The correspondence is detailed in "The Correspondence between Governor and Mr Lang," *Sydney Morning Herald,* May 14, 1932, 13; Twomey, "The Dismissal of the Lang Government"; and in Bethia Foott, *Dismissal of a Premier (The Philip Game Papers)* (Sydney, NSW: Morgan, 1968), 209–210. Also see Evatt, *Dominion Governors,* 164–165 and Killey, *Constitutional Conventions,* 207.

45. John Kerr gave an interview to Suzanne Lunney in 1976 that is held in the National Library of Australia. But while the interview is expressed to be "Available" in both recorded and transcript form, requests for that material are denied due to "access conditions relating to this material." That is, "Written permission required from Sir John Kerr's executor for research, personal copies and public use until 2041." See National Library of Australia, *John Kerr Interviewed by Suzanne Lunney [sound recording],* 1976. https://catalogue.nla.gov.au/catalog/2074277.

46. *Talking Shop* (1987).

47. Kerr, "Kerr Rejects 'ambush' Myth," 72.
48. *Talking Shop* (1987), 23.30-23.50.
49. Kerr, "Kerr Rejects 'ambush' Myth," 75 (Emphasis original).
50. *Four Corners* (1995), 22.40–22.46.
51. Mason, *Conversations with Kerr* [7] that can be found in Kelly & Troy Bramston, *The Dismissal,* 391.
52. Mason, *Conversations with Kerr* [26] that can be found in Kelly & Bramston, *The Dismissal,* 396.
53. Mason, *Conversations with Kerr* [31] that can be found in Kelly & Bramston, *The Dismissal,* 397.
54. Mason, *Conversations with Kerr* [7] that can be found in Kelly & Bramston, *The Dismissal,* 391.
55. Mason, *Conversations with Kerr* [34] that can be found in Kelly & Bramston, *The Dismissal,* 398.
56. Kerr, *Matters,* 309–310.
57. *Talking Shop* (1987), 24.50–25.00.
58. *Four Corners* (1995), 33.45–34.10.
59. *Four Corners* (1995), 33.30–33.45.

Chapter 10

1975

And the Errors of Whitlam

Figure 10.1 ALP political badges from the 1975 election; from the collection of the author. Image taken by the author.

While most discussions of the 1975 dismissal have concentrated on errors or perceived duplicity of those who ambushed and disposed of Whitlam and his government (that is, Kerr, Barwick and Fraser), there is one other issue that few have recognized or discussed – the errors that Whitlam himself had made. And he made many. As this chapter will indicate, Whitlam's errors, particularly those made on November 11, were of such significance that, had Whitlam chosen to operate very differently on that day, he still may have saved his government and been reappointed as prime minister. But to understand that issue, it is first necessary to understand what Whitlam did once he was sacked by Kerr, which occurred at around 1 to 1.10 pm on November 11, 1975.[1] And then, to consider what he might have done.

To find out what he did, and did not do after his dismissal, the best evidence is found in the works by those who were there, particularly in Whitlam's *The Truth of the Matter*, and in the earliest post-dismissal biography of Whitlam written by his great speech-writer, Graham Freudenberg. And from those sources, we find that Whitlam's first action was to return to the prime minister's residence, the Lodge, and to telephone his wife, Margaret, who was then at the prime minister's official residence in Sydney, Kirribilli House.[2] Her response was simple although it was also, as Whitlam recognized, both unconstitutional and ineffective – 'Why didn't you just tear it up?'[3]

His next telephone calls were to his key contacts, and in Whitlam's account, the first of them was his department head, John Menadue,[4] and then his Principal Private Secretary, John Mant.[5] Freudenberg records that those calls were made at 1.15 pm but he also maintains that he was one of the first two summoned by Whitlam.[6]

Despite that difference, there is no disagreement as to what occurred next. Whitlam asked his first two key contacts to come to the Lodge, but without telling them why. Mant was also asked to call other essential ALP colleagues and for them to also come to the Lodge.[7] And then Whitlam sat down to have a steak.[8] As he later recalled, 'The condemned man ate a healthy meal, although, on this occasion, the normal order was reversed. I had my steak *after* the execution'.[9] That line seems to indicate that Whitlam had then believed that there was little he could do about his dismissal other than lunch and theatrics. If that is the case, this may well explain what next occurred; but that is also, as we will see, far from accurate.

The first to arrive at the Lodge, according to Freudenberg, were Mant and Freudenberg, and it was only then that Whitlam told them that he had been sacked – which he later repeated to his other colleagues and advisers when they arrived. But they had little time to advise Whitlam at that meeting. Fred Daly, the Minister for Administrative Services, recalls that he was told of the meeting at 1.20 pm and that the length of the meeting was less than twenty minutes, as he arrived at the Lodge at 1.40 pm, and left prior to 2.00 pm.[10] And as those attending were not advised prior to their attendance what the purpose of the meeting was, they were not much help in assisting Whitlam. Indeed, once Whitlam told them that they had been sacked by Kerr, they were left, as Freudenberg recalls, in a catatonic state,[11] or, as Daly more colourfully put it, they were like 'stunned mullets'.[12] As a result, as Whitlam accepts, little was gained from this meeting. He records its discussion as being 'rather disjointed and fairly desultory'.[13] It seems, however, that Whitlam expected little from his advisers. According to Kelly and Bramston, Mant considered that Whitlam's approach at that meeting was 'symptomatic of the whole problem' of Whitlam's government: 'there was no sense of team because Gough's view was that everyone else was largely useless and they were pissants – and he was right'.[14]

And those disjointed and desultory 'pissants' at the Lodge on that day included, as well as Menadue, Mant, Freudenberg and Fred Daly; the deputy prime minister, Frank Crean; the attorney-general, Kep Enderby (who Kelly and Bramston assert, somewhat harshly, was 'an incompetent');[15] the Speaker of the House, Gordon Scholes; and the ALP's national secretary, David Combe.[16] Notable by their absence is the lack of any senators at that meeting, even though the Supply Bills were still in the Senate.

Three things need to be seen about Whitlam's actions that afternoon. The first is that he told no one before the meeting, other than his wife, that he had been dismissed. As a result, none of Whitlam's key advisers knew, at least from Whitlam[17] about Kerr's actions, or what to do about them, until they arrived at the Lodge. As such, Whitlam had further limited the ability of his 'useless' advisers to advise him.

Second, when they did arrive at the Lodge, the concentration of the meeting ignored the powers of the House, where the important supply legislation still sat – the Senate. Instead, the concentration was on the reaction in the House of Representatives that afternoon, but also on the irrelevancy of seeking constitutional assistance to save the dismissed government from someone with no power to assist; that is, the Queen.

Third, and most importantly, the Lodge meeting also did not consider how the powers in the Lower House may still have helped and possibly saved the Whitlam government – even at that late stage.

But to appreciate the second and third points, a bit more explanation is needed.

POWERS OF THE SENATE

Whitlam gave no attention to how he could still gain control over supply or even to the role that the Senate could still play. To Kelly and Bramston, 'Nothing better illustrated his lack of contingency planning'[18] than this flaw. And that failure can be seen from (to use Mant's word) the 'pissants' that Whitlam invited to the Lodge to plan the ALP's response to Australia's greatest constitutional crisis, including no Labor senators. That absence was, as the then Clerk of the Senate J. R. Odgers said, 'extraordinary'.[19] Labor's Senate Leader, Ken Wriedt, in particular, was not invited or told of the dismissal; and the reason for that remarkable error was a combination, according to Kelly and Bramston, of Whitlam's low opinion of Wriedt as a 'backslider', and

Whitlam's myopic concentration on the Lower House as the 'only place that had any meaningful role'.[20] In Hocking's view, this was 'a matter of logistics as much as flawed political strategy'.[21] Whether the first of those assessments is accurate or not, the second is clearly correct, as well as being something of an understatement. And that can be seen when we consider what occurred in the Senate that afternoon.

Oddly, Michael Sexton SC, the current NSW Solicitor-General, who was then working in the Attorney-General's office, has asserted that there was a senator included at the Lodge meeting, being Senator Jim McClelland (then Minister for Labour and Immigration). This statement was included in his book, *The Great Crash*[22] and in his chapter in Troy Bramston's 2013 book, *The Whitlam Legacy*.[23] If this is true, it provides some defence to Whitlam for his lack of information to Labor senators. But it is puzzling why Whitlam would have told just one senator, and a very junior one at that (Jim McClelland had only been a minister for less than a year),[24] while not advising the Labor leadership in the Senate, being Senator Ken Wreidt, or the Manager of Government Business in the Senate, Doug McClelland (no relation to Jim). However, the Sexton version has larger problems, as it is not reflected in the accounts of those who were actually at the Lodge meeting. Neither Whitlam,[25] Freudenberg[26] nor Menadue[27] recall any senator being at the Lodge meeting on that day, much less have included Jim McClelland – which seems to indicate that the Sexton version regarding McClelland is, at least, questionable.

But it seems even less than that when the account of Jim McClelland is considered. It rejects the Sexton story. In his political autobiography, published in 1988, *Stirring the Possum*, McClelland gives his account of what he did on the day of the dismissal:

> A few minutes after 1 pm on 11 November I was sitting in my broom closet of an office trying to combine the digestion of some ministerial files with some soggy Parliament House sandwiches. My staff was out to lunch so when the phone rang I answered it myself. It was Lionel Murphy ringing from the High Court. He told me in tones of horror and disbelief that his daughter had just informed him on the phone that the Whitlam government had been dismissed. 'Don't believe it, Lionel', I said, 'There are all sorts of silly rumours flying around'.
>
> A few moments later a member of my staff put his head around my door and said: 'No need to worry about those files, boss. We're all out of work.' I went to my drinks cabinet and poured myself a triple whisky. At the same time, as it later transpired, Gough having returned to the Lodge, was tucking into a big steak. I have sometimes wondered what it would take to put him off his food.[28]

There are some obvious problems with this account, such as how would Lionel Murphy or his daughter know about the sacking 'A few minutes after 1 pm' when the sacking was happening at that time. Any information regarding Whitlam's sacking flowing to Lionel Murphy's daughter, or to McClelland's unnamed staff member, must have occurred much later, and it seems difficult to see how it could have been at any time earlier than 1.30 pm. In any case, it remains unclear why Murphy's telephone call 'in tones of horror' was limited to McClelland and, more importantly, why McClelland confined his response, as Hocking put it:

> to go to his drinks cabinet 'pour myself a triple whiskey' and say nothing. McClelland did not reveal this to any of his Senate colleagues, returned to the Senate after lunch and voted for the Whitlam government's budget bills, knowing that this would grant Supply to the Fraser government.[29]

The McClelland account confirms the extraordinary lack of organization and effectiveness on the Whitlam front bench. But it also confirms that the Sexton version of the Lodge meeting and its attendees simply cannot be correct.[30]

In the Senate, after the luncheon break, as Freudenberg recalls it, Wriedt was 'in total ignorance' about the dismissal. As such, he:

> was delighted when Senator Withers told him that the Budget would at last be allowed to pass. Wriedt thought that the crisis was over and that the expected had at last happened and the Opposition had caved in.[31]

A more detailed version was provided by Kelly and Bramston:

> The Senate had resumed at 2 pm in a state of confusion. The government leader, Ken Wriedt, was not told of the dismissal. The Senate president, Justin O'Byrne, was not informed. Nor did the manager of government business, Doug McClelland, know. The opposition senators, however, led by Reg Withers, did know.[32]

According to those two authors, Wreidt did suspect that something may have gone wrong, saying to his deputy, Don Willesee, and to Senator Doug McClelland:

> 'There's something strange here', he said. 'I cant see why they've changed their minds.' Wriedt walked across to [Labor's] John Button. 'There's a story going around that the government's been sacked,' Button told him. 'Don't be bloody ridiculous' Wreidt said. 'Send somewhat to check it.'[33]

Here we have different accounts of what happened next. One is from a note for the file prepared by parliamentary liaison officer, M. J. Hanson, dated

November 20, 1975, on which Kelly and Bramston have relied.[34] According to Hanson's contemporary account, he had been advised by his counterpart in the House at around 2.00 pm of the dismissal, and he advised Wriedt, who sought confirmation from the prime minister's office. Hanson also told Doug McClelland, but he was unable to confirm the news. By 2.10 pm (Sexton says 2.15 pm),[35] 'clarification arrived from Whitlam's office that the government had been dismissed. This was conveyed to Wriedt and McClelland'.[36] However, Hanson made, according to Kelly and Bramston, an additional and confusing comment: 'At no stage had they received any communication from Mr Whitlam's office advising that Mr Fraser was now Prime Minister and that they were no longer Ministers.'[37] How that can be if Whitlam had been dismissed, Hanson, Kelly and Bramston do not explain. It remains puzzling, if this account is accurate, why Wriedt did not, at least, appreciate the significance of the information that Hanson said he received from the PM's office. That is, once he had been told by the prime minister's office that the head of the government had been dismissed, why Wriedt would then not have realized that the dismissal would have had some relevance to the office that he held.

Wriedt's version, however, is very different. According to the version he provided for Nolan's book on *The Dismissal*, he made no reference to any information from the PM's office, but he refers to a query he received at 2.16 pm from Senator Button. Button had heard from a couple of journalists that Whitlam had been sacked[38] and, according to Wriedt, Button expressed the view that 'there were rumours that the government had been dismissed'. But to Wreidt, 'I simply did not believe it'. And in Wriedt's view, expressed in 2005, he 'would not act on the basis of rumour' and he would not have 'adopted any procedure in the Senate that was contrary to [the budget bills] . . . without an official communication from the House'. On that day Wreidt remained: 'quite confident that if anything of substance affecting Message No 406 [the message to pass the two appropriation bills] I would have been advised, probably by a visit from the Prime Minister'.[39] And as that hadn't happened, at 2.20 pm Wriedt reintroduced the supply bills, and within four minutes, that motion was voted on. Both sides of the House supported and passed supply for the new government led by Malcolm Fraser, although that was not appreciated by, at least, almost half of them.

Whatever version of the information that went to Senator Wriedt during that twenty-minute period on November 11 is accurate, we will never know. But it seems clear that Hanson's other observation regarding the 'pervading sense of "confusion" in the Senate that afternoon'[40] was correct. And it also seems apparent that the high level of confusion among ALP senators would not have occurred had the prime minister invited any of them to the Lodge after his dismissal. But he didn't.

In Kelly and Bramston's view, the passage of the supply bills through the Senate was the end of Labor's chances of survival. Once the Senate provided supply, 'Labor's only hope of thwarting Fraser had been extinguished'.[41] And in their more recent book, they expressed a similar view, 'When Fraser became Prime Minister on 11 November he only needed to pass Supply in the Senate'.[42] This is, however, not correct as there may have been other steps, using the powers of the Lower House, that Whitlam should have taken, or at least considered, had he given more thought to the relationship between the elements of Australia's Parliament.

But before discussing this, it is necessary to discuss what Labor could have done in the Senate had Whitlam included Wriedt in his group of stunned mullet confidants at the Lodge. This was discussed as early as 1976 by Lloyd and Clark in their *Kerr's King Hit* when they said:

> If Supply had not gone thorough so quickly at 2.20pm Fraser would have had some difficulties. If Labor had delayed supply by using the forms of the Senate even to the point of physical disruption, the 'No confidence' would have had much more substance. Fraser would have been without supply and with his Government defeated in the House of Representatives. . . . With Fraser having difficult in fulfilling the Governor-General's basic requirement – the passing of supply – it is possible that Kerr would have to reassess the situation later in the afternoon.[43]

Lloyd and Clark did, however, consider that Labors' tactics were only a short-term delay – as in their view 'Labor Senators could not have delayed the budget bills for more than a few hours at the most, but the effort should have been made; it might have turned the tables'.[44]

This, however, seems an undue limitation on the Senate's power and influence. The Labor senator and minister in the Whitlam government, John Wheeldon[45] advised the *Australian* newspaper in 1985 that:

> If the Labor senators had known what was known to Whitlam there would have been many means open to us to stop the Bills, including, for example, adjourning the Senate. If this had happened Kerr and Fraser would have been in such a mess that we would have profited from it.[46]

It is true that Labor was in a minority in the Senate, but the coalition also did not have an absolute majority in that House. At that time, the Senate's membership was 60 senators, 30 of whom were Coalition senators, 27 were government senators, and there were three independents. However, of those three senators, one (Senator Field from Queensland) had been given leave of absence on October 1, 1975, due to a High Court challenge to his eligibility to sit in the Senate, and the other two independents had voted consistently with the government on the appropriation bills.[47] That gave the opposition a slender majority of just one on supply issues, but not an absolute majority. And that slender majority required all opposition senators to stand by their leader and not 'cross the floor'. And, as the Parliamentary study of crossing the floor conducted by McKeown and Lundy in 2020[48] points out, Members of Parliament from both the Liberal Party and the National (Country) Party, unlike the ALP, are not subject to any formal pledge to vote and support party policy. And Coalition MPs are also, unlike the ALP MPs, not subject to automatic expulsion or suspension from their parties for crossing the floor. As a result, as McKeown and Lundy calculated, the vast majority of MPs having crossed the floor were from those two Coalition parties: 'the Coalition accounted for 90.2% of the individual MPs who crossed the floor compared to Labor's 9.8%'.[49]

But even if, in 1975, all Coalition senators had chosen not to cross the floor, as Fraser would have hoped, that would not have prevented the powers of the Senate from being used to hamper the change of government. This issue was dealt with, in some detail, in the 1991 edition of Odgers' *Australian Senate Practice.*[50]

> If the Senate had been informed of the dismissal of the Whitlam Ministry, the course of events might have been different. For example, the Australian Labor Party Senators could have delayed the calling on of the Appropriation Bills by moving motions to bring on other business. Having a majority, the Liberal-National Country Party Senators would eventually have taken charge of the business of the Senate, but they would have had problems. If Senator Withers had moved the motion proposed by Senator Wreidt [that is, that the Standing Orders are suspended and that the Appropriation Bills be passed with no further debate or amendment],[51] and if the motion had been opposed by the Australian Labor Party Senators, it would have failed unless carried by 31 affirmative votes being an absolute majority for the suspension of Standing Orders without notice as required by SO 448. To muster 31 votes, the support of Senator Steele Hall (Liberal Movement) or Senator Bunton (Independent) would have been required. There were, therefore, procedures and circumstances which might have upset any timetable for a dissolution of the Parliament on 11 November 1975, but the final act could only have been delayed, not changed.[52]

As Odgers said, this Senate delay of the supply bills would have only been for the short term at most, but that short-term delay itself may well have been sufficient to upset the Kerr plan, which was 'If . . . the reserve powers were to be exercised and a general election produced before Christmas, 11 November would be the last day for decision'.[53] Delaying the budget in the Senate for even a day may well have prevented that from occurring.

POWERS OF THE LOWER HOUSE

But if Labor had not adopted delaying measures in the Senate, there may have been more it could still have done. And, again, Odgers suggests how that could have been done. That is:

> the House could have instructed the Speaker that the Bills were not to be presented to the Governor-General for assent.[54]

Before discussing this method, however, it is necessary to review what occurred on November 11, 1975, after Whitlam's dismissal by Kerr at or around 1.00 pm. Those salient events are:

- That Fraser was appointed as a so-called caretaker Prime Minister at or before 1.30 pm.[55]
- The Senate reconvened at 2.00 pm, and had passed the supply bills by 2.24 pm, when the sittings of the Senate were suspended.
- Meanwhile, the House of Representatives had also reconvened at 2.00 pm. It initially continued to debate the censure motion of the Whitlam government moved that morning by Fraser, even though by 2.00 pm Whitlam was no longer Prime Minister. Nonetheless, that debate still continued after 2.00 pm with the speech by the former Deputy Prime Minister, Frank Crean, who still referred to the coalition as the Opposition, indicating that he had not appreciated or understood what he had heard earlier in the Lodge meeting.[56] In any case, that debate was ended with a division which the former government, the ALP, won by 7 votes, 63 to 56. It was only then, at 2.34 pm, that Fraser advised the House that the governor-general had commissioned him to form a government until elections could be held.[57] He advised the House that the 'purpose of the commission is to permit a deadlock between the Houses of Parliament to be resolved and to return Australia to stable government' and advised that he had agreed to act in a caretaker capacity. He also stated that he had agreed with the governor-general to 'immediately seek to secure the passage of the Appropriation Bills which are at present before the Senate', at which point Whitlam interjected with the comment 'They have been passed'.[58] This indicated that Whitlam's ability to procure information was far greater than it was for dissemination. But it also indicated that Whitlam had the relevant facts which he could still have used to save his government.

Fraser then moved that the House adjourn, which the House rejected by 9 votes.[59] After that, Whitlam moved the following motion:

> That this House expresses its want of confidence in the Prime Minister and requests the Speaker to immediately advise His Excellency, the Governor-General, to call the honourable member for Werriwa to form a government

a motion that the new, Fraser-led government lost, after a very short debate, by 10 votes.

After that, the Speaker advised the House that:

> It would be my intention to convey the message of the House to His Excellency at the first opportunity.[60]

The House then received the appropriation or supply bills back from the Senate before the House was suspended at 3.15pm.[61]

What next occurred is best described in Whitlam's account:

> Immediately the standing orders were suspended for me to move the motion against Mr Fraser's appointment, Mr Scholes requested his private secretary Mary Harris to contact the Governor-General's official secretary for a tentative appointment so that he could convey the resolution of the House to the Governor-General as soon as the House rose following the passage of the motion. When he returned to his suite following the passage of the motion Mrs Harris told him that the official secretary had been reached and had said that the Governor-General was very busy and might not have time for additional appointments. The Governor-General was clearly making it as difficult for the Speaker to see him in the afternoon as he made it me to speak to him in the morning.[62]

But a meeting was arranged for 4.45 pm that afternoon for the Speaker to meet with the governor-general. However, before that occurred, the governor-general had dissolved the Lower House, making the House's no-confidence motion in the Fraser government, as Smith observes, 'futile'.[63]

This is where Whitlam and the Speaker of the House of Representatives, Gordon Scholes, might still have saved the day, but most accounts fail to recognize this. Most considerations of the 1975 dismissal and its causes would agree with the view of Kelly and Bramston that 'When Fraser became Prime Minister on 11 November he only needed to pass Supply in the Senate'.[64] But for those who took or still take this view, they have forgotten to wonder how the supply bills got to the governor-general for Assent. They have failed to appreciate that the devil is in the detail – and that detail, on November 11, 1975, may have been seen in a procedural rule that may have been the key tool that Whitlam and Scholes could have considered and used that afternoon.

This procedural rule is found in the Standing Orders of the two Houses, the House of Representatives and the Senate. Constitutionally, Standing Orders are of pretty low significance. They are not part of the *Constitution*, and they are much less important, in most circumstances, than legislation. Indeed, they are not 'part of the general law',[65] and if you go to the web page where Commonwealth statutory laws are kept, the Federal Register of Legislation, you won't even find them.[66] Standing Orders are, however, based on the *Constitution*. Section 50 provides that:

> Each House of the Parliament may make rules and orders with respect to –
>
> (i) The mode in which its powers, privileges, and immunities may be exercised and upheld:
> (ii) The order and conduct of its business and proceedings either separately or jointly with the other House.

And it is from such procedural rules that Whitlam might have saved the day. That is because of what Standing Order 265 of the House of Representatives required. In 1975 that Standing Order provided:

> *265* Every bill originated in the House of Representatives which has finally passed both Houses, shall be presented by the Speaker to the Governor-General for Her Majesty's assent, having been first certified by the signature of the Clerk as having originated in the House, and as having finally passed both Houses.[67]

The Standing Orders of the Senate were and are to the same effect. The then Senate Standing Order was SO 234, which in 1975 read:

> *234* When any such Bill shall have been passed by the Senate with or without Amendment, it shall be returned to the House of Representatives by Message, with the Clerk's certificate that 'This Bill has been agreed to by the Senate without Amendment', or 'with the Amendments indicated by the annexed Schedule', as the case may require; and the concurrence of the House of Representatives shall be desired to such Amendments.[68]

The effect of these Standing Orders is that when a bill that began in the House of Representatives has been passed by the Senate, it does not go directly to the governor-general for Assent but it is returned to the Speaker of the Lower House. It is then the Speaker's obligation to present the bill to the governor-general for Assent – there is no time requirement under the Standing Orders. So, a Speaker, particularly a compliant Speaker such as Gordon Scholes, could have delayed the presentation for hours, days, weeks, or whatever time the Speaker considered necessary for his other obligation under the Standing Orders – to obtain the Clerk's certification that the bill had passed both Houses. And until the supply bills were provided to the governor-general *by the Speaker,* Fraser's ability to provide supply was hampered and possibly prevented – and Kerr was not able to dissolve the Lower House.

As Bill Hayden, a later holder of the office of governor-general, has expressed it,

> Had this occurred chaos could have ensued. The Fraser minority government would then have been without supply. On Kerr's interpretation of a legitimate government being one that could deliver supply, it would have been without legitimacy. This could have left the parliament jammed in grid lock, the community startled and confused and Kerr's plans in tatters.[69]

This is the tool that Whitlam and Scholes could have used, or at least considered.

The late Geoffrey Sawer, then professor Emeritus at Australian National University, made this point in his 1977 work *Federation Under Strain.*[70] As he said, 'neither the Constitution nor the common law impose any duty on the House or its officers to transmit Bills to the Governor-General'.[71] That work identified the relevant standing orders and observed, but sadly with no further explanation, that Scholes 'is thought to have had some doubts about sending the Bills on but he acted in accordance with the Standing Orders'.[72]

Sawer's view may have been based on the views expressed by Scholes in the *Australian* Newspaper of November 1, 1976. Scholes then said that he 'held on the certificate for a while' and 'considered holding it longer. But I decided to let it go – because I could not believe that Kerr would refuse to see me'. But by 1976[73] Scholes also added that:

> Given the chance again and knowing the way I was treated by Kerr – I would neither have signed the certificate nor put it through. I would have taken it to Yarralumla with me and used it as a bargaining point. I am not sure of the technical position on this: but if I had not signed, it would have stopped Supply going forward – and could have made a significant difference to events.[74]

And in Sawer's view, that 'significant difference' was that Labor could have at least delayed and possibly prevented the passage of supply, but only 'if Mr Whitlam and his colleagues had anticipated and planned with more imagination and skill'.[75]

The Speaker also could have, given the unusuality of the circumstances, and as Odgers and Sawer have reminded us,[76] referred the issue back to the House for its directions. As Professor Low (one of the few others who have recognized the significance of this error) observed in 1988:

> Had the Speaker withheld the Bills until he had seen the Governor-General and/or had referred them back to his own House – as would not indeed have been

> unprecedented – the day's outcome could have been disruptively different. But he signed them, and as soon as they got to Government House, Kerr did as well. Australia's government accordingly had supply.[77]

If Scholes had referred the issue back to the Lower House for its direction, it could have resolved, as Sawer observed, 'to suspend the Standing Orders and direct both the Speaker and the Clerk – undoubtedly officers of the House and no one else – to refrain from transmitting the Bills to the Governor-General'.[78] We would then have had a modern and antipodean variation of the great dispute between Charles I and the English Parliament that occurred on January 4, 1642. On that day, Charles I, supported by 400 armed men, entered the chamber of the House of Commons, seeking to seize five members whom the Monarch accused of treason. But when Charles asked the Speaker, William Lenthall, where those five were, the Speaker famously replied: 'I have neither eyes to see nor tongue to speak in this place but as this House is pleased to direct me, whose servant I am here',[79] emphasising that his allegiance was to the liberty of Parliament rather than to the will of the Monarch.

If the Speaker had not provided the supply bills to the governor-general for Assent, Kerr's options would then have rapidly diminished. Transmission of the supply bills for Assent would have been hampered and possibly prevented, and the new prime minister would have had some difficulty in complying with the condition he set out in his letter to the governor-general of November 11, 1975:

> I further confirm that upon the granting of Supply, I shall immediately recommend to Your Excellency the dissolution of both Houses of this Parliament.

However, Michael Sexton SC has taken a different view. He has expressed the view that:

> As for the Speaker's certification in relation to the Bills, a refusal by him to provide this document would not have prevented the Bills being taken to the Governor-General for his assent.[80]

He seemed to have based this conclusion on his earlier expressed view from his book *The Great Crash*: that 'the Speaker's certificate is usual, it is not strictly necessary. A refusal to sign would not have stopped the transmission of the bills to Kerr'.[81] But Sexton provides no explanation or justification for these passages, which seem to have ignored the wording of the Standing Orders, the power of the Lower House to direct the Speaker, as well as, as we will see, the different conclusion that even Whitlam himself later reached.

His argument may, however, be supported by a broader view of the governor-general's powers – that he could have granted Assent to the bills based on the parliamentary record. As Sawer has also observed, 'The Constitution contains nothing which explicitly requires a Bill to come to the Governor-General from the House in which it originates, generally or in relation to money Bills'.[82] But Sawer also seems to have considered that the governor-general must receive a bill for Assent from a House, a view that seems inherent in the following observation:

> An argument that only the House in which a Bill originates can transmit it to the Governor-General could be built on s, 58 of the Constitution, which requires the Governor-General to *return* a Bill which he wishes amended to the House in which it originated.[83]

But if Sawer was incorrect then, so long as the bills were 'presented' as s 58 of the *Constitution* requires,[84] and Fraser would seem capable of doing this despite whatever the Lower House or the Speaker has decided, Kerr could still have provided Assent to the bills.

The Standing Orders may also not be definitive of the control of the legislation they relate to. As McLelland J said in *Namoi SC v Attorney-General (NSW)*, 'the very nature and function of Standing Orders of a legislative House indicates that they should be considered as directory, rather than mandatory'.[85] And, as Professor Twomey has recently concluded, 'Failure to comply with a Standing Order in the passage of a Bill will not affect the validity of the resulting Act'.[86] Courts also will not interfere with parliamentary procedures other than, as Mahoney P observed in *Egan v Willis*, 'special cases'.[87] And, a special case will exist, as Barwick CJ said in *Cormack v Cope*, 'if the constitutionally required process of law-making is not properly carried out'.[88] Whether there is a 'special case' here remains unclear. Cases on Standing Orders are largely confined to the judicial consideration of whether a Court would interfere when the Standing Orders regarding one of the elements of the Parliament may not have been complied with. But here, we are discussing the transmission of bills from one element of the Parliament[89] (the House of Representatives) to another (the governor-general). Whether this would be considered, as Barwick CJ put it, as 'intra-mural' (that is, 'within the walls')[90] of Parliament or not remains unsure.[91] But Barwick also expressed the view, in *Cormack v Cope*, that:

> there is no parliamentary privilege which can stand in the way of this Court's right and duty to ensure that the constitutionally provided methods of law-making are observed.[92]

It is, however, clear that a number of commentators, including Sawer, Odgers, Low and, also Whitlam (eventually, as we will see), regarded the interference in the transmission of the bills from the Lower House as being 'effective'. That can be seen from Sawer's view when he said that a House of Representatives' direction to the Speaker to refrain from transmitting the bills to the governor-general 'would not have been the end of the matter'. But his sole qualification was not that the governor-general could bypass the decision of the Lower House, but that 'it would have been equally open to the Senate majority to suspend the Standing Orders . . . in order to direct the President and Clerk to certify that the Bill (already carrying a certificate of passage by the Representatives . . .) had passed the Senate, and to convey the Bill directly to the Governor-General for his assent'.[93] From that, his view seems reasonably clear that, at least in Sawer's opinion, the only way the governor-general could have received bills for Assent was from one of the two Houses.

Whitlam has also accepted that more thoughtful use of the powers of the Lower House could have derailed the Kerr actions. As he said (even if this concession is buried towards the rear of his book on the dismissal):

> With the wisdom of hindsight we can all see that it would have been wiser if Mr Scholes had taken the Appropriation Bills together with the resolution of the House to his appointment with the Governor-General, instead of sending the Bills ahead of time with the usual message. *This would have been a legitimate and even against Sir John Kerr, an effective tactic.*[94]

This is more than a recognition of Scholes' failure to use a disruptive political device. And that is because the only way that Scholes' retention of the supply bills in his meeting with the governor-general could have been 'effective' was if Kerr had accepted that without the supply bills held by the Speaker, Assent to those bills could not be provided. That is, Whitlam seems to have considered that Kerr would not have the constitutional power to provide Assent without the bills being presented by one of the Houses. Accordingly, if Scholes had retained the bills, Assent would not be possible unless Kerr first reappointed Whitlam.

Whatever accuracy there is to the broader Sexton view of the governor-general's Assent powers, the Speaker did not take any actions to delay presenting the supply bills to the governor-general. Whitlam's account, however, suggests that Scholes may have almost stumbled onto the necessary solution. That occurred after the Speaker's secretary, Mary Harris, was attempting to arrange a time for a meeting between the Speaker and the governor-general after the no-confidence motion in the new Fraser government had been passed but found little willingness from Government House due to, so-called, other business of the governor-general. As a result, Scholes came up with the one method to alter the position of the governor-general, and that was a constitutional threat that the new Fraser government may well have not wanted. That is, according to Whitlam:

> Mr Scholes then told Mrs Harris to inform the official secretary that unless an audience was granted he would recall the House and inform the members and seek further guidance on subsequent action.[95]

As a result, 'The official secretary soon telephoned back with an appointment.'[96] This readiness to avoid a recall of Parliament may indicate that Kerr was aware of the weakness of his position and was concerned that Whitlam might also became aware of it if he properly assessed the powers that were still available to him. This is, of course, speculative, as Kerr's views on this issue are uncertain. All that can be said is that Kerr did seem to have some doubts on this issue. But what thought he had given to his power to provide Assent if the Lower House blocked transmission of the bills to him, we will simply never know. All we know is that he did consider that the Labor Party might have taken some steps 'which might have resulted in the grant of supply being delayed or prevented'. He did not seem to question the effect of those steps, but only felt (accurately) that they were 'unlikely' to be taken. But if those steps were taken, 'they would have to be faced, as they occurred, by the caretaker Government and perhaps by me'.[97] And that's it!

Nonetheless, it is apparent that Kerr did not provide Assent to the bills immediately after they had passed the Senate at 2.24 pm. Instead, he seems to have felt it necessary to await the delivery of the supply bills to Government House from the House of Representatives endorsed 'with the Speaker's request that the Governor-General sign them' before Assent was provided and before he issued his proclamation dissolving both Houses. That delivery began at 3.40 pm when one official, Gordon Clarence Pike, from the Lower House played a significant, if now largely forgotten role in the events of the 1975 dismissal when he took the endorsed supply bills to Government House. As Whitlam recorded, 'Mr Pike reached Government House at 3.50 pm. Mr Fraser's car was already there. The Governor-General was as prompt in complying with the Speaker's request for him to sign the bills as he was being dilatory in complying with the Speaker's request to receive the message from the House'.[98] And as a result of Mr Pike's trip, Kerr did not need to test whether he could provide Assent to bills which the House had decided not to present. Fraser had provided Supply. And that allowed Kerr to then dissolve both Houses, which he did at around 4.30 pm.[99] Whitlam had missed his last possible weapon.

What was the cause of Whitlam's errors of November 11? Was it, as he put it, a matter that required the wisdom of hindsight? Or was it a failure of planning on Whitlam's part? According to Kelly & Bramston, Whitlam's planning was based on having the supply bill passed. They quote Mant, Whitlam's Principal Private Secretary, as saying, in relation to the Lodge discussions: 'So we sat around and the focus of conversation was all about getting supply passed and moving of a vote of "confidence"'. If that happened, Whitlam believed that 'Then Kerr will have to dismiss Fraser'.[100] No-one seems to have anticipated what would happen if Fraser's primary aim was to have an election, and to do that, he also needed the supply bill passed. As Fraser later told the House:

> It will be my sole purpose to ensure that Australia has the general election to which it is constitutionally entitled and which has so far been denied it.

But no one at the Lodge seems to have anticipated that Fraser's actions would be what he stated in his letter to the governor-general of November 11, 1975:

> I further confirm that, upon the granting of Supply, I shall immediately recommend to Your Excellency the dissolution of both Houses of this Parliament.[101]

Supply was, therefore, the key to the Fraser approach and his undertaking to the Governor General. So, if Whitlam was going to save his government, he needed to ensure that Fraser did not have and use that key. And as we have seen, he still had the weapons to defer and possibly prevent it. But he didn't use those weapons or even consider them. And the responsibility for that failure is Whitlam's alone.

Kelly and Bramston, however, seem to argue that the use of the Lower House would only have been available if the 'prophetic' recommendations of the Prime Minister's and Attorney-General's departments had been accepted. That is, according to them, Menadue had said that the Departments had recommended to Whitlam:

> inserting 'clauses in the Appropriation Bills, insisting the Bills be returned from the Senate to the House before they were presented to the Governor-General for Assent'.[102]

This is precisely what SO 265 did (and what happened on November 11), although this seems unknown to those authors. Their misunderstanding of this issue may well be because Whitlam's Department Head, John Menadue, continues to believe that the proposition of the Departments was for an amendment to the supply bills to require that they be returned to the Lower House after passage by the Senate. As he recently said to the ABC's Alex Mann:

> The cabinet did consider that perhaps the appropriation bills should be amended so that after they were passed in the Senate they would be returned to the House of Representatives before they went to the Governor-General for signature. The cabinet considered that and decided that that would be too provocative for the Senate.[103]

This statement is simply incorrect, and the proposition was both unnecessary and unworkable. Why would a provision in a bill that is not yet a law be binding on anyone, much less a House of Parliament?

The position of the Departments was, however, somewhat more subtle than Menadue seems to have appreciated. According to the 1997 recollections of Clarrie Harders, who had been the head of the Attorney-General's Department under Whitlam:

> The Departments did foresee that the Governor-General might dismiss Mr Whitlam and they prepared a plan which, had it been implemented, and had it been legally valid, would have kept the Appropriation Bills in the control of the House of Representatives. This would have been done by including a provision in the Appropriation Bills to the effect that a resolution of the House of Representatives would have been required to draw money out of the Consolidated Revenue Fund.[104]

As a result, as he recalled in 1996:

> any deferral by the Senate would have been circumvented by the ultimate control of the bills and also any dismissal of the Government would have been circumvented by the control of the bills being kept in the governing house, as Mr Whitlam saw it.[105]

As a result, as Harders, said:

> This would have prevented the leader of the Opposition being in a position to advise the Governor- General, which he did do before the dismissal, and in compliance with a request from the Governor- General that he, the leader of the Opposition, Mr Fraser, should be in a position to guarantee the passage of Supply. Fraser would never have been able to do that if the Governor-General had been confronted with a position in which the control of the bills remained with the House of Representatives.[106]

The difficulty with this proposal was its legality. Although Kelly and Bramston considered that this plan was 'unusual but legal',[107] Harders was more uncertain as to its legality. As he made plain when he wrote in 1997, 'I do not know whether it was or not'.[108]

Whitlam, however, rejected the departmental plan, but it was never clear why. As Harders wrote in 1996:

> I did never ascertain why the suggestion that came from the Prime Minister's Department and the Attorney-General's Department about keeping the bills in the control of the House of Representatives was not taken up by the Government.[109]

Menadue also raised this option with Whitlam in a two-page note on October 2, but it was, again, not accepted.[110] Why it is not clear, but it could be an example of poor planning on the part of Whitlam. Alternatively, if the reasoning in Menadue's note was as questionable as his recent explanation of the concept, it is not surprising that Whitlam rejected it.

But the failure of the government to adopt the departmental solution did not prevent the Lower House from attempting to rely on the operation of SO 265 and use any powers that still may have remained with that House to defer and possibly prevent the submission of the supply bills to Kerr for assent. But that required something that never occurred – for Labor to realize the power that it still potentially had.

WHY WERE THESE MEASURES NOT USED?

Clearly, Whitlam never gave any thought to the Lower House powers that may have been used to save his government, but he later accepted, as seen earlier, that those powers would have been an effective tactic.[111]

As to his failure to advise the Senate, Freudenberg accepted that Whitlam's error was: 'difficult to excuse but easy to explain: nobody around the table at the Lodge thought of the Senate'.[112] Senator Wheeldon, however, took a very different approach. While he initially accepted that Whitlam's failure to advise the Senate was 'one of those accidents which from time to time play a trick on history', he later reviewed his understanding (and his own rage) when he had been 'reprimanded by one of Whitlam's former secretaries' (unnamed) who told him that this was not just an error or an oversight, but was 'the result of a master plan conceived over lunch at the Lodge by the sacked prime minister and his staff'.[113] If Wheeldon was correct, Whitlam's failure seems one not just of arrogance or inadvertence, but more like incompetence.

Whitlam, in 1995, attempted to defend his failure to make use of the Senate in 1975, arguing that Labor senators voting against the Budget in the Senate '"would not have worked" because Independent senators Steele Hall and Cleaver Bunton would not have altered their previous votes in favour of the Budget, and "nor should they have"'.[114] This, of course, is pure speculation and it also fails to consider the possibility of any nervous coalition senator crossing the floor. But it may be true, or it may not be. We will never know as it was never tested. It does not, however, explain or justify Whitlam's failure to even consider the powers of the Senate after he had been dismissed; his failure to include any senators in his planning leading to his dismissal; and his extraordinary failure to even let any Labor senators know that he had been dismissed, errors that made any possible use of Senate powers impossible.

Professor Hocking, however, attempted to justify Whitlam's concentration on the Lower House due to Kerr's secrecy and Fraser's duplicity. In her view, 'Whitlam was at a single, fatal, disadvantage: he did not know that Malcolm Fraser was already Prime Minister'.[115] Kelly expressed a similar view in his *The Unmaking of Gough*.[116] In Hocking's more detailed view, Whitlam was 'stunned to hear Fraser call himself head of Government'[117] which happened at 2.34 pm.[118]

This attempted justification simply cannot be true as it requires Whitlam to have ignored the information provided to him, including the content of Kerr's letter to Whitlam, the letter that did the sacking. In that letter, which Whitlam received at or around 1.00 pm, the governor-general told Whitlam, in the last paragraph, that:

> I propose to send for the Leader to the Opposition and to commission him to form a new caretaker Government until an election can be held.[119]

Now Whitlam was not aware that Fraser was already at Government House when he received that letter. But it is absurd to conclude that he would not have read Kerr's letter and had not understood it for what it said. From that last paragraph, Whitlam should have understood, and there is no evidence otherwise, that Fraser would be commissioned later that day and may well have been before the time the House of Representatives reconvened that afternoon. Whitlam may well have been tactically unwise on November 11, but he was neither blind nor illiterate. Moreover, Whitlam has subsequently written that: 'it was essential to the success of the operation that I leave Government House dismissed and Mr Fraser should leave it as Prime Minister'.[120] Are we to believe, as Hocking and Kelly seem to require us, that Whitlam did not realize this until 2.34 pm?

This might be possible, but for the other sources of information to Whitlam that Hocking and Kelly have ignored. David Smith (Kerr's Official Secretary) maintains that he telephoned department head, John Menadue at 1.45 pm 'to tell him that the Whitlam government had been dismissed and that Fraser had been commissioned to form a government'.[121] And Menadue confirms this. According to his autobiography, *Things You Learn Along the Way*, he received a phone call:

> at about 1.45 pm. David Smith, the Governor-General's Official Secretary, told me that the Whitlam Government had been dismissed and that Fraser had been commissioned to form a government.[122]

The time of this call was probably much earlier than the time that both Smith and Menadue claim it was.[123] And that is because of everything that we know occurred after that call that afternoon until Malcolm Fraser made his announcement at 2.34 pm. That is, at the time of Smith's call, Menadue was eating his sandwich lunch in his office[124] and his first reaction after the call was to ring two senior public servants[125] to tell them that 'the Prime Minister has been dismissed and that Malcolm Fraser is the new Prime Minister'.[126] Such phone calls would not have taken less than 5 minutes in total. Then, he received a call that advised him that Whitlam wanted to see him 'urgently'[127] before he went to the now former prime minister's residence, the Lodge (a drive which Menadue estimates at seven or eight minutes).[128] Then he talked to Whitlam, received two further calls from his office, the gap between which was either 10[129] or 15[130] minutes, before he left the Lodge. And after he left, as Whitlam says, the Lodge meeting then 'turned to parliamentary tactics'.[131] And that involved Whitlam drafting a motion before he returned to Parliament House by 2.00 pm, the time when the debate in the House of Representatives recommenced.

Whitlam may well have been late for that session, but given the three divisions in the House prior to 2.34 pm in which Whitlam voted,[132] it seems that any lateness could not have been extensive, and no more than, at most, 15 or 20 minutes. All of those events could not have fitted into the 15 minutes between 1.45 pm and 2.00 pm; and are barely possible in 30 or 35 minutes only if Menadue's attendance at the Lodge was much less than the 15 minutes gap he has estimated between his secretary's calls to him while he was there,[133] or that the time that Whitlam's devoted attendance to 'parliamentary tactics' was remarkably short.

But whatever time the Smith/Menadue call was, it is clear that Menadue had been told before he saw Whitlam at the Lodge that Fraser was prime minister. Are we to believe that information highly relevant to Whitlam would not have been provided to him by the person who was the second telephoned after his dismissal? Is it credible that when Whitlam told Menadue and others that 'The bastard's done a Game on me',[134] Menadue would not have then told Whitlam that he had been advised that 'Fraser is the new Prime Minister'. Was this information so important that he felt it necessary to earlier advise those two senior public servants prior to meeting with Whitlam, but when it came to Whitlam himself, it now became merely an optional extra?

But the call from Smith is not the only one of relevance that indicates Hocking's argument clearly cannot be correct. According to Menadue's biography, while at the Lodge he received two calls, this time from his Secretary, Elaine Miller,[135] who said that:

> Mr Fraser wanted to see me. I said, 'Tell him you can't find me'. She rang about 15 minutes later and said, 'This is a message from Mr Fraser. Could you tell John Menadue that the *Prime Minister,* Mr Fraser, wants to see you urgently' [emphasis original].[136]

Menadue then left Whitlam, telling him that he had been 'summoned'.[137] He accepts that he should have told more to Whitlam than what he had said – which was 'that I was being called by Mr Fraser and I was sorry, I had to leave'.[138] But it is clear that Menadue had been told both before and while he was with Whitlam by both the governor-general's office and by his own office that Fraser had been appointed as prime minister. For us to then believe Hocking's argument that Whitlam did not know that Fraser was prime minister until Fraser told the House of Representatives at some point around 2.34 pm requires us to conclude that both Smith and Menadue are incorrect or that Menadue had received the information but, for some unfathomable reason, omitted to tell Whitlam. Neither of those options is credible.

As to Whitlam's later account in *The Truth of the Matter*, he agrees that Menadue 'withdrew' before the Lodge meeting discussed parliamentary tactics, but he did not explain this further.[139] But it seems difficult to believe, in the unlikely event that Menadue had not told Whitlam what he had been told *twice*, why Whitlam would still not have realized or at least suspected why Menadue would then leave him to see Fraser. As Menadue had told Whitlam that he had been 'summoned',[140] who could have summoned a head of a department from his meeting with Whitlam other than his new ministerial head? For us to accept that Whitlam did not appreciate the reason why Menadue had withdrawn from the most urgent of all the meetings that Whitlam had ever called is simply not believable.

SCHOLES, WHITLAM AND THE QUEEN

Instead of relying on those potential powers of the Senate and House of Representatives that may have saved the Whitlam government, the emphasis of the defeated ministers was based on their flawed and pointless attempt to rely on Royal interference to overrule the governor-general's decision.

That can be seen, first, in the motion that Whitlam prepared at his Lodge meeting after he had been dismissed, which was to seek royal assistance:

> That this House declares that it has the confidence in the Whitlam govt and that this House informs HM the Queen that if HE the G-G purports to commission the hon member for Wannon as PM, the House does not have confidence in him or in any govt he forms.[141]

Fortunately, this is not the motion that Whitlam did move; instead, it is one based on a flawed assumption that Kerr's decision was one that the Queen could and would remedy and repair. However, this motion was not a good start to saving his government. The motion is, in fact, a constitutional absurdity. The immediate executive powers in Australia are held, not by the Queen, but by the governor-general, and this is made plain by sections 2 and 64 of the *Constitution*. Section 64, in particular, allows the governor-general to appoint ministers and states, 'Such officers shall hold office *during the pleasure of the Governor-General*'.[142] Moreover, the Australian Parliament has specifically dealt with the powers of the Queen. Aside from the Queen's power to appoint and dismiss the governor-general under section 2 of the *Constitution*, the Queen's direct powers over Australia were limited. As such, section 2 of the *Royal Powers Act 1953* (Cth) states that:

> (1) At any time when the Queen is personally present in Australia, any power under an Act exercisable by the governor-general may be exercised by the Queen.

So, if Whitlam's draft motion was passed in the manner that it left the Lodge and Fraser was appointed as prime minister (as he had already been), was Whitlam's best response to ask Her Majesty to fly to Australia to exercise her few remaining statutory powers to undermine the constitutional powers (whether exercised wisely or not) by the governor-general?

But that was not the end of the former government's attempt to involve the Monarch in overruling the governor-general. On the day of the dismissal (at 4.15 am London time), Whitlam telephoned Martin Charteris and spoke as a private citizen. He told Charteris that supply had been passed and that the Lower House had passed a no-confidence motion in relation to the Fraser government. Although Whitlam 'did not ask me to make any approach to the Queen, or indeed to do anything other than the suggestion that I speak to you [John Kerr] to find out what was going on', Whitlam also said that 'now Supply had been passed he should be re-commissioned as Prime Minister so that he could choose his own time to call an election'.[143]

On November 12, the Speaker, Gordon Scholes, also wrote to the Queen asking her to: 'act in order to restore Mr Whitlam to office as Prime Minister in accordance with the expressed resolution of the House of Representatives'.[144] More constitutional nonsense – which the Palace recognized, but with more subtlety, in its response of November 17, 1975:

> As we understand the situation here, the Australian Constitution firmly places the prerogative powers of the Crown in the hands of the Governor-General as the representative of The Queen of Australia. The only person competent to commission an Australian Prime Minister is the Governor-General, and The Queen has no part in decisions which the Governor-General must take in accordance with the Constitution. Her Majesty, as Queen of Australia, is watching events in Canberra with closest interest and attention, but it would not be proper for her to intervene in matters which are so closely placed within the jurisdiction of the Governor-General by the Constitution Act.[145]

Even after the election on December 13, Whitlam wrote to the Palace seeking to challenge the actions of Sir John Kerr, 'as representative of the Crown'[146] which the Palace felt necessary to correct, making the point that the Monarch's powers are limited:

> The constitutional role of the Governor-General and his reserve powers stem not from his position as The Queen's personal representative, to which he is appointed on the advice of the Prime Minister, but rather from what is written in the Constitution Act as applicable constitutionally.[147]

As the late Professor George Winterton observed in 2003: 'the Queen's decision was clearly correct and derives support from an opinion the Solicitor-General Byers had given the Whitlam Government ten weeks earlier'.[148] The effect of that opinion was referred to in Kerr's account as:

> the executive power of the Commonwealth exercisable by the Governor-General under chapter II of the Constitution (including the power of dismissing Ministers under s 64) and also the powers relating to the dissolution of Parliament conferred by section 5 and section 57 could not be made the subject of instructions from the Queen.[149]

Nonetheless, the emphasis of the dismissed government remained based on a flawed and ineffective approach of involving the Monarch. It was not prepared to accept that the problem was entirely home-grown – based on the powers which the *Constitution* had given to the governor-general and not the Queen. And it flowed from the man that Whitlam had recommended and advised to fill that office. But there was nothing that London could do, even if it wished, to resolve or repair the dismissal once it had occurred.

Instead of relying on the Palace for a result it could not constitutionally provide, a better result would have been for Whitlam to give some reliance to the powers remaining in the two Houses before they were dissolved. But Whitlam, Scholes and the remainder of the dismissed government ignored those powers – and with that failure, any chance of success was lost. The game was over.

NOTES

1. Whitlam, *The Truth,* 277; Kelly & Bramston, *The Dismissal,* 224.
2. Freudenberg, *Certain Grandeur*, 394.
3. Hocking, *His Time* (2012), 338.
4. Whitlam, *The Truth,* 158. Kelly & Bramston, *The Dismissal,* 226. Menadue, however, maintains that the call came not from Whitlam, but from his driver. See Menadue, *Things You Learn,* 162.
5. Whitlam, *The Truth,* 158. Kelly & Bramston, *The Dismissal,* 226.
6. Freudenberg, *Certain Grandeur*, 394.
7. Whitlam, *The Truth,* 158.
8. Freudenberg, *Certain Grandeur*, 394.
9. Whitlam, *The Truth,* 158.
10. Daly, *Curtin to Hawke*, 231–232.
11. Freudenberg, *Certain Grandeur*, 395.
12. Kelly & Bramston, *The Dismissal,* 226; Freudenberg, *Certain Grandeur*, 395; Whitlam, *The Truth,* 159.
13. Whitlam, *The Truth,* 158.
14. Kelly & Bramston, *The Dismissal,* 136.
15. Kelly & Bramston, *The Dismissal,* 137 and 138.
16. Hocking, *His Time* (2012), 338.
17. Menadue, however, as we will see, was aware as he had been advised by David Smith that Whitlam had been dismissed and Fraser appointed – see Menadue, *Things You Learn,* 162.
18. Kelly & Bramston, *The Dismissal,* 226.
19. Odgers, *Senate Practice* (1991), 87.
20. Whitlam, *The Truth,* 158.
21. Hocking, *His Time* (2012), 338–339.
22. Sexton, *Great Crash*, 245.
23. Sexton, "The Dismissal," 294.
24. See the tables in *Whitlam Legacy,* Appendix 3, which detail the content of Whitlam Cabinets.
25. Whitlam, *The Truth,* 158.
26. Freudenberg, *Certain Grandeur*, Loc 395.

27. Menadue, *Things You Learn,* 162–163.

28. James McClelland, *Stirring the Possum* (Ringwood, Victoria: Penguin, 1989), 185.

29. Hocking, *His Time* (2012), 345–346.

30. Also see Ken Wriedt, "Meanwhile Back in the Senate," in *Where Were You?,* ed. Nolan, 51, 53.

31. Freudenberg, *Certain Grandeur*, 396.

32. Kelly & Bramston, *The Dismissal,* 229–230.

33. Kelly & Bramston, *The Dismissal,* 230.

34. See Kelly & Bramston, *The Dismissal,* 230–232.

35. Sexton, "The Dismissal," 294.

36. Kelly & Bramston, *The Dismissal,* 231.

37. Kelly & Bramston, *The Dismissal,* 231 relying on the record made on November 20 1975 by MJ Hanson, Senate Parliamentary Liaison Office.

38. Button, "Out of the Blue," 33.

39. Wriedt, "Back in the Senate," 52.

40. Kelly & Bramston, *The Dismissal,* 230–231.

41. Kelly & Bramston, *The Dismissal,* 231.

42. Kelly & Bramston, *Truth, Palace Letters,* 50.

43. Lloyd & Clark, *Kerr's King Hit,* 231.

44. Lloyd & Clark, *Kerr's King Hit*, 231.

45. Senator from Western Australia (1965–1981) and Minister for Social Security (June 6 to November 11, 1975) and Minister for Repatriation and Compensation (June 12, 1974 to November 11, 1975).

46. John Wheeldon, "If Labor Senators had known . . .," *The Australian*, November 11, 1985, 11.

47. See discussion in chapter 5.

48. Deirdre McKeown and Rob Lundie, "Crossing the Floor in the Federal Parliament 1950–April 2019," *Parliament of Australia, Research Paper*, March 12, 2020.

49. McKeown & Lundy, "Crossing," 1.

50. Odgers, *Senate Practice,* 87–88.

51. Odgers, *Senate Practice,* 87.

52. Odgers, *Senate Practice,* 88.

53. See Kerr, *Matters,* 297–298.

54. Odgers, *Senate Practice,* 88.

55. Whitlam, *The Truth,* 277.

56. Commonwealth of Australia, *Parliamentary Debates*, *House of Representatives*, November 11, 1975, 2925.

57. Commonwealth of Australia, *Parliamentary Debates*, *House of Representatives*, November 11, 1975, 2928.

58. Commonwealth of Australia, *Parliamentary Debates*, *House of Representatives*, November 11, 1975, 2928.

59. Commonwealth of Australia, *Parliamentary Debates*, *House of Representatives*, November 11, 1975, 2929.

60. Commonwealth of Australia, *Parliamentary Debates, House of Representatives*, November 11, 1975, 2932.

61. Commonwealth of Australia, *Parliamentary Debates, House of Representatives*, November 11, 1975, 2932.

62. Whitlam, *The Truth,* 161.

63. Smith, *Head of State,* 256.

64. Kelly & Bramston, *Truth, Palace Letters,* 50.

65. See *Clayton v Heffron* (1960) 105 CLR 214, 240 (Dixon CJ, McTiernan, Taylor and Windeyer JJ). Also see *Namoi Shire Council v Attorney-General* (NSW) [1980] 2 NSWLR 639 (McLelland J) and Anne Twomey, "Minority Government and the Validity of Standing Order Requirements for Absolute Majority Votes" (2019) 30 *Public Law Review* 142 for a useful discussion of the scope of standing orders.

66. See Federal Register of Legislation, https://www.legislation.gov.au.

67. This Standing Order has ceased, but its replacement, SO 175, is to the same effect:

> *175. House bills presented to Governor-General*
> When a House bill has finally passed both Houses, the Clerk shall certify this, and the Speaker shall present the bill to the governor-general for the Queen's assent in accordance with section 58 of the Constitution.

68. This SO has been repealed, but the contents of which are now covered by SO 131.1, which now reads:

> When a bill has been passed by the Senate with or without amendment, it shall be returned to the House of Representatives by message, with the Clerk's certificate that the bill has been agreed to by the Senate without amendment, or with the amendments indicated by the annexed schedule, as the case may require, and the concurrence of the House of Representatives shall be requested for such amendments.

See Parliament of Australia, Annotated Standing Orders of the Senate, https://www.aph.gov.au/About_Parliament/Senate/Powers_practice_n_procedures/aso/so131; and see Odgers, *Senate Practice,* 1083.

69. Hayden, *Hayden*, 298.

70. Sawer, *Federation Under Strain.*

71. Sawer, *Federation Under Strain,* 169.

72. Sawer, *Federation Under Strain,* 169.

73. When interviewed by Garry Sturgess in 2010 (Scholes, "Oral History," Session 3, 38–40), however, Scholes denied any knowledge of how that could have been done or anything else to intervene, which may well indicate that, by then, his memories of 1975 were somewhat hampered, as he was then 79 years of age.

74. Quoted in L. J. M. Cooray, *Conventions, The Australian Constitution and the Future* (Sydney, New South Wales: Legal Books, 1979), 141 & 160, from *Australian* Newspaper, November 1, 1976, 9.

75. Sawer, *Federation Under Strain,* 169.

76. Odgers, *Senate Practice,* 88; Sawer, *Federation Under Strain,* 169.

77. Donald Anthony Low, "The Dismissal of a Prime Minister: Australia, 11 November 1975," in *Constitutional Heads and Political Crises,* ed. Donald Anthony Low (New York: St Martins Press, 1988), 90, 101.

78. Sawer, *Federation Under Strain,* 169.

79. See Antonia Fraser, *Cromwell, Our Chief of Men* (London: Phoenix, Weidenfeld and Nicolson Ebook, 2011), 97, Kindle.

80. Sexton, "The Dismissal," 295.

81. Sexton, *Great Crash*, 249.

82. Sawer, *Federation Under Strain*, 169.

83. Sawer, *Federation Under Strain*, 229, fn 64 – emphasis original.

84. Section 58 requires that:

> When a proposed law passed by both Houses of the Parliament is presented to the Governor-General for the Queen's assent, he shall declare, according to his discretion but subject to this Constitution, that he assents in the Queen's name, or that he withholds assent, or that he reserves the law for the Queen's pleasure.

85. *Namoi Shire Council v Attorney-General* (NSW) [1980] 2 NSWLR 639, 644.

86. Anne Twomey, "Minority Government and the Validity of Standing Order Requirements for Absolute Majority Votes" (2019) 30 *Public Law Review* 142, 153.

87. *Egan v Willis* (1996) 40 NSWLR 650, 673.

88. (1974) 131 CLR 432, 453.

89. *Constitution of Australia*, s 1.

90. (1974) 131 CLR 432, 453.

91. Here, it is necessary to thank Professor Greg Taylor for his views. He strongly regards this issue as one where the governor-general could have provided assent regardless of any actions of the Lower House or the Speaker.

92. (1974) 131 CLR 432, 453 [21].

93. Sawer, *Federation Under Strain,* 169.

94. Whitlam, *The Truth,* 165–166 – emphasis added.

95. Whitlam, *The Truth,* 161.

96. Whitlam, *The Truth,* 161.

97. Kerr, *Matters,* 368.

98. Whitlam, *The Truth,* 161–162.

99. Whitlam, *The Truth,* 278.

100. Kelly & Bramston, *The Dismissal*, 226.

101. See Kelly & Bramston, *The Dismissal,* 374.

102. Kelly & Bramston, *The Dismissal,* 139.

103. John Mendadue, *Transcript of interview* conducted by Alex Mann for the ABC's podcast, *The Eleventh*, which can be found at https://johnmenadue.com/wp-content/uploads/2020/03/John-Menadue-transcript-ABC-Series-1.pdf, accessed January 24, 2023.

104. Clarrie Harders, "The Loans Affair: An Insider's View," in *Power, Parliament and the People,* ed. Michael Coper and George Williams (Annadale, NSW: Federation Press, 1997), 161, 163.

105. National Library Association, Oral History – "Clarrie Harders interviewed by John Farquharson, Clarrie Harders," transcript, Australian Society Oral History Project, sound recording, December 16, 1996, Session 3, 49 emphasis added. https://nla.gov.au/nla.obj-220645788/listen.

106. NLA Oral History, "Transcript of Clarrie Harders Interviewed by John Farquharson," 49.

107. Kelly & Bramston, *The Dismissal,* 139. Their understanding of the plan was also a confused understanding closer to Menadue's incorrect description than that of Harders – as it required, according to Kelly & Bramston "the bills to be endorsed another time by the House after Senate passage."

108. Harders, "Loans Affair," 163.

109. NLA Oral History, "Transcript of Clarrie Harders Interviewed by John Farquharson," 49.

110. Kelly & Bramston, *The Dismissal,* 139.

111. Whitlam, *The Truth,* 165–166.

112. Freudenberg, *Certain Grandeur*, 396.

113. John Wheeldon, "If Labor Senators," 11.

114. Ian Henderson, "Whitlam Censures his Critics," *The Australian,* November 13, 1995, 4. According to Henderson, Whitlam also evidently argued that "'If we had not passed the Budget, we could not have sacked Fraser' with a no-confidence motion." This argument, if made, is confused as a no-confidence motion in the Lower House was not dependent on the budget being passed.

115. Hocking, *His Time* (2012), 340.

116. Kelly, *Unmaking,* 356.

117. Hocking, *His Time* (2012), 341.

118. Commonwealth of Australia, *Parliamentary Debates*, *House of Representatives*, November 11, 1975, 2928.

119. See Kelly & Bramston, *The Dismissal,* 369.

120. Whitlam, *The Truth,* 155.

121. Smith, *Head of State,* 251.

122. Menadue, *Things You Learn,* 162.

123. In the Australian Broadcasting Corporation podcast, "The Eleventh," 17 March 2020, in *The Eleventh*, Episode 6, Australian Broadcasting Corporation, podcast audio, at 17:00, Menadue then recalled that the telephone call from Smith followed "Almost immediately" Whitlam's sacking.

124. Menadue, *Things You Learn,* 162.

125. Fredrick Wheeler, Secretary of the Treasury, and Alan Cooley, Chairman of the Public Service Board.

126. Menadue, *Interview.*

127. Menadue, *Things You Learn,* 162. Menadue considers that the call was from Whitlam's driver, while Whitlam recalled that he had called Menadue – see Whitlam, *The Truth,* 158.

128. As stated by Menadue in the ABC podcast, "The Eleventh," 18:45-18:50.

129. Menadue, *Interview.*

130. Menadue, *Things You Learn,* 162.

131. Whitlam, *The Truth,* 159.

132. Commonwealth of Australia, *Parliamentary Debates*, *House of Representatives*, November 11, 1975, 2926 & 2927.

133. Discussed below.

134. As quoted in Menadue, *Things You Learn,* 162.

135. Menadue, *Things You Learn,* 163.

136. Menadue, *Things You Learn,* 163.

137. Menadue, *Interview.*

138. Menadue, *Things You Learn*, 163.

139. Whitlam, *The Truth,* 159.

140. Menadue, *Interview.*

141. Whitlam, *The Truth,* 136 & 159; Kelly & Bramston, *The Dismissal,* 375–376.

142. Emphasis added.

143. See letter from Charteris to Kerr, November 17, 1975. NAA, *The Kerr Palace Letters,* AA1984/609, Part 2.

144. Kelly & Bramston, *The Dismissal,* 381.

145. Kelly & Bramston, *The Dismissal,* 382. Quoted in Kerr, *Matters,* 374–375.

146. See letter from Whitlam to Charteris, December 26, 1975, in Kelly & Bramston, *The Dismissal,* 383–385, 385.

147. See letter from Charteris to Whitlam, January 12, 1976, in Kelly & Bramston, *The Dismissal,* 388–389.

148. George Winterton, "1975: The Dismissal of the Whitlam Government," in *Australian Constitutional Landmarks,* ed. H. P. Lee and George Winterton (Cambridge: Cambridge University Press, 2003), 229, 242.

149. Kerr, *Matters,* 332. Winterton also refers to the Byers opinion as being dated September 5, 1975, and also unpublished. See Winterton, "1975: The Dismissal," 257, n 125.

Chapter 11

1975

And the Errors of the Conspiracy Theorists

Figure 11.1 Badges with the Images of the Late Queen and the CIA. From the collection of the author. Image taken by the author.

There can't be a crisis without a conspiracy or two. Just as the Kennedy assassination in 1963 led to endless and complex arguments that the CIA, the mafia or even Vice President Johnson was responsible for that death in Dallas, the dismissal of Whitlam by the governor-general in 1975 has also gained some conspiracy propositions, but they are more interesting for discussion than accuracy. And the best (or worst) ones are that Kerr was either a 'CIA flunky' or that he was driven by a Royal Family conspiracy.

CIA CONSPIRACY?

Allegations of this type of conspiracy derive from the diverging approaches of two countries: the then very conservative and expansionist United States, which was then led by the Republican Party's Richard Nixon, and the more left-leaning Australia under Gough Whitlam. Since the end of the 1940s, the American/Australia relationship had been marked by a very cooperative and conservative Australia supporting the United States on all overseas measures, a position most notably put by Prime Minister Harold Holt in 1966, as Australia standing: 'All the way with LBJ'. All this changed, however, with the election of Gough Whitlam in 1972, and the relationship between the two countries soured, largely because the ALP was regarded as both inexperienced and 'socialistic'; those concerns were further increased after Lionel Murphy's raid on ASIO[1] (discussed in chapter 4). Nonetheless, there is no evidence of such a US conspiracy in the Whitlam dismissal, other than allegations made by one former American intelligence employee, Christopher Boyce, supported by the views of some Australian journalists, particularly Ray Martin[2] and the late John Pilger.[3]

Both journalists have asserted that the CIA was behind the Whitlam dismissal, although, as Martin accepts, there is no 'smoking gun'. Pilger, however, argued that the CIA was the cause, and that was largely because that organization believed that Whitlam was intending to end Australia's agreement with the US for the Joint Defence Facility located at Pine Gap, which is near the central Australian city of Alice Springs.

> For the CIA, December 9 remained a critical date. The agency was certain Whitlam would announce the cancellation of the Pine Gap agreement on that day. If the conservative coalition was to be elected in time to 'protect the sanctity of the bases', an election would have to be held before the Christmas holiday period.[4]

But that justification simply cannot be the case unless the CIA had ignored what Whitlam had already made public. On August 21, 1975, in answer to a parliamentary question from a Liberal MP regarding the future of Pine Gap, Whitlam was plain that the facility was to continue. As he said:

> (2) The agreement (Treaty Series 1966, No. 17) can be terminated by a year's notice given on or after 9 December 1975 by the government of Australia or the government of the United States. Neither government proposes to give notice of termination.
>
> (3) The government intends that the facility should continue to be operated jointly in accordance with the agreement.[5]

As to Boyce, he was, in the 1970s, a very young man employed by a corporation related to the CIA, TRW Inc. His work was in that company's 'Black Vault', which was, as he asserts, an 'encryption operation supporting satellite surveillance' of the Soviet Union. For that purpose, he had access to USA information sources, including those collected at the facility at Pine Gap. From that employment, Boyce became concerned regarding the United State's motivations and intentions. In particular, he found that the United States 'was not willing to live up to our agreement to share all information gathered at Pine Gap with our Australian allies', as it did not trust the elected Labor Government under Gough Whitlam, considering it to be 'a threat to American interests'. That was because 'the Whitlam Government was socialistic',[6] and because, as Henry Kissinger, Nixon's National Security Advisor, bluntly put it, 'He is a bastard'.[7] As such, 'The CIA wanted Whitlam out'.[8] And for that purpose the United States was undermining Australia's system of government, and that included, as the CIA resident to this project had told Boyce, that Australia's governor-general was 'our man Kerr'.[9] Boyce concluded, as he later said, that Kerr was nothing more than a 'CIA Flunky'.[10]

This lack of honesty with the United States's supposed friend and ally led Boyce to become disenchanted with his country, beginning together with his friend, Daulton Lee, to sell security information collected at TRW to the Soviet Union. This was a short, nerve-wracking but somewhat profitable career, until they were caught and imprisoned in 1977.

According to the book detailing the rise and fall of Boyce and Lee, called *The Falcon and the Snowman* by Robert Lindsey (which later became the basis for a movie in 1985 starring Timothy Hutton as Boyce and Sean Penn as Lee), the CIA's undermining of Australia also involved the dismissal of the Whitlam government. According to Lindsey's account

> In early November, the Prime Minister said in a speech that he had confirmed reports the CIA had indeed built the [Pine Gap] facilities. This official acknowledgement of the CIA's role in Australia intensified the crisis atmosphere within certain components of the CIA, where it was feared the political brouhaha could explode and force closing of the bases.[11]

This led to the involvement of the governor-general, who had been briefed by Australian 'military and intelligence officials' about 'the CIA's grave apprehension that public discussion of the [Pine Gap] facilities could be disastrous'.[12] According to Freudenberg, that briefing occurred just a few days before Whitlam's dismissal, on November 8.[13] Moreover, on the day prior to that dismissal, according to Lindsey, the Australian Security Intelligence Organisation, or ASIO (the Australian equivalent to the CIA), had also received a cable from the CIA expressing concern regarding the government's plans concerning Pine Gap:

> CIA IS PERPLEXED AS TO WHAT ALL THIS MEANS. DOES THIS SIGNIFY SOME CHANGE IN OUR BILATERAL INTELLIGENCE SECRITY RELATED FIELD. CIA CANNOT SEE HOW THIS DIALOGUE . . . CAN DO OTHER THAN BLOW THE LID OFF THOSE INSTALLATIONS IN AUSTRALIA.[14]

The CIA's concern was that, according to Lindsey, 'On November 11, Prime Minister Whitlam had scheduled another speech in which he was to discuss CIA and the mysterious installations in the Outback [*sic*]'. The CIA's security concern with Whitlam and his speech was, however (according to Lindsey), resolved because Whitlam 'never got a chance to deliver it. On the day the speech was to be delivered, Governor-General Sir John Kerr removed him from office'.[15]

This version has gained some acceptance as being accurate. As Alex Mann said in his ABC series, *The Eleventh*: 'And on the very day that he was dismissed as Prime Minister, Whitlam was planning to stand up in Parliament and confirm the identity of a former CIA agent'.[16] And for some others, those supposed facts have also evolved further to suit the conspiracy argument and conclusion. For example, according to Freudenberg, the November 10 cable had ceased to be a CIA message expressing concern about what the Australian government may have been doing, but now became:

> an extraordinary cable from the ASIO officer in Washington to ASIO Headquarters, dated 10 November, the CIA believed that Whitlam was about to reveal the names of current CIA operatives in Australia; the CIA was threatening to break its intelligence links with Australia.[17]

The truth is, however, much more pedantic. And it arose, not from issues prompted by the ALP regarding CIA operations or Pine Gap, or from any desire of the prime minister to release any information regarding those facilities or that organization or any agents, but from questions made to the prime minister by the leader of the Country Party, Doug Anthony, which the prime minister considered he was obliged to answer.

The first of those questions that Anthony made was prompted by Whitlam's statement at an ALP rally at Port Augusta on Sunday, November 2, 1975, which associated Anthony with CIA funding: 'I have had no association with CIA money in Australia as Anthony has'. There was no mention of CIA operations or agents in Whitlam's comment. But, as Whitlam later wrote, on the following Tuesday, Anthony further developed the issue when he raised this issue in Parliament: 'if his claim is based on letting my house in Canberra nine years ago to an American, does the Prime Minister claim the man was a CIA officer? If so, will he prove that claim'.[18] And Whitlam's reply included the following:

> The right honourable gentlemen has confirmed everything that I believe. His tenant and his host was a member of the CIA when he was in Australia. Nobody would believe that the right honourable gentlemen was not aware of that fact. . . . I have nothing more to add at this stage.[19]

On the following day, in response to a 'Dorothy Dixer' question from the ALP member for the seat of Macquarie, Tony Luchetti, Whitlam added more, to the apparent embarrassment of Anthony, when he said:

> I am reluctant to expand too much on matters of security. My predecessors have always refused to confirm or deny such matters. Nevertheless, yesterday in apparent innocence, the Leader of the National Country Party did refer to such matters. In fact he asked me to apologise to the person concerned. I would point out that I never mentioned the person concerned myself. I never mentioned his position myself, and I never mentioned the places of his employment myself. The right honourable gentleman, however, did mention all these things. There was no denying the accuracy of what he said because he knew that I knew and he knew therefore that he might as well come clean.[20]

Whitlam went on to quote '*in extenso* from today's editorial in the *Australian Financial Review*' when it stated that:

> Yesterday in Parliament the Leader of the National Country Party, Mr Anthony, suggested that the Prime Minister of Australia, Mr E G Whitlam, should apologise to an official of the Central Intelligence Agency of the United States for involving that man in a domestic controversy.
>
> The man, Mr Anthony informed Parliament, was a family friend even though he did not know he was an official of the CIA.
>
> To put it bluntly the man was a spy, a spook, a man with allegiance to a foreign Government, who befriended Mr Anthony when he was the Deputy Prime Minister of Australia.
>
> The duty of this man, Mr Richard Lee Stallings, a quite senior man in the CIA, was to report back to his superiors every remark he gleaned from Mr Anthony, who was at the time the second most senior man in the Australian Government.[21]

As can be seen, Whitlam was not naming or planning to name any current or former CIA agent beyond quoting assertions made in the *Financial Review*. But that was not the end of the matter as, on the following day, Thursday, November 6, Anthony placed one further parliamentary question on the

Notice Paper, which confirmed the name of that former CIA agent. Whitlam recorded the question as:

> (1) Has his attention been drawn to a report on page 1 of *The Australian* of Thursday, November 6, 1975, in which a United States State Department official is reported to have said that Mr Richard Stallings has never worked for any United States intelligence agencies?
> (2) If so, will he provide substantiation of his claim that Mr Stallings was in fact an officer of the United States Central Intelligence Agency in 1966–1967?[22]

Richard Stallings, the subject of this question and of the *Financial Review* editorial of November 5, had been, according to the historian professor James Curran, 'the first head of the Pine Gap intelligence facility'[23] as well as being Anthony's tenant. But as Whitlam was dismissed on November 11, he did not get the opportunity to answer Anthony's second question. Nonetheless, the answer that he planned to give was to include the following: 'I did not disclose Mr Stallings was a CIA agent. The right honourable gentlemen did that'.[24]

The questions made by Anthony did raise security issues, and, as Hocking records, the Secretary of the Department of Defence, Sir Arthur Tange, made 'most concerted efforts' to attempt to convince both Anthony and Whitlam to withdraw on national security grounds, but 'neither would yield'.[25] But those security issues would not have been raised had Anthony not pressed on with his questions. Moreover, Whitlam's answers and planned answers did not, despite what Lindsey alleges, 'discuss CIA and the mysterious installations in the Outback'. And neither did they 'confirm the identity of a former CIA agent'. All they did was to repeat what two newspapers and the Leader of the Country Party had already made public.

While, no doubt, the CIA was not pleased with this public discussion of their operations or of Mr Stallings' name, there was little reason to expect that any 'lid' should be 'blown off' the Pine Gap facilities by Whitlam's answers, or any reason for the United States to break its intelligence links with Australia. But even if that was the CIA's intention, the idea of Kerr dismissing Whitlam based on a briefing conference of November 8 and a cable of November 10 is difficult, if not impossible, to accept. It both minimizes, if not ignores, all of the concerns, planning and discussions that Kerr had undergone over the last few months, as well as the serious economic and constitutional consequences of the Senate's blockage of supply that the dismissal was to avoid (as discussed earlier in chapter 6).

Moreover, it makes the reason for Kerr seeking legal advice from Barwick on November 9 (discussed in chapter 8) questionable or, even more concerning, knowingly deceptive. This is because if Kerr was operating as the CIA's supposed 'flunky' when he dismissed Whitlam, as Boyce alleges, Kerr's request to Barwick for his advice regarding the constitutional justification for Whitlam's dismissal can only have been made as a cover to disguise Kerr's actual national security purposes. If Barwick was aware of Kerr's supposed CIA reasoning and relationship, it seems that he must also have shared in Kerr's supposed deception.

The better view, however, seems to be that of the dismissed Prime Minister Gough Whitlam who has consistently rejected any CIA or USA involvement in his dismissal. In his view, 'I am profoundly, almost preternaturally reluctant to use the term "conspiracy," whether referring to collusion between Kerr, Barwick and Fraser or to allegations of possible CIA involvement'.[26] Moreover, in relation to the immediate relevance of the CIA to his dismissal, he considered, in 1985, that this episode has:

> lent colour to allegations that the CIA had been eavesdropping on me and my Ministers and had influenced the Governor-General, Sir John Kerr, to sack us. . . . It is not a fact, however, that Kerr, fascinated as had been with intelligence matters, needed any encouragement from the CIA.[27]

ROYAL CONSPIRACY?

A much more substantial conspiracy argument is that the governor-general, in making the decision to dismiss Whitlam, did not act alone. Instead, he acted, as Hocking asserts, only after the 'British authorities pressed . . . Governor-General Sir John Kerr in person and through intermediaries on his "duty" to protect the Queen'.[28] In Hocking's view, Whitlam's dismissal 'was the culmination of months of political subterfuge, planned in secrecy and executed in deception'.[29] At its crudest, the claimed conspiracy can be seen in the observations recently given by John Menadue, that 'The Queen was into it', and that 'She acted disgracefully in the dismissal of the Whitlam government'.[30] Menadue, however, made that allegation, despite what he had earlier written in his autobiography, which he now seems to have forgotten:

> The Palace was not amused by what Kerr had done. I learned of this later from a note from Tim McDonald, the Official Secretary at Australia House, London, who relayed to me a discussion he had had with Sir Martin Charteris, who was personal secretary and political adviser to the Queen at the time. The discussion that McDonald had with Charteris was within a few weeks of the dismissal. Commenting on the Whitlam dismissal, Charteris said to McDonald that 'the Palace shared the view that Kerr acted prematurely. If faced with a constitutional crisis which appeared likely to involve the Head of State, my advice would have been that [the Queen] should only intervene when a clear sense of

> inevitability had developed in the public that she must act. This had been Kerr's mistake'. A clear sense of inevitability had not been arrived at.[31]

Much of this Royal conspiracy argument, however, would not have been present but for some of statements, some very incorrect, made by John Kerr regarding the making of his decision to sack Whitlam. Those statements were included in his book, *Matters for Judgment.* And they include his published view that he: 'did not tell the Queen in advance that I intended to exercise these powers on 11 November. I did not ask her approval. The decisions I took were without the Queen's advance knowledge'.[32]

He considered, according to that account, that 'she could become involved if she had advance knowledge of my intention to exercise the reserve powers'.[33] According to Kerr, his 'view was that to inform Her Majesty in advance of what I intended to do, and when would be to risk involving her in Australian political and constitutional crisis in relation to which she had no legal powers; and I must not take that risk'.[34] And that was because 'to do nothing, having once been informed of my intentions, could also have resulted in criticism of the Monarchy'.[35] Moreover, 'Had the Queen been told, there would have been nothing legally that Her Majesty could do about the crisis except conceivably to offer advice'.[36] As such, Kerr's *Matters for Judgment* account was that 'As the Queen could not validly give me instruction as to how I should exercise my powers under s 64, I must not burden her with prior knowledge of my actual intention to act under that section'.[37]

These statements form the basis of what Professor Hocking considers the 'long standing historical "truths"' of the Queen's lack of involvement in Whitlam's dismissal. But, as the documentation between Kerr and the Palace has revealed, there is much inaccuracy in Kerr's public observations, as the Palace knew well before November 11 that Kerr was considering using his reserve powers to dismiss Whitlam.

Hocking became aware of the inaccuracy of Kerr's account when her research found certain documents from Kerr that indicated that the Palace was well informed that Kerr was considering the dismissal of Whitlam well before that dismissal occurred. The first of those documents was a journal that Kerr composed in early 1980, which included his account of his earlier conversation with the then Prince Charles, now King Charles III, from either August or September 1975.[38] In that conversation, as Hocking describes it, Kerr 'confided to Charles that he was considering dismissing the government and his great fear that Whitlam might recall him'. And Charles's reaction was, according to Kerr's journal:

> But surely Sir John, the Queen should not have to accept advice that you should be recalled at the very time, *should this happen when you were considering having to dismiss the government.* [*sic*][39]

In Hocking's view, this was a 'startling proposition' and one that, to her, indicated 'a return to the imperial power of the Crown over the appointment of dominion governors-general . . . and a direct intervention in the Australian political process'.[40] Moreover, according to Kerr's account, Prince Charles relayed the conversation to the Queen's private secretary, Sir Martin Charteris, and 'from Charteris the details were passed on to the Queen'.[41] Hocking notes that Kerr's 1980 account ceased on March 13, 1980, with what Hocking describes as a 'lengthy entry' bringing it to a 'meandering end'.[42] But in that final entry to the account, Kerr recalls that Martin Charteris had said that 'if the kind of contingency in mind were to develop . . . the Queen would try to delay things'. To Hocking those words were 'shocking', indicating 'a new history: one of intrigue, deception and dismissal' and one that would show that the Palace were 'complicit'.[43] To Hocking, if Kerr's account was accurate, 'the Palace had re-entered the Australian domestic political space as though it were still the imperial master and Australia a mere colonial upstart'.[44]

It is, however, difficult to see how Hocking could remain of this view, or why she should be shocked given the understanding of others regarding the removal of governors-general. That included former holders of that office, William McKell and Bill Hayden, both of whom had been senior Labor parliamentarians before being appointed as governor-general. They were of the view that the Queen was not a mere rubber stamp for the wishes of her prime ministers, and should not be. As Bill Hayden[45] said in 1998, and well before Hocking discovered Kerr's journal, that 'In 1975, if the prime minister of the time had been inclined to sack the governor-general, I am certain, with good reason, that the advice to the palace to withdraw the commission would not have been proceeded with'.[46] In Hocking's view, however, for the Queen to even 'discuss the question of the governor-general's tenure with anyone other than her "Minister in the dominion concerned" – the Australian prime minister . . . was an unassailable breach of that elemental relationship, and an affront to our national autonomy'.[47] On that basis, to Hocking, not only was the Queen to be no more than a very responsive rubber stamp for the Australian prime minister, but she was not even able to discuss any advice that she had or may receive on that subject with anyone else. The Queen's task, in Hocking's view, was, it seems, nothing more than 'act[ing] immediately on the prime minister's advice'.[48] There are, however, no authorities to support such a minimum and pointless role for the Monarch. For example, Anne Twomey, in her extensive study of the reserve powers, considered whether the monarch has a reserve power to reject advice to dismiss a governor-general.[49] And she reached two alternative answers:

- 'The orthodox view . . . that while the Queen may exercise her powers to encourage and warn, she must ultimately accept formal advice concerning the removal of a Governor-General'[50] [emphasis added]; or

- 'at least in rare circumstances, the Queen would be justified in refusing to act, such as where the advice to dismiss was made by a Prime Minister to prevent his or her own dismissal or where it was made to "subvert the constitution"'.[51]

As can be seen, neither alternative supports Hocking's very limited immediate and non-consultation power.

Nonetheless, Hocking considered that the passages in 1980 Kerr's Journal indicated that there must be more in the 1975 dismissal story to find, given what she regarded as the 'hint of their explosive content'[52] suggested by those passages. She also located one other document in the National Archives that she found of concern. That document contained Sir John's notes on a 'single, slightly crumpled sheet of foolscap paper (see figure 11.2)'[53] that was included in five pages of largely handwritten material that Kerr considered as relevant to be archived and were not otherwise in the public record. They included the words of Roy Jenkins as to the role of a government facing blockage of Supply (see chapter 5),[54] and his handwritten entries relating to the 'Dismissal' which included three scribbled references relating to his conversations with the Prince of Wales: 'New Guinea – Prince of W', 'My relations with the Prince of Wales' and 'Prince's conversation with MC'.[55]

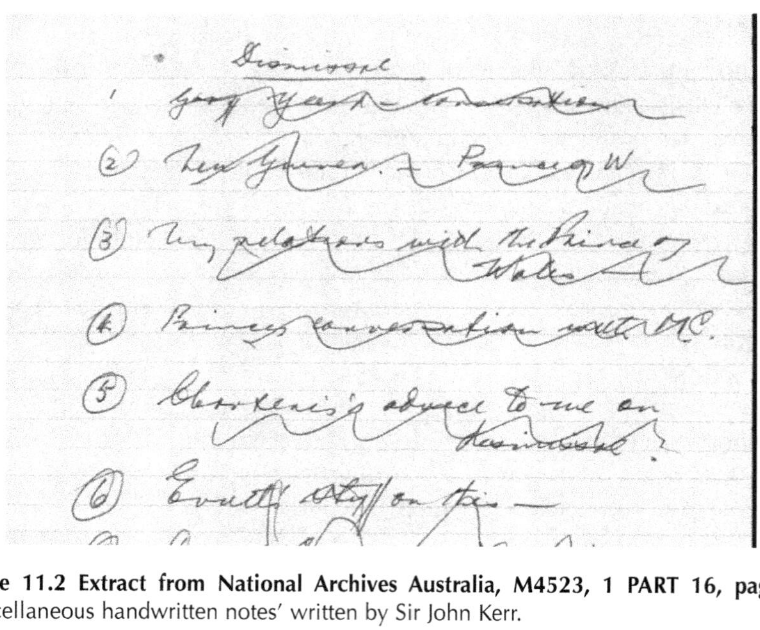

Figure 11.2 Extract from National Archives Australia, M4523, 1 PART 16, page 2. 'Miscellaneous handwritten notes' written by Sir John Kerr.

But to Hocking, the most important entry in that scribbled document was one which she regarded as the 'six of the most important words in the history of the dismissal'.[56] That is, Kerr had also written: 'Charteris' advice to me on the dismissal'.[57] From those few words, Hocking concluded that 'Not only did the Palace know about the prospect of Kerr's dismissal of the Whitlam government, but the Queen's private secretary, Sir Martin Charteris, had given Kerr "advice" about it'. As a result, in her view, 'The chain of communication from Kerr to the Palace and back could hardly have been clearer'.[58] To Hocking, as she earlier said in 2015, the Charteris advice 'can only be seen as an unqualified royal green light to Kerr's dismissal of Whitlam'.[59]

But to clarify that position, Hocking sought the documents that would tell the full story of the Palace's involvement in the dismissal – the correspondence between Kerr and the Palace leading up to and following that event. Hocking considered that those documents would be 'integral to our history'[60] as it was 'obvious that the Palace letters would have an extraordinary story to tell about the dismissal'.[61] But to obtain those documents, she needed to overcome the refusal of the Australian National Archives to release the documents, a refusal that was caused due to what she described as 'The Queen's embargo'.[62]

Fortunately, that was not enough to stop Hocking. She felt that, 'as a historian and as an Australian whose history these letters tell', the Queen's embargo was both 'a personal affront and national humiliation'.[63] As a result, she spent much time and energy bringing her claim to the High Court to challenge the embargo – and she was successful. On May 29, 2020, the High Court ruled that the correspondence between Kerr and the Palace was to be regarded as Commonwealth records and that the director-general of the National Archives was to reconsider Professor Hocking's request for access to the deposited correspondence.[64] And when that occurred, the Palace letters became available to the public.[65]

But, sadly for Hocking, given all the work that she had undertaken to obtain the Palace letters, when the letters were finally released, interesting though they were, they did not support her view that the Palace had approved, encouraged or sought Whitlam's dismissal. What they do indicate is that the Palace did know that Kerr had been considering dismissing Whitlam (despite what Kerr had written in his book). But they also make clear that the Queen did not persuade or embolden Kerr to take that step, and was not aware of Kerr's decision to terminate Whitlam's appointment.

As Kelly and Bramston conclude from the letters, 'Neither the Queen nor the Palace authorised the dismissal or advised Kerr how to conduct the dismissal. There was no "royal green light" from the Palace'.[66] Moreover, Kelly also interviewed the former Labor prime minister (and the one whom Whitlam has regarded as the prime minister 'who had most faithfully carried on his legacy'),[67] Paul Keating, after the release of the Palace Letters, and he unequivocally rejected Palace involvement in the dismissal. As he said, the Queen 'has never contrived, on this occasion or others, over the long course of her reign to undermine governments'.[68]

Hocking, however, has continued to argue that the Palace/Kerr correspondence 'have shattered these claims of royal neutrality and non-involvement, revealing the intensely pollical nature of the correspondence'.[69] To her, they tell a 'story of deception, collusion and intrigue', which she regards 'as disturbing as it is undeniable'.[70] As she had earlier said, in 2017:

> The recent revelation of British involvement in the dismissal of the Whitlam government demolishes some long-standing historical 'truths', notably that the Queen was not involved. Despite repeated public and parliamentary denials, it is now clear that British authorities pressed Kerr in person and through intermediaries on his 'duty' to protect the Queen, in a staggering breach of Australian sovereignty.[71]

And later in that article, she said: 'This communication between Charles, the Queen's private secretary and the Governor-General, is politically and constitutionally shocking. It reveals the Palace to be in deep intrigue with Kerr in the weeks before the dismissal – unknown of course to the Prime Minister, Gough Whitlam'.

To continue to maintain this argument, however, Hocking has adopted some very odd positions. In addition to her highly problematic view that the 'reserve powers' are either a 'fiction'[72] or are 'contested and controversial'[73] (views that are discussed and rejected in chapter 3), she has also maintained the highly doubtful concept that the reserve powers are both 'antithetical to democratic governance'[74] and have died off through lack of use:

> Many believe that, with the passage of time, and the infusion of the sentiments of responsible government through the parliament as the embodiment of the popular will, the notion of the Crown's reserve powers . . . was antithetical to democratic governance and had long since fallen into desuetude.[75]

But this 'atrophy' argument has long been rejected, as seen in the most recent analysis of reserve powers by Professor Anne Twomey,[76] which Hocking does not include in her discussion. In Twomey's view, 'The fact that a power has not been exercised for a long time is merely evidence of its intended rare use – not that it has fallen into desuetude'.[77] Twomey also quotes Lord Balfour[78] who considered in 1913 that the monarch's powers, while rarely used:

> have not on that account become obsolete or fallen into desuetude. The contrary doctrine seems indeed absurd; since it would deprive the sovereign of every power which he does not habitually exercise. It is surely obvious that if a

> prerogative ought rarely to be used, it cannot become obsolete, merely because it is rarely used.[79]

Those views reflect those of other established earlier constitutional authorities, such as Sir William Anson, the author of *The Law and Custom of the Constitution,* who was 'not ready to admit that under such circumstances, these prerogatives have been atrophied by disuse'.[80] Keith, another authority that Hocking does not mention, also wrote in 1936:

> The fact that a power exists only for wise employment in grave circumstances does not mean that it is obsolete, as is sometimes suggested. The mere fact that a safeguard exists is often and perhaps always will be sufficient preventive of such restrained action as would bring the safeguard into operation.[81]

As a result, as Twomey has accurately concluded, 'The fact that the reserve powers have not been exercised in the United Kingdom would appear to be testament to their existence and their effectiveness, as political participants have behaved in such a way as to avoid their exercise'.[82]

Hocking's appreciation of the constitutional powers also seems to be somewhat erratic, and that can be seen from her view that the Palace's objectionable elements in the Palace letters include the Queen's 'failure to warn the Prime Minister about the possibility of his dismissal'. In Hocking's view, 'For a constitutional monarch who must remain politically neutral at all times, this was unconscionable'.[83] Her view seems to have remained the same as her earlier 2015 view, that the Palace, despite its neutrality, should have taken an active role and interfered in Australia's system of government by warning Whitlam of Kerr's proposed actions.

> By failing to inform the Prime Minister of their discussion with Kerr and by failing to alert Whitlam to Kerr's canvassing of his dismissal, the Palace not only abetted Kerr's deception, it was complicit in it.[84]

But for a person who also maintains that the Palace should not interfere in Australia's system of government and should always operate in accordance with 'royal neutrality',[85] this seems a bizarre and inconsistent suggestion. Either the Queen is neutral, or she is not. And if she is neutral, she has no place in undermining the exercise of powers by the person who is constitutionally empowered to exercise those powers. In addition to indicating a lack of appreciation of the difference between consultation with the Palace and receiving its direction, Hocking's argument seems to indicate that she considers that royal neutrality should only apply when the result is one that she supports.

The second odd position that Hocking took was that she was remarkably selective in the material that she relied on; and there is no better example of that than a paragraph from the letter of November 5 to Kerr from Sir Martin Charteris, the Queen's Private Secretary, which Hocking omits to refer to. In that paragraph, Charteris said:

> I think it is good that people should know that The Queen is being informed but, of course, this does not mean that she has any wish to intervene, even if she had the constitutional power to do so. The crisis, as you say, has to be worked out in Australia.[86]

This omitted paragraph makes it very clear, if clarification was necessary, that the Queen did not want the nature of her consultation with the governor-general to be kept a secret from the public (as distinct from its content); that the Queen did not wish to intervene in Australian constitutional matters; that she accepted that she did not have the constitutional power to do so; and, as Charteris accepted, 'The crisis . . . has to be worked out in Australia'. This, however, did not support Hocking's Palace involvement argument.

Hocking's apparently selective approach can also be seen from the few letters she sought to use to support her Palace involvement claim, and how she used, or did not use, the content of those few letters. It is remarkable about how few letters she has relied on. Of the many letters and documents issued after the High Court decision, more than 70 letters and notes were dated on or prior to November 11, 1975.[87] And of those 70 plus letters and notes, Hocking relied on just four.

Her main attention was given to the letter of September 24, 1975, from Martin Charteris to John Kerr and, in particular, to the handwritten addition included by Charteris that draws attention of the governor-general to the book by Eugene Forsey.[88]

> P. S. I suppose you know Eugene Forsey's book 'The Prerogative of the Dissolution'? [*sic*].[89] I believe he lays it down as a principle that if Supply is refused this always makes it constitutionally proper to grant a dissolution.[90]

She criticizes this note on a number of points. First, Charteris was not a lawyer but, she considered, was a friend of Forsey. Then, Forsey's appreciation of Australia's constitutional structure was, 'at best limited'. She regards Forsey merely a 'particular theorist in a contested field', a 'constitutional conservative' and a 'royalist radical'. As a result, she considers Charteris's note 'not only inappropriate' but also 'clearly directive'.[91] In her view, Charteris was telling Kerr what to do, and the basis for the actions.

But is that so? In relation to Hocking's assertion of Forsey's 'ignorance of the Australian circumstances', this evidently is derived from some form of assessment drawn by a Canadian under-secretary for external affairs, made in November 1975 and relates to Forsey's alleged lack of appreciation of the constitutional basis of Australian half senate elections.[92] Whether that is true or not is of little importance as Forsey's expertise was not on the structure of the *Australian Constitution*, but in his knowledge of the doctrine of reserve powers. Hocking, however, seems to have minimized that expertise based on her description of Forsey as being only a 'particular theorist in a contested field'.[93] What Hocking omits is that in 1975 there were very few books of any merit on the subject of reserve powers. And the key books in that little list were, first, Dr Evatt's 1936 *The King and His Dominion Governors,* and second, Forsey's 1943, *The Royal Power of Dissolution of the Parliament in the British Commonwealth.* And both books accepted that the reserve powers existed. The importance of those two books can be appreciated from the foreword to the combined reprint of those two works in 1990, written by the great proponent of an Australian republic, critic of Kerr for his 1975 actions, and himself, a great expert in the field of reserve powers, the late Professor George Winterton.[94] In that foreword, Winterton referred to those two works as being 'of this century's greatest works on the reserve powers of the Crown'[95] and that 'it would be rare to find a recent discussion of the reserve powers which does not refer to at least one of these books'.[96]

As to Hocking's view that Forsey was just a 'conservative, pro-monarchist theorist',[97] she seems to misunderstand if not misrepresent Forsey and his position. As Winterton has recognized (but Hocking seems to have ignored), Forsey was, like Evatt, a socialist. And as to Hocking's view that Forsey was 'very pro-monarchy' or 'very conservative in constitutional matters'[98], or a 'royalist radical', Winterton also seems unlikely to agree, as he considered that Forsey was both 'a great opponent of the "rubber-stamp" theory of vice-regal power' and 'no proponent of vast, unlimited reserve powers'.[99] As Winterton pointed out, reliant on the views of Donald Creighton, Forsey's approach was based on his unusual, if not unique, combination of both 'social radicalism' with 'constitutional traditionalism'.[100] As Creighton has said:

> As a historian and political scientist, Eugene stands quite alone in Canada. His combination of scholarly and literary qualities is unique. His historical traditionalism and social radicalism forms an incomprehensible mixture which completely baffles most Canadian critics. They are simply not equipped, intellectually, to cope with him.[101]

Hocking seems equally baffled by Forsey.

But she still made her 'Most critical' opposition to the use of Forsey: that Forsey and Evatt had reached very different conclusions on the 'constitutionality and propriety of the [Canadian] Governor-General's 1926 dissolution of the Canadian House of Commons'.[102] Hocking takes the view that that Canadian constitutional crisis is 'seen as most comparable to the situation in Australia in 1975', which is very puzzling in that the 1926 crisis did not involve the blockage of supply by the Upper House and did not involve the governor-general dismissing the head of government without warning, the two most central and problematic actions that occurred in 1975. In fact, 1926 has very little in common with 1975 other than they both involved the exercise of the reserve powers; 1975 being concerned with the governor-general's power to sack a prime minister, while 1926 was concerned with the reserve power to reject advice to dissolve the Lower House.[103]

The Byng/King 1926 circumstances are only relevant to 1975 when considering the scope of the reserve powers. That is, to what extent can they be exercised contrary to Ministerial advice, or is the governor-general now the equivalent of a mere rubber stamp? Hocking, of course, takes the view that the rubber stamp approach is correct; a view which, as the discussion in chapter 3 demonstrates, is, at least, problematic.

As to whether Charteris's note was 'clearly directive', this is simply not supported by the words and expressions used. For a non-lawyer, such as Charteris, to refer to an experienced former Supreme Court chief justice, Sir John Kerr, and a legal book (and by using its incorrect title) is not indicative of any clarity or any direction, but of what only can be seen as what Charteris seems to have hoped as a helpful suggestion for research regarding one of the few persons with demonstrated expertise on the reserve powers, and nothing more.

The next letter that Hocking relies on is the letter dated October 27, 1975, from Kerr to Charteris. Towards the end of that lengthy, six-page letter, which Kerr wrote between October 27 and 30, Kerr sought Charteris's view as to whether any decision he might make could 'affect the monarchy'.[104] This question Hocking takes exception to as it, according to her, 'invites the Palace to contribute directly to whatever action he is to make'. This, however, is not consistent with what Kerr said.

The text of this letter is not, however, quoted at length in either Hocking's book or in the treatment of Kelly and Bramston. As such, the paragraphs in that letter that are the basis of Hocking's concern read as follows:

> There is one point I should like to raise. There has been the odd reference in the press to The Queen having been kept informed and this has been confirmed by the Palace. I appreciate that, except on such matters as those upon which the Prime Minister advises Her Majesty direct, she would be anxious – or at least so I assume – for this crisis to be worked out in Australia. However anything I may do or not do could indirectly affect the Monarchy in Australia and I should

welcome any observations on a private and personal basis which you may care to make and which, as you see it, should be taken into account in the interests of the Monarchy in Australia.

In mentioning this I have no desire to escape from any responsibility which the Constitution places on my shoulders or to lessen it or have some excuse for any particular course I may take, but I feel that I should consider, in deciding what I ought to do, anything which may directly or indirectly affect The Queen.

As to Hocking's concerns, they seem unjustified. First, Kerr asked for Charteris's observations, not on behalf of the Queen or the Palace, but 'on a private and personal basis'. Second, and more importantly, Kerr made it clear, in the next paragraph, that he had 'no desire to escape from any responsibility which the Constitution places on my shoulders or to lessen it or have some excuse for any particular course I may take'. His intention was not to seek, expressly or impliedly, any direction from the palace, but instead he sought observations of any matters that may directly or indirectly affect the Queen, that he 'should consider, in deciding what I ought to do'.[105]

Nonetheless, Kerr's concerns were much broader than what they should have been. That is, a governor-general's primary, if not total concern, should have been the impact of any decision he may make on Australia and its citizens, regardless of any impact on the Monarch. And, as Hocking accurately said in 2017, 'The Governor-General of Australia has no duty "to protect the Queen"'.[106] But the response to Kerr, on November 5, was that there were no extraneous or what was formerly known as Imperial matters for Kerr to be concerned about. As Charteris said:

If you do, as you will, what the constitution dictates, you cannot possibly do the Monarchy any avoidable harm. The chances are you will do it good.[107]

So, what is the problem? Hocking takes exception to Charteris' final sentence,[108] and does so by arguing, somewhat oddly, that 'Kerr's decisions were in this sense entirely bound by considerations of his view of the interests of the Queen and what was best for the monarchy'.[109] But that is precisely what Charteris had expressly denied on November 5. As Charteris said, Kerr's task was to do 'what the constitution dictates'.

Hocking also considered that Kerr, by seeking Charteris' advice, 'The Queen's private secretary has now usurped Kerr's Australia's constitutional advisors'.[110] But that indicates that Hocking fails to appreciate the nature of the reserve powers. That is, this view indicates that she either continues to reject the validity of the concept of reserve powers, despite the weight of the prevailing academic authorities, or that she has simply does not appreciate the nature of 'reserve powers'. As pointed out in chapter 3, reserve powers are not powers which the governor-general's constitutional advisers or anyone else can control. They are powers which the governor-general exercises on his or her own responsibility.[111]

Hocking, however, attempts to reinforce her position by reference to other items in the letters in reply from Charteris, of November 4 and 5 (the last two letters that Hocking refers to).[112] She quotes Charteris from his letter of November 4 as saying 'definitely that the contested and controversial reserve powers do exist: "those powers do exist . . . but to use them is a heavy responsibility"'.[113] This is a remarkably inaccurate statement. First, as we have seen, the reserve powers were not in 1975, 'contested and controversial'. They may not have been known to many in the public and the press; but of those who have studied and written on that concept, like the former Labor leader and High Court Justice, Dr Evatt; the Canadian academic and parliamentarian, Eugene Forsey; and the leading academic and Kerr's successor as Australia's governor-general, Sir Zelman Cowen, they clearly existed, even if there was much disagreement as to how they operated. Indeed, it would seem difficult to locate any academic work studying the reserve powers prior to 1975 that contested or denied the existence of those powers. Even Dr Markesinis, who Hocking attempted to use to support her argument regarding the reserve powers, was not prepared to deny their existence. While he said in 1972, that 'It may be that the whole operation of discussing the limits of the reserve powers of the Crown is nowadays . . . an idle exercise', he qualified those views by also saying *'for most purposes'*.[114] As Professor Twomey recently told Paul Kelly, 'There is nothing shocking or surprising about the statement by Charteris that the reserve powers exist. This has always been the position taken by the Palace. It is not possible to say that such powers do not exist, when they are still being exercised in numerous countries'.[115]

But the second, and possibly the greater concern with Hocking's quotation, is that she misquotes Charteris by omitting what seem to be salient words regarding Charteris' intention and purpose, presumably because they do not suit Hocking's argument. Charteris did use the words that Hocking quotes: 'those powers do exist', but they were prefaced by Charteris with two other words, and those words were 'I think'. These two words clearly indicate that Charteris's observation to Kerr was something less than being made 'definitely'. But Hocking omitted those words.

Hocking seeks to fortify her position by pointing out that in the letter of November 5, Charteris ended his letter with a quotation from what Hocking describes as the 'conservative recipient of the Canadian governor-general's largess in 1926', Arthur Meighen, who had, as Hocking put it, 'an extremely positivist view of an interventionist governor-general'. Meighen's words were, as Hocking points out, said by Charteris to be 'good stuff', thereby, it seems, supporting what she considered as the Palace's view that Kerr should intervene. The words re-stated by Hocking from Charteris's supposed endorsed Meighen quote were:

> The sphere of discretion left to a Governor-General under our constitution and under our practice is a limited sphere indeed, but it is a sphere of dignity and great responsibility. Within the ambit of discretion residing still in the Crown in England, and residing in the Governor-General in the Dominions, there is a responsibility as great as falls to any estate of the realm or to any House of Parliament.[116]

There is, however, little of concern that can be seen in these quoted words. Indeed, if there is any concern to Hocking, it seems to be solely limited to Meighen's and, therefore, Charteris' support for the existence of the reserve powers. But, as we have seen when we discussed the nature of reserve powers in chapter 3, the clear academic position, particularly prior to 1975, was that those powers clearly existed. Meighen's words were merely consistent with that view.

But a more significant response to Hocking's criticism is that Charteris' 'good stuff' reference seems not to have been in relation to the continued existence of the reserve powers. Instead, it may well have been made in relation to the next paragraph from Meighen; a paragraph that includes constraints on the use of those reserve powers. Hocking, however, has omitted, for reasons best known to her, these words from her discussion. So here they are:

> Within the sphere of that discretion the plain duty of the Governor-General is not to weaken responsible government, not to undermine the rights of parliament . . . it is to make sure that responsible government is maintained, that the rights of parliament are respected, that the still higher rights of the people are held sacred. It is his duty to make sure that parliament is not stifled by government, but that every government is held responsible to parliament, and every parliament held responsible to the people.[117]

All of this seems to clearly indicate that what Charteris and Meighen were saying was that the reserve powers are to be rarely used, and when used, they still need to protect responsible government, the rights of parliament, and those of the people. This makes Hocking's latter assertion that 'some commentators who have described Charteris as here advising Kerr to be cautious' as being 'completely untenable'[118] as clearly unsound. Caution is clearly what the words that Hocking chose to omit from her November 5 quotation said and intended.

Hocking, however, regards the letters of November 4 and 5 as 'the ballast that Kerr needs', and she considered that they provided the 'confidence that his dismissal of the Prime Minister would not be disavowed by the Palace'.

This view makes little sense, as it seems to be based on the incorrect assumption that the Queen had the legal and constitutional power to 'disavow' the dismissal. But the Queen neither had, nor desired, such power. To repeat the language from the letter of November 5, which Hocking failed to refer to, it was made very clear that the Queen did not have any 'wish to intervene' in Australian constitutional matters and she did not have 'the constitutional power to do so'. As Charteris in that letter said, 'The crisis . . . has to be worked out in Australia'.

So, of all the material released as a result of Hocking's successful High Court application, these are the only letters regarding the dismissal of Whitlam that Hocking was able to provide to give any support for what she had earlier said was the Palace's 'unforgiveable breach of our independence and our national sovereignty'. But as can be seen, even from those letters, even when selectively quoted from, as Hocking seems to prefer, there was still no Palace 'Green light' for Whitlam's dismissal and no breach of Australian sovereignty. Indeed, that 'Green Light' conclusion cannot be reached when the full text of the Palace/Kerr letters is considered.

As most of those documents, while available for public inspection, are not all included in popular works on 1975, it was considered advisable to include the following passages from letters from the Queen's private secretary, Martin Charteris, to the governor-general, to indicate the neutral position taken by the Palace in 1975:

Letter of October 23, 1975[119]

> We must of course still hope that the crisis will somehow become defused and I am sure you are all doing all that you can, properly, to see that this happens. I fear, however, that you are dealing with two resolute and obstinate men, neither of whom will find it at all easy politically or temperamentally to withdraw from the positions they have taken up.[120]

Letter of October 27, 1975[121]

> The impression here is that the political battle is swinging in the Prime Minister's favour. I suppose there was always a good chance that the Opposition's threat to deny supply in the Senate, in the face of the convention not to do so, would boomerang on them and, of course, in this sort of political in-fighting, Mr Whitlam is tremendously formidable.
>
> I was extremely interested in the Prime Minister's new tactic which you describe in your letter.[122] It sounds very ingenious, but I have, of course, no idea whether it would work.

Letter of November 4, 1975[123]

> With the greatest respect, I am sure you are right in taking the line that your crisis has not yet crossed the line from the political onto the constitutional arena. Mr Fraser wants to believe it is already a 'constitutional' crisis because he wants to win. If the tide of public opinion continues to flood against him he may well modify his view, and look for a way of retreat.
>
> Again, with greatest respect, I think you are playing the 'Vice-Regal' hand with skill and wisdom. Your interest in the situation has been demonstrated, and so has your impartiality. The fact that you have powers is recognised, but it is also clear that you will only use them in the last resort and then only for constitutional and not for political reasons.

Letter of November 17, 1975[124]

> If I may so with the greatest respect, I believe that in NOT informing The Queen what you intended to do before doing it, you acted with perfect constitutional propriety but also with admirable consideration for Her Majesty's position.

What these paragraphs demonstrate is that the Palace:

- was in no way supporting Fraser or encouraging Kerr to do so;
- emphasised that while the reserve powers exist, they should only be used 'in the last resort';
- recognised that the powers to be exercised were those of the Governor-General, and not those of the Queen; and that
- the Queen had no knowledge of the Governor-General's decision to dismiss Whitlam before it was made.

While the Palace letters can be criticized for not emphasising the governor-general's right to warn, a right that, as pointed out in chapter 9, should have been central to Kerr's discussions with Whitlam, they otherwise do not support any of Hocking's colourful, but somewhat fictional conclusions. There was simply no 'deception, collusion and intrigue'; no 'litany of institutional improprieties'; and no 'breaches of the essence of the vice-regal relationship'.[125]

As a result, the conclusion of the former Labor prime minister and pro-republican, Paul Keating, was plainly correct when asked by Paul Kelly whether the Queen has always done the right thing by Australia. His response was clear and unequivocal: 'I do'.[126]

NOTES

1. These issues are discussed in Mann's "State Secrets," 24 March 2020 in *The Eleventh*, Episode 7, Australian Broadcasting Commission, podcast audio.

2. As seen in "SBS Dateline Exclusive Interview with Christopher 'Falcon' Boyce" (2014), Youtube, https://www.youtube.com/watch?v=mmElu9tx2S0, 11.40-12.20, accessed December 30, 2022; and in Mann "State Secrets," 24 March 2020 in *The Eleventh*, Episode 7, Australian Broadcasting Commission, podcast audio.

3. John Pilger, *A Secret Country* (London: Vintage, 1992), chapter 5.

4. Pilger, *Secret Country,* 193.

5. Commonwealth of Australia, *Parliamentary Debates*, House of Representatives, August 21, 1975, 468. The questioner was Tony Stanley MP (Chisolm, Victoria). Also, see Gough Whitlam, *The Whitlam Government, 1972–1975* (Ringwood, Victoria: Penguin, 1985), 50.

6. Christopher Boyce, "Introduction" to Christopher Boyce, Cait Boyce & Vince Font, *American Sons, The Untold Story of the Falcon and the Snowman* (Glass Spider Publishing, 2013–2018), 6, 7.

7. Quoted in James Curran, *Unholy Fury* (Carlton: Melbourne University Press, 2015), 403.

8. Robert Lindsey, *The Falcon and the Snowman* (Harmondsworth: Penguin, 1980), 83.

9. Boyce, "Introduction," 8.

10. "SBS Dateline Exclusive Interview with Christopher 'Falcon' Boyce" (2014), Youtube, https://www.youtube.com/watch?v=mmElu9tx2S0, 10.25, accessed December 30, 2022.

11. Lindsey, *Falcon and the Snowman*, 158.

12. Lindsey, *Falcon and the Snowman*, 157.

13. Freudenberg, *Certain Grandeur*, 387. Pilger asserts that Kerr was briefed on Sunday, November 9. See Pilger, *Secret Country*, 193.

14. Quoted in Lindsey, *Falcon and the Snowman*, 157.

15. Lindsey, *Falcon and the Snowman*, 158.

16. Mann, "State Secrets," at 6.15-6.20.

17. Freudenberg, *Certain Grandeur*, 387.

18. Commonwealth of Australia, *Parliamentary Debates*, House of Representatives, November 4, 1975, 2722. And see Whitlam, *Whitlam Government,* 50 and Brian Toohey, "Arthur Tange and Gough Whitlam Spy Mystery: Was there a Crucial Information Gap?" *Financial Review*, November 6, 2015.

19. Whitlam, *Whitlam Government*, 51. And see Commonwealth of Australia, *Parliamentary Debates*, House of Representatives, November 4, 1975, 2721.

20. Commonwealth of Australia, *Parliamentary Debates*, House of Representatives, November 5, 1975, 2790.

21. Commonwealth of Australia, *Parliamentary Debates*, House of Representatives, November 5, 1975, 2790.

22. Whitlam, *Whitlam Government,* 51.
23. Curran, *Unholy Fury,* 443.
24. Whitlam, *Whitlam Government,* 51.
25. Hocking, *His Time* (2012), 294.
26. Whitlam, *The Truth,* 158, xxii.
27. Whitlam, *Whitlam Government,* 52.
28. Jenny Hocking, "'A Royal Green Light': The Palace, the Governor-General and the Dismissal of the Whitlam Government," in *Pearls and Irritations,* John Menadue's Public Policy Journal, October 23, 2017, https://johnmenadue.com/jenny-hocking-a-royal-green-light-the-palace-the-governor-general-and-the-dismissal-of-the-whitlam-government/, accessed, January 3, 2023.
29. Hocking, "A Royal Green Light."
30. Menadue, *Interview.*
31. Menadue, *Things You Learn,* 165–166.
32. Kerr, *Matters,* 330.
33. Kerr, *Matters,* 331.
34. Kerr, *Matters,* 330.
35. Kerr, *Matters,* 330.
36. Kerr, *Matters,* 330.
37. Kerr, *Matters,* 332.
38. Hocking, *Dismissal Dossier,* 13 and Hocking, *Palace Letters,* 19.
39. NAA, *Journal for 1980, maintained by Sir John Kerr,* M4523, 1 Part 17, 137. Quoted in Hocking, *Palace Letters,* 18 and in Hocking, *Dismissal Dossier,* 14, but without the words "at the very time." The emphasis is also Hocking's.
40. Hocking, *Palace Letters,* 19.
41. Hocking, *Palace Letters,* 19.
42. Hocking, *Palace Letters,* 20.
43. Hocking, *Palace Letters,* 21.
44. Hocking, *Palace Letters,* 22.
45. The last Treasurer in the Whitlam government, before succeeding him as the parliamentary leader of the Labor Party between 1977 and 1983, then became governor-general.
46. Quoted in Killey, *Constitutional Conventions,* 209.
47. Hocking, *Palace Letters,* 22.
48. Hocking, *Palace Letters,* 22.
49. That can be found in Twomey, *Veiled Sceptre,* 823–834.
50. Twomey, *Veiled Sceptre,* 823.
51. Twomey, *Veiled Sceptre,* 823–824.
52. Hocking, *Palace Letters,* 23.
53. Hocking, *Palace Letters,* 24.
54. See NAA, *Miscellaneous handwritten notes,* M4523, 1 Part 16, 5.
55. See NAA, *Miscellaneous handwritten notes,* M4523, 1 Part 16, 2.
56. Hocking, *Palace Letters,* 24.
57. Hocking, *Palace Letters,* 24. See NAA, *Miscellaneous handwritten notes,* M4523, 1 Part 16, 2.

58. Hocking, *Palace Letters,* 25.

59. Hocking, *Dismissal Dossier*, 24. Also see similar words said in 2017 in Hocking, "'Royal Green Light'."

60. Hocking, *Palace Letters,* 23.

61. Hocking, *Palace Letters,* 21.

62. Hocking, *Palace Letters,* 24.

63. Hocking, *Palace Letters,* 23.

64. *Hocking v Director-General of the National Archives of Australia* (2020) 271 CLR 1. Also see Anne Twomey, "Before the High Court: *Hocking v Director-General of the National Archives of Australia*: Can Kerr's Correspondence with the Queen be Kept Secret Forever?" (2020) 42(1) *Sydney Law Journal* 97.

65. The names of the documents released by the National Archives of Australia are listed in six summaries that can be found at National Archives of Australia, *The Kerr Palace Letters*, AA1984/609, https://www.naa.gov.au/explore-collection/kerr-palace-letters.

66. Kelly & Bramston, *Truth, Palace Letters,* 194.

67. Troy Bramston, "Preface to the Revised Edition," in *The Whitlam Legacy* xii, xvi.

68. Quoted in Kelly & Bramston, *Truth, Palace Letters*, 33.

69. Hocking, *Palace Letters,* 230.

70. Hocking, *Palace Letters,* 231.

71. Hocking, "'A Royal Green Light'."

72. Hocking, *Palace Letters,* 204.

73. Hocking, *Palace Letters,* 208.

74. Hocking, *Palace Letters,* 203.

75. Hocking, *Palace Letters,* 203. Hocking does not specify who the "Many" are.

76. Twomey, *Veiled Sceptre*, 30–35.

77. Twomey, *Veiled Sceptre*, 31.

78. Lord Arthur Balfour, Prime Minister, Great Britain, 1902–1905.

79. Quoted in Twomey, *Veiled Sceptre*, 31 and in Bogdanor, *Monarchy and the Constitution,* 127.

80. Quoted in Bogdanor, *Monarchy and the Constitution*, 125.

81. Quoted in Twomey, *Veiled Sceptre*, 32.

82. Twomey, *Veiled Sceptre*, 31.

83. Hocking, *Palace Letters,* 216.

84. Hocking, *Dismissal Dossier*, 25.

85. Hocking, *Palace Letters,* 230.

86. This letter can be found in Kelly & Bramston, *Truth, Palace Letters,* 209–210.

87. See the various documents issued by the National Archives of Australia can be found in NAA, *The Kerr Palace Letters,* AA1984/609.

88. This letter can be seen in Kelly & Bramston, *Truth, Palace Letters*, 199.

89. The correct title of Forsey's book is *The Royal Power of Dissolution of Parliament in the British Parliament.*

90. Hocking, *Palace Letters,* 201.

91. Hocking, *Palace Letters,* 202.

92. Hocking, *Palace Letters,* 202 and 251 (n 22).

93. Hocking, *Palace Letters,* 202.

94. George Winterton had been professor of law at the University of New South Wales and then a Professor of Constitutional Law at the University of Sydney. He is the author of several notable works including:

- *Parliament, the Executive and the Governor-General: a constitutional analysis* (Melbourne: Melbourne University Press, 1983).
- *Monarchy to Republic: Australian Republican Government* (Oxford University Press, 1986 & rev ed, 1994).
- *"1975: The Dismissal of the Whitlam Government"* in *Australian Constitutional Landmarks*, eds. H. P. Lee & G. Winterton (Cambridge University Press, 2003), 229.

95. George Winterton, "Foreword," in *Evatt and Forsey on the Reserve Powers* (New South Wales: Legal Books, 1990), vii.

96. Winterton, "Foreword," ix.

97. Hocking, *Palace Letters,* 229.

98. Hocking, *Palace Letters,* 228.

99. Winterton, "Foreword," x.

100. Winterton, "Foreword," vii–viii.

101. Donald Creighton, "Eugene Alfred Forsey: An Introduction," in Eugene Forsey, *Freedom and Order, Collected Essays* (Toronto: Carleton Library, 1974), 1, 18. Also see Eugene Forsey, *A Life on the Fringe, The Memoirs of Eugene Forsey* (Toronto: Oxford University Press, 1990).

102. Hocking, *Palace Letters,* 202.

103. 1926 is discussed in Killey, *Constitutional Conventions,* 171–3 & 224.

104. Quoted in Hocking, *Palace Letters,* 207.

105. Letter from Kerr to Charteris, October 27, 1975, 4.

106. Hocking, "'A Royal Green Light'."

107. Letter from Charteris to Kerr, November 5, 1975, a copy of which can be found in Kelly & Bramston, *Truth, Palace Letters,* 209–210.

108. The title of chapter eleven of Hocking's *Palace Letters* is "You will do it good."

109. Hocking, *Palace Letters,* 222.

110. Hocking, *Palace Letters,* 207.

111. See the discussion of reserve powers in Killey, *Constitutional Conventions,* ch. 7.

112. These letters can be seen in Kelly & Bramston, *Truth, Palace Letters,* 208–210.

113. Hocking, *Palace Letters,* 208.

114. B. S. Markesinis, *The Theory and Practice of Dissolution of Parliament* (Cambridge: Cambridge University Press, 1972), 121. Emphasis added.

115. Quoted in Kelly & Bramston, *Truth, Palace Letters,* 40.

116. Quoted by Hocking, *Palace Letters,* 209.

117. From a letter from Charteris to Kerr, November 5, 1975, a copy of which can be found in Kelly & Bramston, *Truth, Palace Letters,* 209–210. The ellipsis in the passage was included in the words used in Charteris' letter.

118. Hocking, *Truth, Palace Letters,* 208.

119. NAA, *The Kerr Palace Letters,* AA1984/609, Part 2.

120. 2nd paragraph of letter of October 23, 1975 from Martin Charteris.

121. NAA, *The Kerr Palace Letters,* AA1984/609, Part 2.

122. That is, Whitlam's alternative financial plan.

123. NAA, *The Kerr Palace Letters,* AA1984/609, Part 2.

124. NAA, *The Kerr Palace Letters,* AA1984/609, Part 2. Quoted in Kelly & Bramston, *The Truth,* 216–217.

125. Hocking, *Truth, Palace Letters,* 231.

126. Quoted in Kelly & Bramston, *Truth*, *Palace Letters*, 33, from an interview in August 2020.

Chapter 12

Was 1975 a Local 'Coup'?

Figure 12.1 ALP Political Badge from the 1977 Election. From the collection of the author. Image taken by the author.

As we have seen, 1975 seems not to have been created, driven or controlled by the Royal family or the CIA, despite suspicions and arguments by some journalists and historians. But the other theory is that the dismissal was the product of a locally driven conspiracy or *coup d'etat.* That conclusion, presented as early as 1976 by Donald Horne in his *Death of the Lucky Country*, a short work 'struck off in three weeks of passion and pain'[1] after the dismissal, where Horne argued that Kerr's actions on November 11 were a locally driven 'time-tabled operation, for which *coup d'etat'* seems a useful description'?[2] Horne was, however, somewhat unclear as to the parties in that *coup*, beyond Kerr and Barwick. But later authors have clarified and extended that supposed *coup* theory to being a 'coup by Kerr, Fraser and some High Court judges', as Whitlam's head of department, John Menadue, has recently expressed,[3] echoing Whitlam's own post-dismissal views that Kerr's actions were 'a coup conceived in secret and executed by ambush'?[4] Former senator John Faulkner[5] and Gough Whitlam in their 2002 film, *Gough Whitlam: In His Own Words*, also assert that the dismissal was the product of 'three central figures who conspired to bring down your government: Kerr, Barwick and of course, Fraser'?[6]

These 'coup' allegations have gained much public acceptance; but for those conspiracy allegations to be true, Faulkner's and Whitlam's 'three central figures' needed to have acted together, and with one common objective – to bring down the Whitlam government. Is this true of those three central figures, Kerr in particular? Was the governor-general, when he dismissed Whitlam, as Faulkner has argued in his volume, *True Believers,* in 2001, 'in collusion with the Chief Justice Sir Garfield Barwick and Opposition Leader Malcolm Fraser to bring Labor down'?[7]

Kerr has denied being in any conspiracy with Fraser (see his letter to Martin Charteris, November 24, 1975).[8] But it is clear that he had separate discussions with both Fraser and Barwick, some of which were known to Whitlam, while others were not; and some were clearly contrary to Whitlam's advice. And that seems consistent with the *coup* allegations.

As to the motivation of the three, Fraser's objective was obvious – it was opportunistic and political, with a clear intent to replace Whitlam as prime minister. And that political objective may also have been held by, or influenced, the chief justice (given his earlier ministerial role in the Menzies Liberal/Country government). But did the remaining member of this supposed tripartite 'conspiracy', John Kerr, also want to 'bring Labor down'?

One person who one would have thought would have agreed, having been one of the central casualties of Kerr's dismissal, believed otherwise. That is, Gough's successor as the ALP leader, and later Australia's twenty-first governor-general, Bill Hayden. In 1975, Hayden had been one of Whitlam's senior and most competent ministers, having been responsible for the development of one of the continuing and lasting benefits of the Whitlam government, Australia's first system of universal health insurance, then called Medibank. Then he became Whitlam's final Treasurer, responsible for the budget that was blocked in the 1975 supply crisis. After the 1975 dismissal, he went on to be the parliamentary leader of the ALP from 1977 to 1983. While he never took the next step to become prime minister, he was Australia's Foreign Minister from 1983 to 1988 in the Bob Hawke-led Labor government before becoming Australia's governor-general. He held that vice-regal office for a much longer term than John Kerr – seven years between 1989 and 1996, the second-longest term of any of Australia's governors-general.[9] And with that experience, Hayden was able to assess Kerr's actions from both the perspective of its victim and from holding the inflicting office.[10]

His view of Kerr was that he had been 'miscast by history'.[11] That, Hayden accepted, is the 'heretics view',[12] particularly in the party that he once led, the ALP; but he considered that Kerr's objective was sensible as he had 'sought to do what he believed was right and proper'. According to Hayden's autobiography, Kerr's problem was not with his objective, but with his methods, and that was because Kerr's 'judgment was flawed'[13] derived from a 'faulty political "feel" for the situation'[14] and from Kerr's lack of firmness, driven by his fear of dismissal by Whitlam.[15]

As to Kerr's action in dismissing Whitlam, Hayden's view was partially supportive of Kerr. He accepted that Kerr was faced with the 'country plunge[ing] deeper and deeper down a sinkhole of economic chaos, while two titans slugged it out in a personal battle over who was to control government'. And he acknowledged that a governor-general 'could not sit idly' but needed to act.[16] Hayden accepts that he 'would, as Governor-General, have been forced to have intervened much as he did' but that he would have done so at a later date[17] and with much more 'directness and clarity in his dealings with Whitlam'.[18]

This is not the popular view of Kerr and his motives, but it is reflected in Kerr's letters to the Palace that Professor Hocking has done so much to make public, letters that were not available in 1996 when Hayden wrote his biography. Those letters are of particular importance in that Kerr was most unlikely to have misled the Palace as to his overriding purpose (although some of the content of his letters has been selectively constructed to support Kerr's actions).

As Hocking said: 'the Palace letters would have an extraordinary story to tell about the dismissal', but if 'only we could see them'.[19] But when we were finally able to examine those letters to ascertain whether Kerr was conspiring with Fraser and Barwick, or the Palace itself, to bring down the Whitlam government, as Hocking would have us believe, the answer is a clear No.

The most relevant period to examine those letters for a consideration of Kerr's reasoning is the second half of 1975, in the period leading up to and immediately after the dismissal and the election. The following is a summary of Kerr's letters between August and December sent to Martin Charteris. These letters are now electronically available to the public on the National Archives of Australia page, *The Kerr Palace Letters*[20] (and the letters in this period are found in Parts 1, 2 and 3 of that collection). Some of the letters can also be found in Paul Kelly and Troy Bramston's *The Truth of the Palace Letters*.[21] However, as many of the letters have not been quoted in popular or academic sources, the following summary will allow readers to appreciate the nature of the correspondence between Kerr and the Palace during this period. The only letters discussed below are those that deal with the supply issue.

AUGUST 1975

August 29[22] – This is the first letter that raises the supply blockage issues. It is four pages and largely concerns the government's budget and the subject of inflation. However, Kerr also raises the issues of the competition between the two parties and a possible supply crisis in the following passages:

> Mr Fraser has accordingly announced that although the Budget will be criticised by the Opposition, and he has criticised it, no election will be precipitated this year unless some unexpected and serious change occurs.
>
> The Prime Minister had expected it to be possible that an election would occur on December 5th, if supply were denied, but Mr Fraser has been leaving the impression that the Prime Minister could juggle the election date so as to avoid an election till February, even if supply were denied.

And he added a postscript to the letter:

> This morning the Prime Minister predicted no election in May next year saying that he thought that the Leader of the Opposition had, in effect, a better sense of values than his predecessor and would wait till 1977.

SEPTEMBER 1975

September 12[23] – This three-page letter dealt with the potential supply crisis in a number of paragraphs and sentences.

In a nutshell, the position is that Mr Fraser has set out to establish a different style and image for himself from that of his predecessor Mr Snedden. He sought to leave the impression that he was in a statesman like way, accepting the view that the Labor Party had won the last election and was entitled to govern for three years. [H]e did it with qualifications, that in the normal course the Government would not be denied supply. This would not happen unless some extraordinary and reprehensible circumstance emerged.

This impression of a temporary truce was reinforced by the Government's Budget which seemed to be a reasonable attempt to control inflation.

Mr Fraser . . . his attitude was that the Opposition should not defeat the Budget in the Senate.

However, since then, the Gallop Polls have indicated the very low state of popularity both of the Prime Minister and the Government and the pressure on Mr Fraser to have the Budget defeated in the Senate is enormous.

I have come to the conclusion that Mr Fraser is really being driven to find an excuse to deny supply and defeat the Budget.

I feel reasonably sure that the Prime Minister believes that if there is to be an election at this stage the loss for his party would be devastating and the Opposition would gain control of both Houses. In this situation he is not in the mood, to coin a phrase, 'to go quietly'.

If the Senate refuses to pass it, the theory is that the Prime Minister will not accept that as a ground for coming to me for a dissolution. . . . He will simply say that the responsibility for funds running out must be borne by the Opposition. . . . Then there will be a battle in the country about who is responsible for the ensuing mess – failure to meet obligations, pay public servants, the Defence Forces and so on.

If the Prime Minister and the Leader of the Opposition get into a battle in which the Senate has defeated the Budget, the Prime Minister refuses to recommend a dissolution, my role will need some careful thought though, of course, the classical constitutional convention will presumably govern the matter.

September 20[24] – In this three-page letter, Kerr comes back to what was then the possible blockage of supply when he discussed the Senate's powers under s 53 *Commonwealth Constitution* and what he might do if that happened. He made it clear that he considered that the Opposition could block supply, but that he considered 'it better to keep my mind and my options open' and that he would not make any decision until 'the last moment'.

The Prime Minister . . . told me that he was minded if the Senate rejected the Appropriation Bills, to present them to me nevertheless for assent with advice that the Senate has no legal power to reject them. He asked me what I would do if he were to take this course. I rather parried this. . . .

The Press is almost universally against Mr Fraser on all of this. . . .

Another point of importance put to me by the Prime Minister . . . was that if I were, at the height of the crisis, contrary to his advice to terminate his commission . . . Mr Fraser would not be able to get supply either because new legislation would probably be necessary and it would not pass the House of Representatives.

One point is that if neither can get supply . . . it is said that only an election can resolve the point and if Mr Whitlam will not advise one I may have to find someone who will.

I have expressed no view about what I may do in various contingencies. I think it better to keep my mind and my options open so that if the worse happens I can decide at the last moment what to do. I am however thinking hard.

September 30[25] – In this four-page letter, Kerr recounted further discussions that he had on the possible supply crisis, noting that the government had a different and new tactic – and that the attorney-general had told him 'privately that he was of the clear view that under Section 53 of the Constitution, the Senate has the legal power to reject the Appropriation Bills'.

The new tactic was a half Senate election – and Kerr discussed difficulties with that approach, in that conducting such an election required writs to be issued by states, not the Commonwealth,[26] and two states (NSW and Queensland) had indicated that they may not agree.

OCTOBER 1975

October 17[27] – In this lengthy, six page letter,[28] Kerr advised that 'the crisis has finally broken' with the deferral of supply the previous day.

In that letter, he gave a history of the Connor/Khemlani loan-seeking affair and discussed the 'temporary' nature of that proposed loan (see chapter 4). He did not, however, question the accuracy or the legal advice regarding the 'temporary' nature of the loan.

He also identified that the prime minister had decided not to call an election but 'has decided to "tough it out"'. Mr Fraser, however, whom Kerr described as 'a very worried man' due to the denial of supply, 'had passed the Rubicon'. According to Kerr, Fraser also accepted that Kerr should not take 'immediate action' but was encouraging the governor-general to take interventionist actions to resolve the dispute, arguing 'that I have ample power, before the chaos develops too far, to dismiss the Government and produce an election'.

This letter also sets out the main issues of most relevance to Kerr's actions in 1975:

- the economic consequences of a government with no supply:

The situation is very serious indeed. As money runs out, many problems will arise, and the reaction of the trade unions has to be considered. There are threats of protest, strikes and industrial 'war'. Mr Hawke, the president of the Australian Council of Trade Unions and of the Australian Labor Party, has threatened industrial action, although the Prime Minister tonight appealed to the trade union movement not to stage a general strike. Senator Wriedt, who is the new minister for minerals and energy, said after he was sworn in, in the presence of the Prime Minister, that he did not agree with the policy of 'toughing it out'. He thought it would be better for the Prime Minister to accept the inevitable, go down to defeat in an election and start laying the foundation for a return to power in due course. He said that he was very worried about what would happen if, step by step we move into chaos. He said he was concerned that there could be violence in the streets.

Two other Ministers have said rather similar things to me in quite a voluntary way in an Executive Council meeting, but nevertheless, Caucus met on Wednesday and gave approval to the Prime Minister's tactics of strongly resisting the denial of supply and refusing to recommend a dissolution of the House of Representatives while asking in due course for a Half Senate election.

My own role continues to be debated, and I attach some clippings which indicate the way in which attention is being directed to the duties, powers and responsibilities of the governor-general.

- the ineffectuality of the half-Senate election proposal of the prime minister:

The Prime Minister hopes, by having an election for what may turn out to be not half but a part of the Senate, in December, to produce a change in the balance of power in the Senate and thus to get his Appropriation Bills passed in December.

However, many people think that he will not succeed in changing the balance of power in the Senate with these tactics and that by the middle of December it should be apparent that he will be unable, if the Opposition holds its ground, to get supply. Before all of this happens, money will have run out and there could be a developing crisis of great magnitude.

- and Kerr's desire to remain in office and, for that purpose, not to warn the prime minister of his proposed actions due to his fear of Whitlam recommending his removal.

Before our dinner last night, which was in honour of the Prime Minister of Malaysia, in the presence of the guest of honour and his wife, and Mrs Whitlam and my wife, the Prime Minister, in what he would claim to have been a jocular fashion, said a propos of the crisis – 'It could be a question of whether I get to The Queen first for your recall or you get in first with my dismissal'. We all laughed.

The Prime Minister and I remain friendly, and our relations are very good. He wants me to be certain to do exactly what he advises, come what may. This is, of course, understandable.

The clippings that were included in this letter, which Kerr referred to, include:

- a piece from the *Australian* newspaper, of October 16, 1975, 'The Uneasy Choices facing Sir John'[29] which quoted:
  - Professor Colin Howard[30] from the University of Melbourne:

    > If Mr Whitlam does tough it out, God knows what will happen as the money dries up. I think Sir John would be obliged to listen very closely to the advice of the Executive Council. But he may also feel compelled to seek outside professional advice.

    However, he considered that if Fraser were appointed as prime minister:

    > Mr Whitlam would immediately move a vote of confidence in the minority Government, which would be carried, and Mr Fraser would have to resign.

  - Professor Alex Castles, from the University of Adelaide, held views were similar to those of Professor Howard and considered that Kerr did not have the power to dismiss Whitlam. In his view, that was 'not on'. He considered that Kerr could not follow the path of Sir Philip Game, who sacked Jack Lang in 1932, as, according to the newspaper, 'Many constitutional lawyers . . . say that Game's action was unconstitutional'.

  The article, however, also states that 'other constitutional experts believe that if Mr Fraser could form a Government for a few fours he could form an Executive Council to advise Sir John to call an election', and those experts seem to include Professor Kevin Ryan[31] of the University of Queensland.
- An article from the *Sydney Morning Herald* of the same day, 'His is the key role'[32] where Ian Hicks interviewed Professor of Law, Patrick Lane of the University of Sydney. In Lane's view, which seems highly persuasive to Kerr[33] given the actions that he later took, was that:

  > The refusal of Supply by a Senate is an accepted way of bringing a Government to the people – not half the Senate but the Government.
  >
  > For Pete's sake, let's stop all this humbugging about convention and law and the done thing, and all this hysteria about crisis and anarchy and civil war.
  >
  > This is a perfectly respectable machinery which, if followed through, just means that the Government is put before the people and the electorate might say 'give them a fair go' or 'they've had a fair go: give us a new Government'.

  As to the governor-general's powers, Lane considered that:

  > here there is a strong convention, it is no humbug – that by convention the Governor-General usually follows the advice of his ministers.

> And there is no question that the Governor-General has a discretion.
>
> the Governor-General, in the sort of circumstances we may find ourselves in, can take advice from people other than his ministers – from the Chief Justice and eminent counsel.
>
> He can seek his own advice – make his own decision.

He also discussed what would happen 'if an impasse arose', and in a conclusion directly at odds with that of Professor Howard mentioned above, Lane accurately predicted what later occurred when he said that:

> He would simply dismiss the Whitlam Ministry, call in the Leader of the Opposition and ask him to form a Government. The Fraser Government would be defeated immediately on the floor of the House and would ask the Governor-General for a double dissolution.

October 20[34] – In this five-page letter, Kerr gave an extensive explanation of the developments, accepting that he may have sent too much material for the Palace and the Queen's needs. He also emphasized what he claimed as both his neutrality in Australian politics, as well as his friendships with both sides of the political debate, which included Robert Ellicott, Senator Ivor Greenwood (shadow attorney-general) from the Liberal Party, as well as with Senator Jim McClelland and J. Riordan from the ALP.

> This is of course known also to Mr Whitlam and Mr Fraser. Sometime I shall tell you something of my own past in and on the fringe of politics on both sides. I do not feel in the least embarrassed by my so called pragmatic political neutrality and criss-crossing past associations.

To Kerr, he maintained what he considered his political neutrality: 'I am and can remain above it all, and obvious neutrality is a strength'.

Kerr provided extensive material regarding the information that the prime minister had given to him, as well as his assessment of the prime minister.

> The Prime Minister's position had hardened and changed considerably in the last forty-eight hours. He has now decided that he will advise no election of any kind whatsoever. On Saturday he told me that he is determined to break the alleged power of the Senate to force an election, at its whim, of the House of Representatives by denying supply. He has come to the conclusion that this is a great moment of history like the position in the United Kingdom in 1909–1910. He has, so he says, finally and irrevocably decided never to take the House of Representatives to the people because the Senate denies it power to govern by cutting off money. He will not do this now, not next May, nor ever. He has said something along these lines publicly and has accused by Mr Anthony, the Leader of the National-Country Party, of attempting to stand over the Governor-General.

> The Prime Minister is in an exuberant, even euphoric, mood. He is campaigning vigorously for public support and believes he is 'on a winner' on the issue of the Senate's power to force the Lower House to the people. Mr Fraser is also campaigning strongly and with considerable financial support, spending much on advertising. This 'campaign' on both sides is being presented by the Press as the beginning of an inevitable election campaign.

He also advised the Palace of Whitlam's alternate means of financing government to overcome the supply blockage.

> He intends to produce a situation under which everyone owed money by the Commonwealth – public servants, troops, police, contractors and so on can be 'lent' by the Banks and the amount owed, backed by Commonwealth guarantee. He claims to have the financial resources ultimately to meet the bill when Mr Fraser finally collapses. Whether he can do this legally will probably be tested in the High Court but he is confident as to his legal grounds though they are subject to further examination.
>
> By this technique he believes he can defuse the issue – no one or almost no one will suffer and Mr Fraser will be out-manoeuvred. More importantly the crisis will, he argues, thus be kept as the political level. There will be no real constitutional crisis, because despite denial of supply he will still be able to govern and there will be no excuse for me to demand evidence from him that he can get supply and no excuse for removing him and sending for someone willing to recommend an election.

He did not express any view to the Palace as to the merits of this alternate technique, or advise what, if anything, he had said to Whitlam about its strengths or weaknesses.

However, he did advise of his exchange with the prime minister regarding his contest with the Opposition. His comments included:

> I said to the Prime Minister today – 'You say you intend to break the power of the Senate to force the Lower House to the people. Ultimately you can do that only be[sic] getting a constitutional amendment or by breaking Mr Fraser'. He said 'I cannot get a constitutional amendment but I can and will break Mr Fraser, if my Party stands behind me and it will'. I replied 'What about his?' He said, 'It will break'.

And

> In the conversation with the Prime Minister previously mentioned he said 'You are in the position of George V'.[35] My riposte was 'But you are not in the position of Asquith. You cannot pack the Senate'. He asserted that the only solution was a political one and he could and would prevail.

Kerr also discussed the Opposition's view that the governor-general could be 'relied upon'. However, Kerr rejected any such relationship with the Opposition:

> The Liberal leaders may believe that I can be relied upon ultimately to get them out of the situation in which they find themselves. However, as you would expect, I intended to be guided by constitutional principle and by that alone.

In this letter, Kerr advised the Palace of Mr Ellicott's opinion that was the basis for the supply crisis and then the dismissal. But he also advised it of the results of recent Gallup Polls, which, at that stage, tended to favour the government, at least as to whether there should be an early election. The poll showed that: 'only 38% support for Labor (up 3%) and 55% for the Opposition parties'. But when the poll asked the question 'Do you think there should be an early election?' the result was '55% said "No" and 42% said "Yes"'. As result, in Kerr's view, 'The big question is what the next poll will show'.

He also advised the Palace of another article containing further opinions from leading constitutional law experts contrary to his position.[36] That is, Professor Colin Howard from the University of Melbourne (again) and Geoffrey Sawer from the Australian National University, both of whom were critical of any intervening actions by the governor-general, arguing that Kerr's role was to mediate between the two parties. Kerr, however, rejected any immediate mediation role for himself:

> I do not propose, at this stage, to try to mediate. It would be misunderstood. The Prime Minister would resent it, but more important, until the Opposition is told of the Prime Minister's latest tactic, and I cannot tell them, they do not know the full legal and political complexity of the position in which they may find themselves. Better to wait till the full political story unfolds by which time we shall be short of a final constitutional crisis. We can then see what Mr Fraser and any wavering Senators may do.

October 22[37] – In this lengthy six-page letter, which also includes passages written on October 23 and 24, the governor-general advised of the current developments in the supply crisis, including his careful consideration of the Ellicott memorandum, and that, on October 21, he had sworn in the newest Minister in the Whitlam government, Paul Keating (who later went on to be Australia's twenty-fourth prime minister between 1991 and 1996).

Kerr also advised the Palace of his long talk with Prime Minister Whitlam on October 21:

> I have been worried for the last twenty-four hours that the Governor-General might appear to the people of Australia to be uninterested in the profound crisis

which is developing. I had of course, up till yesterday, said and done nothing publicly. It has been my intention and still is, to do nothing constitutionally at this time but the growing expression of the point of view that the Governor-General should mediate or intervene to help produce a solution forced me to consider whether I could do anything at all. As examples of the sort of articles being written I attach one by Professor Julius Stone[38] of the University of New South Wales in yesterday's Sydney Morning Herald and one from Professor Sawer in today's Canberra Times.[39]

When talking to the Prime Minister yesterday I said to him that it seemed to me the crisis at the moment is still a very serious political crisis, but that it has not crossed the threshold yet into a true constitutional crisis, because the Senate has only deferred the Budget, not finally rejected it, and money has not started to run out. Even if money were to run out, the Prime Minister believes he has an option with the Federal Banks backed by Commonwealth guarantee which will help him to carry on, but that is not public.

I suggested to the Prime Minister that he should agree to me seeing the Leader of the Opposition with a view to raising the question whether the Leader of the Opposition is determined to cross the threshold from a political crisis to a constitutional crisis. He would do this, if he is going to do it, by producing what in the course of time would be a rejection of supply either by active rejection or by continued deferral up to the point of time when money runs out. I thought it might be possible subtly to direct a conversation with the Leader of the Opposition to the point where he might see that he has to withdraw from the brink, having done all he could do to force Mr Whitlam to an election. He could take whatever political capital he could out of the Prime Minister's refusal to go to the people. This would allow the main issue in the country to return to the economic problems instead of being clouded, even dominated, by the constitutional issue.

He also discussed his conversations with the Leader of the Opposition:

The Prime Minister agreed to me seeing the Leader of the Opposition, not of course for the purpose of getting advice from him, but simply to do my best to ascertain the likely future course of events. Accordingly, I invited the Leader of the Opposition to call which he did last night. I spent an hour with him. He maintained that the intention of his Party was quite firm and irreversible and that if the Appropriation Bills were re-presented, as is happening, they would be deferred as often as they were presented.

He, of course, believes that there is already a serious constitutional crisis but in any event accepts, from what he says and from what the Prime Minister says, that such a crisis is inevitable.

In this letter, the governor-general also accepted that he is 'entitled to advise and warn the Prime Minister', but he did not explain how he intended to exercise that right. Kerr did, however, include some further information regarding Gallup Polls and how they were still moving against the Leader of the Opposition.

> This morning's press seems to be taking the line that Mr Fraser has made a mistake and that a back-lash is developing. He conceded to me that the next Gallop poll will show some swing against him. Some believe it will be a big swing.

In the second-to-last sentence from that passage, Kerr seems to be referring to Fraser when he used the word 'He'. Accordingly, Kerr seems to have accepted that Fraser was taking a political and constitutional position with Fraser knowing not only that he did not have the confidence of the Lower House but also that his course was likely to be contrary to the will of the public. This prediction seems confirmed by an article that the governor-general attached with the next letter, from the *Australian Financial Review* from October 30 – 'Polls Suggest that Mr Fraser Should Retreat'. In that article, it states that the Age-Herald Poll 'reveals that a substantial majority of the electorate – 70.4 per cent – believe that supply should be allowed to pass'. It also noted that the Morgan Gallup Poll[40] indicates that Fraser's personal popularity had also fallen from 52% to 35%. As a result, the article concluded that 'Mr Fraser and his colleagues should at least sit down and reconsider their decision to block supply'.[41]

October 27[42] – In this lengthy, six-paged letter, which also included passages written on October 29 and 30, part of which was quoted earlier in chapter 11, Kerr considered that 'both sides are appealing to the people for my support'. He summarized the current position as he saw it in the following paragraphs:

> The crunch will not come, so far as I am concerned, until the state of public opinion becomes much clearer. If it becomes obvious that Mr Fraser has made a serious mistake he may wish to retreat and allow supply to pass. There is a suggestion that he may hope to be helped to retreat by some 'advice' from me.
>
> If it appears that the state of public opinion is that a high proportion of people believe that Mr Whitlam should go to an election, the question will arise as to what I should do on the assumption that supply is rejected and the money is about to run out or has already done so. He will have tactics for obtaining credit for public servants and others inconvenienced. How this affects the matter has yet to be ascertained.
>
> In Australia, the Senate is said by most lawyers to have a legal right to reject supply though this has just been denied by a very able judge, in today's 'Age'. Assuming however that the Senate has the legal power to reject supply, whether it should do so is a political question involving argument about whether there is a constitutional convention that it should not do so. Some say it should never

> do so, others say that it should do so only in extraordinary and reprehensible circumstances which it is claimed have arisen.
>
> As I see the matter, it is not for me certainly at this stage, to judge the political question especially as there is a political background going back to the Federation debates in the '90's as to what was the State compact on money bills. . . .
>
> It could easily happen that Parliament will, by the end of November, have finally and unequivocally denied supply and the Government will be attempting to govern without it. This will be so if one of the quite likely courses of events takes place, that is to say, if total deadlock persists. In such a situation it will become necessary to consider whether the Prime Minister and his Government should resign or recommend a dissolution. I should have to consider whether I should have to ask for this.
>
> I do not need to spell out the problems involved in such a course of action if the Prime Minister refuses to do either of these things as he says he will. On these questions, some opinions expressed by Sir Paul Hasluck in his Queale Memorial Lecture in 1972 have been widely canvassed. In case you do not have a copy of this lecture I attach one together with a summary of it published in the Australian of Friday last.

That reference from Hasluck that Kerr refers to relates to Hasluck's view that the governor-general in abnormal times can present 'the crisis . . . to the nation for determination. . . . by forcing a crisis'.[43]

> Not everyone agrees with Sir Paul Hasluck but in conditions of momentous deadlock over supply the question whether the Hasluck doctrine should be accepted and a final constitutional crisis precipitated by Vice-Regal act will have to be thought about. This would force an election. Any Vice-Regal decision either to act or not to act in this kind of situation will be, I suppose, the subject of debate and criticism. I am simply looking into the future and exploring options.

Kerr's advice to the Palace was that he had made no decision as to the course he would take – 'I have still not made up my mind'. He also went on to make a fairly poor prediction of future events when he said, 'I am remaining calm about it all and seek no "man of destiny" role in all of this'. But he also made it clear that he had:

> no desire to escape from any responsibility which the Constitution places on my shoulders or to lessen it or have some excuse for any particular course I may take, but I feel that I should consider, in deciding what I ought to do, anything which may directly or indirectly affect The Queen.

Kerr also pointed out two competing factors – Fraser losing further ground in opinion polls, and his concern that if a half-Senate election was called, 'there is no guarantee that supply will be granted even to get the country through the period of the campaign'. That can be seen from the passage that he added on October 29:

> The controversy rages as before. My impression is that Mr Fraser has lost ground in the struggle and this was today confirmed by the latest Gallup Poll. I enclose the details which speak for themselves. Since the date of the poll (18 October) I think Fraser has lost more ground.

And one he added on the following day:

> This morning's paper disclosed a new poll conducted in the capital and major provincial cities. This shows that 70% of Australia's capital city voters believe the Senate should allow Supply to pass, and 54% believe that Labor should continue to govern, rather than resign and hold a general election. There is apparently quite a big swing against Mr Fraser and in favour of the Government. The swing is not yet enough to produce a victory for Mr Whitlam were there to be an election but as you know now that the gap has been significantly narrowed, the campaign itself could produce a further swing. However, Mr Whitlam has not yet moved in the direction of accepting that the time is ripe for a double dissolution nor even, though this is much more possible, for a Half Senate election this week or early next week. If there is to be such an election before Christmas he really should move in the next few days. Even if he seeks a Half Senate election there is no guarantee that supply will be granted even to get the country through the period of the campaign. Such an election would, if it were held, probably take place on 6th or 13th December.

NOVEMBER 1975

November 6[44] – In this three-page letter,[45] Kerr summarized his discussions with the prime minister, the leader of the Opposition, the treasurer (Bill Hayden) and the attorney-general (Kep Enderby) that occurred on November 3 and 6.

> As to Mr Fraser, he indicated that he regarded the position as being so serious that the Senate would go on deferring Supply indefinitely and that his Party would hold together for this purpose. This was a factual statement in which he merely repeated to me what he was saying publicly, but I judge he meant it.
>
> As to the Prime Minister, his position remains the same though he is obviously in two minds about whether he will recommend a Half Senate election early or late. . . . In any event he has not yet made up his mind.

His explanation of his discussions with the treasurer and the attorney-general concerned the government's alternate manner of funding itself if normal supply was exhausted, including its effectiveness and its legality. Kerr expressed some concerns to the Palace as to the validity of this measure, noting that:

> There is every prospect that it will be challenged by someone in the High Court and I would assume that the Chief Justice would do his best to have an urgent hearing of the matter.

And:

> it obviously is an unsatisfactory way of carrying on Government both because of what has been described as its messy elements and because it does not cover all of the requirements of the Government under existing legislative provisions which need to be supported by Appropriation Acts including the health scheme 'Medibank'.

His conclusion was his first indication to the Palace of any intervening decision that he may make.

> The crisis is now a very serious one and if both parties and their leaders remain adamant, an important decision one way or the other may have to be made by me this month. I may say that Public Servants and others, with some exceptions, will probably be able to be paid until the last pay period in November but there will not be Supply, unless the scheme with the bank works, for the first pay in December, namely the 11th December.

That was the last letter to the Palace prior to the dismissal. And while it was sent on the 'decisive day' (see chapter 6), it did not indicate to the Palace that he had made any decision to sack the Whitlam government or indicate that he was going to take that step or any other step on November 11. All the Palace knew was that Kerr had accepted that he might have to make 'an important decision one way or the other . . . this month'.

November 11[46]- This two-page letter,[47] the text of which was made public in 1975 and is available in a number of sources, outlines the course that Kerr took and his reasons for taking it. In that letter, Kerr made it clear that he took the dismissal step to resolve the deadlock between the two Houses; that the Palace was informed by a telephone call from David Smith made after Whitlam had been dismissed; and that:

> I should say that I decided to take the step I took without informing the Palace in advance because under the Constitution the responsibility is mine and I was of the opinion that it was better for Her Majesty not to know in advance, though it is, of course, my duty to tell her immediately.

November 17[48] – In this three-page letter,[49] Kerr explained the reason why the dismissal occurred on November 11. In his view:

> November 11 was the last day for action if an election of any kind was to be held before Christmas. This was due to practical matters connected with the Electoral Office, December 13 was the last practical date for actually holding an election. A half Senate election without supply (with or without all the States participating) would have meant a very black Christmas. The Senate might I suppose have given in, but after three refusals of Supply and with the then Leader of the Opposition asserting that it definitively would not be granted for a half Senate election I felt I had to act. There is a grey area or twilight zone for personal discretion about the seriousness of the situation warranting a forced dissolution. Many people whose judgment I trust, including Sir Robert Menzies, agree that I really had no choice and that it was right to act. I am sure I had to get the matter to the people. The historians and academics can argue about it for years.

He also discussed whether he would remain in that office and that:

> I have accordingly given some consideration to whether or not I should, here and now, announce that come what may in the election I shall commission the new Prime Minister and then resign.
>
> I have discussed this with the present Prime Minister, Mr Fraser who is emphatically and unreservedly against me taking any such course (a) on the ground that it would in all probability be misunderstood by the electorate despite all attempts on my part to clarify my motives (very many people he says would believe that I had either changed my mind or felt that I should not have done what I did) and (b) that if he wins he would wish to urge me to remain on as Governor-General and would, if it became relevant, so advise Her Majesty.
>
> I have decided to let things rest for the time being. This will enable me to see how the opposition to my action develops and how big an issue it becomes in the campaign, but I should like to assure Her Majesty that I shall put the Monarchy and the Governor-Generalship first and I should not wish to stay on here, even if pressed to do so by Mr Fraser if he wins, if I judge that tensions might adversely affect the basic institution of the Monarchy and the Governor-Generalship.

November 20[50] – In this lengthy six-page letter, Kerr spent much time explaining various elements of what he described as the 'psychological factors involved in what happened in November 11', and it included his misleading comments regarding his failure to warn Whitlam that are discussed in chapter 9.

He also discussed his now strong view that Whitlam's alternative financial measures would not work and 'the chaos and confusion would be enormous'. He also attempted to explain why he did not express his view clearly to Whitlam.

> I believe that apart from a high order of brinkmanship on other matters, Mr Whitlam made a fundamental mistake in believing, as he apparently did, that I would let him do exactly what he advised and let him govern without supply and without going to the people.
>
> At all times during the crisis he stated in the clearest terms that he intended to govern without supply and would never recommend a dissolution of the House or a double dissolution whilst supply was denied. He said both publicly and privately that it was his intention to break the power of the Senate over money bills forever. There could be no doubt, and I had no doubt, of the absolute irreversibility of this decision. Mr Whitlam was engaged in a crusade based upon a single minded determination to destroy the power of the Senate on money bills. No one talking to him privately at that time could come to any other conclusion. The matter was not discussable. He was prepared and said he was prepared to take the country through makeshift banking arrangements, if he could achieve this, over Christmas and on the new year – governing without supply.

November 24[51] – In this four-page letter, Kerr explains how the 1975 dismissal was impacting him. He discussed the Whitlam 'rage' speech, the reaction of his old but now former friend, Senator Jim McClelland, who had broken off relations between them, and an article in the *New Statesman* by a former neighbour of his, Allan Ashbolt,[52] who evidently wrote that Kerr was 'mad, not perhaps clinically mad but, as he put it, at least as mad as George III'. Kerr, however, did not keep a copy of that article on file.[53]

He also included a very puzzling paragraph, which seems clearly inconsistent with the desire that he had earlier expressed, on November 17, to protect the Monarchy from making difficult decisions.

> The question arises as to what I should do in the event of a Whitlam victory. I opened this subject up with you before as a hypothetical question. My mail is starting to show indications of a desire on the part of correspondents that I should not resign. This does not operate, in any significant way, upon my mind but I have been thinking that, for the sake of history, I ought to consider forcing Mr Whitlam, it he wins, to ask Her Majesty for my dismissal.

Despite this possible course:

> I would not allow the position to develop to the point where she would have to take such advice. If she were minded upon receipt of a request for my dismissal to communicate with me before feeling it necessary to act, I should do what I could to answer whatever it was that Mr Whitlam had said to justify dismissal but would wish to resign and would do so.

This paragraph (and the next letter) indicates that Kerr:

- had no difficulty in putting the Monarch and the Governor-Generalship in the centre of a political dispute regarding his future, despite his earlier views on November 17; and
- appreciated that the removal of a Governor-General is not just an automatic process based on a telephone call from the Prime Minister. This, therefore, seems inconsistent with his primary justification for his earlier secrecy from Prime Minister Whitlam.

November 28[54] – This was, as Kerr said, 'a relatively short note attaching a few clippings' from the press. In this two-page letter, Kerr did, however, again discuss his future if Whitlam wins the election. He again had little apparent difficulty in bringing the Monarch into the centre of a dispute where his interests were concerned when he suggested that: 'if Mr Whitlam wins I should just allow him to advise The Queen to dismiss me', but only, as Kerr added, 'if he dares'!

He went on to add:

> Some people think that I should announce now that I shall not resign thus forcing Mr Whitlam, under pressure from the Press, to say how he proposes to cope with that situation, before the election is over. There could be some ground for taking such a step having regard to the editorial in the *Australian* of 27 November. This editorial, though anti-Whitlam, takes it for granted that his victory would inevitably mean that I would have to resign.
>
> The real point about all of this is, I suppose, whether a statement now to the effect that I have no intention of resigning whatever happens in the election could be regarded as too political. On the other hand, it may be said that it puts Mr Whitlam under too much pressure, on the other, it could be said that I have no intention of resigning in the event of a Whitlam victory, that I stand firmly on the correctness of my decision. This would be implied in the stated intention not to resign. Some would believe that failure to make this clear is a sign of weakness.

He ended his views with his '*dominant* consideration [that] has to be in the long term interests of the Monarchy and of my office'. Yet in the next sentence, he still considered that 'If I am to indicate publicly an intention of not resigning it would have to be done next week'. That is, in the week prior to the national election, making any public statement by him and his refusal to resign if Whitlam wins both a central election issue and one that only the Monarch could resolve!

DECEMBER 1975

December 5[55] – This very short two-page letter, written shortly prior to the election, advises the Palace that there is 'not much to report from here at this stage'. Its main relevance is that Kerr included some further articles from the press, including one from the *Financial Review* which, as Kerr puts it:

> does its best, in an absurdly tenuous way, to suggest that the C.I.A. conceivably might have been associated with the events here. In this article they repeat an assertion which has been made occasionally during the last couple of years that I have had intelligence connections. This is simply false.[56]

December 16[57] – The final letter to the Palace for the year is short, by Kerr standards (three pages), and continues to present the election and its result in the manner most favourable to him and included the following observations:

> The constitutional issue virtually died after the first week and a half and economic matters dominated the debate thereafter. However, . . . there is some remaining bitterness.
>
> The truth, of course, is that governments are, generally speaking, defeated rather than oppositions elected. The former government was undoubtedly defeated because voters did not want what it was offering.
>
> My own view is that the electors were really voting positively for a way of life which they want.
>
> The Australian people are, I think, basically conservative in what they want out of life. . . . When the Whitlam Government was elected in 1972 it was my impression that it was elected, not to conduct a social revolution but rather to administer the country, more or less as it had always been administered, but with some new progressive elements on the social welfare side. The enormous frenzy of change, I believe, proved to be far too much for ordinary people to comprehend and, when it was accompanied by heavy inflation and unemployment, much of the change itself proved unattractive.
>
> As I say, my impression is that people turned with some relief to the ways of life which they understand. . . . I cannot help but draw the conclusion that the

> people positively voted as sweepingly as they did by way of approval of what the Senate had done and what I had done.
>
> On the east coast the importance of the Senate is not well understood as it is in the smaller states and in rural areas. Whether I am right or wrong about this, the exercise of the reserve powers which has to be very rare and which I much disliked resorting to has not, I believe, resulted in a weakening of the basis upon which it rests.
>
> There is no chance of our Constitution being amended either to cut down the powers of the Senate or of the Governor-General. I hope, certainly so far as the Governor-General is concerned, that there will be no need to resort to the reserve power for many a year if it ever becomes necessary again to do so at all. I always realised that if it were used, and its use not endorsed with sufficient strength by the people, my own position would be inevitably involved. One of the reasons why the reserve powers can occasionally be used, outside the United Kingdom, is because the Governor-General can be replaced. I cannot envisage it ever having to be used in the United Kingdom itself but the fact that it exists is important in the United Kingdom and its nature can occasionally be illustrated in other parts of The Queen's realms.

The final letter that needs to be referred to was written in the following year, on *January 22, 1976*[58] which Kerr wrote in long-hand due to his lack of any typewriter. In this six-page (and difficult-to-read) letter, Kerr outlines his defence of his 1975 actions that he would later expand into his book *Matters for Judgment.* And in that letter, Kerr acknowledged that he 'did not tell Mr Whitlam that I intended to dismiss his government until the point of time came when I was about to do it'. And he gave his reasons:

> You know the reason. I believed he would seek to have me dismissed on the instant if I gave him any foreknowledge.

As to his reasons for all his actions in the dismissal, he also rejects any conspiracy with Mr Fraser, concluding that:

> It is simply false to say that I did what I did motivated by a desire to help Mr Whitlam's opponents.

What we can see from all of these many letters that Kerr sent to the Palace leading up to and after the dismissal of Gough Whitlam, letters that Professor Hocking has spent so much time and energy to have revealed (and for which she needs great credit), is that they do not support the primary arguments and conclusions that she continues to present. Not only do these letters provide no support for any Palace-led or inspired plan to dismiss the Whitlam government, but they also do not support any *coup* or conspiracy between the governor-general with the chief justice and the then leader of the Opposition, or with anyone else; and there is nothing in these letters to indicate that Kerr's actions were in any way designed to be supporting Fraser nor in opposition to Whitlam. Kerr was careful to describe to the Palace the changing elements in the debate, detailing his lengthy discussions with both Fraser and Whitlam, and emphasising both his views of the strengths and weaknesses of both Fraser's and Whitlam's positions, as well as details of critical academic views regarding Fraser and an interventionist governor-general. And that included the views of academics who disagreed with his approach, as well as details of polls that were not supportive of the Opposition. He also included his assessment of the attitude of Fraser and made it clear that, so far as he was concerned, his role was to exercise what he considered were his constitutional powers, not to be a resource for the Opposition.

The letters also make it apparent what the issues central to Kerr's consideration of his priorities were. And they seem to have been: first – to find a solution to what he considered the serious financial and social consequences to the nation and its community of a government planning to operate with no supply. That he regarded as a crisis, having described as early as September 12 as 'the battle in the country about who is responsible for the ensuing mess – failure to meet obligations, pay public servants, the Defence Force and so on'. And that 'mess' would occur if, as he pointed out in a number of his letters, including October 17, when the 'money runs out'. By October 22, he considered that 'the profound crisis which is developing' had been caused by the adamant and immovable actions of the two political leaders, Fraser and Whitlam. As he said on November 6, in his last letter prior to the dismissal, 'if both parties and their leaders remain adamant, an important decision one way or the other may have to be made by me this month'.

Kerr's second decisive issue was to make his own decision to resolve the supply crisis, a decision based on his own assessment of the law and the circumstances, and not based on any direction from the Palace or anywhere else. As he made clear on November 11, he took the decision without informing the Palace in advance 'because under the Constitution the responsibility is mine'. And as he made clear in his letter of October 20, his actions were also not based on any desire for him to be 'relied on' by the Opposition, but on what he considered as 'constitutional principle and by that alone'. And as he said in his handwritten letter on January 22, 1976, 'It is simply false to say that I did what I did motivated by a desire to help Mr Whitlam's opponents'. His intention was, as he said as early as September 20, 'to keep my mind and my options open so that if the worse happens I can decide at the last moment what to do. I am however thinking hard'. He also considered, somewhat naively, that his strength came from, as he said on October 20, what he regarded as his 'pragmatic political neutrality and criss-crossing past associations' which, he considered, would allow him to 'remain above it all, and obvious neutrality is a strength'.

Kerr's third issue in his dismissal decision was to protect his possession of the office that he held by not advising Whitlam of his thinking or that he was intending to terminate his commission. That led to his problematic approach of minimizing his function of warning his prime minister of the actions he would and did take, despite Bagehot, and despite his acceptance on October 22, that he was 'entitled to advise and warn the prime minister'. However, he never made any warning that was or could have been apparent to Whitlam. His concern was limited by his assessment of Whitlam, as was made clear on November 20 when he discussed his conclusion that Whitlam was engaged in a 'crusade based upon a single minded determination to destroy the power of the Senate on money bills'; that Whitlam was absolutely irreversible on that decision; and that '*The matter was not discussable*'.[59] And as he later said, on January 22, 1976, any advance advice to Whitlam of his actions was confined 'until the point of time came when I was about to do it'. And the reason for this very limited warning, if warning it was, was to protect his ability to hold his office – '*I believed he would seek to have me dismissed on the instant if I gave him any foreknowledge*'.[60]

And his final issue was to present his material and argument in the most supportive manner, which includes being highly selective with exclusions of not only any discussion of Bagehot and his discussion of the right to warn but also his failure to discuss the advice he had received from Governors Cutler and Winneke, as well as that received from Mason, that a warning to Whitlam should have been provided.

Kerr can be criticized, as he should be, for his selectivity as well as his failure to warn Whitlam of his thinking and intentions regarding his proposed action, and for his decision to intervene weeks before any vice-regal action was essential. But there is nothing in this correspondence that indicates, in any way, that Kerr was operating in any conspiracy with anyone. Moreover, Kerr's correspondence with the Palace clearly supports Bill Hayden 'heretic's' conclusion that Kerr has been 'miscast by history',[61] as he was not engaged in any secretive *coup*. He was seeking to 'do what he believed was right and proper' to protect Australia from the 'sinkhole of economic chaos'. He was attempting to find a solution to a 'crisis' that, as the Queen's Private Secretary, Sir Martin Charteris said on November 5, 1975, 'has to be worked out in Australia'.[62] And he was trying to find an Australian solution to an Australian problem. But he just did all of that very badly.

NOTES

1. Freudenberg, *Certain Grandeur*, 402.
2. Horne, *Death of the Lucky Country*, 12.
3. Menadue, *Interview*.
4. Quoted in Kelly & Bramston, *The Dismissal,* 292.
5. Senator for NSW between 1989 and 2015.
6. *Gough Whitlam: In His Own Words,* Ronin Films, 2002, at 56–57 minutes. That film can be seen on Youtube: https://www.youtube.com/watch?v=WmhvM_ALc5A – accessed January 31, 2023.
7. John Faulkner, "Remembrance Day, 1975," in *True Believers* 119.
8. See Kerr to Charteris, November 24, 1975, in NAA, *The Kerr Palace Letters,* AA1984/609, Part 2 in which Kerr advises that:

> Some people are asserting, including a very old friend of mine who has now, of course, broken off relations with me as I am concerned forever – I refer to Senator James McClelland – that I have been in conspiracy with Mr Fraser from the beginning. This is false as Senator McClelland knows because he was party to some of the compromise activities in which I engaged.

Also see his letters of October 20, 1975, and of January 26, 1976.

9. The only governor-general with a longer term is Lord Gowrie VC, who held the office for 9 years between 1936 and 1945.
10. From which he had learnt "much about the nature and potentials of that office." See Hayden, *Hayden*, 238.
11. Hayden, *Hayden*, 239.
12. "1975: A Heretic's View" is the title of Part IV of Hayden's autobiography.
13. Hayden, *Hayden*, 238.
14. Hayden, *Hayden*, 238.
15. Hayden, *Hayden*, 292.
16. Hayden, *Hayden*, 238–239.
17. Hayden, *Hayden*, 238.
18. Hayden, *Hayden*, 294.
19. Hocking, *Palace Letters,* 21.
20. NAA, *The Kerr Palace Letters,* AA1984/609, https://www.naa.gov.au/explore-collection/kerr-palace-letters.
21. Kelly & Bramston, *Truth, Palace Letters,* 199–227.
22. NAA, *The Kerr Palace Letters,* AA1984/609, Part 1.
23. NAA, *The Kerr Palace Letters,* AA1984/609, Part 1.
24. NAA, *The Kerr Palace Letters,* AA1984/609, Part 1.
25. NAA, *The Kerr Palace Letters,* AA1984/609, Part 1.
26. See *Australian Constitution* s 12.
27. NAA, *The Kerr Palace Letters,* AA1984/609, Part 2.
28. The full text of this letter can be found in Kelly & Bramston, *Truth, Palace Letters,* 202–207.

29. Graham Williams, "The Uneasy Choices facing Sir John," *The Australian*, October 16, 1975, 11.

30. Hearn Professor of Law, University of Melbourne between 1965 and 1990 and Dean of the Law School between 1978 and 1983. He was also General Counsel to the Commonwealth attorney-general during the Whitlam government between 1973 and 1976 and was the author of leading texts on a number of areas of law, including Constitutional Law and Criminal Law. His highly critical views of the actions of Kerr and Barwick can be seen in Howard & Saunders, "The Blocking of the Budget," 286–287.

31. Garrick Professor of Law, University of Queensland (1969–1974 and 1979–1985), and later a judge of the Supreme Court of Queensland (1984–1994).

32. Ian Hicks, "His is the Key Role," *Sydney Morning Herald*, October 16, 1975.

33. See Kerr, *Matters*, 257.

34. NAA, *The Kerr Palace Letters,* AA1984/609, Part 2.

35. This discussion concerns the constitutional crisis in the United Kingdom when the budget of 1909 was blocked by the House of Lords. It involved two general elections in 1910 before the House of Lords accepted the views of the House of Commons. It is the subject of Roy Jenkins' *Mr Balfour's Poodle* (London: Collins, 1968).

36. Warren Owens and Martin Saxon, "PM Confident of Budget Victory," *The Sun-Herald*, October 19, 1975, 1 & 4.

37. NAA, *The Kerr Palace Letters,* AA1984/609, Part 2.

38. Then Professor of Law, University of New South Wales and Emeritus Professor of Jurisprudence, University of Sydney. The Institute of Jurisprudence at that university is now named after him. He wrote one of the articles that Kerr attached to this letter – Julius Stone, "Why not a Moratorium?," *Sydney Morning Herald,* October 21, 1975.

39. Geoffrey Sawer, "Political Confrontation: A Modest Proposal for a Way Out of the Mire," *Canberra Times*, October 22, 1975.

40. The full details of this poll were included in the article "ALP Labors in Lib's Wake," *The Bulletin,* October 25, 1975, that was attached to Kerr's letter of October 27.

41. "Polls Suggest Mr Fraser Should Retreat," *Australian Financial Review,* October 30, 1975.

42. NAA, *The Kerr Palace Letters,* AA1984/609, Part 2.

43. See Hasluck, *Office of the Governor-General,* 14.

44. NAA, *The Kerr Palace Letters,* AA1984/609, Part 2.

45. The full text of this letter can be found in Kelly & Bramston, *Truth, Palace Letters,* 211–213.

46. NAA, *The Kerr Palace Letters,* AA1984/609, Part 2.

47. The full text of this letter can be found in a number of sources including Kelly & Bramston, *Truth, Palace Letters,* 214–215.

48. NAA, *The Kerr Palace Letters,* AA1984/609, Part 2.

49. The full text of this letter can be found in Kelly & Bramston, *Truth, Palace Letters,* 218–220.

50. NAA, *The Kerr Palace Letters,* AA1984/609, Part 2.

51. NAA, *The Kerr Palace Letters,* AA1984/609, Part 2.

52. Kerr incorrectly gives his name as "Alan."

53. Charteris did, however, read Ashbolt's article, advising Kerr on December 3 that he had "read Alan [*sic*] Ashbolt's shameful article in the New Statesman." He was supportive of Kerr when he also wrote that "If anyone is nuts he is! I am sorry you have been subjected to this monstrous attack buttressed as it is by a farrago of misrepresentation and absurdities." See Letter from Charteris to Kerr, December 3, 1975, in NAA, *The Kerr Palace Letters,* AA1984/609, Part 2.

54. NAA, *The Kerr Palace Letters,* AA1984/609, Part 2.

55. NAA, *The Kerr Palace Letters,* AA1984/609, Part 2.

56. The article referred to is Brian Toohey, "The CIA and Whitlam's Dismissal," *Australian Financial Review,* December 5, 1975, 1 & 10.

57. NAA, *The Kerr Palace Letters,* AA1984/609, Part 3.

58. NAA, *The Kerr Palace Letters,* AA1984/609, Part 3.

59. Emphasis added.

60. Emphasis added.

61. Hayden, *Hayden*, 239.

62. This letter can be found in Kelly & Bramston, *Truth, Palace Letters,* 209–210.

Chapter 13

1975

The Devil Is in the Details

Figure 13.1 ALP Political Badges, Largely from the 1970s. From the collection of the author. Image taken by the author.

THE CONSEQUENCES OF THE DISMISSAL

When the 1975 election that was called after the Whitlam government was dismissed, the Liberal/Country Party Coalition, led by Malcolm Fraser, was very well organized. They were ready and prepared for the election – while the Labor Party was not. The Liberals already had an election slogan, 'Turn on the Lights' and they had impressively designed election campaign badges with a cartoon electric globe on a blue background to illustrate their election message – 'So that we may live again'. And it was all supported by a very smooth television advertising campaign with an election song sung by an even more impressive and better-known singer than the ALP had used in 1972 – the then very young, 22 years old, Renee Geyer. And when the election was conducted on December 13, 1975, the conservative coalition won, and they did so very easily, with Labor losing 30 seats, sliding to a very low representation in the House of Representatives of 36 seats, way behind the Liberal/Country Parties Coalition with its 91 seats.

To a lot of Australians, however, the election and the way it was brought about was not an exercise in illumination but was a trip to an area that none thought we would see in Australia – an elected government disposed of by the wealthy and the Crown through the application of rules that most did not know existed and fewer had any idea how they worked. Rage was ignited, and that rage has not, for many Australians, disappeared, even with Fraser's electoral loss in 1983. In the election that year, the coalition lost office, this time to a less hectic but much better organized ALP, now led by Bob Hawke. But the party under Hawke's leadership was now much less reformist than the aims and aspirations of Whitlam and those who had supported his 'It's Time' government.[1] Whitlam, however, remained a reformist, even a political crusader, reminding Australia's Special Broadcasting Service television program, *Issues 85*, ten years after his dismissal, that 'The Labor Party is a Party of reform or it is nothing'.[2]

All those who had maintained their rage since 1975 were, however, pacified, at least to some extent, when Malcolm Fraser wept on national television when conceding his election defeat.[3] It was something, but it was not a return of Gough.

SO, WHY DID THE DISMISSAL OCCUR?

When we go to the primary sources, we see that while the 1975 dismissal was a national tragedy, it was not a *coup* or conspiracy, local or foreign, to bring down the Whitlam government. It was not, as seen in chapter 11, and despite the allegations of Christopher Boyce and others, caused by any CIA plan or direction, and Kerr was certainly not a 'CIA Flunky'.[4] As Whitlam himself has consistently concluded, Kerr needed no encouragement from the CIA for his actions.[5] And we also find from the material discussed in that chapter, despite the view of certain hopeful Australian republicans, the dismissal of Whitlam was also not known, planned or driven by Buckingham Palace. It was, to the Palace, a 'crisis' that, as the Queen's private secretary, Sir Martin Charteris, said to John Kerr on November 5, 1975, 'has to be worked out in Australia'.[6] And it was. It was a local affair; and while the governor-general had advised the Palace of the direction of his thinking, he had not sought or received any express or implied direction from the Palace, and he had not advised the Queen that he had made his decision, what it would be, or when it would be exercised. As Charteris said on November 17, by 'NOT informing the Queen what you intended to do before doing it, you acted with perfect constitutional propriety but also with admirable consideration for Her Majesty's position'.

The constitutional responsibility for the dismissal of Whitlam was solely Kerr's, and as chapters 8 and 9 make clear, he was also not directed by Mason, Barwick or anyone else in his actions. As Kerr himself said in his lengthy letter to the Palace written between October 27 and 30, he had 'no desire to escape from any responsibility which the Constitution places on my shoulders or to lessen it or have some excuse for any particular course I may take'.

Kerr decided, as pointed out earlier, particularly in chapters 6 and 12, to take those actions due to his concerns about the impacts on the community of a government governing without supply. This was a sensible objective for a governor-general. As the minister whose budget was blocked in 1975 who went on to be both Whitlam's successor as the Parliamentary leader of the ALP, and later, Kerr's successor as Australia's governor-general, Bill Hayden has said, Kerr was facing a 'vexatious situation' and could not 'sit idly by as the country plunged deeper and deeper down a sinkhole of economic chaos'.[7]

EVERYONE GOT IT WRONG!

So, if the 1975 dismissal tragedy was not caused by any foreign or local conspiracy, then why did it occur? The answer to that question is that the events of November 11, 1975, happened because those centrally involved got it all wrong. They simply blundered in their handling of that event. These errors occurred for a number of reasons, but central to them was the complexity and lack of clarity of the rules that applied.

Australia's Constitution is, as I have elsewhere written, a remarkably misleading document,[8] and one of its misleading elements is its treatment of what appears to be the extensive powers and functions of the governor-general provided by the governor-general (see chapter 3). It obviously does not refer to any constitutional conventions controlling the exercise of those powers and functions, and there was, particularly before 1975, little written on such nebulous but, in that year, essential subjects of the governor-general's reserve vice-regal powers and functions. As a result, when issues regarding the exercise of those reserve powers arose, disagreements as to the scope of those rarely discussed powers were not unusual; and as 1975 demonstrated, there was and remains much disagreement, even among the experts in the field, as to what was the correct course of action to be taken, with little clarity as to how to resolve such disagreements.

So, in that regime of unclear and obscure rules, the consequence is that there would be blunderers: decision-makers who just get the rules wrong, and that clearly occurred in 1975.

And of those who blundered in November 1975, the most important were made by three particular individuals.

The first was the man who dismissed the prime minister, the governor-general, Sir John Kerr. The problem that the governor-general faced was how he was to deal with his prime minister who sought to govern without supply rather than face the electorate. This was a serious problem for Kerr and for the country. But Kerr's blunder was in the steps that he took to deal with that serious problem. Kerr claims that he 'had not set out to play a dramatic or controversial role' in the dispute, but he found the circumstances he faced made it necessary for him to intervene. He claimed to the *Bulletin* in 1985, 'As events turned out, I had no choice'.[9] But as we have seen, Kerr's 'no choice' conclusion is just incorrect.

First, as we have seen from chapter 9, he did have a choice as to when he would intervene, as the funding for government had not expired on November 11. He sacked Whitlam well before it was ever necessary, and by acting so early he deprived the Parliament and the political system of up to an additional 20 days when funding was still present, and when it could all have been sorted out without his intervention.

Second, he did have a choice as to the warning provided to Whitlam before he sacked him. But, as we saw in chapters 7 and 9, he chose not to provide any warning, keeping his thoughts and plans entirely secret from the prime minister until he exercised them. Kerr took those pre-emptive and secret actions for the following reasons, none of which are justifiable.

First, his unwillingness, if not his cowardice, in refusing to engage with his head of government, regarding him as being so 'implacable' that important constitutional issues were no longer 'discussable'.[10] That dialogue-avoiding approach seems derived from what the victor in the 1975 dismissal, Malcolm Fraser, later described as Kerr's 'weakness in character',[11] a weakness which allowed Kerr to conclude that his only 'neutral and intelligent course' and his 'proper behaviour . . . [was] to stay at my post and not invite dismissal' and that he 'should keep silence about my thinking unless and until I decided I must act'.[12] Whitlam substantially agreed with that Fraser conclusion, regarding Kerr and his actions as indicating that 'he was a weak man, and a deceptive man and a dishonourable man'.[13]

The second reason for Kerr was because he considered that his non-dialogue course was consistent with the role of the governor-general. That conclusion, however, could only be reached by his very selective approach to legal principles that he adopted. Not only had Kerr rejected and did not refer in his memoirs or in his correspondence with the Palace, to the advice that he had received from the experienced governors of the States of New South Wales and Victoria, Cutler and Winneke, and from his friend and colleague, the future Chief Justice Anthony Mason who all had advised him that he had a duty to warn Whitlam of his proposed actions (as seen in chapters 8 and 9. But he also made no reference to the nineteenth-century constitutional author, Walter Bagehot. And Bagehot had made the concept of the three rights that the Monarch and all Governors held famous: the right to be consulted, the right to encourage and the right to warn – rights that Bagehot regarded as so essential that 'A king of great sense and sagacity would want no others'.[14] Kerr instead, with less sense and sagacity than Bagehot, took the view that no effective warning[15] was necessary as Whitlam 'accepted that I had the reserve powers and might conceivably exercise them' and that 'He never questioned me on my views'.[16] This limiting of his warning to only be given if asked for is clearly wrong, undermining and minimising Bagehot's fundamental rights. Kerr considered that his role was not to provide a warning as if he did, Whitlam may well have sought to remove Kerr from office. Kerr preferred maintenance of office rather than engaging with his head of government, and that seems to have been largely caused because Kerr simply did not appreciate the rules.

The second central blunderer was the man who advised the governor-general, the then chief justice, Sir Garfield Barwick. Despite the various criticisms of popular and pro-Whitlam authors who have argued that the chief justice should not have been able to advise the governor-general, there was never any constitutional reason in 1975 that should have prevented the chief justice from providing his constitutional advice to the governor-general, as that practice was consistent with the practice adopted by previous High Court chief justices since Federation (as discussed in chapter 8).

The problem with Barwick's advice, however, was not in his constitutional ability to do so, but in the accuracy of his constitutional analysis. That is, he took a remarkably unusual position on Australia's parliamentary democracy, considering that it required government to have the confidence of both

Houses when supply was in dispute. But, as Professor Sawer has said, Barwick's advice:

> Confuses the law and the conventions of the Constitution so as to produce a fallacious statement of the relevant convention. He does this by asserting an analogy between the United Kingdom position of a government in relation to the House of Commons, and the position of an Australian government in relation to both Houses.

To Professor Sawer, this analogy was erroneous, as 'The "responsibility" of an Australian Commonwealth government is solely to the House of Representatives'.[17] In addition, Barwick also supported his odd theoretical view by, as we have seen, no accurate appreciation of the constitutional history of Australia. He did not know, at least in 1975, that supply had been blocked by Upper Houses many times in Australian States both before and after federation, and on none of those occasions had that led to the dismissal of government. And his remarkably confident view, the basis of his advice to Kerr, was both simplistic and incorrect: 'until 1975, no Prime Minister in any Westminster system, including the United Kingdom, has refused to resign or advise dissolution if unable to secure supply'.[18] Barwick's advice may well have been based on his political preference or bias against Whitlam, but he was far too good a lawyer to have made this basic error if he knew what the history actually was. It was not until 20 years after the dismissal that he became even partially aware of this error, but then he attempted to write off instances that did not fit with his analogy as solely from Victoria and from 'frontier days'.[19] But, as seen in chapter 8, there are far more instances of supply disputes than those from Victoria or from a 'frontier' period.

But Kerr and Barwick were not the only persons involved in 1975 who blundered in their appreciation and application of the rules. The *third central blunderer* is the person who should have taken, at least, equal responsibility for the eventual result of the 1975 dismissal (but not its immediate cause), but who has largely avoided any blame. That is, the third man who blundered into the 1975 constitutional crisis is the one who was *its central victim, Gough Whitlam.* Whitlam's error was not only because he surrounded himself with, as his private secretary, John Mant, has put it – 'largely useless . . . pissants'.[20] And it was also not only because he clearly misunderstood and minimized Kerr and the office he held, incorrectly considering the new governor-general, as Bill Hayden saw it, as just 'a man of putty'.[21] But beyond those fairly considerable blunders, it was because of the steps that he could have taken to save his government, but did not; steps that would have delayed and may have prevented Kerr's dismissal of Whitlam and his appointment of Fraser from being effective. As Hayden later said, if Whitlam had taken this course, Kerr's plans would be 'in tatters'.[22]

As we have seen in chapter 10, the course that Whitlam should have taken, once dismissed, was to use the powers that the Parliament still had to delay and arguably prevent the new Fraser government from being able to provide supply. Fraser's actions required him to be able to provide supply and to do so quickly. As the then manager of Opposition business in the House of Representatives, and later leader of the Country Party Ian Sinclair[23] told Troy Bramston in 2015, on November 11, 1975, he was:

> trying to make sure we got the House up at the end of the day for an election. If Gough had told his Senate leader, Ken Wreidt, about the dismissal, it could have been a difficult situation for us. It was Gough's great failure to advise his senators what had happened. If we didn't have supply, there was no government. If supply was not passed, then we had not fulfilled the essential remit from Kerr. The outcome on that day may well have been different.[24]

Similarly, in Malcolm Fraser's 2013 recounting of events, he also made it clear the urgency of his gaining supply:

> I went to my office and said that I had been sworn in as Prime Minister. And I said to Reg [Withers], 'how soon can you get the budget through the Senate, because that is one of the commitments?' And he said, 'Oh, by tonight'. And I said, 'that's not good enough, you've got five minutes'.[25]

But Whitlam failed to appreciate Fraser's urgent need for the passage of the Supply bills. His best course to save his government would have commenced with attempting to delay the passage of the supply bills through the Senate. And if an Upper House delay had not resolved his dismissal, then once the supply bills had eventually passed through that Upper House, his next step should have been to use the powers of the House of Representatives over the supply bills. According to the Standing Orders of both Houses,[26] the House of Representatives would then have controlled the supply bills, and with that power and control, it could have elected to refuse to deliver those bills to the governor-general for Assent.

However, Whitlam, with his minimised view of the importance of the Senate, combined with his arrogance over his colleagues, failed to even consider the powers that remained in the two Houses that may have saved his government. He did not invite any senators to his post-dismissal steak lunch at the Lodge, so ALP senators knew nothing of Whitlam's dismissal and Fraser's appointment. As a result, they were caught completely unawares when the Liberal and Country Party senators were prepared to pass the supply bills at 2.20 pm on November 11, 1975. As to the powers of the Lower House, Whitlam's concentration was not on what was arguably his largest possible weapon to protect his government, the House of Representatives' control over the supply bills once they had passed through the Senate. Instead, his plan was based on the doubtful method of the Queen reinstating, or pressuring Kerr to reinstate Whitlam following a no-confidence motion in Fraser.[27]

A better and more effective plan, as Whitlam later conceded, was for the Speaker Gordon Scholes to have retained the supply bills instead of forwarding them to the governor-general for Assent. Scholes should have taken them, together with the House of Representatives' no-confidence motion regarding the new Fraser government, to his meeting with the governor-general and not provided them for Assent until the governor-general had acted on that no-confidence motion by reappointing Whitlam.[28]

Later, in 2005, Whitlam claimed that he had been the 'last Prime Minister of Australia to defend and protect the rights and authority of the House of Representatives',[29] but as we have seen from chapter 10, there was much more that he could and arguably should have done to protect the rights of the Lower House. But he didn't, and that seems because his actions, his blunders, were substantially caused by the fact that he either was simply not aware of, or did not give sufficient attention to, how the rules that applied worked.

Had Whitlam taken those steps, delaying and/or preventing supply bills from being presented to the governor-general for Assent, the options for the newly formed Fraser government would have been drastically restricted. By 3.15 pm on November 11, the new Prime Minister Fraser had already been denied the confidence of the Lower House, and now would not have been able to provide what Fraser had promised: the supply bills for Assent.

There was, however, one possible exception, but only if the governor-general felt he was both able and willing to give Assent to bills that the Parliament had refused to present to him. But that is a question which Kerr's various writings on 1975 simply do not answer or even consider.

Whitlam, however, was not the only one who failed to recognize the potential government saving solutions that he should have attempted. Indeed, there is very little to indicate that anyone else involved in 1975, including Kerr, Barwick, Mason or Ellicott had ever given any thought to that issue beyond the urgent need for the new government to gain supply from the Senate. The most we have is Whitlam's assertion that he added to his account in 2005, that the Clerk of the Senate, James Odgers, was in the first week of November 'notoriously involved in giving tactical advice to the Opposition' and he did so by being 'closeted with' Kerr's Official

Secretary, David Smith. Whitlam, however, provides no source for this allegation or any explanation of why he would conclude that a conversation between Odgers and Smith should be regarded as either 'notorious' or as 'tactical advice to the Opposition'.[30]

It seems, however, that had the governor-general, or the chief justice, or any one of Fraser's colleagues been aware of the process by which the supply bills needed to pass before they were given Assent, then it seems that they would also have concluded that Prime Minister Whitlam would use the powers in the two Houses as the best means of protecting his government. As Menadue later observed: 'If it was apparent that a dismissed Labor government could deny supply to Fraser because of its ongoing House of Representatives majority then' in his view, 'it is most unlikely, in my opinion, that the Governor-General and Mr Fraser would have contemplated the action that was finally taken'.[31] Kelly and Bramston considered this as 'an arguable proposition';[32] but it is much more than that as even Whitlam later accepted: 'This would have been a legitimate and even against Sir John Kerr, an effective tactic'.[33]

If that realization was ever reached by Kerr, or Barwick or Fraser, that would have been sufficient for a change of plan, restricting them to either of the following courses.

The first was for the supply blockage tactic to be reassessed and possibly reversed. That is, if Kerr, or Barwick or Fraser, or any of his Party colleagues had realized and recognized what Whitlam could have done to protect his government, the effect would have been for Fraser to be forced to acknowledge that his supply blockage approach was, at best, a highly risky and tentative solution, liable to confusion or defeat if Whitlam used the tools in his hands to their full effect.

The second alternate approach was to press on with the supply blockage tactic, regardless of its inherent risks. This requires making that tentative tactic even more high-risk, as its success would now be reliant on not only Whitlam not recognising what he may have done, but also that no one else would realize it, or if they did, they would not reveal the inherent weakness in that plan to Whitlam or to the public. Now, the first of those conditions was fulfilled in that, as we have seen, Whitlam operated both arrogantly and unwisely. But as to the second, would Kerr, at least, have made such a fundamental constitutional decision based on such a problematic and unpredictable expectation?

There is, however, one other factor that needs to be considered that is relevant to whether Kerr, Barwick or any of the other central participants in the 1975 drama appreciated the Lower House powers that Whitlam could have used. And it arises from the apparent mystery that no one, other than Whitlam, even discussed this issue in their later accounts. Possibly, this may be because they regarded the issue as of no relevance, considering that Kerr could have given Assent regardless of any direction that the House of Representatives had given. This conclusion seems odd, particularly after the comments of both Sawer and Odgers that identified the powers remaining in the Lower House that could have been used 'to delay or prevent the passage of supply by hindering the transmission of the Bills to the Governor-General'.[34] Moreover, Kerr seems to have selectively excluded that consideration from his account. This seems apparent when one reads his *Matters for Judgment* and sees that he referred to many other arguments made by Sawer in his *Federation Under Strain*, but not this one. That can be seen from table 13.1, which lists all of the items from Sawer's book that Kerr used and relied on to support his approach.

Table 13.1 Sir John Kerr's Reliance on the Arguments Made by Professor Geoffrey Sawer in *Federation under Strain*

Kerr page references in Matters for Judgment *to Sawer's* Federation under Strain	*Subject Matter*	*Sawer,* Federation under Strain *pages*
66–1	Evatt's and Forsey's opinions on the power of governors	154–5
73–4	Menzies comments on the action of Sir Philip Game in 1932	164
224–6	The governor-general's attendance at Executive Council	98–103
234–5	The Loans Council and the loans affair and justiciability	74–5; 164
325–326	Alternate financial arrangements	Appendix 3 (pages 212–17)
317	Senate's power to reject and defer supply	117; 127–8
332	The Queens lack of power to appoint prime minister	147
336	The 'Constitution preservation' test for the governor-general	163–4
338	Section 57 power – double dissolution	59–61
365	Fraser not taking responsibility for the dismissal	142

Source: (Melbourne University Press, Carlton, Victoria, 1977).

Kerr's considerable reliance on the Sawer book to support elements of his approach, while ignoring this important potential defect, seems to indicate that Kerr recognized, but only after the dismissal, the significance of Sawer's argument. But it also seems to indicate that he felt that the best way of avoiding that problem was just to ignore it. And given the lack of attention given to this argument since 1975, this seems to have largely worked, for Kerr at least.

Otherwise, the failure of those centrally involved in discussing the powers that Whitlam and the Lower House could have used seems to indicate that Kerr, Barwick, Fraser and each of the other central players in the 1975 drama have, like Whitlam, just missed that issue. If not, then the only alternative explanation seems to have been that they did recognize what Whitlam should have done, but they uniformly chose not to discuss it in their later accounts. But that uniform failure also require an additional element to the already high-risk and unpredictable approach discussed earlier. That is, in addition to an expectation that Whitlam would not recognize what his best course was to save his government, and that no one else would have told him, there now seems a need for some form of agreement between those central decision-makers that required absolute secrecy by each to ensure that all later discussion of what had occurred, including in the governor-general's advice to the Palace, would ignore the issue. That is, that plan, as well as having been one of high risk and unpredictability, would also have required Kerr to mislead the Crown[35] as well as the people of Australia. But all of this seems highly fictional, if only because Kerr, even if he was conspiracy-minded, was unlikely to have been willing (or brave enough) to have gone that far.

It also seems that if Kerr had actually recognized the weapons that Whitlam potentially had available to him, the governor-general's best approach to resolve the supply crisis would have been very different from the one he used. Unless he was in some form of collusion with Fraser and Barwick (and there is nothing to support such a conclusion), Kerr would not have needed to maintain either his undesirable secrecy from his prime minister or his ambush method of termination. Instead, his method of resolution would have started with a direct discussion with the Leader of the Opposition regarding his concerns that the supply blockage tactic of the Opposition would not actually work. He could have advised Fraser that, even if Fraser had been appointed as prime minister, that appointment would rely on Fraser's ability to provide supply, and Kerr would question how Fraser would be able to achieve that result given that the House of Representatives would then control the supply bills once they were passed by the Senate. Unless the Opposition was able to change the Standing Orders of the Senate to allow the bills to be submitted for Assent directly by the Senate (which would seem difficult, if not impossible, when the coalition had no absolute majority in that House), or unless Kerr himself was both able to (despite the views of Sawer) and was prepared to Assent to a bill that the Lower House had refused to present, there was not much room left for Fraser.

All these theories and arguments are, however, based on at least, some of the central decision-makers recognizing what the dismissed prime minister could or should have done. But the better view is that they all just didn't see it. There is simply nothing to support the conclusion that Kerr or Barwick or Fraser or Mason had any greater appreciation than Whitlam or Speaker Scholes of what Whitlam may have done to save his government. Clearly, Whitlam did not recognize the potential powers of either House, at least on November 11, 1975; and that was caused by a combination of his arrogance as well as the lack of clarity of the rules themselves. And there is simply no basis to consider that any of the other participants had any better appreciation of the obscure rules on November 11, or had considered how legislation gets to the governor-general for Assent.

The result is that the 1975 tragedy occurred not merely because of any great duplicitous vice-regal coup or conspiracy, but because of a combination of errors caused by a series of confusing events, with the central one being that no one recognized how the rules worked. And with that ignorance or confusion, Kerr, Whitlam, Barwick and everyone else centrally involved just blundered through the events of 1975. By their joint and several blunders, they created Australia's great constitutional crisis, a crisis that should never have occurred had any of them appreciated what the applicable rules were.

THE DISMISSAL – LESSONS THAT SHOULD BE LEARNED

So, if the dismissal of the Whitlam government occurred because no one appreciated what the constitutional rules meant, and that failure includes no one appreciating what Whitlam himself could and should have done to save his government, what lessons should we have learnt from 1975?

And there seems to be, at least, two.

The first arises from the significant constitutional problems regarding the roles of both the governor-general and the prime minister that the dismissal of the Whitlam government has revealed. The result that we should learn from those problems is that the Australian constitutional rules should be clearer and better known.

As we have seen, the events of 1975 are still the subject of confusing and incorrect popular analysis of their fundamentals, demonstrating, despite the work of Dr Evatt and other later authors, that the problems regarding the meaning and application of constitutional conventions and the reserve powers remain. As Professor Bailey said in 1936, in his Introduction to the

First Edition of Evatt's work, the subject of reserve powers was then one of 'immense amount of sheer uncertainty and confusion in which the whole subject is involved'.[36] And as that uncertainty has in no way diminished in the last 85 years, Evatt's 1936 solution to that problem still remains the best way of overcoming that 'sheer uncertainty and confusion'. That is, codification of conventions and the reserve powers. As Professor Bailey then said: 'the reserve powers of the Crown should be subjected to the normal and natural process of analysis and definition and reduction to rules of positive law'.[37] Moreover, given the procedural rules that Whitlam, Kerr, Barwick and Mason failed to even consider prior to and after Whitlam's dismissal, codification would also be appropriate for the relationship between the various elements of the Parliament (the Monarch, the Senate and the House of Representatives),[38] specifying which body controls bills at different stages of a bill's passage through the Parliament.

The other remaining message of this great Australian constitutional crisis is that the victim of the dismissal, the dismissed Prime Minister Gough Whitlam should no longer be regarded as just the undeserved political and constitutional casualty of 1975. Although he was clearly and unjustifiably the central victim of the actions taken on November 11, 1975, he should also have been recognized as part of the list of those responsible for the results of what happened on that day given what he did not do with the powers left available to him when he still had the opportunity. That is, he should now be remembered not just as one of Australia's great reformers, which he was, nor as just the central sufferer from Sir Kerr's unjustified constitutional ambush, which he also was. But he should also be remembered, to adapt an Australian football idiom, as the prime minister who 'dropped the constitutional ball' when he failed to use or even consider the powers that were still available to him from both Houses that would have hampered and may well have prevented Kerr's dismissal of him from being successful.

Whitlam's preferences, however, were elsewhere; his lunchtime steak at the Lodge, while he surrounded himself with ill-informed 'pissants' as advisers, and relied on the constitutional irrelevancy of the Queen saving his government (as discussed in chapter 10) rather than using Parliamentary powers to save his government. That was all part of Whitlam's fundamental constitutional blunder; and by doing so, the fate of his government was sealed.

So, for all those who have been dutifully maintaining their respective rages since Whitlam's request on November 11, 1975, particularly those who have continued to believe that the governor-general was in some form of conspiracy with the leader of the Opposition and/or chief justice; or those who consider that he was being instructed or directed by his old friend, Anthony Mason; or others who regard him as either a flunky to the CIA, or under the instructions of the late Queen – the examination of the events of

1975 discussed in this work should be sufficient for them to, at least, pause and reconsider whether their long-standing rage has been misdirected and misplaced. Their anger and frustration, their rage, regarding the actions taken by those responsible for the cause of the government's dismissal, particularly Kerr, Barwick and Fraser, still remains largely relevant, even if somewhat inflated, as both Kerr and Barwick did not commit all of the various constitutional sins of which they have been accused. But it is here suggested that some, if not all, of that maintained anger and frustration should be directed elsewhere – to the man whose failure to save the sacked Labor government when he might have done so was crucial to the success of Kerr's dismissal, the dismissed Prime Minister Gough Whitlam. Painful though this may be for many, as this work has sought to demonstrate, Kerr's dismissal of Whitlam would have been much more difficult to achieve, and may have been impossible, had Whitlam given much less attention to his lunchtime steak and to his stunned pissant colleagues and much more to constitutional rules, vague though they often are, and had realized that 'the devil is in the details'.

Whitlam's significant blunders in his response and reaction to his dismissal, however, ignored the necessary constitutional minutiae that might have saved his government. Unlike the various actual and claimed faults of others involved, particularly those of Kerr and the chief justice, most of the many errors of the dismissed prime minister have been overlooked and forgotten by history and the public. But that is the regrettable and also the ignored reality of the Australian 1975 constitutional crisis. This continuing ignored reality continues to confuse and distract Australia's understanding of its greatest constitutional crisis when Sir John Kerr dismissed Gough Whitlam, misplacing much of the 'maintained rage' for the divisive constitutional acts taken on November 11, 1975.

NOTES

1. See the interview with Whitlam ten years after his dismissal conducted by the Special Broadcasting Service – Gough Whitlam interview, by Margaret Throsby, Mungo MacCallum, Michelle Grattan and Max Teichmann. *Issues 85*, Special Broadcasting Service (SBS), November 11, 1985, particularly 13.00-15.00. Youtube – https://www.youtube.com/watch?v=uA6T8yhuurM.
2. Whitlam interview (SBS, 1985) –12.55-13.05.
3. See "From the Archives, 1983: It's Hawke . . . and Fraser Quits," *Sydney Morning Herald*, March 5, 2020.
4. "SBS Dateline interview with Boyce," 10.25.
5. Whitlam, *Whitlam Government,* 52.
6. This letter can be found in Kelly & Bramston, *Truth, Palace Letters,* 209–210.
7. Hayden, *Hayden,* 238–239.

8. Killey, *Naked Australian Constitution*, ch 4.
9. John Kerr, "Kerr Breaks his Silence: 'Why I was right to sack Whitlam,'" *The Bulletin*, September 3, 1985, 66, 73.
10. Letter from Kerr to Charteris, November 20, 1975, seen in Kelly & Bramston, *Truth, Palace Letters,* 221, 223 & 225.
11. Fraser & Simons, *Malcolm Fraser,* 357.
12. Kerr, *Matters,* 309–310.
13. *Four Corners* (1995), 37.05-37.15.
14. Bagehot, *English Constitution*, 111.
15. Markwell and possibly Kerr have argued that on November 11, 1975, Kerr had given Whitlam a very limited warning, but this seems a reconstruction and seems not to be correct. That matter is discussed in chapter 7. See Markwell, *Australian Experience*, 153 and Kerr, *Matters,* 358–359.
16. Kerr, *Matters,* 309.
17. Quoted in Whitlam, *The Truth,* 191 and was based on the views of Sawer, *Federation Under Strain*, 158.
18. Barwick, *Sir John*, 55. He also repeated this conclusion on page 115.
19. Barwick, *Radical Tory*, 282.
20. Kelly & Bramston, *The Dismissal,* 136.
21. Hayden, *Hayden*, 278.
22. Hayden, *Hayden*, 298.
23. Ian Sinclair led the National Party between 1984 and 1989.
24. Kelly & Bramston, *The Dismissal,* 232.
25. *Whitlam: The Power & the Passion*, directed by Paul Clarke (Australian Broadcasting Corporation, 2013) DVD, Episode Two, Chapter Six, 0.43-0.44.
26. See SO (House of Representatives) 265 and SO (Senate) 234 discussed in chapter 10.
27. See the draft motion prepared by Whitlam on November 11, 1975, in Kelly & Bramston, *The Dismissal,* 375–376 discussed earlier in chapter 10.
28. Whitlam, *The Truth,* 165–166.
29. Whitlam, *The Truth,* xxiv.
30. Whitlam, *The Truth,* xxiv.
31. Quoted in Kelly & Bramston, *The Dismissal,* 140.
32. Kelly & Bramston, *The Dismissal,* 140.
33. Whitlam, *The Truth,* 165–166.
34. Sawer, *Federation Under Strain,* 169. Also see Odgers, *Senate Practice,* 87–88.
35. Unless the Crown was also part of the "conspiracy" and was happy for the communications from the governor-general to it to be misleading, this seems so fictional and absurd that it does not require discussion.
36. K. H. Bailey, "Introduction to the First Edition," in Evatt, *Dominion Governors* (2nd edition), xxxvii.
37. Bailey, "'Introduction,' to the First Edition," in Evatt, *Dominion Governors,* xxxvii.
38. *Australian Constitution*, s 1.

Bibliography

ABC News. "Malcolm Fraser on his Legacy and Modern Politics." YouTube, filmed in 2010. https://www.youtube.com/watch?v=V21t-wJrXgE.

Allard-Tremblay, Yann. "Proceduralism, Judicial Review and the Refusal of Royal Assent." (2013) 33 *Oxford Journal of Legal Studies* 379.

Ananian-Welsh, Rebecca and George Williams. "Judges in Vice Regal Roles." (2015) 43 *Federal Law Review* 119–146.

Australian Electoral Commission. "House of Representatives-Two Party Preferred Results 1949 – Present." December 10, 2019. https://www.aec.gov.au/Elections/federal_elections/tpp-results.htm.

Australian Government. Department of Prime Minister and Government. *Guidance on Caretaker Conventions, 2021.*

Ayers, Philip. *Owen Dixon.* Carlton, Victoria: Miegunyah Press, 2003.

Bagehot, Walter. *The English Constitution.* Glasgow: Fontana/William Collins, 1983, reprint of the 2nd 1872 edition.

Bailey, K. H. "Introduction to the First Edition." In H. V. Evatt, *The King and his Dominion Governors* (2nd edition), xxxv–xxviii. Reprinted in *Evatt and Forsey on the Reserve Powers* (Sydney: Legal Books, 1990).

Barwick, Garfield. *A Radical Tory.* Annandale, NSW: Federation Press, 1996.

Barwick, Garfield. *Sir John Did His Duty.* Wahroonga, NSW: Serendip Publications, 1983.

Blaxland, John. *The Protest Years: The Official History of ASIO, 1963–1975.* Crows Nest, NSW: Allen & Unwin, 2015.

Bogdanor, Vernon. *The Monarchy and the Constitution.* Oxford: Clarendon Press, 1995.

Bogdanor, Vernon and G. Marshall. "Dismissing Governor-Generals." [1996] *Public Law* 205–213.

Bongiorno, Frank. "The Origins of Caucus 1856–1910." In *The Story of the Federal Parliamentary Labor Party, True Believers,* edited John Faulkner and Stuart MacIntyre, 3–16. Crows Nest, NSW: Allen and Unwin, 2001.

Boyce, Christopher, Cait Boyce & Vince Font. *American Sons, The Untold Story of the Falcon and the Snowman.* Ogden, Utah, USA: Glass Spider Publishing, 2013–2018.

Bramston, Troy. "Prologue, The Whitlam Ascendency." In *The Whitlam Legacy,* edited by Troy Bramston, 1–15. Leichardt, NSW: Federation, 2015.

Bramston, Troy. "The Whitlam Government Through the Cabinet Papers." In *The Whitlam Legacy,* edited by Troy Bramston, 96–111. Leichardt, NSW: Federation, 2015.

Bramston, Troy, ed. *The Whitlam Legacy.* Leichardt, NSW: Federation Press, 2015.

Brazier, Rodney. *Constitutional Practice, The Foundations of the British Government.* Oxford: Oxford University Press, 3rd edition, 1999.

Brazier, Rodney. "The Monarchy." In *The British Constitution in the Twentieth Century*, edited by Vernon Bogdanor, 69–95. Oxford: The British Academy by Oxford University Press, 2003.

Bridge, Carl. *Makers of the Modern World, William Hughes, Australia.* London: Hause Publishing, 2011.

British History Online. *House of Lords Journal*, 18 (11 March 1708): 504–506. https://www.british-history.ac.uk/lords-jrnl/vol18/pp504-506.

Brodie, Scott. *Statesmen, Leaders and Losers, The Twenty-Three Prime Ministers of Australia.* Sydney, NSW: Dreamweaver, 1984.

Buckley, Ken, Barbara Dale & Wayne Reynolds. *Doc Evatt: Patriot, Internationalist, Fighter and Scholar.* Melbourne, Victoria: Longman Cheshire, 1994.

Button, John. "Out of the Blue." In *The Dismissal: Where Were you on November 11, 1975?,* edited by Sybil Nolan, 31–36. Carlton, Victoria: Melbourne University Press, 2015.

"Caretaker Conventions and Other Pre-Election Practices." *Department of Prime Minister and Cabinet*, Annual Report, 1986–87, 39–49.

Carleton, James, ed. *The Wit of Whitlam.* Carlton, Victoria: Melbourne University Press, 2015.

Coleman, Robert. *Above Renown.* South Melbourne, Victoria: Macmillan, 1988.

Commonwealth of Australia. *Parliamentary Debates*, House of Representatives: 1970 – August 25; 1975 – June 4; July 9; August 21; October 9 & 16; November 4, 5, 6 & 11; and 1995 – June 7.

Commonwealth of Australia. *Parliamentary Debates*, Senate*:* 1973 – March 8, 1973; 1974 – April 10, 1974; and 1975 – October 16; November 11.

Constitutional Clarion. "The Night of the Long Prawns – Senate Manipulation during the Whitlam Era." *YouTube*, May 20, 2024. https://www.youtube.com/watch?v=Ofjuyl82IXM.

"Constitutional Experts Scoreboard," from "November 11 in Retrospect; Was Kerr Right?" *The Bulletin*, August 4, 1976.

Cooray, L. J. M. *Conventions, The Australian Constitution and the Future.* Sydney, NSW: Legal Books, 1979.

Costar, B. J. "Gair, Vincent Clare (1901–1980)." In *Australian Dictionary of Biography*, National Centre of Biography. Canberra, ACT: Australian National University, published first in hardcopy 1996. Vol 14. https://adb.anu.edu.au/biography/gair-vincent-clare-vince-10267. Accessed online May 12, 2023.

Cottle, Drew. "Greenwood, Ivor John (1026–1976)." In *The Biographical Dictionary of the Senate,* Parliament of Australia (online). https://biography.senate.gov.au/greenwood-ivor-john/. First published in *The Biographical Dictionary of the Australian Senate, 1962–1983,* vol 3, 77–82. Sydney, NSW: University of New South Wales Press Ltd, 2010, 77–82.

Creighton, Donald. "Eugene Alfred Forsey: An Introduction." In Eugene Forsey, *Freedom and Order, Collected Essays.* Toronto: Carleton Library, 1974.

Cremean, Damien J. "State Chief Justices As Lieutenant Governors: Federal Jurisdiction." (2010) 18 *Australian Journal of Administrative Law* 3–6.

Crockett, Peter. *Evatt: A Life.* Melbourne, Victoria: Oxford University Press, 1993.

Crommelin, Michael. "Book Review – Constitutional Conventions and the Headship of State: Australian Experience by Donald Markwell." (2017) 40 *Melbourne University Law Review* 1132–1141.

Crommelin, Michael. "Powers of the Head of State." (2015) 38 *Melbourne University Law Review* 1118–1139.

Crommelin, Michael and Gareth Evans. "The Exploration and Adventures with Commonwealth Powers." In *Labor and the Constitution,* edited by Gareth Evans, 24–75. Melbourne, Victoria: Heinemann, 1977.

Curran, James. *Unholy Fury.* Carlton: Melbourne University Press, 2015.

Daly, Fred. *From Curtin to Hawke.* South Melbourne: Sun Books, South Melbourne, 1984.

Davey, Paul. *Ninety Not Out: The Nationals 1920–2010.* Sydney, NSW: UNSW Press, 2010.

Department of Prime Minister and Cabinet. "Special Article, Caretaker and Other Pre-Election Practices." In *Department of Prime Minister and Cabinet, Annual Report, 1986–87.* Canberra: Australian Government Publishing Service, 1987.

Donaghue, Stephen. "In the Matter of The Validity of the Appointment of Mr Morrison to Administer the Department of Industry, Science, Energy and Resources." August 23, 2022. https://www.pmc.gov.au/news/solicitor-general-opinion-matter-validity-appointment-mr-morrison-administer-department.

Evans, Gareth, ed. *Labor and the Constitution: 1972–1975.* Melbourne, Victoria: Heinemann, 1977.

Evatt, H. V. *Australian Labour Leader: The Story of W A Holman and the Labour Movement.* Sydney, NSW: Angus and Robertson, 1940.

Evatt, H. V. *Evatt and Forsey on the Reserve Powers.* Sydney, NSW: Legal Books, 1990.

Evatt, H. V. *Rum Rebellion: A Study of the Overthrow of Governor Bligh by John Macarthur and the New South Wales Corps.* Sydney, NSW: Angus and Robertson, 1978, reprint of the original 1938 edition.

Evatt, H. V. *The King and his Dominion Governors.* Oxford University Press, 1936, reprinted in *Evatt and Forsey on the Reserve Powers.* Sydney: Legal Books, 1990.

Evatt, H. V. *The Royal Prerogative.* North Ryde, NSW: Law Book Company, 1987.

Evatt, H. V. *The Tolpuddle Martyrs: Injustice within the Law. A Study of the Case of the Dorsetshire Labourers.* Sydney, NSW: Sydney University Press, 2009, republication of original 1937 edition. Kindle.

Everett, William. "The Last Royal Veto." *The Atlantic,* December 1903.

Farmer, Richard. "Gough Whitlam: The Campaigner." In *The Whitlam Legacy,* edited by Troy Bramston, 58–63. Leichardt, NSW: Federation, 2015.

Faulkner, John. "Remembrance Day, 1975." In *The Story of the Federal Parliamentary Labor Party, True Believers,* edited by John Faulkner and Stuart MacIntyre, 118–119. Crows Nest, NSW: Allen and Unwin, 2001.

Faulkner, John and Stuart Macintyre, ed. *The Story of the Federal Parliamentary Labor Party, True Believers.* Crows Nest, NSW: Allen & Unwin, 2001.

Federal Election Commission. *Federal Elections 2016, Election Results for the US President, the US Senate and the US House of Representatives.* Washington: Federal Election Commission, 2017.

"Federal Executive Council Handbook, 2021." Australian Government, Department of Prime Minister and Cabinet. https://www.pmc.gov.au/sites/default/files/resource/download/executive-council-handbook-2021.pdf.

Final Report of the Constitutional Commission. Canberra, ACT: Australian Government Publishing Service, 1988.

Foott, Bethia. *Dismissal of a Premier (The Philip Game Papers).* Sydney, NSW: Morgan, 1968.

Forsey, Eugene. *A Life on the Fringe, The Memoirs of Eugene Forsey.* Toronto: Oxford University Press, 1990.

Forsey, Eugene. *Freedom and Order, Collected Essays.* Toronto: Carleton Library, 1974.

Forsey, Eugene. "Introduction – The Present Position of the Reserve Powers of the Crown." In *Evatt and Forsey on the Reserve Powers,* xi–ciii. Sydney, New South Wales: Legal Books, 1990.

Forsey, Eugene A. *The Royal Power of Dissolution of Parliament in the British Commonwealth.* Canada: Oxford University Press, 1943 & 1968.

Four Corners. "The Dismissal of Gough Whitlam on the 11th of November 1975." Australian Broadcasting Commission, 1995. https://www.youtube.com/watch?v=09bb1uETzfE&list=PL18SxApCKfY6M9jrv3rNWXOQ7DV9rhzhF&index=10&t=1469s.

Frank, Thomas. *People Without Power: The War on Populism and the Fight for Democracy.* Brunswick, Victoria: Scribe Publications, 2020.

Fraser, Antonia. *Cromwell, Our Chief of Men.* London: Phoenix, Weidenfeld and Nicolson Ebook, 2011, republication of original 1973 edition. Kindle.

Fraser, Malcolm. "Towards 2000: Challenge to Australia." The Fifth Alfred Deakin Lecture – 20 July 1971. The Malcolm Fraser Collection, University of Melbourne. https://library.unimelb.edu.au/asc/collections/highlights/collections/malcolmfraser/resources/postparliamentspeeches/towards-2000-challenge-to-australia.

Fraser, Malcolm and Margaret Simons. *Malcolm Fraser, The Political Memoirs.* Carlton, Victoria: Miegunyah Press, 2010.

Freeman, Joanne. *Field of Blood.* New York: Picador, 2018. Kindle.

Freestone, Robert & Richard Whitington. "Urban Planner and Policy Leader 'made a difference.'" *Sydney Morning Herald*, July 19, 2021.

French, Robert. "The Chief Justice and the Governor-General." (2009) 33(3) *Melbourne University Law Review* 647–656.

Freudenberg, Graham. *A Certain Grandeur, Gough Whitlam's Life in Politics.* South Melbourne, Victoria: Sun Books, 1978.

Gageler, Stephen. "Australian Government Solicitor, No 1: What is it to be a Government Lawyer, Australian Government Solicitor." https://www.ags.gov.au/publications/agsmagazine/issue-1/guest-case-studies. Accessed May 27, 2023.

"Geoffrey Sawer – Emeritus Professor, Lawyer and University Administrator." ANU Emeritus Faculty Oral History Project, The Australian National University, Emeritus Faculty Inc. https://openresearch-repository.anu.edu.au/handle/1885/13027. Accessed September 17, 2022.

Gibbs, Harry. "The dismissal and the Constitution." In *Power, Parliament and the People*, edited by Michael Coper and George Williams, 146–154. Annadale, NSW: Federation Press, 1997.

"Gough Whitlam's Post-Dismissal Press Conference," November 11, 1975. WhitlamDismissal.com. https://whitlamdismissal.com/1975/11/11/whitlam-post-dismissal-press-conference.html/.

Gough Whitlam: In His Own Words. Ronin Films, 2002. Youtube. https://www.youtube.com/watch?v=WmhvM_ALc5A. Accessed January 31, 2023.

Gray, John. *Lawyer' Latin: A Vade Mecum.* London: Robert Hale, 2002.

Haigh, Gideon. *The Brilliant Boy, Doc Evatt and the Great Australian Dissent.* Cammeray, NSW: Scribner, 2022.

Harders, Clarrie. "The Loans Affair: An Insider's View." In *Power, Parliament and the People*, edited by Michael Coper and George Williams, 161–164. Annadale, NSW: Federation Press, 1997.

Harders, Clarrie. "Oral History," interview conducted by John M Farquharson in the Law in *Australian Society Oral History Project*, National Library of Australia. Sound recording, December 16, 1996, Session 3. https://nla.gov.au/nla.obj-220645788/listen.

Hartcher, Peter. "It's Not My Party and I'll Quit if I Want To." *Sydney Morning Herald*, May 27, 2010, 15.

Hasluck, Paul. *The Chance of Politics.* Melbourne: Text Publishing, 1997.

Hasluck, Paul. *The Office of Governor-General.* Carlton, Victoria: Melbourne University Press, 1979.

Hawker, Geoffrey. "Field, Albert Patrick (1910–1990)," Parliament of Australia, *Biographical Dictionary of the Australian Senate (online).* https://biography.senate.gov.au/field-albert-patrick/. First published in *The Biographical Dictionary of the Australian Senate, 1962–1983*, vol 3 (Sydney: University of New South Wales Press Ltd, 2010), 371–375.

Hayden, Bill. *Hayden, An Autobiography.* Pymble, NSW: Angus & Robertson, 1996.

Heanue, Siobhan. "Stroke of Genius: the legacy of Blue Poles." *ABC News,* August 29, 2012. https://web.archive.org/web/20121101101757/http://www.abc.net.au/

news/2012-08-28/stroke-of-genius-the-legacy-of-blue-poles/4228672, viewed August 23, 2022.

Heard, Andrew. *Canadian Constitutional Conventions, The Marriage of Law and Politics.* Ontario: Oxford University Press, 2nd edition, 2014.

Hearn, William. *The Government of England, Its Structure and Its Development.* Melbourne, Victoria: Longmans Green and Co, 1887.

Heenan, Tom. "Burchett, Wilfred Graham (1911–1983)," in National Centre of Biography, *Australian Dictionary of Biography*, Canberra ACT: Australian National University, published first in hardcopy 2007, Vol 17. https://adb.anu.edu.au/biography/burchett-wilfred-graham-12265/text22015. Accessed online May 12, 2023.

Henderson, Anne. *Menzies versus Evatt, The Great Rivalry of Australian Politics.* Redland Bay, Queensland: Connor Court, 2023.

Henderson, Gerard. "Evidence, Memory and The Dismissal." Review of *The Dismissal* by Kelly and Bramston; *Where Were You*, edited by Nolan; and *Dismissal Dossier* by Hocking. *The Sydney Institute*, February 2, 2016. https://thesydneyinstitute.com.au/blog/evidence-memory-and-the-dismissal/.

Henderson, Gerard. "Whitlam's Opposition." In *The Whitlam Legacy*, edited by Troy Bramston, 83–95. Leichardt, NSW: Federation, 2015.

Hocking, Jenny. "'A Royal Green Light': The Palace, the Governor-General and the Dismissal of the Whitlam Government." In *Pearls and Irritations*, John Menadue's Public Policy Journal, October 23, 2017. https://johnmenadue.com/jenny-hocking-a-royal-green-light-the-palace-the-governor-general-and-the-dismissal-of-the-whitlam-government/.

Hocking, Jenny. *Gough Whitlam, A Moment in History.* Carlton, Victoria: Miegunyah Press, 2008.

Hocking, Jenny. *Gough Whitlam, His Time.* Carlton, Victoria: Miegunyah Press, 2012.

Hocking, Jenny. *Gough Whitlam, His Time.* Carlton, Victoria: Miegunyah Press, 2014. Kindle.

Hocking, Jenny. "Introduction: History by Numbers." In *The Dismissal: Where Were You on November 11, 1975?,* edited Sybil Nolan, 14–29. Carlton, Victoria: Melbourne University Press, 2015.

Hocking, Jenny. *Lionel Murphy: A Political Biography.* Cambridge: Cambridge University Press, 1997.

Hocking, Jenny. "Scholes, Gordon Glen (1931–2018)," Australian Dictionary of Biography, National Centre of Biography, Australian National University. https://adb.anu.edu.au/biography/scholes-gordon-glen-28243/text35926, published online 2021. Accessed online June 23, 2024.

Hocking, Jenny. *The Dismissal Dossier.* Carlton, Victoria: Melbourne University Press, 2015.

Hocking, Jenny. *The Palace Letters.* Melbourne, Victoria: Scribe, 2020.

Hogen, Michael. "Education Policy." In *The Whitlam Legacy,* edited by Troy Bramston, 186–195. Leichardt, NSW: Federation, 2015.

Horne, Donald. *Death of the Lucky Country.* Harmondsworth: Penguin Books, 1976.

Horner, David. *The Spy Catchers: The Official History of ASIO, 1949–1963.* Crows Nest, NSW: Allen & Unwin, 2015.
Hough, David & Kay Walsh. "Withers, Reginald Grieve." *The Biographical Dictionary of the Australian Senate*, Online Edition.
Howard, Colin. *Australian Federal Constitutional Law.* Sydney, NSW: Law Book Co, 1985.
Howard, Colin & Cheryl Saunders. "The Blocking of the Budget and Dismissal of the Government." In *Labor and the Constitution: 19720–1975,* edited by Gareth Evans, 251–287. Melbourne, Victoria: Heinemann, 1977.
Howard, John. *Lazarus Rising.* Sydney, NSW: HaperCollins, 2010.
Hughes, Robin. "Australian Biography: Jim Cairns – Transcript." National Films and Sound Archive of Australia. NFSA ID: 420890, recorded May 22, 1998. https://www.nfsa.gov.au/collection/curated/australian-biography-jim-cairns#field-file-transcript.
"It's Time: Audio, Video and Lyrics." November 13, 1972, WhitlamDismissal.com. https://whitlamdismissal.com/1972/11/13/its-time-audio-video-lyrics.html/.
Jennings, W. Ivor. *Cabinet Government.* Cambridge: Cambridge University Press, 1947.
Jenkins, Roy. *Mr Balfour's Poodle.* London: Collins, 1968.
Judicial Decisions:
Australian Communist Party v Commonwealth (1951) 83 CLR 1.
Clayton v Heffron (1960) 105 CLR 214.
Commonwealth v Kreglinger & Fernau Ltd (1926) 37 CLR 393.
Grollo v Palmer (1995) 184 CLR 348.
Hilton v Wells (1985) 157 CLR 57.
Hocking v Director-General of the National Archives of Australia (2020) 271 CLR 1.
Jones v Commonwealth (1987) 61 ALJR 348.
Kable v DPP (1996) 189 CLR 51.
Medical Board of Victoria v Meyer (1937) 58 CLR 62.
Namoi Shire Council v Attorney-General (NSW) [1980] 2 NSWLR 639.
NSW v Commonwealth (1915) 20 CLR 54 ('*The Wheat Case*').
Queensland v Commonwealth (1977) 139 CLR 585 ('*Second Territory Senators' Case*').
R v Kirby; Ex parte Boilermakers Society of Australia (1956) 94 CLR 254.
Re Resolution to Amend the Constitution [1981] 1 SCR 753.
Wainohu v NSW (2011) 243 CLR 181.
Western Australia v Commonwealth (1975) 134 CLR 201 ('*First Territory Senators' Case*').
Wilson v Minister for Aboriginal and Torres Strait Affairs (1996) 189 CLR 1.
Kumerasingham, Harshan. "Viceregalism." In *Viceregalism: The Crown as Head of State in Political Crises in Postwar Commonwealth*, edited by H. Kumarasingham, 18–78. Cham: Palgrave, Macmillan, 2020.
Kelly, Paul. *The Unmaking of Gough.* Sydney, NSW: Angus & Robertson, 1976.
Kelly, Paul. *The Unmaking of Gough.* St Leonards, NSW: Allen & Unwin, 1994. Kindle.

Kelly, Paul & Troy Bramston. *The Dismissal in the Queen's Name.* Australia: Penguin, 2015.

Kelly, Paul & Troy Bramston. *The Truth of the Palace Letters*. Carlton, Victoria: Melbourne University Press, 2020.

Kemp, David. "Red Felt on Green Paper." In *The Dismissal: Where Were You on November 11, 1975?,* edited by Sybil Nolan, 56–62. Carlton, Victoria: Melbourne University Press, 2015.

Kerr, John. *Conversation with Sir Anthony Mason during October-November 1975.* National Archives of Australia, M4523, 1 Part 14.

Kerr, John. "Kerr Breaks his Silence: 'Why I was right to sack Whitlam'." *The Bulletin*, September 3, 1985.

Kerr, John. "Kerr Rejects 'ambush' Myth: 'PM knew I could sack him'." *The Bulletin,* September 10, 1985.

Kerr, John. *Matters for Judgment.* Melbourne, Victoria: Macmillan, 1979.

Kerr, John. "Sir John Kerr Speaks to Geoffrey Robertson." Interview by Geoffrey Robertson. *Talking Shop,* Australian Broadcasting Commission, 1987. https://www.youtube.com/watch?v=J_K0ljE_6Y8.

Kerr, John. "Statement by the Governor-General, November 11, 1975."

Killey, Ian. *Constitutional Conventions in Australia.* North Melbourne, Victoria: Australian Scholarly Publishing, 2009 & 2012.

Killey, Ian. "Letters: The Whitlam Shambles." *Quadrant*, July–August 2005.

Killey, Ian. *The Naked Australian Constitution.* Lapham, Maryland: Lexington, 2022.

Laing, Rosemary, ed. *Odgers' Australian Senate Practice as Revised by Harry Evans.* Canberra, ACT: Department of the Senate, 14th edition, 2016.

Lane, Patrick. *A Manual of Australian Constitutional Law.* Sydney, NSW: Law Book Co, 1984.

Langan, Bernard. "Pickwickian Figure Helped Shape Nation; OBITUARY." *Sydney Morning Herald,* January 19, 1999, 4.

Lawson, Henry. "Freedom on the Wallaby." *The Worker*, May 16, 1891.

Legislation:

Appropriation Bill (No. 1) 1975-76.

Appropriation Bill (No. 2) 1975-76.

Constitution Act 1934 (Tas).

Constitution Act 1975 (Vic).

Commonwealth of Australia Constitution.

Lim, Brendan. *Australia's Constitution After Whitlam.* Cambridge: Cambridge University Press, 2017.

Lindsey, Robert. *The Falcon and the Snowman.* Harmondsworth: Penguin Books, 1985.

Lloyd, Clem & Andrew Clark. *Kerr's King Hit.* Stanmore, NSW: Cassell Australia, 1976.

Long, David. *Australia's American Constitution and the Dismissal: How English Legal Science Marred the Founders' Vision.* Lapham, Maryland: Lexington, 2021.

Love, Peter. *Labour and the Money Power: Australia Labour Populism.* Carlton, Victoria: Melbourne University Press, 1984.

Low, D. A. *Constitutional Heads and Political Crises.* New York: St Martin's Press, 1988.

Mackerras, Malcolm. "Victories, Defeats and Electoral Politics." In *The Whitlam Legacy*, edited by Troy Bramston, 64–82. Leichardt, NSW: Federation, 2015.

Malcolm, David K. "Role of the Chief Justice." Law Society of Western Australia, *Lunch with the Press*, May 5, 2004. https://www.supremecourt.wa.gov.au/_files/Law%20Society%20Press%20Lunch%205%20May%2004.pdf.

Mann, Alex. *The Eleventh.* Podcast audio series, Australian Broadcasting Commission. Originally broadcast between February 25 and March 24, 2020. https://www.abc.net.au/radio/programs/the-eleventh/episodes.

Manne, Robert. *The Petrov Affair.* Text, Melbourne, 2004.

Markesinis, B. S. *The Theory and Practice of Dissolution of Parliament.* Cambridge: Cambridge University Press, 1972.

Markwell, Don. "Griffith, Barton and the Early Governor- Generals: Aspects of Australia's Constitutional Development." (1999) 10 *Public Law Review* 280.

Markwell, Don. "On Advice from the Chief Justice: A Reply to Gareth Evan' Challenge." *Quadrant,* July 1985, 38.

Markwell, Donald. *Constitutional Conventions and the Headship of State; Australian Experience.* Redland Bay, Queensland: Connor Court Publishing, 2016.

Mason, Anthony. "A New Perspective on Separation of Powers." (1996) 82 *Canberra Bulletin of Public Administration* 1–9.

Mason, Anthony. *Conversations With Sir John Kerr Relating To His Termination of The Commission of The Prime Minister (The Hon E G Whitlam AC QC) on 11 November 1975* (2012).

Mason, Anthony. "The Convention Model for a Republic." (1999) 10 *Public Law Review* 147–149.

McClelland, James. *Stirring the Possum.* Ringwood, Victoria: Penguin Books, 1989.

McCullough, Colleen. *The Courage and the Will.* London: Weidenfeld and Nicolson, 1999.

McGarvie, Richard E. *Democracy, Choosing Australia's Republic.* Carlton, Victoria: Melbourne University Press, 1999.

McKenna, Mark. "Kerr's Ghost: The Office of Governor-General in Australia After 1975." In *Viceregalism: The Crown as Head of State in Political Crises in Postwar Commonwealth*, edited by H. Kumarasingham, 412–446. Cham: Palgrave, Macmillan, 2020.

McKeown, Deirdre and Rob Lundie. "Crossing the Floor in the Federal Parliament 1950–April 2019." *Parliament of Australia, Research Paper.* March 12, 2020.

McKinnon, Frank. *The Government of Prince Edward Island.* Toronto: University of Toronto Press, 1951.

McMullin, Ross. *So Monstrous a Travesty.* Melbourne, Victoria: Scribe Publications, 2004.

McMullin, Ross. "Ward, Edward John (Eddie) (1899–1963)." *Australian Dictionary of Biography*, National Centre of Biography, Australian National University. https://adb.anu.edu.au/biography/ward-edward-john-eddie-11959/text21435, published first in hardcopy 2002. Accessed July 19, 2022.

Menadue, John. *Things You Learn Along the Way.* Melbourne, Victoria: David Lovell Publishing, 1999.

Mendadue, John. *Transcript of Interview* conducted by Alex Mann for the ABC's podcast, *The Eleventh.* https://johnmenadue.com/wp-content/uploads/2020/03/John-Menadue-transcript-ABC-Series-1.pdf.

Murphy, John. *Evatt, A Life.* Sydney, NSW: NewSouth, 2016.

Murray, Robert. *The Split: Australian Labor in the Fifties.* Melbourne, Victoria: Cheshire, 1970.

Museum Victoria. Collections, "Malcolm Fraser, Tobhar, Australia, circa 1980." Item SH 950049. https://collections.museumsvictoria.com.au/items/258900.

Nairn, Bede. *The "Big Fella."* Balmain, NSW: Ligature, 2021.

National Archives of Australia. *The Kerr Palace Letters,* AA1984/609. https://www.naa.gov.au/explore-collection/kerr-palace-letters.

National Archives of Australia. *Journal for 1980, Maintained by Sir John Kerr,* M4523, 1 Part 17.

National Archives of Australia. *The Ellicott Memorandum – or Press Statement,* M4523, 1 Part 12.

National Centre of Biography. *Australian Dictionary of Biography.* Canberra, ACT: Australian National University, 2006–2023.

National Library of Australia. *John Kerr Interviewed by Suzanne Lunney [Sound Recording],* 1976. https://catalogue.nla.gov.au/catalog/2074277.

Nolan, Sybil, ed. *The Dismissal, Where Were You on November 11, 1975?* Carlton, Victoria: Melbourne University Press, 2005.

Oakes, Laurie. *Crash Through or Crash.* Richmond, Victoria: Drummond, 1976.

O'Brien, Peter. *Villain or Victim?* Redland Bay, Qld: Connor Court Publishing, 2022.

Odgers, J. R. *Australian Senate Practice.* Canberra, ACT: Royal Australian Institute of Public Administration (ACT Division), 6th edition, 1991.

Office of Police Integrity. *Report on the Investigation into Operation Clarendon,* Session 2006-08, PP 79. Melbourne: Victoria Government Printer, June 2008.

Parliament of Australia. *Annotated Standing Orders of the Senate.* https://www.aph.gov.au/About_Parliament/Senate/Powers_practice_n_procedures/aso/so131.

Parliament of Australia. *Biography for Ellicott, the Hon Robert James, AC, KC.* https://parlinfo.aph.gov.au/parlInfo/search/display/display.w3p;query=Id%3A%22handbook%2Fallmps%2FYF6%22.

Parliamentary Library. *Fraser's Shadow Ministry.* https://handbook.aph.gov.au/ShadowMinistry/25.

Parliamentary Library. *Parliamentary Handbook,* "Shadow Ministers in the Fraser Shadow Ministry from 21.03.1975 to 11.11.1975." https://handbook.aph.gov.au/ShadowMinistry/25.

Parr, Adriane. "ALP Its Time." National Films and Sound Archive of Australia, NFSA 253356. https://www.nfsa.gov.au/collection/curated/alp-its-time.

Penniman, Howard R., ed. *Australia at the Polls: The National Elections of 1975.* Washington, DC: American Enterprise Institute for Public Policy Research, 1977.

Pilger, John. *A Secret Country.* London: Vintage, 1992.

Poynter, J. R. "Sir Kenneth Clinton Wheare (1907–1979)," in National Centre of Biography, *Australian Dictionary of Biography*. Canberra, ACT: Australian National University, published first in hardcopy 2002, Vol 16. https://adb.anu.edu.au/biography/wheare-sir-kenneth-clinton-12005. Accessed May 12, 2023.

Press Articles:

"ALP Labors in Lib's Wake." *The Bulletin,* October 25, 1975.

"An Arrogant Silence." *Canberra Times,* July 4, 1975.

"From the Archives, 1983: It's Hawke ... and Fraser Quits." *Sydney Morning Herald,* March 5, 2020.

"It's Government by Crisis. What they Said." *The Age*, October 16, 1975, 1.

"Mr Hughes and the Labor Party, PLL Dominance." *The Age,* September 16, 1916, 11.

"November 11 in Retrospect; Was Kerr Right?" *The Bulletin*, August 4, 1976.

"Polls Suggest Mr Fraser Should Retreat." *Australian Financial Review,* October 30, 1975.

"Solicitor General Explains Opinion: Did Not Deny Crown's Power." *Sydney Morning Herald*, November 19, 1975, 10.

"Son: No Profit for Me." *The Age*, July 3, 1975, 3.

"The Cairns Letters." *The Age,* July 3, 1975.

"The Correspondence between Governor and Mr Lang." *Sydney Morning Herald,* May 14, 1932, 13.

"The Federal Crisis, The Labor Party Split, Mr Hughes and Supporters Leave Caucus." *The Age*, November 15, 1916, 7.

Amphlett, Patricia. "Timely Campaign Signalled Start of Whitlam's Cultural Sea Change." *Sydney Morning Herald,* November 12, 2012.

Cole-Adams, Peter and Ben Hills. "Cairns, the Full Story." *The Age,* July 2, 1975.

Henderson, Ian. "Whitlam Censures his Critics." *The Australian,* November 13, 1995, 4.

Hicks, Ian. "His is the Key Role." *Sydney Morning Herald*, October 16, 1975.

Hills, Ben. "Cairns' Son in Arab Plan." *The Age*, July 1, 1975.

Hills, Ben and Staff Reporters. "I Made Up $4m Story: Cowls." *The Age,* July 3, 1975.

Jost, John. "Connor Denied Loan Charges." *The Age*, October 9, 1975.

Jost, John. "It's Government by Crisis. Comment: The Buck Stops when the Money Runs Out." *The Age,* October 16, 1975.

Morris, Linda. "Jackson Pollock's Controversial Blue Poles Valued at $500 million." *Sydney Morning Herald,* January 30, 2023.

Oakes, Dan. "Nixon Duped by Corrupt Ex-policeman, Says OPI." *The Age*, June 27, 2008, News, 1.

Quick, John & Robert Randolph Garran. *The Annotated Constitution of the Australian Commonwealth, 1901*. Reprinted with forewords by Maurice Byers (1994) and Geoffrey Sawyer (1976). Sydney: Legal Books, 1995.

Owens, Warren & Martin Saxon. "PM Confident of Budget Victory." *The Sun-Herald*, October 19, 1975, 1 & 4.

Pelly, Michael. "Palace Gave Kerr Green Light to Sack Whitlam." *Financial Review*, July 14, 2020.

Sawer, Geoffrey. *Federation Under Strain.* Carlton, Victoria: Melbourne University Press, 1977.

Sawer, Geoffrey. "Political Confrontation: A Modest Proposal for a Way Out of the Mire." *Canberra Times,* October 22, 1975.

"SBS Dateline Exclusive Interview with Christopher 'Falcon' Boyce." 2014, Youtube. https://www.youtube.com/watch?v=mmElu9tx2S0. Accessed December 30, 2022.

Scholes, Gordon. "Oral History," interview conducted by Garry Sturgess. National Library of Australia, *Old Parliament House Political and Parliamentary Oral History Project.* Sound recording. August 6, 2010. https://nla.gov.au/nla.obj-218960066/listen.

Schneider, Russell. "Oral History." Interview with by Barry York, *Museum of Australian Democracy at Old Parliament House,* April 1, 2015. https://oralhistories.moadoph.gov.au/russell-schneider.

Sexton, Michael. *The Great Crash.* Melbourne, Victoria: Scribe, 2005.

Smith, David. "Letters: Whitlam Could Have Had More Time." *Quadrant,* September 2005.

Smith, David. *Head of State: The Governor-General, The Monarchy, The Republic and the Dismissal.* Sydney, NSW: Macleay, 2005.

Solomon, David. "ALP Shows its TV Talent Line-up." *Canberra Times*, August 1972.

"Son: No Profit for Me." *The Age*, July 3, 1975.

Stone, Julius. "Why not a Moratorium?" *Sydney Morning Herald,* October 21, 1975.

Strangio, Paul. *Keeper of the Faith, A Biography of Jim Cairns.* Carlton, Victoria: Melbourne University Press, 2002.

Stubbs, Matthew. "The Constitutional Validity of State Chief Justices Acting as Governor." (2014) 25 *Public Law Review* 197.

Tiffen, Rodney. "Scandals." In *The Whitlam Legacy,* edited by Troy Bramston, 158–165. Leichardt, NSW: Federation, 2015.

Toohey, Brian. "Arthur Tange and Gough Whitlam Spy Mystery: Was there a Crucial Information Gap?" *Australian Financial Review*, November 6, 2015.

Toohey, Brian. "The CIA and Whitlam's Dismissal." *Australian Financial Review*, December 5, 1975.

Twomey, Anne. "Advice to the Governor-General on the Appointment of Kevin Rudd as Prime Minister." (2013) 24 *Public Law Review* 289–304.

Twomey, Anne. "Advice to Vice-regal Officers by Crown Law Officers and Others." (2015) 26 *Public Law Review* 193–296.

Twomey, Anne. "Before the High Court: *Hocking v Director-General of the National Archives of Australia*: Can Kerr's Correspondence with the Queen be Kept Secret Forever?" (2020) 42(1) *Sydney Law Journal* 97–108.

Twomey, Anne. "Changing the Leader – The Constitutional Conventions Concerning the Resignation of Prime Ministers and Premiers." (2011) 39(3) *Federal Law Review* 329–360.

Twomey, Anne. "Constitutional Convention and Constitutional Reality." (2004) 78 *Australian Law Journal* 798–811.

Twomey, Anne. "Dicey on Brexit and the Conservative Nature of Referendums." (2019) 93 *Australian Law Journal* 981–984.

Twomey, Anne. "From Bagehot to Brexit: The Monarch's Rights to be Consulted, to Encourage and Warn." (2018) 107(4) *The Round Table* 417–428.

Twomey, Anne. "Legal Advice by Judges on the Exercise of Reserve Powers" [2016] *Public Law* 285–303.

Twomey, Anne. "Mason's Role in the 1975 Dismissal 'unprecedented'? Hardly." *Conversation,* August 31, 2012.

Twomey, Anne. "Minority Government and the Validity of Standing Order Requirements for Absolute Majority Votes." (2019) 30 *Public Law Review* 142–159.

Twomey, Anne. "Prorogation: Can it Ever Be Regarded as a Reserve Power?" (2016) 27 *Public Law Review* 144–154.

Twomey, Anne. "Sir Maurice Byers Lecture 2020: 'Maurice Byers – Legal Advice in the Constitutional Maelstrom of the Whitlam Era'" [2020] (Summer) *Bar News* 36–42.

Twomey, Anne. "The Dismissal of the Lang Government." In *State Constitutional Landmarks*, edited by George Winterton, 129–160. Annandale, NSW: Federation, 2006.

Twomey, Anne. "The Exercise of Reserve Powers in Victoria from 1912–1955." (2014) 39 *Australian Bar Review* 198–214.

Twomey, Anne. "The Governor-General's Role in the Formation of Government in a Hung Parliament." (2011) 22 *Public Law Review* 52–74.

Twomey, Anne. "The Justiciability of Prorogation." (2019) 93 *Australian Law Journal* 913–917.

Twomey, Anne. "The Queen's Letters." (2019) 93 *Australian Law Journal* 267–269.

Twomey, Anne. "The Race to the Palace from Tuvalu: What Happens When a Prime Minister and a Governor-General Try to Dismiss Each Other?" In *Viceregalism: The Crown as Head of State in Political Crises in Postwar Commonwealth*, edited by H. Kumarasingham, 474–503. Cham: Palgrave, Macmillan, 2020.

Twomey, Anne. "The Reserve Powers in Times of Political Crisis: The Dutton/Turnbull Leadership Challenge and Royal Assent to the Medevac Bill and Brexit Bills." (2021) 49(1) *Federal Law Review* 96–121.

Twomey, Anne. "The Unrecognised Reserve Powers." High Court Public Lecture, November 14, 2012.

Twomey, Anne. *The Veiled Sceptre*. Cambridge: Cambridge University Press, 2018.

University of Western Australia. "Australian Politics and Elections Archive 1856–2018." https://elections.uwa.edu.au/listelections.lasso?ElectionType=2.

"Vale Professor Emeritus Colin Howard QC." University of Melbourne, Melbourne Law School, *MLS News*, Issue 6, October 2011. https://law.unimelb.edu.au/alumni/mls-news/issue-6-october-2011/vale-professor-emeritus-colin-howard-qc.

Walker, Ross. *Harold Holt, Always One Step Further.* Collingwood, Victoria: Latrobe University Press, Black Inc, 2022.

Waterford, Jack. "Ellicott Resigns from the Bench." *Canberra Times*, January 19, 1983, 1.

Waugh, John. "Blocking Supply in Victoria." (2002) 13 *Public Law Review* 241–245.

Waugh, John. "Evading Parliamentary Control of Government Spending: Some Early Case Studies." (1998) 9 *Public Law Review* 28–42.

Welsh, Rebecca Ananian & George Williams. "Judges in Vice Regal Roles." (2015) 43 *Federal Law Review* 119–146.

Wheeldon, John. "If Labor Senators had Known …." *The Australian*, November 11, 1985.

Wheeler, Fiona. "Sir John Latham's Extra Judicial Advising." (2011) 35 *Melbourne University Law Review* 651–676.

Whitlam: The Power & the Passion, directed by Paul Clarke (Australian Broadcasting Corporation, 2013), DVD.

Whitlam, Edward Gough. "Go to the Documents," National Bi-annual Postgraduate History Conference, University of Melbourne, July 20, 2001, *Whitlam Institute Collection.* https://rosetta.westernsydney.edu.au/delivery/DeliveryManagerServlet?dps_pid=IE51463. Accessed May 16, 2023.

Whitlam, Edward Gough. "Gough Whitlam's Eulogy for Lance Barnard: 'My Oldest and Best Mate.'" WhitlamDismissal.com. Accessed June 22, 2024. https://whitlamdismissal.com/1997/08/15/whitlam-eulogy-for-lance-barnard.html.

Whitlam, Gough. Interview, by Margaret Throsby, Mungo MacCallum, Michelle Grattan and Max Teichmann. *Issues 85*, Special Broadcasting Service (SBS), 11 November, 1985. Youtube. https://www.youtube.com/watch?v=uA6T8yhuurM.

Whitlam, E. G. "Speech by The Prime Minister Mr. E.G. Whitlam, Q.C. M.P., at The Unveiling of The Eureka Flag, Ballarat Fine Art Gallery. Ballarat, 3 December 1973." In Australian Government, Department of Premier and Cabinet, *PM Transcripts.* https://pmtranscripts.pmc.gov.au/release/transcript-3092.

Whitlam, Gough. *The Whitlam Government, 1972–1975.* Ringwood, Victoria: Penguin, 1985.

Whitlam, Gough. *The Truth of the Matter.* Carlton, Victoria: Melbourne University Press, 2005.

Whitlam, Gough and Tom Hughes. "An Adviser Who Gave His All." *Sydney Morning Herald,* March 10, 1997, 17.

Williams, George. "Law Reform and the Constitution." In *The Whitlam Legacy,* edited by Troy Bramston, 280–289. Leichardt, NSW: Federation, 2015.

Williams, Graham. "The Uneasy Choices Facing Sir John." *The Australian,* October 16, 1975.

Winterton, George. *Monarchy to Republic.* Oxford: Oxford University Press, 1994.

Winterton, George. *Parliament, the Executive and the Governor-General.* Carlton, Victoria: Melbourne University Press, 1983.

Winterton, George. "1975: The Dismissal of the Whitlam Government." In *Australian Constitutional Landmarks,* edited by H. P. Lee and George Winterton, 229–261. Cambridge: Cambridge University Press, 2003.

Wriedt, Ken. "Meanwhile Back in the Senate." In *The Dismissal: Where Were You on November 11, 1975?,* edited by Sybil Nolan, 51–54. Carlton, Victoria: Melbourne University Press, 2015.

Wright, Raymond. *A People's Counsel.* Melbourne, Victoria: Oxford University Press Australia, 1992.

"Zines, Leslie Ronald (1930–2014)." *Obituaries Australia,* in National Centre of Biography, Australian National University. https://oa.anu.edu.au/obituary/zines-leslie-ronald-17895/text29475. Accessed May 12, 2023.

Index

Page references for figures are italicized.

About the Author

Ian Killey PSM is an experienced Australian public lawyer. Following his lengthy career in the Victorian public service, during which he held positions such as General Counsel to the State's Department of Premier and Cabinet and General Counsel to its Ombudsman. He completed a PhD at Victoria University studying the constitutional relationship between police and government. He then began tertiary teaching, first at that university and then at the Australian Catholic University, mainly in the fields of public law and legal foundations.

He has also produced a number of other works on Australian Public Law, including the recently published *The Naked Australian Constitution* (2022), as well as *Constitutional Conventions in Australia* (2009 and 2012) and *Police and Government in Australia* (2019) and is the co-author of textbooks on constitutional law including *Australian Constitutional Law and Government* (2021).

www.ingramcontent.com/pod-product-compliance
Ingram Content Group UK Ltd.
Pitfield, Milton Keynes, MK11 3LW, UK
UKHW020839290926
15470UKWH00004B/1435

9 781666 930320